Hal Wallis

Hal Wallis

Producer
to the Stars

Bernard F. Dick

The University Press of Kentucky

Publication of this volume was made possible in part
by a grant from the National Endowment for the Humanities.

Editorial and Sales Offices: The University Press of Kentucky
663 South Limestone Street, Lexington, Kentucky 40508-4008
www.kentuckypress.com

08 07 06 05 04   5 4 3 2 1

Library of Congress Cataloging-in-Publication Data

Dick, Bernard F.
  Hal Wallis : producer to the stars / Bernard F. Dick.
     p. cm.
  Includes bibliographical references and index.
  ISBN 0-8131-2317-8 (Hardcover : alk. paper)
  1. Wallis, Hal B., 1899-1986. Motion picture producers and
directors—United States—Biography. I. Title.
  PN1998.3.W343D53 2004
  791.4302'32'092—dc22   2003024584

This book is printed on acid-free recycled paper meeting
the requirements of the American National Standard
for Permanence in Paper for Printed Library Materials.

Manufactured in the United States of America.

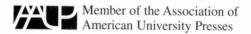 Member of the Association of
American University Presses

For John E. Burke

Contents

Photographs follow pages 82 and 178

Preface

"COLD," DOUGLAS DICK SAID, affecting a shudder, as if a blast of arctic air had invaded the Gardens at Glendon, a far-from-frigid Los Angeles restaurant within walking distance of UCLA. I understood his response to the name of Hal Wallis, even though it was 11 July 2001. Dick had experienced the Wallis chill in the mid-1940s when he came to Hollywood for his film debut in Wallis's production of *The Searching Wind* (1946). I encountered it two decades later—in June 1978, when I was preparing a paper on Paramount for delivery at the Modern Language Association. Knowing that Wallis had been based at Paramount from 1944 through 1969, I wrote to him requesting an interview, which was granted on 9 June 1978.

His office was at 9200 Sunset Boulevard, just beyond the point where Hollywood dissolves into Beverly Hills. What struck me immediately about Wallis was his head, which looked like a piece of sculpture, as if his body were merely a column supporting it. Then the head spoke: "I don't allow recorders." I replied that I had none. No reaction. I began my questions, always looking down at my pad to avoid staring at his head. "What was your first film for Paramount? *The Affairs of Susan* or *Love Letters* (both 1945)?" "*The Affairs of Susan*" was the terse reply. "What about *You Came Along* (1945)?" "Later." "And your directors? You used Lewis Allen for several films." "He was a good action director." I said nothing. Lewis Allen? Action? *The Perfect Marriage* (1946)? *Desert Fury* (1947), perhaps. Comparisons between Warner Brothers, where he started, and Paramount, where he spent a quarter of a century as the studio's preeminent producer? "I had complete autonomy at Paramount. I could match the people with the properties." "How would you characterize a Hal Wallis production?" "Movies about mature, realistic people." It was only when I asked if he thought he had transferred the Warner style to Paramount that Wallis looked reflective. Finally, he answered, "Possibly."

Wallis had little to say. He was courteous but aloof, as if he had agreed to the interview because he felt unthreatened by an academic. There would be no prying into the past, no questions about liaisons. In short, no dirt. But also no information.

It is strange how an unsatisfactory interview can spark a writer's curiosity about his subject, whose head suggested an archive with files carefully labeled and indexed. But there was no access to it that day. Twenty years later, discovering that a Hal Wallis archive existed at the Center for Motion Picture Study (CMPS) in Los Angeles, I hoped that amid his numerous papers, I might learn what I never did on that June day in 1978: namely, how a Chicagoan, who relocated in Los Angeles only because his mother's tuberculosis necessitated a change of climate and who entered the movie industry because his sister, who happened to be Jack Warner's secretary, got him a job managing one of the theaters in the Warners circuit, became one of Hollywood's most creative producers.

Although the young Wallis would occasionally pop into a Chicago nickelodeon, he much preferred live entertainment—preferably theater, with vaudeville as second choice. Show business was a diversion, not a career. If Hal Wallis had never gone into pictures, he would probably have ended up as the founder of an household appliance company, since his last job before leaving for Los Angeles was selling stoves. In that event, the Wallis stove would have been unlike any other.

I have tried to strip away the layers of myth, hype, and gossip that went into the forging of the Wallis persona, which has incurred so many type-overs that it resembles a text written over another so that the first can only be read after the second has been deciphered. A man of a thousand faces? Hardly. Several? Certainly.

In 1980 Wallis wrote an autobiography of sorts in cooperation with Charles Higham, whose numerous books on film and studio history made him the voice of Hollywood during the 1970s and 1980s. The result of their collaboration, *Starmaker* (1980), was aptly titled but strangely lacking in the kind of information usually found in works of this sort. For example, Wallis never mentioned his parents' names, although he wrote glowingly of his mother and sympathetically of his father, who deserted the family when Wallis was a teenager. He had no problem admitting that his family was Jewish, but he failed to mention that his father's surname was originally Walinsky. In fact, Wallis eventually decided against the use of family names, except those of his sisters Minna and

Juel and his uncle Maurice, who merits only a caption under a picture of himself and his nephew in baseball uniforms.

Starmaker was originally intended to be much more inclusive. CMPS's Wallis Collection includes a typescript of the first chapter, "The Early Years," which provides considerably more information than its later version in *Starmaker*. Wallis relied heavily on a tape recorder to tell his story, and the tapes were then transcribed and edited. There is a partial tape transcription in the Collection, containing material that also never reached the printed page. It is hard to believe that these omissions were the result of editorial decisions by Higham or Wallis's publisher, Macmillan; more likely they were Wallis's.

As a producer, Wallis avoided the kind of publicity that dogged Hollywood celebrities, who found their peccadilloes turned into scandals and learned that their private lives were in the public domain. Wallis preferred certain aspects of his life to remain in shadow; to him, an autobiography was a form of chiaroscuro; instead of light alternating with shade, detail is balanced by selectivity, and disclosure by discretion. *Starmaker* was never intended to be a "Hal Wallis Tells All." If it had been, we would have learned more about the man and his Hollywood.

Yet we still can. Since the jettisoned pages have the power to bring Wallis out of his penumbra into a light that neither flatters nor distorts, I have drawn upon them, always indicating their source, so that there is no confusion between the unpublished material and the published text.

Acknowledgments

I WAS ESPECIALLY FORTUNATE in having the cooperation of Martha Hyer Wallis, who not only provided me with many of the extraordinary photos that appear in this book but also answered numerous questions by phone and mail.

I must also express my personal thanks to the following persons: Robert Blees, for his guidance and, above all, friendship; John E. Burke, for forty years of exchanging film and theater lore; Ned Comstock of the University of California's Cinema/TV Library, for alerting me to the Jack L. Warner Collection, from which I learned much about the complex relationship between Wallis and Warner; Douglas Dick (no relation), for sharing his memories of the man who launched his career, not knowing it was the prelude to a radically different one; Tony Greco, for tapes of Wallis's 1945–50 Paramount films; Barbara Hall, head of Special Collections at the Center for Motion Picture Studies, for making the Wallis Collection so accessible; Mother Dolores Hart, whom I first saw as Dolores Hart in the movies and on stage, for her prayers and memorable conversations about everything from Elvis Presley to Mike Curtiz; Randi Hockett, director of the University of Southern California Warner Bros. Archives, for her assistance in negotiating the collection; Kristine Krueger of the National Film Information Service for answering some rather arcane questions; Joan Leslie, for her recollections about working with Mike Curtiz; Kristine Miller, for a candid phone interview about being a Wallis discovery; Jay Ogletree, for providing me with background information about *Becket, Anne of the Thousand Days,* and *Mary, Queen of Scots;* Katherine Restaino, my wife, without whom research would be the equivalent of transcribing manuscripts in a medieval scriptorium; and Lizabeth Scott, who showed me another way of looking at a man whom others considered cold and aloof.

Before there was networking, there were friends with contacts.

Through Robert Blees, I was able to meet Walter Seltzer, who guided me through the labyrinth of Wallis's life, providing me with information that only someone who spent a lifetime in the industry would have. I have indeed been blessed. Unless otherwise indicated, the photos in this book are courtesy of Martha Hyer Wallis.

CHAPTER ONE

Child of the Tenements

Hal Wallis was fond of saying that his birth coincided with the start of the twentieth century. Actually, he was off by two years. According to Wallis's death certificate, he was born on 8 October 1898. The place was Chicago, "Hog Butcher to the World," as Carl Sandburg christened it in his famous 1916 poem "Chicago." Sandburg was ambivalent about Chicago: he saw it as "wicked" and "crooked," yet vibrant with the "stormy, husky, brawling laughter of Youth." Wallis would probably have agreed, although he never bore the "marks of wanton hunger" that Sandburg observed on the faces of the city's underclass. Wallis's parents, however, did.

In *Starmaker* Wallis's Chicago boyhood is reduced to five pages, perhaps because he did not consider those years formative, even though they provided the refining fire from which one of Hollywood's golden boys emerged. Some—but not all—of the gaps in Wallis's early life can be filled in; unfortunately, turn-of-the-twentieth-century Chicago was not noted for meticulous record-keeping.[1] This was especially true when the Walinskys anglicized their names and became the Wallises. Hal Wallis was originally Harold Walinsky, a fact known only to a few of his associates. Wallis preferred that the past live up to its name.

"Father was Russian and Mother was Polish."[2] Their names, Jacob Walinsky and Eva Blum, are known only from the 1920 census, not from *Starmaker*. Why Wallis rendered his parents nameless is not hard to explain; the screen of privacy that he placed between his personal and his public lives was not an iron curtain but more of a silken one, which, if properly lit, would become transparent. Wallis must have known that his parents' names were not buried in some registry, never

1

to be exhumed; more likely, he felt that "mother" and "father" were sufficient. He was the starmaker; Jacob and Eva, the starmaker's parents.

Jacob was a tailor by trade and a gambler by addiction. Although
Jacob the tailor rarely practiced his trade, his gambling alter ego more
than made up for it, but he failed miserably, frequently placing his family in jeopardy because of his habit. Eva, however, "was a beautiful
woman, one of nature's aristocrats [with] chestnut hair, blue eyes, fair
skin and a sweet expression."[3] In pages that never saw publication, Wallis celebrated his mother as an exemplary parent who made sure that her
children had enough to eat, regardless of the family's limited and at
times nonexistent finances. Eva's maternalism extended to the children
in the various cold-water tenements where they lived; the aroma from
her pies no sooner reached the other apartments than the children would
be trooping into her kitchen.

Wallis's second wife, Martha Hyer Wallis, recalled her husband and
his sister Minna mentioning "Minsk" when speaking of their parents'
origins.[4] One of Wallis's many deletions from the *Starmaker* typescript
was a reference to Minsk as his parents' birthplace. That was partially
correct. Indeed, in 1872 Jacob was born in Minsk, the capital of what is
now Belarus, formerly Belorussia. However, Belorussia had been part
of Poland (more accurately, Poland-Lithuania) until the partitioning
(1772–95), which left Russia with the eastern part of the country, including Belorussia. Whether Jacob considered himself Polish or Russian is unknown. Since Belorussia had been Russianized, along with
the other parts of Poland-Lithuania that were annexed, Jacob's language
was Russian; so was the spelling of his name, which was probably Vo-
linskij, suggesting a family connection with Volhynia (Wolyn in Polish,
Volyn in Russian) in western Ukraine.[5]

Thus, Jacob Walinsky was only nominally Russian. His roots were
clearly Polish, as were those of his wife, Eva Blum, despite her Ger-
manic surname. Eva was born in 1873 in Kovno, now Kaunas in central
Lithuania. Kovno, another victim of the partitions, then belonged to
Russia; like Minsk, it had once been part of Poland-Lithuania. Kovno
was an important Jewish cultural center, not as famous as Vilna, "the
Jerusalem of the East," but still respected for its outstanding Hebrew
schools. Tragically, the Holocaust almost decimated Kovno's Jewish
population; of the forty thousand Jews in Kovno at the outbreak of World
War II, only two thousand survived.

Although *Blum* suggests German or perhaps Austrian origins, the name would not have been that unusual in Kovno. There had been a German presence in Poland since the thirteenth century. After the Tartar invasions had devastated vast sections of the country, the Poles encouraged German settlements to make the land habitable again. Furthermore, Poland (that is, Poland-Lithuania) had been divided up three ways, with Russia getting eastern Poland; Prussia, western Poland; and Austria, southern Poland. Originally, Eva's ancestors might have come from western or southern Poland and then moved east, settling in Kovno and perhaps relocating in Minsk. It was not uncommon for Jews to change their name as they moved from one part of the former Polish commonwealth to another or, even if they did not move, to adopt a name that was less likely to mark them as Jews. One of the great stars of the Yiddish theater, Jacob Adler, was born in Odessa. *Adler* may have sounded German, but the actor's roots lay in Mother Russia.

If Jacob and Eva met in Minsk, they most likely married there.[6] At the time, they were in their late teens. They must have emigrated to America shortly after their wedding. When their first child, Minna, was born in 1893, they were living in Chicago; Eva was barely twenty, and Jacob was a year older. Chicago was not an arbitrary choice: Eva's brothers were there, and the young couple needed all the support they could get.

When Jacob and Eva arrived in Chicago about 1890, they settled on the West Side, a predominantly eastern European Jewish enclave of two-story shanties or "double deckers" for the fortunate and rear tenements in foul-smelling alleys for the rest. Whether Jacob and Eva first lived in a double decker or a rear tenement is unknown. Garment workers gravitated to the latter.[7] Since Jacob rarely had an opportunity to practice his trade and was reduced to working in sweatshops, he and Eva might well have experienced life in a rear tenement. But Eva was determined that their children would not live in such squalor, and that they would not go hungry. Even Wallis admitted he never went hungry—but that was not for publication.[8]

Eva never enjoyed robust health. She contracted tuberculosis, which became so severe in 1919 that she had to be placed in a sanitorium. Eva's tuberculosis was not so much the result of the Chicago winters, as Wallis has suggested, as of the unsanitary conditions that prevailed on the West Side. Inadequate (or nonexistent) bathing facilities, the lack of heat and refrigeration, the stench from the outhouses, and the garbage left rotting in alleys produced a variety of diseases, including smallpox and tuberculosis. Eva was fortunate in having caring children, who more than compensated for her wastrel husband.

"Our furniture was heavily mortgaged. Often it was removed because payments had not been made."[9] The payments had not been made because Jacob was gambling away most of his salary. Even a decent-paying job at Gimbel's department store, where he was put in charge of alterations, did not solve Jacob's problem; in fact, the additional money might have exacerbated it. When Jacob was unable to pay the rent, he would move his family to another tenement, always in a neighborhood populated by Polish and Russian Jews. Wallis recalled living in walk-ups on Newbury Avenue, Albany Avenue and Independence Boulevard near Albany Park, Fifty-fifth and Independence Boulevard, and Fifty-fifth and Michigan, which bordered on Roseland, an ethnic neighborhood on the far South Side.[10] Once, Jacob even packed his wife and children off to Milwaukee, presumably because he had found work there. But soon they were back in Chicago at another West Side address.

Those years, with their frequent dislocations, were ones that Wallis preferred to ignore after becoming an established film producer. In 1944 he did not appreciate receiving a "Hello Hal" letter from Sylvia Zeidman, recalling the "good old days" when they were neighbors on Ashland Boulevard on the West Side (and hinting that as an adoptive New Yorker she had "some ideas that would be useful for a New York picture"). Zeidman received a curt reply, informing her that all story suggestions must go through the studio.[11] So much for the good old days.

Wallis was the youngest of three children and the only male. His sister Minna (1893–1986) was the oldest; next came Juel (1895–1953), and finally Harold (1898–1986), soon to be known as Hal. When he was born, the surname was still Walinsky. There is no way of knowing when it became Wallis. Jacob and Eva might have been influenced by the decision Eva's relatives, the Sapersteins, made when they changed their name to Saper, believing that they would encounter less job discrimination. If Jacob Walinsky was serious about graduating from the sweatshops, he might have thought Jacob—or Jake—Wallis stood a better chance than Jacob Walinsky.

As was often the case in eastern European households, both Jewish and Christian, education was the prerogative of the male. Thus Minna and Juel were not encouraged to continue their education beyond grade school. Wallis would have completed high school had Jacob not fallen into a state of depression, brought on by the belief that his obsession with gambling made him a failure as a husband and father. He could not even take pride in his new position in Gimbel's tailoring department, which at least freed him from the sweatshops. The best job he ever had neither cured his gambling fever nor assuaged his guilt. Unable to face his family, Jacob Walinsky deserted them. The year was 1912. All that is known of Jacob past that point is that eventually he moved to Canada, where he died on 14 September 1930.[12]

At the time of his father's desertion, Wallis was fourteen, having just completed his first year at McKinley High School. He would not be returning in the fall. A scenario familiar to countless families left fatherless was played out in the Wallis household: in the absence of the father, the children rallied around the mother, and everyone went to work—including the son, who could no longer remain in school. In a sense, Jacob's desertion was a blessing. Although there would be one last move, this time to Thirteenth Street and Independence Boulevard, there would be no more uprooting, no more rooms without furniture, no more money worries. His desertion was also inevitable. If guilt and gambling had not caused Jacob to walk out, the tension between himself and Minna would have. It may even have been a contributing factor.

Minna was the most aggressive of the children; her steely determination served her well in Hollywood, where she became one of the industry's most powerful agents. Home life in Chicago provided her with a survival kit, to which she was continually adding. As the oldest, she considered herself a matriarch-in-the-making, assuming greater authority as Eva's health worsened.

Wallis has written compassionately about his father. Although he could not condone what his father had done, he did not excoriate him, either. Perhaps Wallis understood that the roots of his father's depression lay in his misunderstanding of the American Dream, which turned Jacob Walinsky into a wage slave, gambling away his salary and his dreams along with it. Then, too, there was his marriage to a woman who appeared to have a German background. Many German Jews felt superior to their Slavic coreligionists, whom they considered refugees from the shtetl. Whether Eva and her brothers felt similarly about Jacob is problematic; however, in his depression, Jacob may well have imagined they did.

When Wallis was gathering material for his autobiography, he asked Minna to share her memories with him. But since Minna's recollections would undermine the image of their father as a tragic figure, they never made the final revision. While Wallis was sympathetic to Jacob, Minna loathed him—and vice versa. She joined the workforce before her brother did, lying about her age to land a job at Marshall Fields (only to be fired when someone discovered she was fourteen). Minna had no patience with a man who was constantly reaching for the brass ring, while his wife and children wondered what their next address would be. At least they knew where their next meal would come from: Eva's kitchen in some tenement or other. Minna could not overlook the toll her father's profligacy had taken on their mother; Jacob could not deal with a daughter who had no respect for her father. Jacob, in fact, once delivered the equivalent of a curse, telling Minna that he hoped she would be married under a black *chope* (canopy).[13] Minna need not have fretted—not that she would have, anyway. Although Minna was rumored to have been the lover of Clark Gable, whom she supposedly discovered, she never married.

Minna also remembered that when their father died, Wallis paid for his burial. Since Wallis knew where and when Jacob died, either he had made contact with his father at some point or had found a way of keeping track of him. In any case, Wallis was a dutiful—and forgiving—son.

Having been thrust into the working world at fourteen, Wallis discovered that for the first time in his young life he had spending money. At first he could only find a job as a gofer in a real estate office at five dollars a week. When an opening arose at Rapid Transit, Wallis saw an opportunity for more money and free trolley rides. He was now making twelve dollars a week and could take advantage of Chicago's excellent transportation system with its trolleys and elevated railway that brought him to the entertainment venues he was so anxious to explore. Live entertainment in any form—not movies—was Wallis's first love. When he could afford it, he would drop by the College Inn in the elegant Sherman House on Randolph Street, an architectural beauty in the Second Empire style, where there was always music. During the time he worked for Rapid Transit, he rode free to the penny arcades and vaudeville houses on South State Street and the legitimate theaters on Randolph Street and Wabash Avenue. Chicagoans loved the theater, and actors felt similarly about the city. Lillie Langtree, the Barrymores, Maud Adams,

Lillian Russell, and Sarah Bernhardt were among the most popular. Wallis does not cite the plays he saw, but he was so taken with the theater that he ushered without pay.[14] If Chicago meant anything to Wallis, it was the place where he discovered the magic of the stage, a lifelong love affair that resulted in numerous film versions of plays, famous and otherwise.

If *Starmaker* had followed the format of the traditional celebrity biography, it would have read like a treatment for a Hal Wallis biopic. FADE IN on the teenage Wallis, fatherless and penniless, except for the nickel that landed on the pavement when it fell through a hole in his pants pocket. The coin was his entrée to a nickelodeon on State Street, where he sat in darkness, so enthralled by what he was watching that he was oblivious to the discomfort of the straight-backed seats and the smell of unwashed bodies. He only knew he had witnessed the birth of an art form, of which he intended to be part.

That was hardly the case. On those few occasions when Wallis saw "the simple movies of the time" (*Starmaker*, 3), he had no idea he would end up in the film business, much less as one of its greatest producers. Chicago's strategic importance as a center of film exhibition and distribution was lost on him, even though when he was growing up there, nickelodeons were cropping up all over, and exhibitors were haunting the exchanges to get decent prints for their theaters. By February 1907 there were 158 nickelodeons in Chicago.[15] One reason for the large number was the absence of blue laws. It was possible for exhibitors to stay open seven days a week, thus allowing Chicago's working class to sample the new medium on Sundays if they were too tired to drop in on a weekday evening.

Wallis may even have been unaware that the Essanay Film Manufacturing Company had its headquarters on Wells Street. Essanay, founded in 1907, capitalized on the popularity of westerns. The exteriors were usually filmed on location, the interiors in Chicago. All this film activity had no effect on Wallis, even though he would have been a prime candidate for a job in a business that required neither education nor prior experience.

During his years in Chicago, Wallis was constantly encountering men who would have a lasting effect on a medium to which he seemed oblivious. In 1917 the Wallis family was living on Thirteenth Street and Independence Boulevard in the same building as Sam Katz. Wallis became friendly with Katz, whose father, a barber, felt that his son should have a musical education, in other words, piano lessons. The education paid off; at thirteen, "Young Katz," as Wallis called him (*Starmaker,* 2), even though Katz was six years his senior, was providing piano accompaniment for the one-reelers at Carl Laemmle's nickelodeon, the White Front Theatre on Milwaukee Avenue. After finishing high school and realizing that all that was needed for a nickelodeon was a storefront and folding chairs, he hopped on the bandwagon.[16] Soon Katz teamed up with the Balaban brothers to form Balaban and Katz, one of the country's biggest theater chains, with forty-five venues in Chicago alone.

Wallis had no idea then of the role one of the Balabans would play in his life. He may have known about the Balabans, who were familiar to the denizens of Chicago's West Side. Like Wallis's parents, Israel and Goldie Balaban were Russian Jews. They ran a grocery story on Maxwell Avenue, an area teeming with fruit and vegetable vendors, whom eastern European immigrants patronized because of their cheap produce. The Balabans had eight children—seven sons and a daughter. Barney became the most famous of the children, serving for three decades as president of Paramount Pictures, the studio that Wallis joined in 1944.

After seeing his first movie in a Chicago nickelodeon, Barney, encouraged by his mother, persuaded four of his brothers—Abe, John, Max, and Dave—to enter exhibition in 1912. The Balabans' first theater was the Kedzie in Chicago's Albany Park, a predominantly eastern European community that was also near one of the various tenements in which the Wallises lived. The Kedzie set the standards for the other theaters, each of which featured something unique. Whereas most exhibitors hired barkers to lure passersby, the Balabans felt the Kedzie deserved a violinist, who would play outside and draw customers with music. The Circle, another Balaban theater, sported a four-piece orchestra and a pipe organ for those who preferred a combination of live entertainment and film. Impressed, Katz joined the Balabans, and together they created the movie palace concept—theaters with the opulence of opera houses, with evocative names such as the Granada and the Grand Central, the latter giving audiences the choice of sitting downstairs, in the mezzanine, or in the balcony.

If the Wallises were living in the same building with the Katzes, it must have been a pleasure dome compared to their former residences.

The Katzes were hardly impoverished; Sam, in fact, was earning four hundred dollars a week from his nickelodeons when he graduated from high school in 1917.[17] That Wallis's family could finally afford a decent apartment was largely due to his new job. Knowing that better-paying positions required the stenographic skills that he lacked, Wallis signed up for evening courses in typing and shorthand. His diploma from the Gregg Stenographic School brought him to the Hughes Electric Heating Company, which produced and marketed electric ranges with the General Electric or Hotpoint labels. As a sales representative with a fifty-dollar-a-week-salary, plus commissions, Wallis found himself traveling through Kansas, Nebraska, and Missouri, learning en route how lonely the itinerant life can be. However, he could not afford to succumb to the usual short-term fixes for loneliness: liquor and sex. He was too busy mastering the technical information in the Hughes manuals, so he could answer questions from prospective buyers. Soon he was comfortable demonstrating the models at high schools, even though he had never had the chance to take physics at McKinley. When Wallis was on the road, he had no idea that he was preparing for a career founded on an ever-changing technology that made Luddites out of those who could not learn it.

Wallis had become such a successful sales rep that, within a few years, he was promoted to assistant sales manager, based in Chicago. Before he had the chance to enjoy the luxury of being back in his hometown, which lately had become a stopover, he was hit with the news that his mother's tuberculosis had become so severe that she could no longer remain in the sanitorium in which she had been placed.

Enter Minna, the matriarch in the wings ready to make her entrance. While her brother was on the road, Minna had some visitors, the Gormans, former Chicagoans who had moved to southern California. They convinced Minna that her mother's health would improve in a warmer climate. Not quite ready to commit to relocation, Minna needed proof. When the Gormans were ready to return to Los Angeles, Minna accompanied them; she even slept on a sofa in their home until she found what she considered suitable accommodations for the family, including her brother.[18]

"Westward, ho!" became her motto, and the others had no other choice but to follow her lead. Wallis managed to get reassigned to southern California, hawking stoves and hot plates—but not for long. Although Minna thrived in California, her brother at first did not. Absent from *Starmaker* is the fact that the new territory to which he was assigned, from central California to the Mexican border, proved so daunting that he headed back to Chicago, hoping to reclaim his old job. But he discovered that it had been phased out because Hughes had merged with the Pacific Electric Heating Company and General Electric to form the Edison Electric Appliance Company, soon to be known as General Electric.[19]

With no other prospects, Wallis returned to Los Angeles and the four-room apartment on Western Avenue where Minna, Juel, and Eva were now living. Minna had not only become the matriarch, with Eva relegated to emerita status, but she was also gainfully employed. Like Wallis, Minna had picked up typing and shorthand, and the skills landed her a job as secretary to Edward Loeb, one of the lawyers in the firm of Loeb, Walker, and Loeb that represented Warner Brothers. When Jack Warner was looking for a secretary, he did not have to look further than Minna; on Loeb's recommendation, Minna was hired. She would not be a secretary much longer; once she discovered Hollywood's dependence on stars, she realized that her forte was not typing but flesh peddling, at which she became quite adept.

Meanwhile, her brother was languishing. As the eldest, Minna felt she had to be protective of him. After all, it was she who spearheaded the move to Los Angeles; it was she who inherited the matriarch's mantle from Eva, who, even when brought to a healthier climate, did not reclaim it. Minna and her brother had a turbulent relationship after they both achieved success in their respective ways—she as an agent who gave spectacular parties and knew everybody worth knowing in Hollywood; he as one of the industry's greatest producers, who was every bit the equal of Irving Thalberg and Darryl Zanuck.

Believing that her brother was meant for something better than selling stoves, Minna searched for a way to bring him into a business that would provide careers for both of them. Minna had already met theater owner H.L. Gumbiner when she was working for Edward Loeb, who was also Gumbiner's lawyer. Gumbiner was so impressed by the way Minna drew up contracts that he exclaimed, "I wish you were a man!"[20] When Minna learned that Gumbiner was looking for someone to manage the Garrick Cinema on Eighth and Broadway in downtown Los Angeles, Minna decided to renew their acquaintance, slight as it was.

She had a man for the job—her brother. Thus, Wallis learned the business the way Carl Laemmle and the brothers Warner did—through exhibition. Although Wallis was merely a manager of a theater that specialized in reruns, he learned how important it was to frequent the exchanges on film row on nearby Olive Street and get enough product so the bill could be changed at least twice a week. He also discovered the publicity value of stills and lobby cards.

Yet he was bored by the routine: mounting stills on cardboard, writing publicity, opening and closing the theater. Minna would not let boredom destroy the goal that she had envisioned for them. Taking advantage of her Warner affiliation, she introduced her brother to Sam Warner, who was in charge of Warner's ever-growing theater chain. Sam, who was always Wallis's favorite among the brothers, was so impressed that he hired him as assistant director of publicity. Working for Hughes had taught Wallis the knack of demonstrating appliances and answering consumers' questions. Now there would be no more demonstrations or explanations. Hal Wallis had now become a publicist.

In one sense, movies were not that different from electric ranges. Every commodity requires promotion. Since most products rarely function as efficiently as the ads claim they do, Wallis understood the importance of hyperbole, which the classical rhetoricians considered a figure of speech rather than a willful exaggeration. Similarly, most films, if left to their own merits (which are often nonexistent), would die at the box office. Like appliances, they need hype.

Since Wallis was no longer on commission as he had been at Hughes, his salary was less than what he was used to earning. When he asked Jack Warner for permission to supplement his income with outside PR jobs, Jack agreed. However, Harry Warner did not, and he fired Wallis. Later, upon Wallis's return to the studio, Jack would become his bête noire. Meanwhile, Wallis had enough confidence in his promotional skills—honed from reading manuals and, when time permitted, fiction— to know they would lead to another job. Immediately, Sol Lesser hired him to handle publicity for his theater chain, West Coast Theaters, as well as for a couple of the films Lesser was producing. To Wallis, it was just another job; he had no idea he was working for one of the industry's first independent producers, who was also an innovator. If Lesser is remembered at all, it is for his Tarzan films and possibly the all-star *Stage Door Canteen* (1943). Yet it was Lesser who introduced a practice that filmgoers now take for granted: the preview. Realizing that industry executives lacked objectivity, Lesser had certain movies previewed in theaters before their release to gauge audience response, which often resulted in a reedited version of a film or a radically different ending. Sending stars out on tour to promote their movies was also a Lesser first.

Wallis did not remain long with Lesser. When Jack realized his brother's mistake, he brought Wallis back to the studio at twice his salary and with a different title: director of publicity. It was now 1925. Two years later, Wallis would marry a movie star.

CHAPTER TWO

Becoming Hal B. Wallis

W HEN WALLIS BECAME PUBLICITY DIRECTOR at Warners, the studio
was considered the creation of upstarts who could not compete with the Big Three: MGM, Associated First National
(which Warner Brothers later absorbed), and Famous Players–Lasky
(soon to be known as Paramount). In time, the Big Three became the
Big Five: MGM, Paramount, Fox, RKO, and Warner Brothers. Hollywood was an invention, according to Neal Gabler: the invention of immigrant Jews and their children, who discovered a business in its infancy,
at a time when as many outsiders as native sons were looking to make
their fortune; a business in which education was irrelevant and being a
Jew was neither a liability nor an occasion for a pogrom.[1]

The history of Hollywood, like that of any cultural institution, is a
blend of fact and myth. The facts have become so mythicized that the
lives of the "Jews who invented Hollywood" have come to resemble the
lives of the saints—inspirational accounts of ordinary people who did
not shrink from challenges that lesser beings could not meet but that
brought them the power and the glory, stopping short of canonization.

The lives of the movie moguls often read like their movies—tales
of triumph over adversity, last-minute recoveries, and lushly orchestrat-
ed comebacks. In a way, their biographies are like medieval exempla,
bedtime fare for American dreamers desperate for success scenarios
with appropriate role models. These scenarios begin with poverty or
privation and proceed through the intermediate stages of rejection, re-
versal, and reinvention, ending in martyrdom or resurrection. None of
the moguls had a privileged life; but, to paraphrase Tolstoy, each life
was unprivileged in its own way. Harry Cohn (Columbia Pictures) was

not an immigrant, although his parents were. The Cohns' four-room apartment on New York's Upper East Side may have been crowded, but it was vastly superior to an eastern European hovel. Nor was living in Nova Scotia unbearable for Louis Mayer (MGM), particularly since he had a doting mother. Adolph Zukor (Paramount) never starved, having learned the fur trade, which he could have parlayed into a profession if the movie business had not panned out. William Fox, whose Fox Film Corporation was the forerunner of Twentieth Century–Fox, could truly lay claim to the hard-knock life—a nine-year-old with a withered arm and a third-grade education, hawking his father's stove polish on the streets of New York's Lower East Side. The plus side was becoming a millionaire at thirty.

The brothers Warner—Harry, Jack, Abe, and Sam—and their parents could honestly say they knew the American dream's underside, and through their own efforts, they reversed it, as if it were the lining in a coat. They emerged from the fiery furnace not only intact but transfigured—and with a resoundingly Anglo-Saxon surname. The fire burned away the past. There were no Warners in the Polish shtetl where the brothers' parents, Benjamin and Pearl, were born in 1857.[2] When Jack Warner Jr. badgered his father about the family name, Jack senior lit a cigarette and responded, "I don't remember."[3]

The past may have been purged, but it failed to eradicate the resentments and rivalries that bedeviled brothers entering a business where there were no precedents except family. Movie families are unique, though: in the absence of a patriarch, one of the brothers claims the seat of honor and the recognition that goes with it. Among the Warners that brother was Jack.

Had Benjamin been born later, he would have been a movie pioneer, like Universal's Carl Laemmle; and his sons would have joined him, as Carl junior had. But Benjamin was not one to remain long in any business if another, more lucrative, beckoned. An expert cobbler, Benjamin was willing to switch from repairing shoes to peddling tin or even selling furs, if it meant more money. Changing jobs often meant relocation, and Ben thought nothing of following the hot tip of the day; if he had to pull up stakes and trek off to Canada to sell furs, so be it.

The Canadian experience convinced Ben that he was not meant for the fur trade. When Ben learned there was a sizable Jewish community in Youngstown, Ohio, the Warners became Ohioans. Ben returned to his old profession and opened a shoe repair business. But his restlessness persisted. Youngstown may have reunited him with his coreligionists, but it did nothing to assuage his fear of spending the rest of his life hammering nails into people's shoes. When Ben decided that there was not that much difference between repairing shoes and trimming meat, he reinvented himself as a combination butcher-greengrocer, so that customers could buy their meat and produce under the same roof.

Had all of the children born to Ben and Pearl Warner survived, they would have numbered at least eight. But poor nutrition, influenza, and peritonitis took their toll. As the twentieth century dawned, there were four brothers—Harry, Jack, Sam, and Abe (who went by the name of Albert)—and a sister, Rose. At sixteen, Abe left Youngstown to become a soap salesman; Harry found work in Pittsburgh, while Jack and Sam remained at home to help their father in his business—but not for long.

In 1904 Pittsburgh proved a revelation to Abe/Al and Harry. The nickelodeons were getting under way, and Pittsburgh, which was then enjoying an economic boom, embraced them. Abe was mesmerized by his first visit to a nickelodeon, whereas Harry was more interested in the money to be made from this new form of entertainment. Many nickelodeons operated from around 10:00 A.M. to 10:00 P.M. with a repeat of the program almost every fifteen minutes. Audiences were not encouraged to linger, nor would they want to. In these "store shows," called such because the theaters were often converted storefronts, there was no ventilation; even during the movie, it was not uncommon for someone to go up and down the aisle with a spray can. Unfortunately, nothing could be done about the patrons' hygiene, especially those for whom bathing was a luxury. Cleanliness, either then or now, has never been a prerequisite for admission.

Body odor did not deter the brothers Warner, who had inherited their father's mania for latching on to the latest craze. However, it was Sam who really loved movies; the others loved the money movies brought in. Sam, who had remained in Youngstown with Jack, learned how to use a projector; he then persuaded his father to buy one from a local exhibitor who was going out of business. Next, the brothers needed something to project, and what better than the wildly popular *Great Train Robbery* (1903)? But where to show it? In the Youngstown area, theater and opera house owners had a real antipathy to the "flickers," which they reluctantly booked between engagements by acting troupes and solo performers merely to keep their establishments from going dark.

Ben Warner was rejuvenated by his children's entrepreneurial spirit; it was the equivalent of the Warner Traveling Players as Harry, Jack, Rose, Abe, and Sam—armed with a projector, a film, and a couple of shorts to fill out the bill—took their picture show to whatever community could provide them with a space, either a theater or, more often, a hall.[4] It had become customary in both nickelodeons and music halls that condescended to show movies to provide live entertainment as well. Generally, someone would sing a popular ballad, encouraging the audience to join in, as the words were projected on the screen. Harry Cohn began this way, as did, surprisingly, Jack Warner, accompanied by Rose at the piano. Sam handled the projection, and Abe sold tickets. If they were booked into a hall where there were no seats, the brothers would head for the nearest funeral parlor and rent folding chairs.

Once exhibition became a family business, there was no going back to shoes and soap; meat was another matter. Ben was not ready to pack up his butcher knives. When the brothers left Ben and Pearl behind, it was to pursue their dream, vertical integration—a term they had never heard, since it had not yet been coined. Yet they were moving toward a company that would combine production, distribution, and exhibition under a single corporate roof. Like Carl Laemmle, who started in exhibition, then advanced to distribution, and finally moved into production, creating a company that evolved into Universal, the brothers Warner decided it was time to stop depending on opera houses for bookings and open their own theaters, the first of which was in New Castle, Pennsylvania.

And just as Laemmle discovered that more money was to be made in distributing movies to nickelodeon owners than in being one himself, so did the brothers Warner, who joined forces with other exhibitors and established the Duquesne Amusement Supply Company, a film exchange based in Pittsburgh. The venture failed for a couple of reasons: one was the high prices that producers began charging when they discovered that sizable profits could be derived from such an exchange; the other (which was more significant) was the competition from the General Film Exchange Company, the distribution arm of the Motion Picture Patents Company (MPPCo). The MPPCo was a monopoly created to restrict film production and distribution to its members, who pooled their patents on cameras and projectors, thereby denying the use of that equipment to the independents.[5]

But by 1912 the MPPCo had been declared in violation of the Sherman Anti-Trust Act, and by 1915 it had faded into history. Regardless, the brothers had by no means abandoned the idea of setting up exchanges in a variety of locations to distribute whatever product they had—their own or that of others. With the shift of production from the East Coast to the West, exchanges in California were particularly desirable, and Sam and Jack, to whom travel was as natural as it was to their father, established some in Los Angeles and San Francisco—the latter being a profitable filmmaking center, although in no way comparable to Hollywood.

The brothers Warner seemed to know how to forge their own fortune. It was not so much that fortune favored the brave, as that fortune favored the knowledgeable. The brothers knew that certain goals were achieved gradually and that establishing a theater chain was one of them. After their first acquisition in New Castle, the brothers began buying up theaters in cities that were known to be movie conscious. Flagship theaters were de rigueur, and the brothers eventually had theirs in Los Angeles at Hollywood Boulevard and Wilcox and in New York on Broadway itself—each called, appropriately enough, the Warner. Eventually, Warners would have to divest itself of its theater chain, but that would only be after Warner Brothers had become a major studio.

Meanwhile, it was relocation time. The brothers, who had traversed the country buying theaters and setting up exchanges, knew it was time to put down roots in Los Angeles. After renting space in various parts of the city, they were able to use the profits from *My Four Years in Germany* (1918), based on the best-seller by the U.S. ambassador to Germany, James W. Gerard, to help pay for a production facility on Sunset and Bronson. *My Four Years in Germany*, which depicted the events leading up to America's entrance into World War I in 1917, grossed $1.5 million; it also prefigured the moviemaking philosophy that Warners adopted during the 1930s and 1940s and that Hal Wallis espoused from the moment he became a producer: topicality is everything. Today's headline can be tomorrow's movie. The same applied to Broadway plays. Since it was impossible to synchronize the closing of a play with the opening of the movie version, Wallis always tried to have the film ready before the play had faded from memory. Usually there was only a lapse of a few years, but even when Wallis had to wait a decade or so, as he did with Tennessee Williams's *Summer and Smoke,* and longer with Maxwell Anderson's *Anne of the Thousand Days*, he capitalized on their Broadway pedigree, promoting the films in such a way that non-theatergoers knew they were seeing something that had originated on the New York stage.

Wallis had probably never even heard of *My Four Years in Germany*. In 1918 he was on the road selling and demonstrating electric stoves, and cracking a book whenever he had time. He had no idea that within a few years he would be in Los Angeles working for the studio that produced what is considered the first feature-length propaganda film. Nor could Wallis have foreseen the role Warners would play in the lives of his sisters. After Minna ceased being Jack Warner's secretary, she became an important talent agent, often working out of an office at the studio. Juel's first husband was Wally Kline, an aspiring writer-producer, remembered (if at all) as the coauthor of the first treatment for the film version of an unproduced play, *Everybody Comes to Rick's*, which became the legendary *Casablanca*. Eva also profited from the Warners connection, albeit indirectly. She opened a luncheonette on Hollywood Boulevard, right next to the Warner theater, which opened in 1926. Little more than a storefront, it attracted such celebrities as Charlie Chaplin and Rudolph Valentino because of its location. Eva had become either starstruck or maternalistic, because the bigger the star, the more often the check bounced. Why pay cash when you could sign a check, especially if the owner's son was a studio hotshot? The restaurant business was not for the great-souled Eva, and the luncheonette soon closed.[6]

The year the Warner opened in Hollywood, Wallis became engaged to the celebrated comic actress Louise Fazenda, a Warners contract player since 1924.[7] Born in 1896 (and thus two years older than Wallis), Louise was a late, as well as an only, child. Planning to become a teacher, she was accepted at Stanford University but discovered she could not afford the tuition. A family friend, a bit player at Universal, took her to the studio one day, and from that moment Louise knew that she would not be spending her life in a classroom. Beginning as a stuntwoman, she went on to become one of Mack Sennett's best-loved performers because of her willingness to do anything for a laugh, including wearing bloomers that kept slipping down her legs.

A Paramount bio distributed after Wallis joined the studio in 1944 described him as so taken with Louise's films that he ran one of them for five weeks at the Tower. That would not have been impossible, since the Garrick, which he managed, had been renamed the Tower. Since the Garrick/Tower specialized in reruns, Wallis might have kept it on so long because it was a cheap rental. But it was probably only part of a bill. Wallis was anything but a romantic. What brought Louise and Wallis together was not the magic of the movies, but a dog. Wallis was saddled with the task of transforming Warners's big moneymaker—Rin-Tin-Tin, a German shepherd with a nasty disposition—into such a sweet-tempered canine that audiences would take him to their heart. But publicists are hagiographers, who make monsters into saints and snarling dogs into household pets. Until the arrival of Rin-Tin-Tin, Wallis's duties were fairly routine: making up press books with stills and plot summaries, arranging interviews, editing trailers, supplying columnists with copy, and welcoming new arrivals at the Pasadena train station, putting down a red carpet if their reputation merited it. Now, Wallis had to turn Rin-Tin-Tin into man's best friend and work out a promotional tie-in with dog food manufacturers to have his face emblazoned on their product.

Louise had been cast in a Rin-Tin-Tin movie, *Lighthouse by the Sea* (1925), with a script by Darryl Zanuck, who was soon to become production head at Warners. In one of her rare dramatic roles, she played the daughter of a blind lighthouse keeper who concealed her father's condition by performing his chores. Rin-Tin-Tin is cleverly worked into the script when a shipwreck survivor takes refuge in the lighthouse with his dog. The survivor falls in love with Louise, who is later kidnapped but rescued by her lover and the fearless Rin-Tin-Tin.

Wallis, who was on location at Laguna Beach with the *Lighthouse* company, was awed by Louise's ability to hold her own with Rin-Tin-Tin, whose salary was higher than anyone else's: $1,000 a week. Wallis began courting Louise, suggesting a ride in his Model T Ford for their first date. If that moment had been captured on film, it would have looked like a piece of Americana out of Booth Tarkington or Sinclair Lewis. It did not take Wallis long to realize that pursuing a movie star required a more sophisticated approach.

Louise was as taken with Wallis as he was with her. They were complete opposites. Cunning yet generous, she was everything Wallis had never encountered in a woman. Eva and Juel came close; in fact, it was Juel's warmth and vitality that prompted Louise to ask her to be maid of honor at their wedding. Since Minna had assumed the role of the terrible mother, eager to control her brother's life as if it were her own, whatever was fun-loving or outgoing in his nature had either been suppressed or undeveloped. An extrovert with a social conscience and a touch of the zany, Louise brought out as much of it as she could. But not even she could defrost Wallis completely.

In 1925, when Wallis and Louise began dating, Sam Warner witnessed a demonstration at Bell Laboratories in New York of a sound-on-disk system called Vitaphone, in which the sound, recorded on 33⅓ rpm disks, was synchronized with the celluloid image by means of an interlocked projector and turntable. Believing that this method of synchronization would not only enhance a film's appeal but also make it possible for exhibitors, unable to afford live musical accompaniment, to offer their patrons a reasonable substitute, Sam persuaded his brothers to adopt the Vitaphone system, thus giving birth to the talkies.[8]

As publicity director, Wallis was expected to write the copy heralding the Warners foray into talking pictures and persuade exhibitors to hop on the sound bandwagon. On 26 April 1925 Wallis's first broadside was ready for circulation: "Warners will enter a policy of talking pictures. Our researches show this is practical and will bring to audiences in every corner of the world the music of the greatest symphony orchestras and the vocal entertainment of the most popular stars of the operatic, vaudeville and theatrical fields."[9] Actually, that was not far from the truth. When *Don Juan* (1926), Warners's first full-length Vitaphone release, premiered at New York's Warner Theatre on 6 August 1926, those who had read Wallis's publicity release were not disappointed. The evening began with the New York Philharmonic playing the overture to Wagner's *Tannhäuser*, followed by a series of musical shorts, including Metropolitan Opera tenor Giovanni Martinelli singing "Vesti la giubba" from Leoncavallo's *Pagliacci*. Reportedly, the synchronization was perfect. When the audience returned after intermission, the main attraction, *Don Juan*, proved no less thrilling; bells tolled, swords clashed, doors slammed, and lips kissed—audibly.

The year 1925 was a hectic one for Wallis. In addition to promoting Vitaphone, he also had to travel to New York to supervise the ad campaign for the new system. But his lengthy absences did not affect his relationship with Louise. By 1926 they were contemplating marriage, despite opposition from Louise's mother and her actress-friend Irene Rich. Legally, however, Louise was still the wife of director Noel Mason Smith, even though they were separated. After Louise obtained a divorce from Smith on the ground of desertion, she and Wallis were free to marry, which they did on Thanksgiving Day, 24 November 1927. Since Wallis's meager digs could not accommodate the two hundred guests that were expected, the ceremony took place at Louise's elegant duplex at 5402 Ninth Street. As Warners's director of publicity, Wallis probably felt he had no other choice but to ask Jack Warner to be best man, especially since he had no brothers or close male friends. Always eager to hog the spotlight, as Wallis later learned, to his profound disillusionment, Warner gladly accepted.

Like so many stars, Louise discovered that the Los Angeles equivalent of gold was property. And she always found the best, in Los Angeles and Palm Springs. Louise frequently rented out the homes she had purchased, making certain they had spacious closets and large windows that would be especially appealing to women. Later, Wallis acquired his wife's knack of finding prime locations—as did Minna, with help from her brother. Meanwhile, Wallis's career was accelerating at a pace that resembled a movie in which time is collapsed and irrelevant events ignored.

Convinced that the silent era was now over, the brothers Warner decided to purchase a two-thirds interest in First National Pictures, later acquiring the remaining one-third from Fox. The First National purchase gave Warners not only a studio in Burbank, in addition to the one in Hollywood, but also a four-thousand-venue theater chain. Since Wallis had developed a reputation for being a quick study, he was made studio manager at First National. It was a vague title, as is often the case, but it reflected the studio's belief in Wallis as a potential production executive—title notwithstanding. Soon the title became meaningful. Wallis had barely settled into the job when he was prevailed upon to replace the "production executive," C. Graham Baker, who had suffered a nervous collapse. Having learned to deal with pressure as a teenager, Wallis succeeded where Baker had failed.

Although Wallis was no longer a publicist, the experience proved invaluable when he moved into production. While many publicists of his generation became producers (William Pine and William Thomas of Pine-Thomas Productions, Hunt Stromberg, Frank Rosenberg, Charles

Einfeld, and others), producers rarely, if ever, became publicists. If a producer had reached the executive suite via public relations, he or she would have no reason to return to the gritty business of selling—which is what a publicist does. A product has to be sold; it must be gift-wrapped with ribbons and bows, on the assumption that customers will buy the package because they believe the container and the contents are more or less identical. With Wallis, there was little difference between building up Rin-Tin-Tin into a friendly German Shepherd and promoting director Ernst Lubitsch as Europe's gift to America, although there was certainly more truth in the latter than in the former.[10]

When Lubitsch arrived at Warners in 1923, it was with the air of a bon vivant entering a deli. Lubitsch had encountered his share of vulgarians in Europe, but nothing could have prepared him for Jack Warner, the reigning king of crass. Still, Warner had to indulge Lubitsch, realizing that the studio needed a major director on the order of Paramount's Cecil B. DeMille or MGM's Clarence Brown, who were capable of making prestige films that were also moneymakers. Lubitsch provided the prestige; Rin-Tin-Tin, the money. Although Lubitsch's early films (e.g., *The Marriage Circle* [1924] and *Lady Windemere's Fan* [1925]) were strikingly literate, they also portrayed love as a game in which the players are equally adept—so much so that, though it may seem that one or the other is losing, both win at the end. Lubitsch aestheticized the physical. He never denied its presence; he merely raised it to a higher level: romance transmuted into *grand amour*—or sex without sweat.

Understanding that he had to sell Lubitsch to the American public, whose views of sex were primitive by comparison, Wallis came up with the phrase *the Lubitsch touch,* to indicate that the director, like Midas, had a special power: he could transform passion into civilized conversation and erotic metaphors, lovemaking into whispers and sighs. The phrase entered the film lexicon, becoming the touchstone for romantic cinema. Even after Lubitsch left Warners, Wallis remained on friendly terms with the director and his wife. By the 1930s Wallis had a beach house at Malibu that he rented to Mrs. Lubitsch. When she asked if she could stay there again in August and September 1937 to recuperate from an illness, Wallis graciously accommodated her. Joan Fontaine, who starred in two Wallis productions, *The Affairs of Susan* (1945) and *September Affair* (1950), characterized him as "a producer of charm and concern."[11] Wallis learned the importance of charm and concern as a publicist; as a producer, he never forgot where he had started. He would still be pitching a product, but one more valuable than a German Shepherd's image.

When Wallis became production manager at Burbank, he at first functioned independently of Darryl Zanuck, who headed production at the Sunset Boulevard studio. The distinction meant little after September 1928, when Jack Warner declared himself production head at First National, with Zanuck reporting to him and Wallis reporting to Zanuck. The reason was not megalomania, characteristic as that was of Jack Warner, but expediency: of the two studios, only Sunset was equipped to make talkies. And since Zanuck was production chief there, it made sense for him to precede Wallis in the chain of command. Moreover, the company's stock had fallen, making it necessary to centralize authority until such time as there was only one studio—the Burbank facility.

After Warners and First National merged in 1931, Wallis knew the organizational chart had changed when he arrived at the studio one day to find a workman painting his new, less prestigious title on his office door. Wallis reportedly sat on the steps and laughed: "It was the first indication I had that I was being supplanted."[12] Zanuck was now production head and Wallis his associate. It was back to studio manager, but not for long. In two years he would have a more imposing title—Zanuck's.

Darryl Zanuck was not one of Gabler's "Jews who invented Hollywood," although he certainly profited from his association with them, especially Jack Warner and William Fox. A Protestant from Wahoo, Nebraska, Zanuck discovered he had a knack for writing—first short stories, then scripts. Soon he was known as one of the fastest scenario writers in Hollywood. When Jack Warner wanted a Rin-Tin-Tin movie, he approached Zanuck, who obliged with *Find Your Man* (1924), which led to Zanuck's becoming a contract writer at the studio. He turned out scripts so rapidly (*Find Your Man* was written in four days) that he was forced to use a variety of pseudonyms, all of which he copyrighted so they could be used again.[13]

Jack Warner was both impressed and intimidated by Zanuck, whose talent compensated somewhat for his cockiness. But it was Zanuck's ability to pinpoint the flaws in a script or the inadequacies in a director—becoming so vocal at times that he was barred from the set—that inspired Warner to make him production head in 1927, regardless of his knack for offending the thin-skinned and mediocre. Product was all, and Zanuck could deliver it.

Product, however—specifically, talkies—had become a problem. Logically, owning two studios should have increased Warners's output—and would have during the silent era. But that era had ended, in great part because of Warners's venture into sound. Warners may have had two studios, but the technology for talkies was available only at one of them; thus sound films could not be made at both Burbank and Sunset at the same time. A compromise was reached that naturally favored Sunset: production at Sunset took place from around dawn to 6:00 P.M.; at Burbank, from 7:00 P.M. to early morning, with sound provided by a telephone hookup with Sunset *(Starmaker,* 20).

The initial tension between Wallis and Zanuck was eventually resolved, as suspicion changed to respect and then to a cautious camaraderie, as opposed to genuine friendship, of which both were incapable. It was more of a student-teacher relationship, with the older Wallis learning from Zanuck, four years his junior, as he sat alongside his mentor in the editing room, picking up tips that he would later use when he inherited Zanuck's job.

Zanuck would not have left Warners, or at least not so early, had the studio not incurred a net loss of $14 million in 1932. When Jack Warner instituted across-the-board cuts the following year, Zanuck refused to implement them and resigned. Although 1933 was the worst year of the Great Depression, Zanuck had no dearth of job offers. When Joseph Schenck, president of United Artists, invited Zanuck to join him in founding a new studio, Zanuck did not hesitate. The studio was Twentieth Century, soon to merge with Fox Film Corporation to become Twentieth Century–Fox, where Zanuck spent the rest of his career.

Zanuck's departure benefited both Wallis and Jack Warner. Wallis was given Zanuck's job and title; and Warner had a less abrasive production head. Warner could also claim that the salary cuts were justified: the studio's 1933 losses were less than half of what they had been the previous year.

Nineteen thirty-three was Wallis's annus mirabilis: he landed a dream job, and he became a father. Louise had been desperate to have a child. In 1930 she heard her biological clock ticking; she was then thirty-four and after three years of marriage had not yet conceived. Educated at a convent school, Louise believed in the power of prayer and began frequenting shrines, hoping to cure what she thought was infertility. A pilgrimage to the shrine of Saint Anne de Beaupré in Quebec proved efficacious. In 1933 Brent, their only child, was born; Louise was thirty-seven, Wallis thirty-five.

Wallis now had a son, who he expected would share his penchant for horseback riding and deep sea fishing, not to mention moviemaking. As it turned out, Brent shared none of his father's interests, particularly film, to which he developed a strong aversion. Although Wallis insisted in *Starmaker* that Brent was a source of joy to himself and Louise, he was always bothered by his son's reclusiveness, which had more to do with Wallis's profession than with Brent's being an introvert. Brent was impervious to the magic of the movies; watching his father edit films at home traumatized him, because Wallis seemed to be imposing narrative continuity on material that, to Brent, looked like a series of pictures without any (*Starmaker,* 94). Obviously, Brent either did not—or could not—comprehend continuity editing.

Brent's inability to be the son of Wallis's dreams may have been due to a number of factors: being a late child; having a father whose schedule only allowed for weekend parenting (and not always then); and having a mother who took her son along on her errands of mercy when, armed with food and literature, she visited the needy, who were usually complete strangers. To be the son of a former madcap turned social worker manqué and a father with a granitelike persona would not have been easy for anyone who would rather sit down with a book.

Wallis, who devoted only two pages to Brent in *Starmaker* (93–94), glosses over his son's college days, which lasted much longer than the usual four-year sequence either because of a stint in the Air Force or because of an active social life. In 1962, at the age of twenty-nine, Brent finally graduated from Stanford with a psychology degree. The previous year he had married Helen Carpenter. Brent's only accomplishment that seems to have made Wallis proud was his Ph.D. in psychology from the University of Florida. If Brent's marriage did the same, Wallis's pride was short-lived; and so was the marriage.

Over the years, the gulf between father and son grew into an abyss; by the 1970s, Wallis rarely spoke of Brent. When Wallis died in 1986, some of his associates were surprised to learn that he even had a son.

But it was different in 1933. Wallis wanted his son to be raised in the best possible environment—in other words, away from Beverly Hills, where he and Louise were then living. It was not that Benedict Canyon Drive was an undesirable address; quite the contrary. It was that Wallis wanted Brent to have a normal childhood—or as normal a childhood as a producer's son could have. And Beverly Hills, home to Hollywood's rich and famous, was not Wallis's idea of normal, either for Brent or for himself. While he was married to Louise, Wallis shunned the kind of socializing common in the industry for reasons ranging from his lack of bonhomie and his grueling twelve-hour days to Louise's feeling of alienation from a Hollywood she no longer recognized. When Brent was born, Louise was appearing only in minor roles; by 1939 she had completely retired from the screen.

When Wallis failed to find his ideal home, he built one. As a former tenement dweller, he appreciated the importance of a house, but only if it was the right kind. Louise had made him conscious of real estate, whether a corner lot, an apartment building, an orange grove, or a piece of commercial property. Wallis bought them all. Louise had done the same, but earlier. Minna, in fact, lived in an apartment building that Louise owned. Louise even had some choice property in Palm Springs that Wallis inherited after her death and tried, unsuccessfully, to sell to a developer for a hotel.[14]

In 1935 Wallis found sixty acres in the San Fernando Valley, which he purchased for $30,000. Wallis knew exactly what he wanted, the way the self-made and the self-educated do from random reading, which often leads to a wealth of information in one or two fields and a peripheral knowledge of others. Wallis had developed a keen interest in things British. He envisioned a large estate with a colonial farmhouse that resembled an English manor, the interior being a blend of British trappings and American chintz. If this seems an odd combination, it reflected the kinds of movies that most appealed to him: films with distinctly American or British themes. *Little Caesar* (1930), *Kid Galahad* (1937), *Four Daughters* (1938), and especially *Yankee Doodle Dandy* (1942) were as characteristic of Wallis as *Anthony Adverse* (1936), *The Adventures of Robin Hood* (1938), and *The Private Lives of Elizabeth and Essex* (1939).

Wallis's Anglophilia explains why, so shortly after the end of World War II, he chose to film the Victorian melodrama *So Evil My Love* (1948) in London. However, it was his trilogy—*Becket* (1964), *Anne of the*

Thousand Days (1969), and *Mary, Queen of Scots* (1971), all filmed on location—that convinced British audiences, including Elizabeth II, of his deep knowledge of their history and culture.

As a self-taught student of British history, Wallis demanded authenticity. Many of the furnishings for the Woodman Avenue home, such as the fireplace and the woodwork, were imported from Britain and presumably came from English manor houses.[15] The interior mirrored the taste of the owners: pewter and English china for Wallis; ceramic dogs on the bedroom dresser for Louise. The living room sported a portrait of Brent above the fireplace. Although most sons would have been delighted to be so prominently displayed, Brent always felt uncomfortable in that room because it exuded such a formal air—which is exactly what Wallis intended.

Anyone passing the impressive colonial at 5100 Woodman Avenue would have assumed from the electric gates that the owner was someone of substance, but not a member of the Hollywood community. That was also true of the interior. The home was a reflection of Wallis, not his profession. There was only one room that had any connection with film— and then only on certain occasions. The Blue Room, as it was called, bore no resemblance to a theater until Wallis was ready to screen the rushes of his films or entertain his family and friends with a weekend movie. Then it was magic time. The Frederic Remingtons came down from the wall, revealing a projection booth; the press of a button activated a hydraulic lift, causing the screen to emerge from beneath the floor. At other times the Blue Room was a low-ceilinged space that could pass for a den.

Beyond the gate was a pool, a small cottage for Louise's mother, a grape arbor, and an orchard of apricot and walnut trees. Louise convinced her husband that he should think of their property as a source of income as well as a home. The apricot and walnut trees, in addition to the orange groves on the other lots they owned in the Valley, made Wallis a gentleman farmer. As a film producer, he generated product; as a land owner, he grew produce. Wallis saw nothing incongruous about the two roles, which had one thing in common: profitability. The apricots were dried, the walnuts harvested, and the oranges plucked and sold to Sunkist. Not just a farmhouse, 5100 Woodman Avenue was an income-producing property.

Wallis needed a wife like Louise when he was wending his way through the Hollywood labyrinth. If the Wallises led a sequestered existence, avoiding Hollywood parties and entertaining small groups at home, it had as much to do with his lack of social grace and dislike—if not contempt—for schmoozing as with Louise's preference for the simple life after years of slapstick and shtick. In a small town like Hollywood, where so much depends on being at the right party with the right persons, Wallis succeeded on his own merits and on his own terms.

Louise shared her husband's pragmatism, although hers was spiritualized by a Catholic education that placed great emphasis on the corporal works of mercy, such as visiting the sick and assisting the needy. Once she retired from the movies, she became active in the UCLA Medical Center's Volunteer Services—dropping in on invalids, even those she did not know personally, and offering some of them financial assistance. Louise and Wallis also understood the importance of hard work—Wallis perhaps better than his wife, whose father had been a grocer, able to provide a home for his family and a high school education for his daughter. But they knew the vicissitudes of fortune because each had witnessed them. Louise saw what happened to such silent stars as "Fatty" Arbuckle, Mabel Normand, and Mary Miles Minter, once their reputations were tainted by scandal. She saw the demise of Mack Sennett's Keystone Company, where she began her career, and then the decline of Sennett himself, whose belief in the superiority of sight gags over plot found few adherents in the sophisticated 1920s. At Warners, Wallis watched as Richard Barthelmess, Lilyan Tashman, and Billie Dove held on to their former fame as if it were a life preserver, unable to accept the fact that they were sinking into oblivion. Louise, at least, made the transition from the silents to sound, but only as a character actress; and it was as a character actress that she exited the screen.

Wallis and Louise also understood the ephemeral nature of fame, which was, ironically, the basis of the star system on which the industry thrived. But in the early thirties, the industry was in trouble. For three years Warners registered only losses: $7.9 million in 1931, $14 million in 1932, and $6.2 million in 1933. The situation was slightly better in 1934: a $2.5 million loss. Small wonder that when the Wallises purchased the acreage on Woodman Avenue, they were hoping to turn a profit, not incur a loss.

One reason Wallis chose the Woodman Avenue location was to keep a distance between himself and Minna, who was living with their mother in one of Louise's apartment buildings in Beverly Hills. The distance was only geographical; Wallis was never able to extricate himself from her embrace, which, to use the idiom of the time, was the equivalent of "smother love." Barreling through airports with her brother and his second wife, Martha Hyer, Minna played herald, telling those in the way to make way for her brother the producer. Dining with Minna would have tried the patience of a monk. Walter Seltzer, Wallis's publicity director, recalled an occasion when he, Wallis, and Minna were together in a London restaurant. She turned on her brother, berating him for never making her a partner in his production company and thereby dashing her hope of their working together.[16] Wallis stared down at the table, enduring her tirade and saying nothing.

Minna may not have been part of her brother's professional life, but she was certainly part of the industry's. Realizing that, as a woman, she would never ascend to the executive suite, Minna turned to flesh peddling. With everyone except her brother, she could suppress her aggressiveness and radiate charm. Thus Minna had no problem ingratiating herself with such powerful agents as Leland Hayward and Myron Selznick, who provided her with enough capital to become the associate of Ruth Collier, a former model and bit player and now a successful agent with an impressive clientele; she also had an impressive address: 8627 Sunset Boulevard.

That became Minna's business address, too; but she also wanted a presence at Burbank. She cajoled her old boss, Jack Warner, into providing her with an office on the Warner Brothers lot, where she could be near her brother and check out the new contract players. Like her brother, Minna looked to the theater for her discoveries. When Minna saw a picture of Clark Gable and read that he would be appearing in the West Coast production of the prison drama *The Last Mile* (1930), in the same role that brought Spencer Tracy such acclaim on Broadway, she set her trap. Gable was her first client and probably her lover. Although Minna got him his first movie role, in *The Painted Desert* (1930), he did not remain her client for long. When Berg-Allenberg, which handled MGM's top stars and directors, beckoned, Gable changed agents, although he continued to remain on friendly—and perhaps amorous—terms with Minna.[17]

Minna's other clients included Myrna Loy, whom she encouraged Jack Warner to put under contract after seeing Loy's picture in a photo gallery; John Barrymore, whose money she managed so that he would not spend it all on liquor; Errol Flynn, who was not her lover; and George Brent, who was.[18]

The Irish-born actor, whose real name was George Brendan Nolan, had been a member of the Abbey Theatre before coming to Hollywood around 1930. Minna sensed a potential star and signed him immediately. We will never know if it was she who persuaded the actor to change his name; but as one who, like many of her clients, underwent a name change herself, it is not unlikely that Minna came up with "George Brent" before her latest discovery appeared in his first major film, *The Rich Are Always with Us* (1932). It may be coincidental—but Martha Hyer Wallis does not think so—that in 1932 Wallis also added the middle initial, *B,* to his name. And on those rare occasions when his entire name appeared in print, it was "Hal Brent Wallis." But usually it was either "Hal Wallis" or "Hal B. Wallis." Was the *B* Minna's idea? Louis Mayer and David Selznick added the middle initials *B* and *O,* respectively, to give their names an air of importance. Harold Walinsky had already become Hal Wallis, so why not Hal B. Wallis? If it were simply *B,* one could say that he was emulating Mayer and Selznick. But unlike their middle initials, the *B* stood for something—Brent, which can serve as either a first or last name. Thus, it is not so odd that it became his son's name. Whoever was responsible for Wallis's newly acquired middle initial and name succeeded in severing the last connection with the Walinskys of Chicago.

CHAPTER THREE

At the Court of the Clown Prince

A S SOON AS WALLIS REPLACED Graham Baker in 1928 as production head of First National, he began looking to the theater for talent, assuming that stage actors would have no difficulty adapting to talking pictures. But that was not always the case; many stage stars—Mary Martin, Ethel Merman, Gertrude Lawrence, Alfred Lunt, Lynn Fontanne, Katharine Cornell, Maurice Evans, and others—fared poorly in Hollywood, either because their elusive magic could not be captured on film or because their acting style was incompatible with a medium where less is more. Others—such as Bette Davis, Claudette Colbert, Humphrey Bogart, John Garfield, and Henry Fonda—made the transition from Broadway to Hollywood by scaling down their theatrical personas without detriment to their art. When they returned to the stage—as Colbert, Garfield, and Fonda regularly did—they could readjust to a medium in which there were neither cuts nor retakes.

Because Bette Davis started in the theater, Wallis understood her tendency to overact. Although he respected her talent, he still believed Davis had to be monitored before she went over the top. Even when she did, Davis performed with such bravura that she seemed to be giving moviegoers Hollywood's equivalent of theater. Ironically, Davis's return to Broadway in *The World of Carl Sandburg* (1960) and Tennessee Williams's *The Night of the Iguana* (1962) revealed a movie star unable to command the stage as she once did the screen. Film turned out to be Bette Davis's natural habitat.

In the 1930s Davis was not the only Broadway refugee to find her niche at Warners; Edward G. Robinson was another. That they both enjoyed their greatest triumphs at the same studio was not accidental. Initially, Robinson was unimpressed by movies, because he believed that film narrative was created by an editor; characterization, by a camera. But what he really found alien was shooting out of sequence—a practice for which there was no equivalent in the theater. After a few disillusioning experiences in Hollywood, Robinson was convinced that movies were not his métier. He headed back to New York in time to land the lead in *Mr. Samuel* (1930), an adaptation of a French drama that seemed oblivious to the stock market collapse the previous year. The title character (Robinson) was a domineering patriarch whose children took over his company after he suffered a heart attack. However, the patriarch not only recovered but also regained control, turning the company around and scoring a $1 million profit in the process. Although *Mr. Samuel* ran for a scant eight performances, Wallis, who caught one of them, was sufficiently impressed to go backstage hoping to persuade Robinson to return to the screen for a role in *Little Caesar* (1930).

Little Caesar spawned Warners's gangster cycle, which other studios soon emulated, much to the consternation of parents and civic organizations; the result was the familiar "crime does not pay" prologue, which did not keep Great Depression audiences from empathizing with the protagonists, as they progressed from robbing gas stations to running crime syndicates. Upward mobility has many forms, as Warners reminded moviegoers, stopping short of endorsing America's latest corporate climbers but not discouraging identification with them, either. That the characters ended up being gunned down was sufficient retribution. But that only occurred at the very end of the movie. Until then, audiences watched in fascination as gangsters flaunted the law and ignored convention, so that it almost seemed a shame that such colorful figures had to pay for doing what many in the audience fantasized about doing themselves.

Wallis had originally offered Robinson the secondary role of Otero, perhaps to test his seriousness, the actor believed.[1] After reading the script, Robinson declined; if he was to appear in *Little Caesar,* it would be as the title character, Caesar Enrico "Rico" Bandello. Once Robinson explained that he envisioned Rico as a man who traversed the same self-destructive path as Shakespeare's tragic figures, Wallis was impressed. He asked Robinson to wait until he conferred with Jack Warner. It was not a long wait. Perhaps Wallis sounded out Warner; more likely, Wallis made his own decision. At any rate, Robinson became a Warners contract player for more than a decade.

Little Caesar would never have been the classic it is without Robinson. The actor lived up to his promise, humanizing a character who was physically unattractive and at times even repellent. Awkward in a tuxedo, ill at ease with women, Rico desperately seeks the friendship of Joe Masara (Douglas Fairbanks Jr.), who prefers being a dancer to robbing night clubs. In an unusually homoerotic scene, Rico makes a pathetic bid for Joe's affection, revealing not only his profound need for male companionship but also his disdain for women. Robinson was so successful in his transformation of Rico from thug to antihero that when he utters his dying words—"Mother of mercy! Is this the end of Rico?"—we feel that blend of pity and fear that tragedy alone can produce. Enough moviegoers hoped it was not the end of Rico, or his kind. And Hollywood was eager to comply.

The *Starmaker* filmography begins with *Little Caesar,* as if it were Wallis's first production. Yet *Little Caesar* did not originate with Wallis, but with director Mervyn LeRoy, who, after reading W.R. Burnett's novel in galleys, had to convince Jack Warner, as well as Wallis and Zanuck, that he was the one to bring it to the screen.[2] Zanuck also took credit for the film, although he later admitted that his contribution was minimal, probably consisting of some uncredited contributions to the script.[3]

Although Zanuck ranked higher than Wallis on Warners's organizational chart, "senior executive" as opposed to "associate executive," he did not interfere with Wallis's production plans at First National. Each headed his own facility: Zanuck, Sunset; Wallis, Burbank. Each had his own slate of pictures. Production files, however, are incomplete, and the self-compiled filmography in *Starmaker* includes films with which Wallis was involved but not necessarily in a supervisory capacity. Thus it is impossible to determine how many movies from, say, 1930 to 1933, were Wallis's and how many were Zanuck's. *The Public Enemy* (1931) was, in every sense, a Zanuck production.[4] So, it seemed, was *I Am a Fugitive from a Chain Gang* (1932), despite its inclusion in Wallis's filmography.[5] *Chain Gang* may have originated with Wallis, who tried to interest Roy Del Ruth in directing it. When Del Ruth (a strange choice for a social consciousness film) declined because of the grim subject

matter, Zanuck stepped in, monitoring each stage of the script's preparation, hiring Paul Muni for the lead, and entrusting the direction to
Mervyn LeRoy, who claimed more credit for the film's success than he
should have: "Taken together then, the daily summary sheets, the memos, the versions of the script, the conference notes, and the other docu-
mentary evidence support Zanuck's contention . . . that he deserved
more of the creative credit for this film than LeRoy did."[6]

The Dawn Patrol (1930), however, was a Wallis, not a Zanuck, film.
Inspired by the success of Wings (1927), which went into general re-
lease in 1929 and became the first Oscar-winner for best picture, Howard
Hughes came up with his own aviation spectacle, Hell's Angels (1930),
at the same time that Warners was putting The Dawn Patrol—another
World War I film about fliers—into production. Hughes, a megaloma-
niac as well as a billionaire, did all he could to sabotage The Dawn
Patrol, even threatening to buy up all the available planes, although
Wallis managed to snag a few for the film (Starmaker, 22). Even then,
Hughes would not relent; he had one of his associates bribe a female
employee at Warners to steal a copy of the script. Once Wallis learned
about it, he hired detectives, who arrested the woman as she was about
to hand the script over to Hughes's emissaries. Hughes then resorted to
litigation, charging Warners with plagiarism and insisting that The Dawn
Patrol be withdrawn from circulation. A court battle ensued, and the
two films were screened for the district court judge. The verdict was
inevitable: the films were similar only in setting, and The Dawn Patrol
went into release.[7]

When Zanuck resigned from Warners on 15 April 1933, Wallis replaced him as production head, but without the title. Titles were fluid at
Warners; the 1933 Film Daily Year Book listed Wallis as "production
supervisor"; the next year, he was "assistant to executive, reporting directly to Jack Warner." Further upgrades followed: associate executive
(1935–36), associate producer (1937), associate executive in charge of
production, 1938–40; and finally executive producer in 1941.

Whatever his title, Wallis pretty much ran production at Warners
from 1933 until he left a decade later. He wielded authority in a variety
of ways, as seen from his memos, which, after Zanuck's departure, became more numerous in keeping with the footer on the interoffice sta-
tionery: "Verbal Messages Cause Misunderstanding And Delays (Please
Put Them In Writing)." Despite his new position, even Wallis had to

admit that Zanuck had already determined the studio's characteristic genres: crime, social consciousness, romantic comedy for diversion, and a unique kind of musical (e.g., *42nd Stree*t [1933] and *Gold Diggers of 1933*) that, unlike RKO's Astaire-Rogers films, acknowledged the existence of the Great Depression without broadcasting it. Reality had entered the musical, but for a relatively short time.

The clearest indication of the kind of producer Wallis was comes from his memos. Since he had never outgrown the penny-pinching mentality of his Chicago boyhood, he had little patience with directors who indulged themselves with take after take, when two or three would have been sufficient. Confrontation, however, was another matter. Wallis would not personally reprimand a director like William Wyler, who thought nothing of shooting thirty-three takes of a scene.[8] In one sense confrontation was not Wallis's responsibility as head of production. He conveyed his displeasure, often in vitriolic terms, to the film's associate producer, assistant director, unit manager, or studio manager, depending on who was supervising the day's shooting.

Wallis was not alone in deploring Wyler's methods while stopping short of taking him to task. When Jack Warner viewed some dailies from *The Letter* (1940), he was appalled at Herbert Marshall's diction; still, he refused to approach Wyler himself, entrusting the task instead to Wallis, in whom Warner placed the utmost confidence—or so he said.[9] Since Wallis had no intention of tangling with Wyler (or of playing scapegoat), he referred the matter to associate producer Robert Lord. Lord must have been effective; Marshall shaped up, but Wyler did not.

Wyler's filming two takes of the same scene in *Jezebel* (1938), when one would have sufficed, infuriated Wallis: "What the hell is the matter with him—is he absolutely daffy?" When Wyler made eleven takes of a scene with Henry Fonda, Wallis wondered if the actor was being punished for having been the first husband of Margaret Sullavan, who had recently divorced Wyler after a year and a half of marriage. "By-gones should be by-gones," Wallis fumed. The director was proceeding so slowly that Wallis snidely remarked that one of the children in *Jezebel* "will be a full-grown man by the time Wyler finishes the picture."[10] Even if Wyler had been aware of Wallis's displeasure, he would not have changed his ways. Wyler knew Warners needed his expertise, which was apparent on Academy Awards night, 23 February 1939, when *Jezebel*'s star, Bette Davis, won for best actress. After Wyler finished *The Letter* (1940), another Davis vehicle and his last film for Wallis (and Warners), Wallis begged Jack Warner not to let Wyler cut the film himself.[11] Wyler apparently had been trying to wrest control of the editing from Wallis, even telling Warner that *The Letter* was ready to be previewed. Wallis knew it was not; when it came to editing, Wallis was a far better judge of deciding which shots should be used and which should be trimmed—even estimating the number of feet he thought should be cut from a particular scene—than either Wyler or Warner. For example, his cutting notes for *Marked Woman* (1937) specify that in the trial scene the cuts of the "hostesses" (i.e., prostitutes) should be no more than two and one-half feet each. That *The Letter* was nominated for best editing suggests that Wallis's judgments were artistically sound.

Even if Wallis had issued a policy statement on shooting economically, there would have been directors who ignored it. Since Wallis had never directed, he could not appreciate the glitches that affect a shoot—anything from sudden illness and technical malfunctioning to flubbed lines and costumes that suddenly seem inappropriate. When the unit or studio manager reported a short day or a half day, Wallis demanded an explanation. During the filming of *The Old Maid* (1939), Wallis was shocked at how little Edmund Goulding shot one day. Since Goulding was a respected director, best known at the time for MGM's *Grand Hotel* (1932), Wallis instructed the associate producer, the German-born Henry Blanke, to remain on the set, keeping tabs on Goulding and prodding him to shoot more film per day and include more close-ups, particularly of Bette Davis—especially at the moment when she realizes she named her daughter Clementine after her lover, Clem.[12]

Blanke, who had once been Ernst Lubitsch's assistant, was now Wallis's. When Wallis ran dailies of *The Petrified Forest* (1936) and spotted a shot of Humphrey Bogart sitting behind a moose head, with the horns seeming to come out of the actor's head, he had Blanke inquire of director Archie Mayo whether this was intentional (obviously knowing it was not). And while Blanke was getting Mayo's answer, Wallis saddled him with an additional task: an explanation of Mayo's shooting scenes from so many different angles. After receiving no response to his 1 November 1935 memo to Blanke, Wallis fired off another three days later: "When I write you these things, I expect you to follow it up and report back to me."[13] The next day an apology arrived from Blanke, who also answered another of Wallis's complaints—namely, Leslie Howard's tardiness—by insisting that the actor made up for it by staying longer on the set.

Wallis leaned hard on Blanke, who came into his own as a producer only after Wallis left the studio in 1944. Meanwhile, Blanke was only a "production supervisor" (actually, an "associate producer"), who often had to perform duties usually relegated to junior executives. After viewing the *Old Maid* dailies, Wallis told Blanke to have the tassels removed from Bette Davis's jacket. When Davis had her hair cut during the filming of *Juarez* (1939), contrary to Wallis's mandate that no actors or actresses cut their hair until after the retakes, he became livid and dashed off a memo to the production manager, Tenny Wright; the head of makeup, Perc Westmore; and, of course, Blanke: "Come up to my office at 11:00 A.M."[14]

Wallis constantly complained about short days and half days. His idea of a day's work was not that of most directors, particularly the auteurs. It was bad enough that while directing *All This and Heaven Too* (1940), Anatole Litvak filmed the same close-up of Bette Davis fourteen times; it was worse that Wallis thoroughly disliked the one Litvak selected, insisting that it be replaced with a medium shot because "it is possible that by that time [Davis] didn't know what she was doing."[15]

"Tola" Litvak was not one of Wallis's favorites. Wallis vetoed his idea of using an elaborate crane shot of Davis going up a staircase, preferring the less expensive method of a cut and a dissolve to the second floor. When Wallis discovered that Litvak had proceeded with the shot, he lashed out at the associate producer, the generally reliable David Lewis: "I simply cannot understand a total disregard of instructions. . . . I want to see you and Litvak at noon to discuss this further."[16]

Ordinarily, directors heeded Wallis's suggestions; those who ignored them did so much to the detriment of their films. There was little Wallis could tell Elliott Nugent about the way he should direct *The Male Animal* (1942), since Nugent not only had coauthored the 1940 Broadway hit with James Thurber but also had played the lead—a mild-mannered English professor whose politics run afoul of the college administration. Apart from carping at the paucity of dailies, Wallis was especially critical of Nugent's direction of a drunk scene between Henry Fonda as the professor, whose happy marriage is threatened by the appearance of his wife's former beau, and Herbert Anderson, as the idealistic editor of the campus newspaper under attack by the board of trustees for its liberal editorials. As teacher and student bemoan their plight, they become increasingly inebriated—this being a time before the drinking age was twenty-one, although Anderson barely looked eighteen. It is certainly one of the most misdirected drunk scenes in film; Wallis was actually kind when he described it as "a little too overdone" and "played at too slow a pace."[17] Instead of heeding Wallis's advice, Nugent, who felt he understood the way the scene should be played, having done it on stage for 187 performances, let Fonda and Anderson deliver their lines in a soporific drawl. An actor of Fonda's stature deserved better direction; and Nugent, who had been working in film for a decade, should have known that while theater is larger than life, film is life writ small.

Wallis could be blunt, flippant, and even insulting—but usually only in memo form. Enraged at the wretched acting by a member of *Marked Woman*'s supporting cast, he asked Max Arnow, "Are you the casting director or what the hell are you?"[18] The same day Arnow responded, offering his "humble apologies" and explaining that the actor playing a gangster had actually been one himself. Although *Juke Girl* (1942) was not a major production, Wallis behaved as if it were. After looking at the *Juke Girl* dailies, he wrote candidly to director Curtis Bernhardt, stating that if Bernhardt shot the script as written instead of reworking it, the movie would come in on budget: "I don't want to take you off the picture, but if you do not improve . . . I will be forced to do so."[19] What he expected of directors was virtually impossible—namely, staying on schedule and on budget, particularly when shooting an epic like *Anthony Adverse* (1936), a sprawling nineteenth-century costume drama with a huge cast, multiple sets (including an opera house), and a glorious score by Erich Wolfgang Korngold.

Mervyn LeRoy, who was assigned to direct the film, seems to have wanted to shoot in continuity, which was both uncommon and fiendishly expensive. Although LeRoy was the kind of director with whom Wallis could be (and often was) frank, on this occasion he let Tenny Wright deal with the matter, since that was the production manager's job; besides, Wright was a former carnival barker and prize fighter and should therefore be able to handle LeRoy.

Wallis was on target when it came to the folly of continuity filming. He saw no reason for LeRoy to go on location in the morning to film long shots of the leads, Fredric March and Olivia de Havilland, on a hay wagon, and in the afternoon return to the set for the next scene, which was an interior. As far as Wallis was concerned, LeRoy had wasted the morning; the long shot of the couple in the wagon could have waited until the company went on location again: "Let's get this settled once and for all," Wallis instructed Wright.[20]

Continuity shooting ceased. But there were other problems. When Wallis produced a film requiring sumptuous sets and costumes, he never succumbed to the "spare no expenses" mentality; quite simply, he could not afford to. Warners weathered the Great Depression by packaging quality in dime store wrappings. Although *42nd Street* and *Gold Diggers of 1933* were budgeted at around $400,000 each, their production values suggested otherwise. Warners was doing what Universal was not. A melodrama like Universal's *Magnificent Obsession* (1935) cost the studio more than $900,000; the musical *Show Boat* (1936), even more: $1.194 million. Yet *Show Boat* was far less elaborate than any of Warners's musicals, the best of which featured Busby Berkeley's geometric arrangements of chorus girls in the shape of revolving wheels and budding flowers. What Universal did wrong—placing films into production with skyrocketing budgets that led to the studio's takeover by Standard Capital in 1936—Warners did right. *Anthony Adverse* became a huge hit and was rewarded at Oscar time, winning for best supporting actress (Gale Sondergaard), best editing (Ralph Dawson), best cinematography (Tony Gaudio), and best musical score (Korngold). That *Anthony Adverse* lost for best picture to Columbia's *Mr. Deeds Goes to Town* did not affect its box office appeal.

When Wallis identified with a film, as he did with *Anthony Adverse*, the memos proliferated. Transformation stories fascinated him—in this case, from a commoner to a gentleman—perhaps because they paralleled his own situation. Wallis wanted perfection, but at bargain prices. When he was handed the budget for *Anthony Adverse*, he immediately reduced it by $75,000 after lowering the estimates for some of the sets.[21]

Wallis always became testy when his instructions were ignored, especially by those who, he felt, "double-crossed" him. *Anthony Adverse* required an opera house sequence, for which Wallis provided specific instructions. Impressed by the opera house in Columbia's *Love Me Forever* (1936), which starred Metropolitan Opera soprano Grace Moore, Wallis knew exactly how the interior should look. He informed Tenny Wright that only two boxes were to be built, allowing for reverse shots as well as high shots of the stage. When Wallis discovered that art director Anton Grot had an elaborate interior constructed, ringed with boxes, he was enraged: "There is no God damned reason for things of this kind happening, and I'm going to do something drastic about it if I have to fire four or five Art Directors . . . because I'm getting disgusted with having meetings and telling people what to build, and then finding the stuff come out on the screen with thousands of dollars spent uselessly."[22]

It was one thing to be an art collector, as Wallis was; it was another to understand the artistic mind. The Polish-born Grot, who had studied illustration and design in Cracow and Koenigsberg, was familiar with opera house interiors and wanted authenticity. While Wallis found it "a ridiculous waste of money" for a hundred or so extras to sit in the orchestra merely to suggest that the opera house had one, it would have seemed odd if the Paris Opéra consisted of only two boxes and a stage. It was not that Grot and LeRoy double-crossed Wallis; it was that they had an artist's view of the film, not a producer's. Perhaps the opera set cost a couple thousand more than Wallis had budgeted; the film cost around $1 million total. Dramatically, *Anthony Adverse* was an epic— an odyssey that took the title character from Italy to France, with stopovers in Cuba and Africa. He finally returned to Paris via the French Alps, after which he was presumably off to America. Financially, *Anthony Adverse* contributed to Warners's net profit of $3.17 million for 1936.

Although Wallis never evidenced any interest in directing, he knew what he wanted from actors. He bemoaned sloppy diction, criticizing LeRoy for allowing the actor playing Anthony as a boy to utter such anachronisms as "I wanna go now."[23] The opposite extreme, affectation, also infuriated Wallis, who repeatedly asked that Olivia de Havilland speak more naturally, "with a little more feeling and not quite so much histrionics."[24] Bette Davis's tendency to overact was a constant thorn in his side. "Hold her down," he ordered Litvak during the filming of *All This and Heaven Too*. He was annoyed that the director had indulged Davis, who was "going overboard again in her precise manner of speaking."[25] Davis must have acquiesced, since she gave one of her less mannered performances.

Nothing escaped Wallis's attention. He wanted a full-length dress for June Lockhart in *All This and Heaven Too* to conceal "her little skinny legs."[26] The handwriting seen on the screen in *Anthony Adverse,* which was set during the Napoleonic era, should be "aged and have some character to it."[27]

Unflattering costumes and excessive makeup were other bêtes noires. Rosalind Russell's eyelashes in *No Time for Comedy* (1940) were so long that they curled, Wallis complained to Perc Westmore. And while on the subject of Russell's appearance, he specified wardrobe changes, demanding that she stop wearing those "large daffy hats she loves" and appear in more flattering outfits, particularly high-necked blouses.[28] Wallis thought nothing of telling Ann Sheridan to lose weight before *Torrid Zone* (1940) began shooting. Furious that she had not slimmed down, he instructed the director, William Keighley, to do something about her "fat" face and Perc Westmore to minimize the size of her lips.[29] Francis Langford's pompadour hairdo in *This Is the Army* (1943) made her face look like a dish.[30] No prostitute wears a coat with a fur collar and carries a muff, Wallis informed Orry-Kelly about Lola Lane's outfit in *Marked Woman*.[31] A new costume was quickly designed. Since Wallis was romantically involved with Lane at the time, he had her photographed in five different hairstyles for *Daughters Courageous* (1939) before he could decide what was the most attractive.[32] Ironically, Lane was not playing the lead; her sister Priscilla was. Wallis, however, was not attracted to the plucky Priscilla; he much preferred her earthy and somewhat blowzy sister.

Having been in the vanguard of the sound revolution, Wallis was especially concerned with the way sound enhanced—or perhaps detracted from—a scene. He was generally pleased with Mike Curtiz's direction of *The Sea Wolf* (1941) (though he thought there were too many high shots of the deck, and he criticized Barry Fitzgerald's slurred speech), but he instructed Blanke to have Curtiz film the climax, in which the *Ghost* is on the verge of sinking, by first shooting close-ups of John Garfield and Edward G. Robinson, so that the sound of the water rushing into the engine room could be added in postproduction; that way, Curtiz could determine how much sound was needed.[33] There may not have been much dialogue in *The Sea Wolf*'s denouement; but what there was, Wallis did not want drowned out.

Even in 1933 Wallis was thinking about forming a cadre of loyal subordinates whose allegiance would be as much to him as to Warner Brothers. With Zanuck's departure, he was now head of production, and he may well have been thinking of a time when he would either be heading a studio or running his own production company. But at present Warners was his home and Jack Warner his boss.

It was probably not coincidental that his cousin, Jack Saper, arrived at Warners shortly after Wallis took over production. Whether Saper came there on his own or by invitation from Wallis is unknown. The latter is the more probable. At any rate, Saper was a film editor by 1936; four years later, he had advanced to unit manager of *Brother Orchid* and *Torrid Zone* (both 1940). It may have been a step upward, but a unit manager is essentially a troubleshooter, doing everything from arranging transportation and accommodations for the cast and crew when they go on location, to solving whatever problems arise during the shoot—in short, the unit manager inherits tasks that producers feel are beneath them.

Naturally, Saper would rather produce; Wallis, however, realized that his cousin, like T.S. Eliot's Prufrock, was meant to serve, not command. Rather than discourage his friend, Wallis made him associate producer of four films: *The Man Who Came to Dinner* (1941), *Navy Blues* (1941), *Larceny, Inc.* (1942), and *Juke Girl* (1942). Still, Wallis had doubts about Saper's being sole associate producer, believing he needed a mentor who would share the title with him. The title itself is a misnomer. "Assistant producer" is more accurate, since an associate producer is just a unit manager with more responsibilities, including keeping a close eye on the budget and, depending on the producer and director, providing creative input. Since Saper was not the creative type, Wallis brought Jerry Wald on board, with the expectation that, as a co–associate producer, Saper would learn from his more seasoned colleague.

It did not matter who the associate producers were. Wallis hovered over the shoot like a spectral presence. Although the *Juke Girl* files in the Warner Brothers Collection contain a memo (8 May 1941) entrusting Saper and Wald with the "joint supervision" of the film, Wallis behaved as if it was *his* movie from the start, threatening to fire director Curtis Bernhardt if he did not stick more closely to A.I. Bezzerides's script and giving him specific instructions for the opening shot (a close-up of a jukebox, followed by a pan over to Ann Sheridan). Wallis made certain that he copied Saper and Wald on every vitriolic memo to Bernhardt, if only to remind them who ran production at Warners. Neither failed to get the point; when additional shots were needed, Saper and Wald compiled a list for Wallis's approval.

Only once did Wallis step out of the picture, at least nominally, to allow Wald and Saper to coproduce *Across the Pacific* (1942), which reunited the *Maltese Falcon* trio—Humphrey Bogart, Mary Astor, and Sydney Greenstreet—with director John Huston. But with Huston again directing, it is hard to imagine Wald and Saper's doing much more than making sure the ship, on which much of the action took place, looked as if it were moving.

Wallis knew that Wald, unlike Saper, was a true producer; thus, while Wald and Saper were receiving joint credit for their films, Wald was receiving sole credit for producing a number of important films, such as *George Washington Slept Here* (1942), *The Hard Way* (1942), *Background to Danger* (1943), and *Destination, Tokyo* (1943). Wald went on to become a major producer at Columbia, RKO, and Fox, but Saper was destined for a less glamorous role. When Wallis was ready to leave Warners for Paramount in 1944, he needed a production manager. Saper did not have to be persuaded; he fit the job description perfectly. Perhaps Saper thought that at another studio there would be more opportunities to produce. Wallis had other plans for his cousin, and producing was not one of them. Keeping an eye on the budget was.

As the 1940s began, Wallis was at his peak. He had assembled a team that proved so loyal that when he made the switch to Paramount in 1944, he took some of them (e.g., Saper; story editor Irene Lee; and his secretary, Paul Nathan) with him. On Oscar night, 23 February 1939, Wallis was given the Irving Thalberg Memorial Award, which Zanuck had received the previous year. That year, Wallis's productions were nominated in almost every category: three for best picture (*The Adventures of Robin Hood, Four Daughters,* and *Jezebel*); one for best actor (James Cagney, *Angels with Dirty Faces*); two for best actress (Fay Bainter, *White Banners;* Bette Davis, *Jezebel*); one each for supporting actor (John Garfield, *Daughters*) and supporting actress (Fay Bainter, *Jezebel*); one for original story *(Angels)* and one for screenplay *(Daughters);* and one each for sound *(Daughters),* art direction *(Robin Hood),* original score *(Robin Hood),* and editing *(Robin Hood).* No studio made a clean sweep that night. Although Bainter lost to Davis for best actress, she went home with an Oscar for supporting actress; the *Robin Hood* trio was similarly honored: composer Erich Wolfgang Korngold, film editor Ralph Dawson, and art director Carl Jules Weyl. Wallis was proud of his five winners, but prouder of his Thalberg Award. That award was inau-

gurated in 1937, the year after Thalberg's death, to single out producers
who had made major contributions to film. Zanuck was the first recipient, Wallis the second. Within a few years, Wallis would again receive
the Thalberg award.

Usually, Wallis was on target, but not about the billing for *High
Sierra* (1941). Wallis was convinced that Ida Lupino, rather than Humphrey Bogart, was the film's true star and should be acknowledged as
such, meaning top billing. Wallis was so impressed by her performance
in *They Drive by Night* (1940) that he believed her name would carry
the film. Ironically, *High Sierra* made Bogart a star and Lupino a respected actress and later one of Hollywood's few female directors—but
not an icon and much less a household word. Lupino was billed before
Bogart when *High Sierra* was first released; the billing was reversed
with the rerelease.[34]

Wallis was also oblivious to the potential of a failed Broadway play
about an heiress who died of a brain tumor. If it had been up to him,
Dark Victory (1939)—which joined the ranks of *Ninotchka, Mr. Smith
Goes to Washington, Gunga Din, The Wizard of Oz, Stagecoach,* and,
naturally, *Gone with the Wind* as Warners's candidate for Hollywood's
annus mirabilis—might never have been filmed. It originated as a 1934
play starring Tallulah Bankhead as the doomed heroine. Bankhead was
respectably reviewed, although the play ran a mere fifty-one performances. Still, *Dark Victory* had the makings of the perfect woman's
picture, as David Selznick realized when he purchased the rights, thinking it would be an ideal vehicle for Greta Garbo. The growing popularity of the woman's film made *Dark Victory* appealing to other stars such
as Katharine Hepburn, Carole Lombard, Rosalind Russell, and Janet
Gaynor, who were eager to play the leading role of Judith Traherne.
Plagued by script and casting problems, Selznick relinquished the rights
to Warners for $27,500—about $10,000 more than what he had paid for
the play.[35] Wallis was lukewarm about *Dark Victory*. When he learned
that Selznick was about to unload the property, he advised Jack Warner
to pay no more than $5,000 for it. Naturally, he was disturbed at how
much it eventually cost.

Although Wallis included *Dark Victory* in his filmography, the movie
owes less to him than to the associate producer, David Lewis, a specialist in the woman's film (e.g., *Camille* [1936] and *The Sisters* [1938]),
who believed more strongly in the property than either Wallis or Jack

Warner—the latter asking ingenuously, "Who the hell wants to see someone dying of a brain tumor?"[36]

Warners was looking for a vehicle for Kay Francis, who was finally
chosen to play the ill-starred Judith, while Bette Davis, the more logical
choice, was assigned to the mediocre *Comet over Broadway* (1938), a
low-grade weepie. After *Jezebel,* Davis had no intention of playing a
woman obsessed with being a Broadway star, especially since she was a
star, albeit in the movies. Francis ended up in *Comet,* which gave off
whatever little light it had and then disappeared into the black hole of
deservedly forgotten films. *Dark Victory* resulted in one of Davis's finest—and unaffected—performances; it also has the distinction of being
the first film to deal openly with terminal cancer as well as one of the
most accurate in doing so. Casey Robinson, Davis's favorite writer, who
provided her with such memorable roles as Charlotte in *The Old Maid*
(1939), Henriette Desportes in *All This and Heaven Too* (1940), and
Charlotte Vale in *Now, Voyager* (1942), consulted several neurosurgeons
to make certain that the symptoms of brain cancer that Judith experiences, and the examination that she undergoes, were medically accurate. Wallis may have green-lighted the film, but it was Lewis and director
Edmund Goulding who saw what Wallis and Warner could not: that
dying can be as much an art as living. Judith's final acceptance of her
condition, and her refusal to burden her best friend and her husband
with a fate that she alone must face, redeemed what otherwise would
have been a three-hankie movie. Rarely have death and transfiguration
coalesced in a single shot as they did at the close of *Dark Victory,* when
Davis's face slowly went out of focus until nothing remained but a luminous screen.

Wallis's production duties were only part of his job; he was also
expected to keep Jack Warner informed of everything going on at the
studio during his absence. When Warner was traveling by train to the
East Coast, as he frequently did with his wife Ann and his masseur
Abdul, he left his itinerary with Wallis, who either communicated with
his boss en route, wiring him in his compartment, or waited until Warner and his entourage were ensconced at the Ritz Towers at Fifty-ninth
and Park or the Waldorf Astoria ten blocks farther south. Whatever taste
Jack Warner may have lacked in film, he made up for in his choice of
hotels.

The Wallis-Warner telegrams attest to Jack Warner's confidence in

Wallis, Wallis's ability to carry out his boss's instructions as well as making independent judgments, and their bond, which seemed to be deepening until it devolved into an employer-employee relationship, then estrangement, and finally animosity.[37]

But in the 1930s Wallis was Warner's Mercury, apprising him of the reviews (selecting only the positive ones), cuts (often specified in feet, as was Wallis's practice), release dates, loan-outs, and titles to be registered; he filed progress reports, informing Warner of major script changes, such as a character's ethnicity—a topic of special interest to Warner, who preferred non-Jewish characters whenever possible to prevent a boycott by anti-Semites. Warner was not alone in muting the Jewish voice in his films. Few movies of the period featured Jewish families; and when they did—for example, in Fox's *House of Rothschild* (1934)— the script downplayed the family's ethnicity to the extent that it became irrelevant, particularly with Loretta Young playing Nathan Rothschild's daughter. Even in Columbia's great postwar success, *The Jolson Story* (1946), the young Al Jolson, having run away from home to become a vaudevillian, is caught and placed in a Catholic orphanage, where he is promptly made a chorister, singing the solo part of the "Ave Maria."

When Broadway producer Herman Shumlin tried to interest Jack Warner in making the movie version of a play, *Sweet Mystery of Life*, that he was planning to produce, Warner maintained that it could only work "by eliminating the Jewish names and giving the characters Gentile names."[38] The film became *Gold Diggers of 1937*, although no one would ever know that the Jews of the original had become conversos.

None of this had much impact on Wallis. He knew his place in Jack Warner's hierarchy, which was vastly different from the studio's organizational chart. Warner had his lieutenants, reporting to him alone, and Wallis was lieutenant first class. His mantra was "Will attend promptly to all matters and will keep you advised," the closing words of many a telegram.

However, after extolling *Black Fury* (1935) as "ONE OF THE GREATEST PICTURES I HAVE SEEN," Wallis added, "AND YOU KNOW I AM NO YES MAN." Wallis's assertiveness probably eluded Warner on this occasion, although it became quite apparent by 1943. Meanwhile, Wallis kept his boss "advised"; no detail was deemed too trivial for Warner's attention. Wallis was so good at his job, in fact, that in July 1935 Warner complained to Joseph Hazen, one of the studio's vice presidents and a board member, about the "tremendous amount of work" he had to do during Wallis's three-week absence.[39]

As a former publicist, Wallis understood the importance of exploitation, although he also believed it should be tastefully done. Movie tie-ins were common (for example, getting a department store to feature replicas of the costumes and accessories from a particular film), yet Wallis urged Warner to veto tie-ins with *A Midsummer Night's Dream* (1935), since they would cheapen the movie's quality, especially in view of its Shakespearean origins. Wallis sent Warner a telegram indicating that he was appalled by the publicity department's creation of a trick dress, similar to the costume Anita Louise wore as Titania, that could be displayed in stores. There is no record of Warner's reply, but it is safe to assume that if Warner had not acceded to Wallis's request, there would have been a follow-up telegram on the subject, emphasizing that *A Midsummer Night's Dream* was a prestige film, not a potboiler.

Wallis's casting suggestions were usually on target, while Warner's were frequently off the wall, including the following ideas: either Jack Benny or Fred MacMurray (*The Male Animal* [1942]), Tallulah Bankhead (*Mr. Skeffington* [1944]), Ida Lupino (*The Corn Is Green* [1944]), and Errol Flynn (*The Constant Nymph* [1943]), in roles that were eventually cast with the right stars: Henry Fonda, Bette Davis (in both *Skeffington* and *Corn*), and Charles Boyer, respectively. Although Warners decided against buying the rights to the Kurt Weill–Moss Hart musical *Lady in the Dark* (1941), Warner was toying with casting either Claudette Colbert or Irene Dunne in the pivotal role of Liza Elliott. Dunne at least could sing; Colbert could not. Warner also could have made the film version of Gershwin's folk opera *Porgy and Bess* in 1943. But he felt the same about an African American project as he did about a Jewish one. "I have definitely made up my mind not to make any all-Negro picture," he informed East Coast story editor Jacob Wilk. Titles were also of little consequence to Warner. When General Sales Manager Gradwell Sears balked at entitling a movie *The Private Lives of Elizabeth and Essex* (1939) because it sounded too British, Warner referred Sears to the English film *Pygmalion* (1938), which was embraced by American audiences: "I personally looked in 4 dictionaries to find what the word—PYGMALION—meant and haven't found out yet, which only proves . . . if you have a good picture you can call it PADDY'S PIG and they will come in."[40]

Wallis may have had his blind spots, but they were fewer than Jack Warner's. Wallis was indifferent to *Dark Victory,* for which Bette Davis campaigned so strenuously—giving what is arguably her best screen performance, vastly superior to the self-caricature in *All About Eve* (1950) that spawned a series of films revealing Davis in various forms of the grotesque, until she became a grotesque. For a theatergoer like Wallis, passing on Lillian Hellman's *Children's Hour* (1934) was a huge mistake. On the one hand, he was turned off by the plot—a female student's accusation that her teachers, Karen Wright and Martha Dobie, were lovers, which led to Martha's suicide. On the other hand, Wallis knew that if Warners bought the rights, the script would have to comply with the Production Code, which forbade any intimation of homosexuality—not that there was that much in the original; however, in 1934, the mere allegation of an "unnatural" relationship was enough to warrant a rewrite. Wallis's telegrams to Warner reflect his ambivalence about the play; fascinated by the theme, while realizing it could never be filmed as written, Wallis suggested that it might work if Karen and Martha were in love with the same man; that would retain the triangular plot but without the lesbian implications. Despite his distaste for the subject matter, Wallis at least knew how to market *The Children's Hour* to a mass audience. Warner was still not interested; Hellman then persuaded Samuel Goldwyn to buy the rights for $50,000, convincing him that she could deliver a script in which Martha was secretly in love with Karen's fiancé, thus removing any hint of lesbianism. *The Children's Hour* became *These Three* (1936), a hit movie as well as an unusual case of fidelity to the original: Martha (sensitively played by Miriam Hopkins) still harbors a love for Karen, which has been redirected toward Karen's fiancé. Moviegoers able to appreciate the many forms of film subtext (particularly body language, glances, and pointed line readings) would sense that in *These Three* Hellman's reconfiguration of the eternal triangle was a way of contrasting two forms of love to comply with the Production Code.

The *Children's Hour* did not mark the end of Wallis's association with Hellman. Whenever he saw a Hellman play whose politics coincided with his, such as *Watch on the Rhine* and *The Searching Wind,* he was more than eager to produce the movie version; and Hellman was more than eager to let him. "Unnatural love" was a subject Wallis did not understand, even though *The Children's Hour* was really a play about

the devastating effect of a lie on three people, one of whom starts believing it and kills herself.

As different as Warner and Wallis were when it came to filmmaking
savvy (in which Wallis clearly had an edge over his boss), they had one
thing in common: frugality. Each regarded himself as the studio's unofficial comptroller. If an actor planned a trip to New York supposedly to
see family but really to audition for a play, Wallis would authorize train
fare only, taking the actor off salary. Knowing that at times Warner acceded too readily to a star's demands, especially if the star had scored
favorably with audiences, Wallis cautioned him against negotiating pri-
vately with Errol Flynn about loan-outs, percentage deals, and bonuses:
"We should keep in mind at all times that we are in the picture business
and all ends should function with that understanding." After inquiring
about the rights to "My Mammy"—the song that Al Jolson had immortalized in *The Jazz Singer,* had reprised in *Go into Your Dance* (1935),
and would be performing again in *The Singing Kid* (1936)—Wallis was
shocked to discover that the price had zoomed to $5,000. Jack Warner
was undaunted: "IF ANYONE OVERCHARGES US THEY WILL NEED US SOMEDAY
AND WILL RETALIATE."[41] One suspects that Warners did not pay the American Society of Composers, Authors, and Publishers (ASCAP) $5,000.
Even so, *The Singing Kid,* Jolson's last film for the studio, was neither a
critical nor a commercial success.

The 1930s were both trying and exhilarating for Wallis, who alter-
nated between being a one-person courier service for Jack Warner and
functioning as his production chief. In 1936, when the intoxicated Busby Berkeley, driving in the wrong lane, crashed into a car and killed
three people, Warner stood by the director and expected Wallis to do the
same. Wallis—who, as a producer, could not help but take a pragmatic
approach to friendship—was fond of Berkeley, not because the director
was particularly likable, but because he edited in camera, coordinating
everything so seamlessly that an editor could easily assemble a cut.
Legally, Berkeley was guilty of vehicular homicide. He even admitted
he had been drinking. Still, the studio provided him with a clever lawyer, Jerry Giesler, whose tactics resulted in a hung jury and a new trial.

As usual, Jack Warner was traveling during the trial, expecting Wallis
to keep him apprised of any new developments. On 24 December Wallis sent Warner a radiogram at the Ritz Towers, informing him that the
jury had been dismissed and that a new trial would be scheduled. Warn-

er immediately wired Berkeley, wishing the director and his mother a
"Merry Christmas" and pledging his support: "AWFULLY SORRY THAT YOU
WERNT COMPLETELY EXHONERATED [*sic*] HAVE FELT CERTAIN . . . THAT YOU
SHOULD HAVE NO FEAR . . . IF THERE IS ANYTHING I CAN DO WAITING TO HEAR
FROM YOU.[42]

Berkeley was relieved to know Jack Warner was behind him, but he
did not realize that, to the studio, he was nothing but a cash cow. Giesler
did his job well, even bringing in tire experts, whose testimony resulted
in an out-of-court settlement of $95,000 that obviously came from Warn-
ers's coffers. Naturally, Berkeley was elated, but his euphoria was short-
lived. In an abortive suicide attempt, Berkeley only succeeded in slashing
his throat, which did not produce the desired effect. He owed Warners
another film, *Garden of the Moon* (1939), which he despised so much
that he deliberately shot few close-ups.

There was life after Warners, but not much of one. Berkeley found
work as dance director at Fox and MGM, going out in a blaze of glory
when he choreographed the 1972 Broadway revival of *No, No, Nanette,*
which reunited him with Ruby Keeler.

Once the Berkeley affair was resolved, Wallis wanted the recognition that he deserved. After returning from a vacation, he expected a
notice to be planted in the trades that carried such information, which
might seem trivial to outsiders but was real news to the Hollywood community. Thus, Wallis was livid in June 1937 when his return from vacation failed to make the *Hollywood Reporter* or *Variety;* he addressed his
complaints to S. Charles Einfeld, director of advertising and publicity,
who was so unnerved that he wrote to Jack Warner, explaining the situation and adding, "I wouldn't mind this happening with a million other
people, but it had to happen with Wallis."[43] Although Wallis knew he
was the equivalent of Jack Warner's answering service, he also knew
that he had fought to improve the Warners image by putting a number of
films into production—largely historical and biographical—that would
give the studio the prestige it needed to compete with MGM, "the Tiffa-
ny of studios," and win over a public that thought of Warners as a studio
that ran to the headlines before it aimed at the heart. Warmth, Warners
definitely lacked. But it could be achieved if history provided the human factor.

History did, but not Warners. The biographical films that Wallis
placed in production (e.g., *The Story of Louis Pasteur* [1935], *Juarez*

[1939], and *Dr. Ehrlich's Magic Bullet* [1939]) were often freighted with self-importance, as if to suggest that audiences had to be educated and entertained simultaneously. In the case of *Louis Pasteur*, the public did not seem to mind; the film's success, which neither Jack Warner ("Who would want to see a movie about a chemist?") or the New York office ("Who'd want to see a picture about pasteurized milk?") expected, led to a film about Florence Nightingale, *The White Angel* (1936) (*Starmaker*, 55). Always a stickler for authenticity, Wallis had director William Dieterle study all the available lithographs and photos of Nightingale; and he had Orry-Kelly replicate the uniforms worn by nurses during the Crimean War (1853–56). Although *The White Angel* had a period look, Kay Francis was unimpressive in the title role; Wallis was furious with Dieterle, who, for some reason, kept switching scenes from day to night; and audiences had to wait fifteen years for a far better film about Florence Nightingale—*The Lady with a Lamp* (1951), in which Anna Neagle gave a glowing performance as the legendary nurse.

Some of Wallis's historical films of the 1930s caused legal problems, even *The Life of Emile Zola* (1937), the best of the lot, in which Paul Muni was far less mannered as the author-activist Zola than he had been as Pasteur. Since *Zola* focused mainly on the Dreyfus Affair and the anti-Semitism that led to Captain Alfred Dreyfus's being sentenced to life imprisonment on Devil's Island, one would have to know that the captain was Jewish to understand the factors surrounding his court-martial. The prologue made it clear that the film was a mix of history and fiction: "This production has its basis in history. The historical basis, however, has been fictionalized for the purpose of this picture and the names of many characters are fictitious." Warners played it safe; an insert of Dreyfus's dossier with the words, "Religion—Jew," highlighted was the studio's way of indicating Dreyfus's religion—but only in print, not in dialogue. Warners may have assumed that with the distinguished Jewish actor, Joseph Schildkraut, appearing as the captain, the knowledgeable would make the connection and others would be too caught up in the drama to notice. Although *Zola* received accolades from the critics and Oscars for best picture, best screenplay, and best supporting actor (Schildkraut), the film encountered numerous problems before and after production.

During what is now considered Hollywood's Golden Age (1930–60), the studios bought numerous properties—published and unpublished novels, fiction and nonfiction in galleys, biographies, magazine articles, produced and unproduced plays; in one case, even a poem was purchased, Edna St. Vincent Millay's "Murder of Lidice," the basis of Douglas Sirk's *Hitler's Madman* (1942) about the Nazis' destruction of the Czech village of Lidice and the extermination of its men.

Many such properties went unfilmed, often ending up in files to which the screenwriters working on similar projects had access; the use they made of them, however, was another matter. Since film is a collaborative art, it is not uncommon for a writer to "collaborate" with his or her source, drawing from it but not always acknowledging the debt. Unlike nonfiction books, screenplays are not footnoted; even then, distinguished historians such as Stephen Ambrose and Doris Kearns Goodwin have, however unconsciously, incorporated material from their sources, sometimes almost verbatim. Thus, unless one has had access to production and story files, it is impossible to know whether the screenwriter has simply adapted the property per se; incorporated material gleaned from treatments or drafts of related projects that, for some reason, were abandoned; or enriched the script with period detail from works of scholarship. Even the credits cannot tell the complete story, since film history is studded with examples of pseudonyms and fronts, especially during the time of the blacklist.

Zola had its share of script and authorship problems. Before the filming, Captain Dreyfus's son Pierre expressed concern about the screenplay. As a loyal French subject, Pierre insisted that the tribunal that sentenced his father to Devil's Island not be depicted as a cabal, despite the captain's exoneration. Once he had Wallis's assurance, he signed a waiver of privacy rights, while declining Wallis's invitation to visit Hollywood. As it turned out, Pierre was quite taken with the film. What Dreyfus relative would not be, given a prologue that insisted that "no identification with actual persons, living or dead, is intended or should be inferred"?

Matthew Josephson and Hans Rehfisch felt differently. Josephson, the well-known author of *Zola and His Time* (1928), charged plagiarism, eventually receiving $10,000 for the rights and a credit: "book by Matthew Josephson." The German playwright Hans Rehfisch was not so fortunate: he fought to get recognition for the use of his play, *The Dreyfus Affair,* eventually receiving a settlement of $5,000 in 1944 (*Starmaker,* 60). In Hollywood, the wheels of justice revolve at varying speeds.

Juarez (1939) was also beset with problems. It could have been an epic about Mexico's national hero Benito Juarez and his successful attempt to destroy the "empire" that Napoleon III had imposed on his country with Maximilian as its bogus emperor, but it became a ponderous spectacle with a miscast Bette Davis as Carlotta, Maximilian's wife, whose mad scene was the forerunner of the antic disposition Davis adopted for the ghoulish *Whatever Happened to Baby Jane* (1962). Although Wallis discusses some of the film's problems in *Starmaker*, he neglects to mention that the $6,000 the studio paid for Franz Werfel's 1926 play, *Juarez and Maximilian* (which Wallis calls *Maximilian and Carlotta*), required an additional $1,200 to the Nazi-controlled publisher, Paul Szolany Verlag, who owned the copyright. Since the Jewish Werfel (often mistaken for a Christian because he had written *The Song of Bernadette*, which was made into a successful 1943 film) would not give Warners the rights if Szolany received any money, Wallis worked out an arrangement with Szolany, giving the publisher 20 percent of the amount Warners paid for the rights—in other words, $1,200.[44]

There were other problems. Muni—a Method actor before the Method was even understood or entered the theater lexicon—wanted to absorb local color while on location in Mexico City. Several rounds of tequilas with Wallis and director William Dieterle persuaded the actor to find the character within himself. That Muni could do, once he felt confident. The confidence was provided by his wife Bella, who, he insisted, must be allowed on the set because of his peripheral vision. When Muni did something with which Bella disagreed, she would shake her head, and Muni would immediately stop even before Dieterle called "Cut!"[45]

Juarez was bedeviled from the start. Even before the disastrous Hollywood preview, which convinced Wallis that he should eliminate two thousand feet of film, there was the specter of plagiarism, which often hovers over movies about historical figures who have inspired biographers, novelists, and playwrights; certain details are often repeated, sometimes in language so similar as to suggest unacknowledged borrowing. Likewise, a plagiarism charge can easily result when a film is released depicting the same period and characters as an earlier one, especially if the material dovetails; and if the charge comes from an independent or international filmmaker, it is taken more seriously than if it is a case of one Hollywood studio threatening to sue another.

Plagiarism was one of the studios' major fears; Warners, which had its share of threatened lawsuits and out-of-court settlements, was not about to engage in a protracted battle with Mexican director Miguel Contrerras Torres, who was planning to release *The Mad Empress*, which covered some of the same ground as *Juarez*. Ordinarily, that would not have been a problem, but five years earlier Torres had made a similar film, *Juárez y Maximiliano* (1934), which he produced, wrote, and co-directed. *Starmaker* (62–63) offers a muddled account of the affair. According to Wallis, Torres sought $1 million in damages, charging both plagiarism and loss of distribution rights. "Nobody connected with our picture *[Juarez]* had ever seen or heard of the Mexican production" (63). Not true. In 1935 Columbia had distributed *Juárez y Maximiliano*. The *New York Times* gave it a respectable review (16 February 1935), commenting on Medea de Novara's uncanny resemblance to Carlotta and commending the film for its authenticity, which came, for the most part, from location shooting. Wallis confused the 1934 film with *The Mad Empress* (1939), which Torres made as a showcase for de Novara, now his wife, focusing mainly on Carlotta's descent into madness. Wallis never mentions *The Mad Empress*, alluding instead to lawsuits, including one threatened by screenwriter Jean Bart, who Wallis would have us believe contributed to the script of the 1934 film. Bart had nothing to do with *Juárez y Maximiliano;* however, she had a great deal to do with *The Mad Empress*.

Torres used the failure of *Juárez y Maximilano* in the States to try to pressure Warners into distributing *The Mad Empress*, which had been made before *Juarez*. Quite possibly, the *Juarez* screenwriters might have seen *Juárez y Maximiliano* during its American release; any writer working on a history-based screenplay in the late 1930s would have been foolish to ignore a potential source, especially since a few strategically placed calls to Columbia could have led either to a print or a script. The issue, then, was not *Juárez y Maximilano*, which was passé, but *The Mad Empress*, which needed a distributor.

Jack Warner cared less about the issues than about alienating Latin Americans. *Juarez* could at least acknowledge Bertita Leonarz Harding's biography, *The Phantom Crown: The Story of Maximilian and Carlotta of Mexico* (1934), and Werfel's play, *Juarez and Maximilian* (1926), as sources; however, *The Mad Empress*'s credits would lead one to believe the film derived from an original screenplay. With three writers credited for each film (John Huston, Aeneas MacKenzie, and Wolfgang Reinhardt for *Juarez*; Jean Bart, Jerome Chodorov, and Torres himself for *Empress*), both teams would invariably have consulted some of the same sources; in the case of *Juarez*, it was not just a novel and a play but a number of scholarly works as well. And since the same characters appeared in both films (for example, Juarez, Maximilian, Carlotta, Porfirio Diaz, Napoleon III, Empress Eugenie, and Marechal Bazaine), comparisons were inevitable.

It would be easy to dismiss *The Mad Empress* as a second-rate *Juarez*, except that it represented the efforts of a number of Hollywood professionals. Jean Bart was a minor playwright and screenwriter. Jerome Chodorov was better known; the year *The Mad Empress* was finally released, Chodorov scored a major success on Broadway with *My Sister Eileen* (1940), which he adapted for the screen two years later, doing the same for several of his other plays including *Tunnel of Love* (1958) and *Anniversary Waltz* (retitled *Happy Anniversary* [1959]). *The Mad Empress*'s cast might have lacked the cachet of *Juarez*'s, but many moviegoers would have recognized some of the actors: Conrad Nagel (Maximilian), Evelyn Brent (Empress Eugenie), Lionel Atwill (Bazaine), and Jason Robards Sr. (Juarez).

Warners finally agreed to distribute *The Mad Empress* rather than risk another plagiarism charge.[46] *The Mad Empress* reached the theaters in 1940, sporting excerpts from Erich Wolfgang Korngold's score for *Juarez*—courtesy of Warners, which was relieved that another legal showdown had been averted. The addition of Korngold did not help the picture; *The Mad Empress* failed to draw an audience. In his *New York Times* review (15 February 1940), chief film critic Bosley Crowther dismissed *The Mad Empress* as "interesting" and lamented its "academic leafing through the familiar pages of history." *The Mad Empress* has vanished into the limbo of lost films; *Juarez*, at least, is still viewable.

As the 1930s came to a close, Jack Warner grew more dependent on Wallis, who, in turn, became increasingly restless. It was not that Wallis felt he lacked prestige; he was, after all, an executive producer at a major studio. Yet he was growing tired of turning out a dozen or so pictures a year, many of which he had no affinity for; his ideal was an arrangement whereby he could produce a few—perhaps four a year—of his own choice, truly making them "Hal Wallis productions." The dream would become a reality in 1942. Meanwhile, it was back to being Jack

Warner's confidant and alter ego; at least that is how Warner perceived their relationship.

The rise of fascism—particularly its most virulent strain, Nazism—stirred up feelings in Jack Warner of which one would have thought him incapable. The same Jack Warner who had no qualms about soft-pedaling Dreyfus's religion in *The Life of Emile Zola* had acquired a conscience now that there was the possibility of America's going fascist—as Italy, Germany, and Spain had in their respective ways. This was one of the few occasions when the Jew in Warner took precedence over the studio head. Of course, one could also argue that Warner was equally concerned about losing major sectors of the international market that were pro–Third Reich. Jack Warner was conflicted: the Jew was warring with the studio head.

Warner expected Wallis to have similar feelings; however, Wallis always placed his work before his religion, which he rarely practiced except on the high holy days. That *The Life of Emile Zola* failed to clarify the racial issues behind the Dreyfus case did not affect Wallis at all, or Warner either. But by 1939 Warner began thinking of Wallis as a coreligionist, assuming he shared the same fears about Nazism, which, in Warner's case, began in 1936 when Nazi thugs kicked a studio employee to death in a Berlin alley because he was a Jew.[47] Two years later, when he and Wallis began work on *Confessions of a Nazi Spy* (1939), the first major exposé of Nazi-directed espionage in America, the bond—or what Warner considered a bond—grew stronger.

Confessions was in every respect a Wallis production, although, one suspects, his commitment to the film was more professional than emotional. He knew the problems: invasion of privacy suits, retaliation by the German-American Bund, boycotts by Nazi sympathizers, and the wrath of the German consul, who did not take kindly to the film's revealing the existence of his country's growing number of concentration camps.[48] Wallis decided that *Confessions* should open with a combination voiceover narration–montage–animated map prologue, a technique that he would repeat in *Casablanca* (1942). Although Wallis originally wanted to use the names of the real-life spies, he soon recognized the legal implications and opted for fictitious names. To dispel the notion that *Confessions* was just another feature film, Wallis altered the main title format (usually, film title, cast, and chief production personnel, ending with the director) by having only the title appear at the beginning, with the rest of the credits relegated to the end of the film.

Warner thought of his collaboration with Wallis on *Confessions* as a confirmation of their friendship, although neither could have predicted that within three years it would end in mutual bitterness. Meanwhile, Warner was in a "Dear Hal" mood when he wrote to Wallis, as he did on 6 March 1939 from New York, ostensibly to voice his concern about *Confessions* running into legal problems because it was so blatantly propagandistic.[49] The real reason, however, was to share his feelings about a rising surge of Americanism and his delight that a Jewish lawyer was suing Fritz Kuhn, head of the Nazi-cloned German-American Bund, for defamation of character.

There was no reason for Warner to burden Wallis with the problems he was having with Eddie Albert's agent, the formidable Leland Hayward, over his client's salary for the movie version of Rodgers and Hart's *On Your Toes* (1939), in which Albert was scheduled for the role that Ray Bolger had created. Yet Warner clearly felt the need to unburden himself; and what better way than in a letter, where one could reveal on paper what might be difficult to express in person. Warner believed he would not have been put in the position of negotiating with Albert and bargaining with Hayward if Wallis had been present: "In behalf of Albert, the guy undoubtedly is a conscientious artist but the next time . . . anyone gets me to see anyone under contract, unless I run into them in a cafe or restaurant, I want you to be there to catch me."[50] One doubts that Jack Warner would have been so open if he and Wallis had been face to face. Naturally, Warner asked Wallis to destroy the letter.

If there was anyone at Warners whom Wallis could rightly call a friend, it was not Jack Warner but director Michael Curtiz. Theirs was not always the most cordial of relationships, yet it was long-lasting because each sensed in the other a kindred spirit. In 1924 Wallis arrived at the Pasadena train station to pick up a Hungarian director by the name of Mihaly Kertesz, who, once he reinvented himself as Michael Curtiz, became Wallis's favorite director; together they made more than twenty pictures for Warners: *Dr. X* and *Cabin in the Cotton* (both 1932); *Mystery of the Wax Museum* (1933); *Captain Blood* (1935); *The Charge of the Light Brigade* and *Stolen Holiday* (both 1936); *Kid Galahad* and *The Perfect Specimen* (1937); *Gold Is Where You Find It, The Adventures of Robin Hood,* and *Four Daughters* (all 1938); *Daughters Coura-*

geous, The Private Lives of Elizabeth and Essex, and *Four Wives* (all
1939); *Virginia City, Santa Fe Trail,* and *The Sea Hawk* (all 1940); *The
Sea Wolf* and *Dive Bomber* (both 1941); *Captains of the Clouds, Yankee
Doodle Dandy,* and *Casablanca* (all 1942); *This Is the Army* (1943);
and *Passage to Marseilles* (1944).

What drew Wallis to Curtiz was his perfectionism, which alienated
anyone who could not, or would not, abide by the director's standards.
However, professionals willing to sacrifice their egos for the good of
the film understood that Curtiz's autocratic behavior was a manifesta-
tion of his genius. It took Wallis and Warners a while to realize that
Curtiz was one of the few contract directors at any studio worthy of the
name *artist.* If Warners expected quality from Curtiz, it came with a
price. Curtiz found a $750,000 budget for a swashbuckler like *Captain
Blood* unacceptable; $950,000 was more realistic, and that is what the
film eventually cost.[51]

Curtiz ignored Wallis's suggestions about Errol Flynn's costumes
for *Captain Blood.* As the title character, Peter Blood, Flynn would be
playing a seventeenth-century British surgeon-turned-pirate in the film
that made him a star—thanks to his agent, Minna Wallis, who persuaded her brother to cast him in the role when Robert Donat bowed out. Hal
Wallis's conception of a pirate was a man in tight pants and a V-necked
shirt with billowing sleeves, brandishing a sword like a gentleman fenc-
er. Curtiz had other ideas. The time is England, 1687; James II's autocratic rule has inspired rebellion—not as widespread as the film would
lead one to believe, but enough to result in an attempt to unseat the
monarch. When one of the rebels knocks at Blood's door late at night,
seeking treatment for a wounded comrade, the doctor (Flynn) first throws
on a dressing gown before seeing his caller, thus declaring himself a
gentleman—a role he will play even when sold into slavery for being a
traitor to the crown. Later, when Blood turns rebel himself and leads his
fellow captives to freedom, they become pirates, making the Caribbean
their private waterway. Now *Captain* Blood, the doctor dons a velvet
coat with lace cuffs when divvying up the loot. Since it had already
been established that Blood was sartorially correct, his attire even as
pirate was in character. Wallis, however, did not think so. "What in the
hell is the matter with you, and why do you insist on crossing me on
everything I ask you not to do?" Wallis exploded—in print, of course—
at Curtiz.[52] Wallis, who took virility seriously, expected Flynn to look

like a man, not a "God damned faggot." Flynn's manhood was never in question; nor was Wallis's or Curtiz's. Since *Captain Blood* was a high-testosterone film, it did not matter what Flynn wore; he looked just as masculine in velvet as he did in a discreetly opened shirt. Flynn even survived a wig that crested in a wave, which would have been the envy of every beautician. A woman could have worn the same hairpiece and would have looked as attractive. If Flynn looked androgynous, he was in good company. Properly lit, an actor's face could appear transfigured, and his hair, real or fake, sculpted in light. In *Camille* (1936), high-key lighting turned Robert Taylor's face incandescent, without robbing it of its virility. Leslie Howard in *Berkeley Square* (1934) or *The Petrified Forest* (1936) did not seem any less a man even though he could have passed as a poster boy for the Romantic movement.

Fortunately, Curtiz did not agree with Wallis's monolithic concept of masculinity, which, in his memo, almost verged on homophobia. Nor did Curtiz soften the violence—in the form of lashings and brandings—that Wallis thought would alienate audiences. In *Captain Blood*, men are whipped and branded on camera. Wallis also had a problem with a scene in which Blood, now personal physician to Port Royal's governor, is summoned to his patient's bedside on the very evening of a midnight escape from the island. Wallis was bothered by the way the shot had been framed—with a lighted candle on the governor's bedroom table and a clock in full view, so that no one could forget that time was of the essence. Wallis expected a close-up of Flynn telling the governor, "I'll have you well by midnight if I have to bleed you to death," apparently forgetting that (1) the audience already knew the time of the escape and (2) if Blood were to "bleed" the governor, he would do it medically. There was no need for audiences to suspect that Blood had the slightest intention of killing a gout-ridden incompetent—and a figurehead, to boot. Curtiz shot the scene as he had composed it: a doctor doing his duty while at the same time keenly aware of the time he must depart. There were no close-ups of clocks or of Blood's anxious face. Blood, after all, had taken the Hippocratic Oath. Perhaps Flynn looked too much the dandy in *Captain Blood* with his tailored jacket, plumed hat, and neck scarf; but when it came time to duel, jacket and hat came off. And if Wallis was disturbed by Flynn's "image" in *Captain Blood,* he need not have worried; the tension between the actor and the "pansy" that Wallis thought he was becoming under Curtiz produced moments of high adventure, as Blood led his fellow slaves out of captivity and into pirating, and high romance, as the woman (Olivia de Havilland) who once bid on him at auction changed from ingenue to lover.

Curtiz turned *Captain Blood* into a moneymaker that made a generation believe in the gentleman pirate, capable of inspiring fantasies—erotic and otherwise. By 1938 Wallis began to adjust to Curtiz's ways, and a genuine friendship developed, based on mutual respect. What turned Wallis around was Curtiz's assuming the direction of *The Adventures of Robin Hood*, after William Keighley had to be replaced. Once Wallis discovered that Keighley had shot "thousands of feet of film with hundreds of people,"[53] only eight or ten feet of which were salvageable, Wallis had no other choice but to replace the director; and what better choice than Curtiz? Still, Wallis did not want Robin Hood depicted as Superman. He urged Curtiz to do something about the scene in which Robin (Errol Flynn), entering the great hall at Nottingham Castle with the body of a "royal" deer that had been killed in Sherwood Forest, deposits the carcass on the banquet table in front of Prince John and his Normans. The act is so audacious, and at the same time amusing, that Prince John invites Robin to join the feast. John's civility is a pretext to trap his nemesis. Once the doors of the hall are bolted, Robin knows his life is imperiled; although Robin is one against many, Ralph Dawson edited the ensuing melee so brilliantly (which the Academy acknowledged by awarding him an Oscar) that Robin's swordsmanship holds off a roomful of effete royalty and bumbling knights. As Dawson cut the sequence, it made perfect sense, once Wallis instructed his editor to delete the shot where Robin seizes a shield to protect himself from the arrows raining upon him.[54] The sequence could accommodate only so much derring-do.

The Adventures of Robin Hood was a triumph for Warners; not only did it reunite Errol Flynn and Olivia de Havilland as Robin and Marian, making them the most attractive couple on the screen, but it also turned out to be the studio's most successful film of 1938 as well as a triple Oscar winner (score, art direction, and editing). And what was an uneasy relationship between Wallis and Curtiz became a genuine friendship, with Wallis continuing to dash off his memos (of which there were fewer to Curtiz) and Curtiz going his own way, but grateful for the input.

Wallis and Curtiz were often seen riding together on the horse trails in the San Fernando Valley; even Wallis had to concede that Curtiz was the better equestrian. Wallis even kept his horses at Curtiz's farm in nearby Canoga Park. The Curtizes were one of the few couples with whom Wallis and Louise socialized. Louise knew Curtiz's second wife, Bess Meredyth, from the days of the silents when Meredyth was a leading scenarist at MGM. It was not coincidental that of the 126 Warner Brothers films listed in the *Starmaker* filmography, twenty-four were directed by Curtiz, including Wallis's favorite, *Casablanca.*

Curtiz's range paralleled that of Wallis; both of them made films of every genre: for example, thrillers (*Dr. X* [1932] and *Mystery of the Wax Museum* [1933]); historical films and biopics (*The Charge of the Light Brigade* [1936], *The Adventures of Robin Hood* [1938]), and *The Private Lives of Elizabeth and Essex* [1939]); swashbucklers (*Captain Blood* [1935] and *The Sea Hawk* [1940]); domestic dramas (*Four Daughters* [1938], *Daughters Courageous* [1939], and *Four Wives* [1939]); musicals (*Yankee Doodle Dandy* [1942] and *This Is the Army* [1943]); romantic melodramas (*Cabin in the Cotton* [1932] and *Casablanca* [1942]); westerns (*Gold Is Where You Find It* [1938], *Virginia City* [1940], and *Santa Fe Trail* [1940]); and war movies (*Dive Bomber* [1941], *Captains of the Clouds* [1942], and *Passage to Marseilles* [1944]). Although Curtiz made only one real comedy under Wallis, *The Perfect Specimen* (1937), he proved he could bring off a piece of fluff like *Janie* (1944)—in which the title character was a teenager who talked in pig Latin on the phone— without pandering to the youth market.

Even after Wallis left Warners, Curtiz continued to display his versatility. He directed Doris Day in her film debut, *Romance on the High Seas* (1948), following it up with *My Dream Is Yours*, both of which turned the former band singer into a movie star. Curtiz, in fact, allowed Day to reveal her talent for drama in *Young Man with a Horn* (1950). The year 1954 saw the release of three vastly different films from three studios: a western, Warners's *Boy from Oklahoma;* a musical, *White Christmas,* which was Paramount's most financially successful film of the year, grossing $12 million domestically; and a historical epic, Fox's *Egyptian,* filmed in CinemaScope—a wide-screen process that exasperated many directors accustomed to the aspect ratio of the rectangular screen. Curtiz directed all three.

Although Errol Flynn made ten films with Curtiz, he rarely spoke well of the director, nor did Bette Davis, who was interested in playing the title role in *Mildred Pierce* (1945), until she discovered that Curtiz would be the director. She never forgave him for referring to her as a "goddamned-nothing-no-good-sexless-son-of-a bitch."[55] But on the whole, actors enjoyed working with Curtiz, whose flamboyance, malapropisms, and mangled but colorful syntax—not to mention his knack for shooting crowd scenes—enhanced his appeal as a technically competent, if eccentric, professional. Joan Leslie, a Warners contract player who costarred in two Wallis-Curtiz productions, *Yankee Doodle Dandy* and *This Is the Army,* found the director "a joy to work under" in the former, "because he loved the story and star [James Cagney]." *This Is the Army* was another matter; Curtiz was dealing with a musical revue in need of a plot in order to succeed as a movie. Curtiz's idea of a musical was one that was script-driven; until Howard Koch came up with a screenplay that could accommodate all of Irving Berlin's patriotic numbers, "he [Curtiz] was very temperamental."[56]

Like his films, Curtiz's temperament was never uniform. Mother Dolores Hart of Regina Laudis Abbey in Bethlehem, Connecticut, remembers two of his myriad faces. As the actress Dolores Hart, she costarred in two of his films, *Kid Creole* (1958) and *Francis of Assisi* (1961). In the former, she again played opposite Elvis Presley, to whom she gave his first screen kiss in *Loving You* (1957). Mother Dolores, who respected Curtiz, recalls that the director was uncommonly kind to Elvis, shepherding him through a complex role that required real acting, of which Elvis proved he was quite capable. When she worked with Curtiz again, it was on location in *Francis of Assisi*. Just before a crucial scene was to be shot inside a local church, Curtiz swaggered in and then suddenly stopped. Removing his hat, he began to weep. The crew was astonished. "What are you staring at?" Curtiz exclaimed, "This is the best goddamn crucifix I've ever seen."[57] Perhaps the cross inspired an emotional response that had more to do with art than religion; Curtiz, after all, was a Hungarian Jew. Perhaps he experienced a kind of epiphany, signaling the end of his directing days. Whatever the case, *Francis of Assisi* was Curtiz's penultimate film. He died in 1962, a year after its release. The following year, Dolores Hart took a limousine to Regina Laudis, marking the end of her film career and the beginning of another life.

The versatility that Curtiz acquired at Warners carried him through the end of the studio system and into corporate Hollywood, which took over starting in the 1960s. Curtiz's last two movies were a biopic and a western, two of the many genres at which he excelled: *Francis of Assisi* (1961) and *The Commancheros* (1962). Both films, however, were released by Twentieth Century–Fox—a studio with which Michael Curtiz will never be identified.

That Wallis and Curtiz remained friends for more than thirty years in a business where friendship is based on expediency resulted from a mutual respect for professionalism, which neutralized two extraordinarily powerful egos. When director Vincent Sherman told a journalist that Curtiz's "whole life was pictures," he could have been speaking of Wallis;[58] and when Wallis called Curtiz "a demon for work" (*Starmaker*, 25), he was also describing himself.

Wallis bristled when Curtiz was dismissed as a director without a signature, unable to inscribe his films with a distinctive hand as Billy Wilder, John Ford, and Alfred Hitchcock had done. Rather, Wallis insisted, Curtiz was guided by the kind of film he was making, thereby giving it the appropriate style.[59] Vincent Sherman felt similarly. Although Sherman was disappointed at not being chosen to direct *Casablanca*, he still defended Curtiz against the charge of being just another contract director: "He was . . . one of the most skillful directors we have ever had, and his use of the camera was superb. How many other directors made such a variety of pictures and so successfully?"[60]

And how many producers during the studio era—apart from, perhaps, Zanuck and Goldwyn—could match Wallis's range and output? Yet Wallis's oeuvre is dominated by a single film that limns an era so accurately that it has tended to overshadow his other productions. If the perennial talk show question, "What is the film by which you would like to be remembered?" had been posed to Wallis and Curtiz, each would have probably answered, "*Casablanca*." They may have had other preferences, but they were realistic enough to know that *Casablanca* was the only film either of them made that found a permanent place in both American mythology and world cinema. Who would argue? Unlike Narcissus, alter egos see their reflections in each other's pool.

CHAPTER FOUR

The End of a Dubious Friendship

O N 12 JANUARY 1942, Hal Wallis, now forty-five, signed a contract with Warners, stipulating that "a 'Hal Wallis Production'
or 'Produced by Hal Wallis' appear as a separate credit at the
end of the main title" and that his name be "equal at least to fifty percent
of the largest type used in presenting the name of any member of the
cast on the screen."[1] As far as Wallis was concerned, the contract made
him an independent producer—free to select four films a year, receiving 10 percent of the gross profits after they had reached 125 percent of
the negative cost. Within eight months, Wallis's contract was renegotiated; that September, he was given a new contract that would run for
four years—with the first-year terms modified, requiring Wallis to put
six, rather than four, films into production: *Now, Voyager; Desperate
Journey;* and *Casablanca* (all 1942 releases); and *Air Force, Princess
O'Rourke,* and *Watch on the Rhine* (all 1943).[2]

The contract was not quite so liberating as it seemed. Wallis may
have assumed he was an independent producer, but he was still working
at Jack Warner's studio; and theoretically, any Warner Brothers film
was one of Jack's. According to the credits, *All This and Heaven Too*
(1940) was "An Anatole Litvak Production," with Hal B. Wallis as "executive producer" and David Lewis as "associate producer." However,
appearing under the title was "Jack L. Warner in Charge of Production."
Simply put, Litvak made the film exactly as he wanted to; Wallis, as
head of production, fumed when his instructions were disregarded; Lewis
took the heat; and Warner took the credit.

Although Wallis called *Yankee Doodle Dandy* (1942) "one of my
favorite pictures as an independent producer" (*Starmaker,* 103), it was

neither a Hal B. Wallis production nor one of the films listed in his 1942 contract. Wallis is credited as *Yankee Doodle Dandy*'s executive producer—the same title he had for *All This and Heaven Too*. The idea for a biopic about playwright-composer-actor George M. Cohan may have originated with Wallis, who probably sensed that Cohan's unabashed patriotism, reflected in such songs as "You're a Grand Old Flag" and "Yankee Doodle Dandy," would be perfect for a flag-waver. Although there was no connection between the life of Cohan, who died of bladder cancer the same year *Yankee Doodle Dandy* was released, and the world war that America entered a few months before the film was completed, love of country is a timeless theme that can be recycled for any occasion. Warners turned *Sergeant York* (1941), ostensibly a film about a World War I hero, into a parable about the transformation of a pacifist into a fighter, implying that if there are no atheists in foxholes, there can be no neutrals in the fight against fascism.

No sooner had Wallis assigned Robert Buckner to write the script for *Yankee Doodle Dandy* than the project began to slip out of Wallis's and Buckner's hands and into those of the star, James Cagney; his brother William, who had become the associate producer; and Cohan himself.[3] As the great comic Jimmy Durante used to lament, "Everybody wants to get into the act!" William Cagney summarily informed Wallis that Rev. Gilbert Hartke, head of the drama department at the Catholic University of Washington, D.C., had produced a play about Cohan at Georgetown University, coauthored by Walter Kerr—later to become one of America's finest theater critics.[4] Father Hartke, it seemed, wanted to be involved in the script. Wallis stood his ground; the studio had all the writers it needed—and, in fact, there would be others besides Buckner, including the ubiquitous Epsteins.

Cohan, who had definite ideas about the way his life should be filmed, not only sent Buckner a chronology but also embarked upon a script; after all, he had written more than thirty-five plays. By now, even William Cagney was alarmed at Cohan's ever-expanding ego. By the end of August 1941 William Cagney, Wallis, and Buckner joined forces, pleading with Cohan to jettison his script and approve theirs, which Cohan finally did—with the understanding that neither of his wives' names be used. Instead, Cohan's wives were reduced to one—Mary, a name that audiences would recognize because it was also the title of one of Cohan's most popular songs. Mary was played winningly by the seventeen-year-old Joan Leslie.

Now, Voyager was another matter. It was truly a "Hal B. Wallis Production," with Jack Warner's name nowhere in the opening credits. Warner tended to be selective about the films to which he would affix his name; yet even when his name appeared, it was merely a self-advertisement, an empty title. Regardless, Wallis was determined to make *Now, Voyager*, the movie version of Olive Higgins Prouty's novel, anything but another woman's film or, to use the less euphemistic term, a three-hankie movie. The story of Charlotte Vale—a repressed Bostonian who succeeds in freeing herself from her tyrannical mother, only to become the lover of a married man, to whose young daughter she eventually becomes a mother substitute—could easily have become a real "weepie," complete with florid acting, ethereal dialogue, and a treacly soundtrack. Consequently, the last actress Wallis envisioned as Charlotte, who metamorphoses from an overweight neurotic to a strikingly beautiful woman of the world, was Bette Davis. His first choices were Norma Shearer and Irene Dunne, both of whom could have portrayed the post-transformation Charlotte, although one wonders how convincing either would have been as the Charlotte who has been made to feel so useless that she has a nervous breakdown and must be institutionalized or the Charlotte whose sexuality is expressed in elliptical dialogue, looks of longing, and a coiled body waiting to unwind. When neither Shearer nor Dunne was available, Wallis turned to Ginger Rogers, influenced, no doubt, by her best actress Oscar for *Kitty Foyle* (1940), another tastefully produced woman's film. Although Rogers was taken with the novel, for some unknown reason she passed on the film, leaving Wallis no other choice but to look internally, since Shearer, Dunne, and Rogers were not Warners contract players. There was only one actress on the Warners lot—or, for that matter, in Hollywood—who could play Charlotte: Bette Davis, about whom Wallis was ambivalent. While he respected Davis's art, he also knew it veered toward excess, as he constantly reminded directors.

Although Davis was not on Wallis's short list, it is to his credit that he offered her a role that, perhaps for the first time in her career, revealed her myriad talents as she changed from a dowdy maiden aunt, bullied by her mother and mocked by her niece, to a glamorous sophisticate who is alternately flirtatious, witty, headstrong, sensuous, and, in the final scenes with her lover's daughter, poignantly maternal. Davis had undergone transformations before—from unconventional Southern belle to selfless heroine in *Jezebel* and from hedonistic heiress to death-accepting cancer victim in *Dark Victory*. Each role had an arc, which Davis traced brilliantly. But now it was a matter of shading. *Now, Voyager* required a more diverse palette; in Davis's case, that palette existed, although its colors were not always evident, partly because some directors found her so intimidating that they indulged her, allowing her mannerisms to become so embedded in her persona that she became the sum of them, and partly because some scripts encouraged her to draw on that repertoire of mannerisms, later sneeringly labeled as "camp."

Either because director Irving Rapper managed to rein Davis in (which he could not do in *Deception* [1946] and *Another Man's Poison* [1952], both of which had mediocre scripts), or because Davis found a part with which she identified so completely that she disappeared into the character, Wallis had little to say about her performance, except for a balcony scene between Charlotte and her architect-lover, Jerry (Paul Henreid). Wallis objected to Davis's delivery of the line "I'm immune to happiness" as "very stagey and artificial."[5] Rapper must have reshot the scene, since it is one of the most moving in the film. Charlotte, experiencing love for the first time in her life, discards her self-pity, which she disguises as stoicism, and begins to weep. When Jerry embraces her, she turns her face away, explaining that she is shedding "tears of gratitude" for the "crumbs" from his—she does not say "table," but the meaning is clear.

Wallis's chief criticism was Rapper's tendency to edit in camera, leaving the editor nothing to work with, in case a close-up was needed. Oddly, this was a quality Wallis respected in Busby Berkeley. Rapper, who came from the theater, tried to recreate the wholeness of a stage performance. Thus, if Rapper could avoid cutting, he did. When Charlotte makes her first appearance, slowly descending the stairs while her mother, her sister, her niece, and a psychiatrist are discussing her condition in the parlor, the camera tracks her, showing nothing but her unattractive shoes. Thus, when Charlotte is finally seen, her frumpy appearance has already been anticipated by her footwear. An editor could add nothing to the shot, since Rapper, focusing solely on the matronly shoes, did not cut until Charlotte entered the parlor.

After her flowering, Charlotte returns to her mother's home, where she is berated for her transformation from resentfully obedient daughter to fiercely independent woman. Refusing to wear the dress her mother has selected for a family gathering, Charlotte retires to the bathroom to change. Rapper frames the shot with Mrs. Vale (Gladys Cooper), her back to the camera, holding on to the bedpost. Shooting through the bend of Mrs. Vale's arm, Rapper allows mother and daughter, neither of whose face is visible, to continue conversing until Charlotte emerges in a dress that clearly does not meet with her mother's approval. It is only when Charlotte strides over to the dressing table that Rapper cuts, making it impossible for an editor to alter his artfully composed long take. Perhaps Rapper should have learned to give his editor more leeway— but not in *Now, Voyager*.

If there is one Warners film that Wallis truly regarded as his, it is *Casablanca*, which opens like a typical studio release—with the studio logo, the heraldic shield with "WB" emblazoned on it. This time, however, "Jack L. Warner, Executive Producer," has been added to the logo. On Oscar night, it became clear whose film *Casablanca* was—or whose film Jack Warner thought it was. Warner's "executive producer" credit, which only succeeded in cluttering the logo, was as much an honorific as his "Lieutenant Colonel" (he achieved that rank courtesy of the Army Air Corps in 1942 for promoting the war effort through film). *Casablanca* had one producer: Hal Wallis.

Even before Wallis signed his new contract, he had found a "Hal B. Wallis Production"—a film that would reflect his personal values as well as his standards of moviemaking. Before *Casablanca* became an iconic film, it underwent a year's gestation period, spawning a mythology that grew up around it like a jungle, requiring travelers to slash their way through the underbrush until they reached a clearing and came to the end of the quest for the lost treasure/sacred tablets/secret formula: in short, the stuff that dreams—particularly those of researchers—are made of.

The *Casablanca* story begins with Irene Lee, who in 1941 was an assistant story editor at Warners. Before she was Irene Lee, she was Irene Levine of Pittsburgh. Fearing an anti-Semitic backlash, she changed her surname to Lee when she set out for New York in the late 1920s hoping for future stardom, which she thought would be hers after testing for a part in Fox's production of Noël Coward's *Cavalcade* (1933).

Although Lee failed to get the role, a chance meeting with director Mervyn LeRoy, who was about to become Jack Warner's son-in-law by his marriage to Jack's daughter Doris, provided her with an entrée to Wallis. LeRoy was so impressed by her astute observations about his film *I Am a Fugitive from a Chain Gang* (1932)—which Wallis considered one of *his* films, although Zanuck was the unheralded producer—that LeRoy arranged for her to meet Wallis, who reacted similarly and made her assistant story editor in the New York office. Lee has always claimed credit for discovering the unproduced play by Murray Burnett and Joan Alison, *Everybody Comes to Rick's,* that became the basis of *Casablanca.*[6] Julius Epstein, one of the credited writers of the *Casablanca* screenplay, not only seconded Lee's claim but also insisted that Lee "was much smarter than Hal Wallis [and was] the one who assigned us [Epstein and his twin brother Philip] to write it."[7]

For every myth there is a countermyth. Around the same time that Julius Epstein discredited Wallis, he praised him to another writer, calling Wallis "a great executive to be able to manage so many pictures and to run a studio the way he did for so many years."[8] Contradictory accounts are part of Hollywood—or any—mythology. Alternative versions with happy endings for narratives full of unrelieved tragedy are common. A person who is repelled by the idea of Agamemnon's sacrifice of his daughter Iphigenia, should try the story of Artemis substituting a stag in her place, allowing Iphigenia to go off either to Aulis or Tauris. In Ambroise Thomas's operatic version of *Hamlet*, Ophelia goes mad but does not die, Hamlet kills Claudius and is proclaimed king, and Gertrude enters a convent. In Gluck's *Orfeo ed Eurydice*, Orpheus neither loses his beloved to a second, and permanent, death nor suffers dismemberment, as he does in Virgil's *Georgics*. Small wonder, then, that Epstein both buries and praises Wallis, oblivious to the fact that by calling Wallis a great producer while claiming that Wallis's story editor was more knowledgeable than her boss, he has undermined his credibility. Contradiction and the inability to decide are not the prerogatives of deconstructionist critics. Like any fabric, memory frays, leaving loose threads that probably should have been pulled off at least for appearance's sake.

Since everyone seems to have a *Casablanca* story, one is left with the problem that teachers of fiction have always faced: the narrator's reliability. Casey Robinson, Warners's highest-paid screenwriter, maintained that he read *Everybody Comes to Rick's* while on a trip to the East Coast with Wallis and urged him to option it.[9] Robinson prepared detailed notes on the *Casablanca* script, explaining how important it is "these days" (i.e., May 1942) for the heroine to leave Casablanca with her resistance fighter husband, instead of her former lover—thus exploding the myth that no one at the studio knew with whom she would be going.[10]

If "history has many cunning passages," as T.S. Eliot wrote in "Gerontion," those attempting to recall an event that occurred almost a half century earlier can easily lose their way in the labyrinth of the past, making more out of less—and vice versa. Lee may well have suggested the Epsteins for the film that became *Casablanca*, but she could not possibly have assigned them to it. No story editor had that kind of clout, particularly one working for Wallis. Furthermore, Lee was based in New York, and the Epsteins in Los Angeles. It is true that the Epsteins were "assigned" to the film—but by Wallis; and so were five other writers— by Wallis.

According to a memo from Wallis's secretary Paul Nathan to Jack Warner (4 February 1942), "Mr. Wallis had discussed *Casablanca* with the Epsteins . . . [and] they are anxious to do this script." Although "Wallis's contract had allowed him to choose the writers, actors and directors for *Casablanca*,"[11] he was no longer production head—a position he relinquished on 12 January 1942 to become an independent—or so he thought—producer. Nathan's memo was merely an attempt to inform Jack Warner of the Epsteins' interest in the film, just in case the brothers were needed for another project. Wallis played by the rules; Warner ignored them. Perhaps more than any other American film, *Casablanca* exists as a vast web where truth and myth are so tightly interwoven that only someone skilled at unraveling, like Homer's Penelope, can separate them. Fortunately, enough production material exists that anyone eager to untangle the skein can begin by pulling some strands— but with the realization that what was woven between 25 May and 3 August 1942 by hands that have long since ceased spinning can never really be returned to a ball of yarn.

Some of the facts can be easily summarized, although they can never explain the mysteries at the heart of the film that have made it a perennial favorite. *Casablanca* did originate as an unproduced play, which might have been mounted in New York if Alison and Burnett had been willing to make the revisions that producers Martin Gabel and Carly Wharton requested. Instead, Alison and Burnett decided to try Hollywood, which proved less demanding. Either the authors or their agent sent the script off to several studios, including Warners, where a copy arrived on 8 December 1941. Three days later, story analyst Stephen Karnot submitted a synopsis to Wallis, calling the play "a box-office natural"; on 22 December Wallis's secretary asked Irene Lee to "get . . . a price" on the play and solicit some reactions.[12] The next day Lee received responses from two producers: Jerry Wald, who was enthusiastic, and Robert Lord, who was skeptical but agreed that it might be worthwhile if the rights came cheap.

The rights were cheap: $20,000. Once Wallis was convinced the play was "a box-office natural," he made the script his top priority—so much so that seven writers were involved in its creation, three of whom received screenplay credit: the Epstein twins, Julius and Philip, and Howard Koch. The other writers included the team of Aeneas MacKenzie and Wallis's brother-in-law, Wally Kline, who wrote a treatment that is now lost; Lenore Coffee, who was merely asked to comment on the drafts that the Epsteins and Koch had written; and Casey Robinson, who devised a way for the film to end on a patriotic note and who also refused credit because he would not allow his name to appear with three others.[13] Although Robinson later insisted that the script was actually his because he had been asked to rework the drafts written by the Epsteins and Koch (who were at the same time reshaping each other's work), he had really been doing what contract writers traditionally did during the studio years: refining their colleagues' work and polishing it until it acquired a uniform sheen.[14]

In 1941 Irene Lee could never have believed that the play that she may or may not have persuaded Wallis to buy would become a cultural touchstone. The day before *Everybody Comes to Rick's* reached Karnot's desk, the Japanese bombed Pearl Harbor, bringing an end to the dream of isolationism and the beginning of an unprecedented patriotism, which often verged on nationalism—much of it fueled by Hollywood. Wallis saw great potential in the play, with its initially apathetic American, Rick Blaine, owner of a Casablanca café, who resumes an affair with his ex-lover, Lois Meredith, now the consort of a world-famous freedom fighter, Victor Laszlo. Although audiences would have liked the curtain to come down on a reunited Rick and Lois, even the playwrights knew that World War II made it impossible for Lois to ditch Victor, whose integrity, not to mention commitment, is far greater than Rick's. Unless Rick develops a political conscience and performs some kind of redemptive act (which he does), any other solution would be an affront to the war effort. To create a script that combined romantic melodrama and wartime propaganda, populated by character types that would become standard in the World War II film (isolationists, collaborationists, neutrals, opportunists, black marketeers, visa-seeking refugees), Wallis could not rely on a single writer. Rather, he decided on a variety of writers, each of whom could add something to the various plot strands. The Epsteins, known for their humor, punctuated the melodrama with one-liners; Koch deepened Rick's characterization by making him a onetime left-winger who fought in the Spanish Civil War and had now soured on life; and Robinson steered the plot in the direction of a wartime melodrama, so that it could be a love story as well as a criticism of neutrality. Robinson, a specialist in the woman's film, who gave Bette Davis some of her best vehicles—notably, *Dark Victory* and *Now, Voyager*—convinced Wallis that the Lois Meredith figure, renamed Ilsa Lund (and played unforgettably by Ingrid Bergman), should at first agonize over dumping Victor for Rick but then decide to stand by the man who supposedly would help turn the tide of the war in favor of the Allies. Although Ingrid Bergman insisted that she never knew whether she would be departing with Rick or Victor, World War II provided the answer, as seconded by the writers. However strongly audiences might have wanted a lovers' reunion, they were even more eager to see a lover shed his self-pity and embrace a cause.

    Casablanca is proof that film is a collaborative art, a phrase that seems a cliché until the facts are checked. The movie itself is a coat of many colors, each individually selected so that the clothier can produce the garment. Wallis was both clothier and producer. Admittedly, his contributions were not as significant as those of the Epsteins, Koch, and Robinson—not to mention director Michael Curtiz. But whether the film the world knows as *Casablanca* would have had the same cachet if the play's title had been retained is problematic; it would certainly never have had the same exotic appeal. It was Wallis who changed the title to *Casablanca* on 31 December 1941; the symbolically inclined might make note of the date Wallis issued a memo informing the various departments that "the story that we recently purchased entitled *Everybody*

Comes to Rick's will hereafter be known as *Casablanca.*" In a way it was the beginning not only of a new year but also of Wallis's freedom from the responsibilities of production head, formerly saddled with a dozen films a year and now enjoying the luxury of making only a few.

On 31 December Wallis could not have known that the title change would prove to be prophetic. Although he was probably thinking of place-name titles of successful films set in North Africa like *Morocco* (1930) and *Algiers* (1937), he had no way of knowing that Casablanca would be in the news throughout November 1942 after it was occupied by the Allies during the North African campaign. The nationwide release of the film on 23 January 1943 coincided with the windup of the Casablanca Conference, where President Roosevelt, Prime Minister Churchill, and Premier Stalin determined the next stages of the war. Wallis also added the classic fade-out line, believing that *Casablanca* should end on an upbeat note without diluting Rick's genial cynicism. As Rick and the prefect of police, Captain Louis Renault (Claude Rains), a self-styled "corrupt minor official," walk off in the fog, two former neutrals about to join the Free French, Wallis had Bogart record one of the most frequently quoted lines from the film: "Louis, I think this is the beginning of a beautiful friendship."[15] It is hard to imagine any of the *Casablanca* writers topping that.

No one in Hollywood had any doubt that *Casablanca* would figure in the Oscar nominations, given the patriotic fervor that gripped the nation—which, in turn, was reflected in the Academy's selection of *Casablanca* for best picture, best screenplay, and best direction. As far as Wallis was concerned, *Casablanca* was a "Hal B. Wallis Production"; Jack Warner's inclusion of his name in the logo as executive producer was nothing more than ego gratification. Wallis may have thought that—but not Warner. Since *Casablanca* came from Jack Warner's studio, it was *his* picture. That was evident at Grauman's Chinese Theatre on Academy Awards night, 2 March 1944, when Jack Warner's egomania morphed into hubris. When director Sidney Franklin announced that *Casablanca* had won for best picture, Wallis, assuming it was his award, immediately rose to accept it, only to discover that Jack Warner had bolted from his seat, beating him to the stage.

Many industry members were shocked at the arrogance of Warner, who upstaged Wallis for a statuette made of plaster rather than the usual bronze—a change necessitated by World War II, when metals took on strategic importance. When Bing Crosby won his Oscar for *Going My Way* (1944), he expressed his gratitude for a "piece of crockery," acknowledging the material that went into the award without minimizing its significance. Wallis would eventually get an Oscar of his own—not in plaster, and at his own expense. When the Academy went back to awarding bronze Oscars, Wallis ordered one for himself.[16]

It was evident that if Wallis were to remain at Warners, he would be in Jack Warner's shifting shadow, despite his new contract. At the time, Wallis concealed his anger; the extent of it was not revealed until he published his autobiography thirty-seven years later. The *Los Angeles Times* did not wait that long. Almost immediately *Times* film critic Edwin Schallert took Warner to task. Wallis, calling on history, came to Warner's defense, reminding Schallert that Warner had also accepted the best picture award for *The Life of Emile Zola* (1937), implying that it was customary for the studio head, rather than the producer, to accept the best picture Oscar.

To a certain extent, Wallis was right, although much depended on the producer's reputation. In 1937 Wallis was not an independent producer; in 1944 he was. At the 1937 Oscar ceremony, when MGM's *Great Ziegfield* was named best picture, Louis Mayer rose to accept the award, noting that at MGM it was common knowledge that "I make all the speeches." Yet Mayer not only asked the director, Robert Z. Leonard, to take a bow but also brought the producer, Hunt Stromberg, up to the dais.[17]

It was generous of Mayer to acknowledge Stromberg, who became an important producer but not one of Wallis's stature. Mayer would not have behaved so condescendingly to someone like Sidney Franklin, a major producer (*Waterloo Bridge* [1940], *Mrs. Miniver* [1942], *Random Harvest* [1942], *Madame Curie* [1943]) but a minor director, whose best-known film is *The Good Earth* (1937). Thus at the 1943 awards banquet, when William Goetz announced that MGM's *Mrs. Miniver* was voted best picture of 1942, Mayer accepted the award but made it clear he was doing so only because Franklin was ill.

That neither Hunt Stromberg nor Sidney Franklin was in Wallis's league was obvious even before the night of 2 March 1944, when Wallis received the Thalberg Award for excellence in filmmaking for the second time. Thus, Wallis believed that if *Casablanca* received the best picture Oscar, he had every right to claim it. The competition was formidable: *For Whom the Bell Tolls, Madame Curie, The Song of Bernadette, Heaven Can Wait, The Human Comedy, The Ox-Bow Incident, The More the Merrier,* and *In Which We Serve.* By 1951 the point was moot: the Academy finally voted to award the best picture Oscar to the producer. But in 1944, who exactly was *Casablanca*'s producer: Jack Warner, with his "executive producer" title affixed to the logo like a cynosure, or Hal B. Wallis, with his penultimate credit declaring the film a "Hal B. Wallis Production"?

There was an ulterior motive for Warner's rush to the stage that March evening to claim the trophy he assumed was his. That the wartime Oscars were made of plaster did not matter. The previous month Wallis gave an interview to the *Los Angeles Examiner* (5 February 1943), in which he supposedly claimed he was the producer of the Irving Berlin flag-waver *This Is the Army* (1943). That same day Warner fired off a blistering memo to Wallis: "I told you from the beginning that you and I are the producers. You had no right to give that story. However, every time my name, or any other name, appears in the paper, you start grumbling. You won't come to the dining room, and I have to phone you two or three times to come to lunch." He ended by reminding Wallis that "there's more going on in the world" and they should discuss the matter "man to man."[18]

Although Wallis denied making such a statement to the *Examiner,* he had said pretty much the same thing two months earlier at a press conference in Cleveland, implying that he was *This Is the Army*'s sole producer and making no mention of Warner.[19] *This Is the Army* was a special case: the film was coproduced by Wallis and Warner, as the credits attest. Given his title, "Lieutenant Colonel" Warner had no intention of being excluded from a film about a branch of the service in which he held rank, however bogus.

Wallis knew there was more going on in the world besides his feud with Warner. Of Wallis's 1942–43 films, three held special significance for him: *Casablanca, This Is the Army,* and *Watch on the Rhine.* Their common theme was patriotism in the World War II sense of combating fascism. Wallis was forty-three when America was forced out of its isolationist torpor on 7 December 1941. Even if he had wanted to enlist, he would have ended up with a fancy title that would have shielded him from the realities of war, as Warner's "Lieutenant Colonel" tag did. Instead, Wallis did his bit by making movies.

Lillian Hellman's *Watch on the Rhine,* winner of the New York Drama Critics' Circle Award for best play, was still a major Broadway attraction when the Japanese bombed Pearl Harbor. On 30 December 1941, Warners reached an agreement with Hellman and the play's producer-director Herman Shumlin (who would also direct the film version) to purchase the rights for $150,000.[20] Wallis agreed with Hellman and Shumlin that Paul Lukas should reprise his role of the freedom fighter, Kurt Müller, which won him such acclaim in the New York production. Lukas, however, though he may have been a fine actor, was not a box office attraction. Wallis wanted a star for Kurt's wife, Sara, an important but subordinate role. Since Bette Davis was the studio's biggest female star at the time, he persuaded her to take the part, appealing to her strong sense of patriotism (Davis called herself a Jeffersonian Democrat), which she revealed when she and John Garfield founded the Hollywood Canteen in 1942, where members of the armed forces could dunk donuts with the stars before embarking for "destination unknown" and an uncertain future.

Although Hellman's lover, Dashiell Hammett, had all but given up writing, doing only occasional polish jobs on scripts, Hellman persuaded Wallis to entrust the adaptation to him, despite the objections of Jack Warner. Warner claimed he was unfamiliar with Hammett's work, apparently forgetting that his studio had produced the highly successful film version of Hammett's *Maltese Falcon* (1941). Contrary to the myth that Hellman got Hammett on the payroll but wrote the script herself, there is ample evidence that the screenplay was indeed Hammett's; that Wallis acknowledged it as such, dubbing it "wonderful"; and that Hellman also got herself on the payroll for a few weeks of script polishing, a skill she probably picked up from Hammett. The skill also brought her a screen credit: "Additional Scenes and Dialogue by Lillian Hellman."

Released in the late summer of 1943, *Watch on the Rhine* was nominated for best picture, best actor (Paul Lukas), best supporting actress (Lucile Watson), and best screenplay. Although Humphrey Bogart seemed a shoo-in for best actor in view of *Casablanca*'s popularity, the Academy preferred Paul Lukas's Kurt Müller to Bogart's Rick Blaine—but not Hellman and Hammett's stinging attack on neutrality, which neither playwright nor adapter softened by reducing antifascism to drawing-room politics. *Watch on the Rhine* received only one Oscar, but the fact that it was nominated for four reflected favorably on Wallis, three of whose productions were honored that evening.

The third was *This Is the Army,* a lump-in-the-throat flag-waver with enough Irving Berlin songs and rah-rah zeal to keep recruiting offices busy for the duration. Although *This Is the Army* only merits one page in *Starmaker,* Wallis treated the film no differently than any of his other productions—except, perhaps, *Casablanca* and *Now, Voyager,* in which he truly believed. He dispatched detailed memos about hairstyles, costumes, added shots, and the staging of the musical sequences. *This Is the Army* may have appealed to Wallis's patriotism, but he soon discovered that Irving Berlin, the people's choice for America's unofficial songwriter laureate, had his own ideas about Casey Robinson's script, which Berlin reworked to such an extent that he opposed Robinson's receiving screen credit. Although Robinson received credit for a script that he would rather forget, audiences rallied around the film, which enriched the Army Emergency Relief fund by almost $2 million, partly because Robinson, the Epstein brothers (who also worked on the script), and Curtiz donated their salaries.[21] Wallis also made his contribution, but he had no intention of working pro bono. Despite his contract, Wallis chose to forgo his share of the profits in favor of a producer's fee of $25,000, proving that patriotism benefits both the patriot and the cause.

Oscar night 1944 was a triumph for Warners. Although *This Is the Army* won only for musical scoring, it had been nominated for interior decoration and sound recording. Still, it was further vindication of Wallis's uncanny ability to divine the public's taste. At the end of the evening, Warners could claim six Oscars, all of them Wallis's productions.

Yet that did not stop Warner from retaliating against what he perceived as an affront to his authority, especially after gossip columnist Louella Parsons quoted Wallis as saying that a forthcoming Warner Brothers film, *The Conspirators,* was his own "story idea." Jack Warner had become so paranoid that he bluntly informed Wallis (28 November 1943) that he was tired of Wallis's claiming credit for such films as *Watch on the Rhine, Princess O'Rourke,* and *This Is the Army:* "I happened to be the one who saw these stories," Warner insisted. In the same memo, he lamented: "You certainly have changed and unnecessarily so."[22]

A week after the *Examiner* piece appeared, Wallis's lawyer, Loyd Wright, had to remind Warner that diminishing the size of Wallis's name in the ads was a violation of his client's contract. Even after the large-type lettering was restored, Warner did not relent. Whenever Wallis and Warner met, Wallis griped about the *Casablanca* Oscar, and Warner found another nit to pick at. In November 1943 Warner criticized Wallis for his supposedly paltry contribution to the War Chest, arguing that if Bette Davis gave $6,000, he should have given $8,000. That same month, Warner refused to give Wallis producing credit for *Saratoga Trunk,* even though its release was being delayed. Warner, whose logical sense was a bit skewed, replied that only stars' names appeared in trailers, not those of producers. Never mind that the issue was newspaper and magazine ads, not trailers. Again Loyd Wright had to intervene by reminding Warner that Wallis's name was also omitted from the print ads.

It was not until Wallis threatened legal action that the *Saratoga Trunk* credit was resolved: the film would be advertised as a "Hal B. Wallis Production" in lettering two-thirds the size of "Jack L. Warner, Executive Producer." When *Saratoga Trunk,* whose release was held up for two years, finally opened in March 1946, Wallis had already made three films at Paramount, and the "executive producer" was left with a movie that turned out to be a major disappointment for fans of Gary Cooper and Ingrid Bergman, both of whom were painfully miscast.

The days when Jack Warner would give Wallis a watch and a vicuna coat for Christmas, as he did in 1939, were over. And soon Wallis's days at Warners would be over as well. Wallis's new contract gave him—or so he thought—power and stature that he had not previously possessed. However, the truth is that his power and stature remained unchanged; and so did Jack Warner's. Although Wallis was not so naive as to think that he and Warner were now equals, he must have at least felt that he had moved up a few rungs on the Warners ladder without quite realizing that he was still stuck on the same rung with a new title. It was like making a lateral move with fewer duties but the same boss.

The new contract brought out a side of Wallis that grated on Warner. Two weeks after he signed the new contract, Wallis wanted a watchman at his home, fearing it could be burglarized during his frequent absences. Again, he complained to Warner that no one met him at the train when he returned from Chicago. Wiring back that the studio had enough problems with stockholders without requesting another expenditure, Warner also criticized Wallis for his pettiness, particularly since the world was at war again: "YOU MUST REALIZE THERES WAR GOING ON AND THESE

MINOR THINGS SHOULD NEVER BE BROUGHT UP. THERE ARE TOO MANY BIG THINGS IN WORLD INSTEAD WORRYING ABOUT PEOPLE MEETING YOU AT TRAIN."[23] The unkindest cut occurred at the end of Warner's telegram, where he reminded Wallis that the "world has been very good to you." As far as Warner was concerned, all that had changed was Wallis's self-image, which had grown far beyond the boundaries that Warner had imposed upon it.

The world and Warner Brothers had treated Wallis well; Wallis, however, considered Jack Warner a small part of his world—a producer's world. Similarly, Jack Warner regarded Wallis as a small part of his—a studio head's world.

By 1944 Warner seemed to be doing everything in his power to make Wallis's life so unpleasant that he would eventually leave the studio. In early March Wallis learned that the writers on his current and proposed productions (*Hotel Berlin, God Is My Co-Pilot, The Corn Is Green,* and *Night and Day*) were taken off assignment. These films were eventually made and released in 1945–1946, but not as Wallis productions; they were produced by Louis F. Edelman, Robert Buckner, Jack Chertok, and Arthur Schwartz, respectively. Warner realized that when Wallis gave up being an executive producer in 1942, he was theoretically an independent producer seeking to green-light his own films. But Warner did not even want Wallis as an independent producer. It was not so much a clash of egos as of wills: Warner could not impose his will on Wallis, and Wallis would not allow himself to be strong-armed by a man for whom he had lost respect.

On 4 April 1944 Warner charged Wallis with failing to meet the terms of his contract by negotiating with other studios. Loyd Wright was quoted as saying that the abrogation of Wallis's contract came as "a distinct surprise," particularly since his client and the studio were negotiating a termination that would be mutually acceptable.[24] However, discussion ended abruptly on the evening of 4 April, and less than a few hours later, the studio released a statement to the effect that it had no desire to hold Wallis to a contract that had become so onerous. That did not mean that Warners would not sue Wallis, who had breached the terms of his June 1942 contract, which was to run for four years.

During the contract dispute, Wallis remained in his office on the studio lot. One day, however, Wallis discovered that Warner had had the lock changed. Wallis then had a desk moved to the nearby lawn. Warner decided that the lawn needed fertilizer and had a truckload of manure dumped on it.[25] In 1945 Wallis's contract was settled in his favor after Warner learned he was powerless to deny Wallis his 10 percent of the gross for *Desperate Journey* and *Now, Voyager* (1942); *Air Force, Princess O'Rourke, This Is the Army,* and *Watch on the Rhine* (1943); and *Saratoga Trunk* (1945). In retaliation, Warner turned on his former secretary, Minna Wallis, who, after becoming a talent agent, often met her clients at the studio. With her brother's departure, Minna found herself without an office.

Even before Warner upstaged him on Oscar night, Wallis was hunting for another studio where he could be an independent producer with as much autonomy as possible at a time when the studio system was still in place. Even if, in 1944, the Academy had had a policy of awarding the best picture Oscar to the producer, it is doubtful that Wallis would have remained at Warners. Jack Warner, in addition to being the "clown prince of Hollywood," as his biographer Bob Thomas christened him, was notoriously petty and vindictive; eventually, he would have been unable to endure further accolades for Wallis and so few for himself. In his autobiography, Warner barely mentioned Wallis, who wrote generously about Warner: "He was good to me. He gave me my break, and he was a great administrator" (*Starmaker,* 13).

A week after his humiliation on Oscar night, Wallis started making plans to leave the studio. Coincidentally, so did Joseph Hazen, a Warners vice president and board member. It was the talkies that brought Wallis and Hazen together. When Warners decided to use the Vitaphone system to make sound pictures, Joseph H. Hazen, a George Washington University law school graduate, drew up the contract between Vitaphone and the studio.

The enormous success of Warners's initial ventures in sound, *Don Juan* (1926) and especially *The Jazz Singer* (1927), convinced the brothers Warner that Joseph Hazen's name could be a worthwhile addition to the legal department, which Hazen joined in 1927. Wallis wrote the publicity releases that heralded Warners's foray into talking pictures, even traveling to New York to supervise the advertising campaign. It was there that he met Hazen, who was as impressed by Wallis's talents as a publicist as Wallis was by Hazen's negotiating genius.

The industry needed that genius in 1940 when the Justice Department accused the vertically integrated studios (MGM, Paramount, RKO,

Warners, and Paramount) of violating the Sherman Anti-Trust Act. The
five studios succeeded in gaining control of 65 percent of the market by
using their theater circuits as conduits for their own films and discrim-
inating against independent exhibitors, who were often forced to wait
for major films until the first runs had ended at the studio-owned theaters. The Justice Department's goal, to sever production and distribution from exhibition, was achieved at the end of the decade—America's
entry into World War II making the matter a low priority for the duration. In the meantime, the industry bought time—thanks, in great part,
to Hazen's legal acumen. Hazen was a member of the committee that
drew up the consent decree, which went into effect on 1 February 1941.[26]
Although hardly a triumph for the exhibitors, the decree was the result
of a compromise between the motion picture industry and the Justice
Department that modified, but did not discontinue, the policies of blind
bidding and block booking. Exhibitors were now not required to bid on
films they had not seen; instead, trade show screenings were arranged
before the films were offered for rental. Exhibitors no longer had to
book as many as ten films to get the two or three they really wanted; the
number was reduced to five. If exhibitors objected to films on moral
grounds, they were not saddled with them. Unwanted shorts and news-
reels were no longer part of the package. Distributors could not play
favorites with exhibitors within the same territory, withholding a film
from one theater owner in order to license it to another—unless there
was a shortage of prints, in which case the point was moot. The Justice
Department agreed to give the studios a three-year grace period before
requiring them to divest themselves of their theaters. The respite only
delayed the inevitable disaggregation.

The year 1947, however, saw the beginning of the end of the studio
system: The Justice Department pursued its investigation of Hollywood's
monopolistic practices, the House Un-American Activities Committee
(HUAC) began hearings about alleged Communist subversion of the
movie industry, and postwar America found other diversions that started with miniature golf and ended with television.

But in 1941 Hazen felt he had done his job, although his committee
had only achieved a stop-gap solution. Hollywood was never concerned
about the long term. World War II meant big box office, with 1946 becoming Hollywood's banner year.

By 1946, however, Wallis and Hazen were no longer at Warners. At exactly the same time as Wallis was planning to leave Warners because of Jack Warner, Hazen was planning to do the same because of Harry, whose financial conservatism he had come to deplore. Their disenchantment with Warners proved to be mutually advantageous. In mid-March 1944, when Wallis discovered that Hazen was leaving the studio, he suggested that they form their own production company. Wallis did not have to convince Hazen, who knew a good deal when he saw one: "Just as music is greater than the sum of its notes, so I think that you and I jointly will add up to more than you and I working separately and apart," Hazen wrote to Wallis.[27] The music grew dissonant in a few years and eventually became cacophonous. Although Wallis would never descend to the depths of vituperation and betrayal that Warner did, he could not tolerate having anyone take credit for one of his accomplishments. Wallis's obsession with receiving his due, a side effect of the *Casablanca* affair, eventually affected his relationship with Hazen, who began taking credit for some of Wallis's coups. The men remained business associates for two decades but did not part as friends. Until separation time, they put up a united front, whose fissures were carefully concealed from the press.

It was different in spring 1944, when the industry learned that Wallis and Hazen were looking for a studio base. There was no dearth of offers; United Artists courted them, as did MGM. The former, however, was really a distribution company, home to a number of independent producers, the best-known of whom were Hunt Stromberg and Walter Wanger. Although Wallis would have outshone both of them, he would still have been another producer, releasing through United Artists. Wallis even received an offer from Nicholas Schenck, president of Loew's, Inc., the parent company of MGM, who recommended that he become MGM production head and Hazen become president. But president of what? MGM did not have a president; it was a subsidiary of Loew's, Inc.

Apparently, Schenck, then sixty-three, hoped Hazen would replace him as president of Loew's, Inc. Although Schenck lived to be eighty-eight, dying in 1969, he had been looking for a successor a quarter of a century earlier. Hazen succeeding Schenck? Perhaps. But Wallis dislodging Louis Mayer, whose name was synonymous with MGM? Even if Wallis had done so, he would have been production chief at a studio that was a subsidiary of Loew's, Inc. In the early 1940s, MGM's idea of

(Above) Wallis the publicist (left), looking unimpressed as Harry Warner welcomes stage star Lenore Ulric to Hollywood in 1923. (Below) Wallis as publicist for Sol Lesser's production of *The Man with the Iron Door* (1924).

On the set of *Page Miss Glory* (1935). *Left to right:* director Mervyn LeRoy, star Marion Davies, Jack Warner, and Wallis.

(Above) Wallis, Bette Davis, and Harry Warner at a Hollywood premiere in the late 1930s. *(Below)* Wallis on the set of *The Sea Wolf* (1941) with (*left to right*) star Edward G. Robinson, his son Manny, and the young Brent Wallis.

Robert Cummings *(left)* with Wallis and Lizabeth Scott on the set of *You Came Along* (1945), Lizabeth's screen debut. Courtesy Academy of Motion Picture Arts and Sciences (AMPAS).

Wallis as guest producer of a 1945 radio version of *Intermezzo* (1939) with Ingrid Bergman and Joseph Cotten.

(Above) The boys' night out. *Left to right:* George Jessel, Ronald Reagan, Wallis, Dean Martin, Jerry Lewis, and George Burns, around 1950. *(Below) Left to right:* Elvis, Tennessee Williams, Colonel Parker, Laurence Harvey, and Wallis around 1960 when Elvis had finished *G.I. Blues* (1960) and Harvey was about to costar with Geraldine Page in *Summer and Smoke* (1961).

Paul Nathan, who served Wallis faithfully for thirty years, Elvis, and the producer in the early 1960s.

(Above) Wallis and Elizabeth Taylor going over a bit part written for her in *Becket* (1964) but later discarded. (Below) Wallis with Robert Redford and Jane Fonda, the stars of *Barefoot in the Park* (1967).

(Above) A chance meeting between Wallis and Charlie Chaplin (left) at England's Shepperton Studios in 1968. (Below) Wallis and Chaplin sharing a laugh in 1968.

(Above) Wallis and Kim Darby during the filming of *True Grit* (1969). *(Below)* Genevieve Bujold (Anne Boleyn) and Wallis on the set of *Anne of the Thousand Days* (1969).

(Above) Wallis, Richard Burton, and director Charles Jarrott during the filming of *Anne of the Thousand Days. (Below)* A luncheon Wallis hosted for Prince Charles during the shooting of *Anne. Left to right:* Charlton Heston, Prince Charles, Wallis, Genevieve Bujold, and Ava Gardner.

Wallis and the
Queen Mother at a
Royal Command
Performance of
Anne in November
1972.

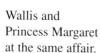

Wallis and
Princess Margaret
at the same affair.

Wallis in the 1930s, photographed by the renowned George Hurrell.

Wallis in the late 1940s.

Wallis in 1970.

Wallis in 1972, Martha Wallis's favorite picture of her husband.

an independent producer was Seymour Nebenzahl, who managed to get the studio to release his production of *Hitler's Madman* (1942), most of which had already been shot before MGM decided to release it, thereby enabling Nebenzahl to use the lot to film additional scenes. Nebenzahl is known, if at all, as the producer of Fritz Lang's *M* (1930); *Hitler's Madman*'s importance lies solely in its being director Douglas Sirk's first American film.

Columbia and Universal had no appeal to Wallis at the time, although, ironically, Wallis would end his career in 1975 at a radically different Universal. Fox was the preserve of the formidable Darryl F. Zanuck. RKO was so unstable, and president George J. Schaefer so autocratic, that the studio had become a revolving door for independent producers. Sam Goldwyn, the most important independent producer in Hollywood, usually released his films through RKO. Wallis wanted a studio where there would be minimal competition—specifically, no Sam Goldwyns. That left Paramount. Barney Balaban, Paramount's president, had no problem bringing Wallis on board. Both hailed from Chicago, where Balaban got his start. Paramount had already experienced its share of independent producers, such as Leo McCarey, who had given the studio the Oscar-winner *Going My Way* (1944). Although McCarey had made some memorable Paramount films in the past (e.g., *Duck Soup* [1933], *Belle of the Nineties* [1934], and *Make Way for Tomorrow* [1937]), he did not intend to make Paramount the home of his short-lived Rainbow Productions, which, during its brief existence (1945–52), released through RKO.

By July 1944 Wallis was ready to set up shop at Paramount. When Hazen came on board, the company's name became Wallis-Hazen, Inc., with Wallis as president and Hazen as vice president and treasurer. However, Wallis-Hazen also included Hal Wallis Productions. Wallis was taking no chances. Although Wallis counted Hazen among his friends, he did not distinguish between friendship and expediency. In 1936 Hazen married Lita Annenberg, the daughter of Moses L. Annenberg, the publishing tycoon. It was the proverbial "brilliant marriage," a union of intelligence and wealth, which allowed Hazen and his wife to become philanthropists as well as art collectors, whose acquisitions included works by Van Gogh, Toulouse-Lautrec, Braque, Kandinsky, and Picasso. In time, Wallis emulated Hazen and began collecting himself. Meanwhile, Hazen was the ideal partner in a venture that, given Hollywood's uncertain future after World War II, could end up like Rainbow Productions or the ill-fated Liberty Films, Frank Capra's inspiration (in cooperation with George Stevens and William Wyler). Liberty's sole release, *It's a Wonderful Life* (1946), needed exposure on television to become a holiday perennial; it had little impact on postwar America.

Wallis knew he could never recreate Warners at Paramount. No longer would he work with such stars as Errol Flynn, Bette Davis, Humphrey Bogart, Edward G. Robinson, Ann Sheridan, Paul Muni, and James Cagney; or such directors as Raoul Walsh, John Huston, Edmund Goulding, Howard Hawks, and William Wyler. But he could apply the formula that had brought him such success in the past: a judicious combination of the old and the new, of contract players and new talent. Although Paramount had contract players that were at his disposal, Wallis also wanted his own discoveries. His new studio's logo was a mountain peak with a halo of stars. Although Wallis knew that no more stars could be added to the logo, that did not preclude his adding them to his—and Paramount's—roster. Having emerged from Jack Warner's shadow, Wallis was ready for starlight.

CHAPTER FIVE

Starting Over

W ALLIS-HAZEN, INC., WAS an alliance of talent (Wallis's), ego (shared), legal expertise (Hazen's), hubris (largely Hazen's), and periodic disillusionment (mutual), which brought the company to the brink of dissolution several times, starting in 1952; but as zero hour approached, Wallis and Hazen opted for reinvention, burying the corporate name and leaving only Hal Wallis Productions. In 1944, however, Wallis-Hazen was "a perfect blendship," as Cole Porter would have said—a blend for which Warners provided the ingredients. To ease the transition from Warners to Paramount, Wallis surrounded himself with as many of his cronies as possible. Although he did not exactly stage a talent raid, he managed to persuade some of his people to join him at Paramount. In addition to Hazen, vice president of the company, there was Jack Saper, who had worked at Warners in various capacities, including editor, unit manager, and finally associate producer of four Wallis films: *The Man Who Came to Dinner* (1941); *Navy Blues* (1941); and *Larceny, Inc.* and *Juke Girl* (both 1942). Saper was more than an employee; he was Wallis's cousin, a fact that Wallis never acknowledged. They grew up together in Chicago, and the young Wallis occasionally stayed with the Sapers—his aunt and uncle on his mother's side—after his father deserted the family. Although Saper was listed on the roster as secretary and assistant manager of Wallis-Hazen, his title was misleading; Saper was really production manager—in short, Wallis's budget officer.

Saper was also Wallis's factotum. Unhappy about the $100 that had been spent on jeans and a plaid skirt, two of Joan Fontaine's less glamorous costumes in *Susan*, Wallis snidely asked Saper why they were not purchased at an Army & Navy store, where they would have cost $7.[1] When Wallis lost his trench coat en route from Zürich to Rome, Saper was expected to file an insurance claim.[2] The memos were always curt. Before Wallis went on location, he had Saper set the timers in his house; during location shooting, Saper was expected to monitor the weather reports as well as scrutinize the budget. A 21 March 1946 teletype to Saper consists of one question, which speaks volumes about the sender: "What did you find out about my glasses?"

Paul Nathan was another Warners defector. After graduating from Los Angeles City College in the mid-1930s, Nathan had no idea he would be spending the rest of his career working for Wallis. First it was at Warners as Wallis's secretary, then at Paramount, and finally at Universal—but in different capacities. After serving in the army in World War II, during which he wrote and directed training films, Nathan joined Wallis at Paramount. In 1945 job descriptions were never very specific; otherwise, few would have vied for Nathan's position—a combination casting director–confidant–adviser. When Wallis's story editor, John Mock—a Texas-born Rhodes Scholar, fluent in French and Spanish, whose plot summaries read like an honors student's essays—departed in 1952, Nathan moved into his job. Although Wallis considered Mock's departure a major loss, he realized he had an acolyte in Nathan, who behaved accordingly.

At first, Nathan was in awe of Wallis, addressing him as "Mr. Wallis," progressing to "Dear Boss" and, after fifteen years, to "Dear Hal." His casting suggestions were often intriguing: Bette Davis, Burt Lancaster, and Lizabeth Scott in *A Streetcar Named Desire*, which Wallis never made; if he had, *Streetcar* would have been vastly different from the 1951 Elia Kazan version with Vivien Leigh, Marlon Brando, and Kim Hunter, all of whom had performed their roles on stage—Brando and Hunter in New York, Leigh in London. Nathan's taste in theater, however, was unreliable: *Guys and Dolls* "was not worth the effort to get seats." As for *Stalag 17*: "Who cares today about men in a Nazi prison camp?"[3] *Guys and Dolls* is a landmark stage musical that remained stage-bound in Joseph L. Mankiewicz's 1955 film version. *Stalag 17*, however, was a middling stage play that became one of Billy Wilder's best films (1953), brought William Holden his only Oscar, and spawned a popular and long-lived television series, *Hogan's Heroes* (1965–71).

Like anyone with producing aspirations, Nathan found it difficult being around Wallis and serving in a subordinate capacity. He tried his hand at writing, but his scripts never reached the screen, although he seems to have contributed to two Wallis productions, *Visit to a Small Planet* (1960) and *All in a Night's Work* (1961). Nathan would have his chance to produce, but it would not be until the end of the 1960s.

Irene Lee, Wallis's assistant story editor and the self-proclaimed discoverer of the play that became *Casablanca*, also jumped ship. Lee, in fact, turned out to be the most famous member of Wallis's entourage. In 1942 she married Aaron Diamond, a real estate developer, whose enormous success enabled them to live the good life, become world travelers, and socialize with presidents, composers, writers, artists, dancers, and scientists. The Diamonds, however, did not believe in stockpiling wealth for their own use or in forging relationships with celebrities so they could drop names at parties. Lee and her husband established the Aaron Diamond Foundation, a major philanthropic organization and a leading supporter of AIDS research, known as the Irene Diamond Foundation since Aaron's death in 1984. If Irene Lee Diamond is known for anything, it is not as Hal Wallis's story editor but as a humanitarian and activist, whose causes have ranged from teacher education to gun control. Although Irene continued to work for Wallis after her marriage, always on the lookout for new talent and filmable properties, the two parted ways when Wallis left Paramount for Universal in 1969.

As a former publicist, Wallis understood the power of PR. He had met Walter Seltzer in 1940 at Warner Brothers, whose publicity department Seltzer had just joined. Seltzer's love affair with film began when he ushered after school in Philadelphia, where he was born, although having a father who operated a theater chain must have influenced his choice of profession.[4] After graduating from the University of Pennsylvania with a journalism degree, Seltzer tried exhibition, briefly working as assistant manager of the Warners theaters in Philadelphia. But like Wallis, who had also been a theater manager, Seltzer soon discovered how important a factor promotion was in a movie's success.

The lure of Hollywood brought Seltzer to Los Angeles in 1935 as publicist for Fox West Coast Theatres. The successful ad campaign he mounted for MGM's *Mutiny on the Bounty* (1935) landed him a job at the studio, where he helped form the public's image of such stars as Mickey Rooney, Myrna Loy, Judy Garland, Clark Gable, and Joan Crawford. Crawford, in fact, was so delighted with the publicity that he generated for her that even when he moved from MGM to Warners, she paid him to be her personal publicist. Interestingly, Wallis too had done some freelancing when he started at Warners.

Pearl Harbor put Seltzer's career on hold. After spending four years in the Marines, he returned to civilian life in 1945, just as Wallis had settled in at Paramount and was in need of a publicity and advertising director. Financially, it was not ideal: three-year contracts with a weekly raise of $25 for the next contract period.

Although Seltzer could have done better offering his services to a major studio, he was attracted to the idea of becoming part of Hollywood's newest producing company, headed by a man with an outstanding record of hits. For the next nine years, he served Wallis, doing what he had done at MGM and Warners: acting as mythmaker to the starmaker and basking in the reflected glory. As Wallis discovered new talent, Seltzer found the right way to showcase it; this may have meant embellishing the truth, but the moviegoing public has never bought truth—only truth cloaked in illusion. If the movies are the dream factory, the buyer is not purchasing a real product.

Seltzer could not turn every one of the starmaker's finds into a household name. But he succeeded more often than he failed: Charlton Heston, Burt Lancaster, Dean Martin and Jerry Lewis, Shirley Booth, Kirk Douglas. No doubt they could have succeeded on their own; but they would not have been as interesting.

Like Wallis, Seltzer discovered the power that lay in producing. Wallis understood Seltzer's frustration at promoting the careers of others, while his own was limited to hagiography. So Wallis made him a production assistant, which turned out to be a meaningless title. Just as Wallis had had to leave Warners, Seltzer had to make his exit, too, although in this instance there was no acrimony—merely the urge to move on.

First, Seltzer joined Burt Lancaster's production company, Hecht-Lancaster, in 1954. Although a producing credit was not forthcoming, Seltzer was rewarded with a new title, vice president of advertising and publicity, after he reawakened a sleeper called *Marty*, which won the Oscar for best picture of 1955.

Once Seltzer realized that, apart from starting his own production company like Wallis, he had no other choice but to join someone else's, he opted for Marlon Brando's Pennebaker Company. He became executive producer of a score of films, including six with Charlton Heston, with whom he struck up a lasting friendship when he first met the actor in 1949: the resulting films included *Will Penny* (1967), *Number One* (1969), *The Omega Man* (1971), *Skyjacked* (1972), *Soylent Green* (1973), and *The Last Hard Man* (1976). Although none of these films represent Heston's best work (i.e., *The Ten Commandments* [1956], *Ben-Hur* [1959], and *Planet of the Apes* [1967]), the actor at least enjoyed a successful career—thanks, initially, to Wallis, as we will see, with the help of his mythmaker, Walter Seltzer.

By July 1944 Wallis had chosen his first three releases: *The Affairs of Susan, You Came Along,* and *Love Letters* (all 1945). *Susan* was romantic fluff, revolving around a stage actress (Joan Fontaine) torn among four lovers. With George Brent as the male lead (and as a Broadway producer, no less), Brent's costar billing and his character's profession solved *Susan*'s plot. *Susan's* director was William A. Seiter, whose forte was light comedy. *Susan*, apparently, was not one of Wallis's favorites, since no reference to either the picture or its director appears in *Starmaker*. The film was given an attractive production, as one would expect of a movie whose title character is a Broadway star. For her efforts, Fontaine received a star's salary: $2,500 a week; Seiter did better, netting twice that amount. Though Wallis was silent about *Susan*, it found favor with the critics and received an Oscar nomination for original story.

For his 1945 releases, Wallis relied mostly on "name" actors. He realized he could not feature a newcomer in his Paramount debut, even though he had one—Lizabeth Scott, whom he was grooming for stardom and who, as a stage actress herself, could have easily played Susan. But for his first Paramount release, Wallis wanted recognizable names, whose star power may not have had the wattage of Bette Davis and Humphrey Bogart but could still draw an audience. Thus, for *Susan*, he chose Joan Fontaine, a 1941 Oscar winner for Hitchcock's *Suspicion;* and George Brent, Minna's former client-lover, still sexy in his midforties. Wallis had encountered both of them at Warners. Fontaine costarred with Charles Boyer in *The Constant Nymph* (1943), which, according to the production files, could have been a Wallis film; however, for reasons that remain unclear, Wallis declined to be credited. Brent was truly a known factor, having appeared in three Wallis films: *Gold Is Where You Find It* (1938), *Dark Victory* (1939), and *The Fighting 69th* (1940). Since Fontaine and Brent were freelancing, neither had to be borrowed.

Love Letters was another matter. In June 1944 Wallis purchased the rights to Chris Massie's novel *Pity My Simplicity* for $35,000.[5] For the leads—an amnesiac known only by the name of Singleton and Quinton, the ex-GI who helps her regain her memory—Wallis envisioned Jennifer Jones and Gregory Peck. Since Peck had just finished making Hitchcock's *Spellbound* (1945), in which he played an amnesiac, he was reluctant to appear in a film with a similar theme. Wallis then approached Joseph Cotten, who, like Jones, was under contract to David Selznick. Jones, in fact, would marry Selznick four years later. Selznick guarded his talent as if they were his property, which, in a sense, they were. Selznick agreed to the loan-out, with these stipulations: that he have final approval of Jones's hairstyle, makeup, and wardrobe; that Lee Garmes be hired as director of photography; that in the main title Jones's name appear first, with Cotten's in the same size lettering; that they be identified as "artists in arrangement with David O. Selznick"; and that Jones be paid approximately one hundred thousand dollars for nine weeks of work. Selznick's salary request reflected Jones's star power. For her first major role, the title character in *The Song of Bernadette* (1943), Jones won the Oscar for best actress, playing a fourteen-year-old French girl whose unwavering belief in a vision of the Virgin Mary in a grotto at Lourdes eventually brings her sainthood and brings Lourdes international fame for its miraculous cures. Although Cotten was not in Jones's league, his popularity grew after Hitchcock cast him against type as a silken-voiced serial killer in *Shadow of a Doubt* (1943).

Even after Wallis agreed to Selznick's terms, he was bombarded with memos, Selznick's favorite means of communication, as if *Love Letters* were Selznick's movie. It was the same when Jones was making *We Were Strangers* (1949) at Columbia; Selznick besieged Harry Cohn with detailed instructions about the way she should be photographed. Selznick may have been an irritant, but he got results. Selznick was delighted with *Love Letters*; Jones was "absolutely sensational," he wrote to Neil Agnew, the vice president of his new production company, Vanguard.[6] If any actress was meant for black-and-white photography, it was Jones, whose dark hair, luminous skin, and high cheek bones allowed for the kind of sculpting that color—particularly Technicolor—could not accomplish. Yet *Love Letters* was not a love affair between the star and the camera. Garmes's expressive and often moody lighting created a tension between the love story that the film purported to be and the "whodunit" that it eventually became. And director William Dieterle resolved the tension by integrating plot and subplot into the romantic melodrama the title implied.

Wallis had great expectations for *Love Letters*. He hired Ayn Rand to adapt Massie's novel. Rand, who around the same time provided Wallis with the script of *You Came Along*, may have had minimal experience in screenwriting; however, her play *The Night of January 16th* had been filmed in 1941; and *The Fountainhead* (1943), the novel that became the cornerstone of her reputation, was on its way to becoming the egoist's manifesto. *Love Letters* also featured an unusually strong supporting cast: Anita Louise, who had been Titania in *A Midsummer Night's Dream*, in the much smaller but important role as Quinton's former fiancée; the genial character actor Cecil Kellaway; and one of Hollywood's grandes dames, Gladys Cooper, always an imposing presence, as Singleton's adoptive parent, who holds the secret to Singleton's memory loss.

For *Love Letters*'s director, Wallis settled on William Dieterle, who had given him several prestigious films when they were together at Warners: *A Midsummer Night's Dream, The Story of Louis Pasteur, The Life of Emile Zola, Juarez, Dr. Erlich's Magic Bullet,* and *A Dispatch from Reuters.* By 1941 Dieterle was freelancing and available for multi-picture deals. After leaving Warners, he was reduced to making such films as MGM's *Tennessee Johnson* (1942), more a piece of Americana than a biopic about President Andrew Johnson; and *Kismet* (1944), whose chief attraction was Marlene Dietrich in gold leg makeup that made it seem as if she had been fitted with gilded prostheses.

Having made *I'll Be Seeing You* (1944) for Selznick—a wartime romance between a woman released from prison for the Christmas holidays (Ginger Rogers) and a soldier suffering from shell shock (Joseph Cotten)—Dieterle seemed the right choice for *Love Letters*. Cotten would again play a recovering vet, this time suffering from postwar malaise. While the woman was the redemptive force in *I'll Be Seeing You,* in *Love Letters* it was the man, who restores an amnesiac's memory by forcing her to confront the past.

When Wallis beckoned, Dieterle came on board, knowing a good deal when he saw one but realizing that theirs could never be a harmonious relationship. Unlike Mike Curtiz, who could be charmingly gruff with his skewed idioms, Dieterle was a sadist. Striding on the set with his signature accessories, white hat and gloves, he would deliberately single out an inexperienced actor for ridicule, knowing that no star would tolerate such behavior. Novices, however, were sitting ducks; for no other reason than the desire to humiliate, Dieterle would so demoralize a performer, as he did Suzanne Dalbert in *The Accused* (1948), that she could barely function.[7] Since Dalbert was playing a college student slighted by a stud who found his psychology professor (Loretta Young) more enticing, Dieterle may have thought that such verbal abuse would improve Dalbert's performance. However, the role was so small that a pouty look—something any actress could affect—would have done the trick.

If Dieterle had become unusually difficult, it was partly because he was rankled by Wallis's inability—or refusal—to replicate the Warners past by making the historical films and biopics that became his specialties. Although Dieterle suspected there would be no more *Pasteurs, Zolas,* or *Juarezes,* he still balked at being reduced to making potboilers. Wallis gave him a few "prestige films"—"prestige" defined in terms of the new economy that allowed for a serious film without big names, like *The Searching Wind* (1946)—but not an epic like *Juarez.*

By 1949 Dieterle had made four films for Wallis, averaging one a year. He began feeling restless because he sensed that, except for *Love Letters* and *The Searching Wind,* the films—*The Accused* and *Rope of Sand* (1949)—could have been directed by anyone. Dieterle was forced to give up the opportunity to work in France because Wallis wanted him for *Dark City* (1950), Charlton Heston's debut film. When *Dark City* was delayed for three weeks, Dieterle expected to be compensated for losing the chance to direct *Montana* (1950) at Warners, proposing that he remain on salary at $1,000 a week until Wallis found him another film. Wallis chose to find him a film; the film was *Dark City,* an assignment that Dieterle reluctantly accepted, while insisting that he "was getting the worst of it."[8]

Wallis had the same kind of love-hate relationship with Dieterle that he had with Hazen. With Dieterle, there was an additional problem: the director's wife, Charlotte—a combination agent-manager-astrologer, who believed that shooting schedules should be determined by the position of the stars. Since Wallis appreciated Dieterle's versatility, even though it could not compare with Curtiz's, he indulged the couple, although he ignored Charlotte's astrally determined recommendations. When the Dieterles were visiting New York in 1950, Wallis had Irene Lee arrange for accommodations at the Waldorf, meet them upon their arrival at Penn Station, and arrange for tickets to *South Pacific* and *The Member of the Wedding*. When Dieterle complained he was not getting full billing for his films abroad, Wallis saw that he did.

But by 1953, disillusionment had set in. Dieterle realized he had no place at Paramount after Wallis chose Daniel Mann to direct *About Mrs. Leslie* (1954) with Shirley Booth and Robert Ryan. The plot of *About Mrs. Leslie,* a backstreet love affair between a married man and a single woman, was reminiscent of *September Affair* (1950), which Dieterle had directed to generally favorable reviews. Dieterle assumed that infidelity is infidelity—a subject he could handle whether the clandestine lovers were an engineer and a concert pianist *(September Song)* or an industrialist and an entertainer *(About Mrs. Leslie)*. Wallis chose Mann over Dieterle, however, because he hoped that Mann, who had directed *Come Back, Little Sheba* (1952), for which Shirley Booth won an Oscar, might provide the actress with another triumph. As it happened, Booth was not even nominated, and *About Mrs. Leslie* failed to find an audience despite respectful reviews.

With Wallis, moviemaking was a matter of expediency. When the sun sets on a talent, one waits for another sunrise. Mann was more than a quarter of a century younger than Dieterle. To Wallis, time's wingéd chariot dogs actors and directors; producers travel in more up-to-date vehicles.

By fall 1953 Wallis had nothing more to offer Dieterle. Wallis was too preoccupied promoting his latest discovery, the team of Dean Martin and Jerry Lewis, to give much thought to Dieterle's bitterness. Eager to get out of his contract (and also to leave Hollywood), Dieterle told his agent, Mike Levee, that he would settle for $25,000, but that he first needed a $10,000 loan.[9] Wallis finally bought him off. Dieterle was advanced $10,000 with the understanding that he stay on for two more years, after which Wallis had the option to cancel his contract and pay him $15,000, bringing the total to the $25,000 that Dieterle had requested. In the meantime, should a film materialize, Dieterle would get $60,000.

There were no further films. Dieterle received his $25,000 and returned to Germany, where he found nothing even remotely comparable to a *Pasteur,* a *Zola,* or a *Juarez*—much less a *Dark City*. He had no other choice but to retire, and he died in 1972.

Neither *The Affairs of Susan* nor *Love Letters* introduced a new star from the Wallis galaxy, which had yet to become visible. *Love Letters* came close with Ann Richards as Dilly, Singleton's friend, who aids Quinton in his search for a woman by the name of Victoria Morland. It was to Victoria that Quinton composed the love letters that her clod of a husband was incapable of writing; Quinton, however, never thought that Victoria would fall in love with the writer, for whom her abusive husband was no substitute. Naturally, "Singleton" turns out to be Victoria, who allegedly killed her husband when he tried to burn her treasured letters—or so the audience surmises until the denouement.

Wallis never had any intention of making a star out of Ann Richards, an Australian actress with an accent that was faintly British but could also pass for upper-class American. Although Richards had played the female lead in King Vidor's *American Romance* (1944), she was the classic case of a talented actress without the star power to carry a picture. Wallis had his stars for *Love Letters,* but he needed someone for Dilly who sounded authentically British and who looked around the same age as Jones and Cotten. Impressed by her performance, Wallis cast Richards as an American diplomat's politically naive wife in *The Searching Wind* (1946), in which she behaved like a woman who was thoroughly at home among European royalty—both real and bogus. Richards did not do badly for a competent actress whom no one would have nominated for stardom: $1,750 a week for *Sorry, Wrong Number* (1948), which was her final film for Wallis. After that, there were a few forgettable pictures and then the inevitable: retirement from the screen.

Wallis's third 1945 film, *You Came Along,* was a showcase for his new star, Lizabeth Scott, in her Hollywood debut. Wallis prided himself on being a starmaker, going so far as to use the term for the title of his autobiography. But a starmaker is not merely a discoverer of talent. Although all of Wallis's discoveries displayed varying degrees of talent, they did not all become icons. For without that golden aura that distinguishes an icon from another religious painting, an actor is just glitter in an overcrowded firmament. That aura is achieved by combining a carefully constructed persona with a vehicle that illuminates it, so that it can shine forth. But no amount of subtly applied makeup or face-caressing lighting can produce the glow that must burn through the haze of the ordinary to transport the actor to the ninth sphere of stardom. Lizabeth Scott had the persona; what she lacked was the vehicle.

CHAPTER SIX

Morning Star

IZABETH SCOTT HAD A PERSONA that, in 1945, would have been unique—a baritonal purr with a creamy huskiness. The problem was that Lauren Bacall, who had made her screen debut a year earlier, had a similar voice, although hers was characterized by a smoky throatiness. At the time both actresses were smokers, but Bacall sounded like one; each syllable seemed to have been coated with tar. When Lauren Bacall married Humphrey Bogart, who spoke in measured syllables that resounded with the wisdom of booze, tobacco, and life, their voices were as suited to each other as they were. In their films together (*To Have and Have Not* [1944], *The Big Sleep* [1946]), *Dark Passage* [1947], and *Key Largo* [1948]), there was an interpenetration of persona and voice.

Bacall achieved stardom at Warners, Wallis's former studio. It is always tempting to imagine what might have been. For the moment, let us suppose that Wallis had swallowed his pride and stayed on at Warners as an independent producer. In April 1943 director Howard Hawks was looking for an actress to play Marie in *To Have and Have Not*. His wife Nancy suggested a *Harper's Bazaar* model, Betty Bacal, née Betty Persky. Hawks was so impressed that he made Betty his protégée, bestowing upon her the name of Lauren Bacall. Had Wallis been at Warners the following year, he would not have had to do the same for Lizabeth Scott, who had already changed her name twice—from Emma Matzo to Elizabeth Scott, and then to Lizabeth Scott.

Even if Lizabeth had been Wallis's protégée at a Warners-based Hal B. Wallis Productions, the studio would have had two actresses with a dark sultriness and voices to match who could double as femme fatales, ladies with a dubious past, or simply tough broads. Lizabeth ended up playing women on both sides of the law; even when Bacall played the dark lady (e.g., in *Young Man with a Horn* [1950]), she never became a femme fatale.

Lizabeth Scott, unfortunately, was always regarded as a Lauren Bacall clone. The truth is that her voice was the product of heredity and voice lessons.[1] Born Emma Matzo, the daughter of a Slovakian mother and an Italian father in Scranton, Pennsylvania, she evidenced an affinity for theater when she was a child. In the 1930s, many parents believed that the only way their children could escape from coal towns like Scranton was to speak properly. It was not that Scrantonians spoke poorly; it was that they carried the baggage of their grandparents' or parents' immigrant past with them. If parents could afford to, they supplemented their children's grade school education with private classes in elocution. Scranton's idea of an elocution school was the living room of a Victorian house where a grande dame would preside, instructing her pupils to round out their vowels and dramatize their recitations. First-graders would learn

> T'wit, t'woo
> I say to you
> I am the owl of Halloween

and

> Poor little upside down cake
> Of all the cares you've got 'em
> Poor little upside down cake
> Your top is on your bottom

There was always a recital in May when the children—those who survived and were impervious to stage fright—would perform for parents and relatives. Elocution school could be either a haven or a nightmare; for young Emma it was a refuge from a city whose distinctive color was gray.

Emma responded well to the lessons, which enhanced the natural resonance of her voice, giving it a breathy theatricality quite different from Bacall's mannered toughness. Her affinity for the stage brought

her to New York in 1941, where she studied at the Alvienne School of
Drama. She was now Elizabeth Scott, ready for the national tour of
Hellzapoppin', minus the original stars, Ole Olsen and Chic Johnson,
but still the "screamlined revue," as the ads read, with Elizabeth feeding
laugh lines to the comics. "Elizabeth Scott" was a perfect stage name
for Emma Matzo, with just the right number of letters to dominate a
marquee. But it was not the name of an actress who was the equivalent
of a set decoration in *Hellzapoppin'*, looking glamorous while the mad-
caps pelted the audience with puffed rice.

Elizabeth Scott considered herself an actress; her first dramatic lead
was Sadie Thompson, Jeanne Eagels's signature role, in W. Somerset
Maugham's *Rain*. Since *Rain* was performed in what was then the equivalent of off Broadway, it went unreviewed. Elizabeth had no thought of
giving up; she had a face, a figure, and a talent, and if theatergoers could
not experience it, magazine readers would. If she wished, she could
have had a future as a model, especially after she began appearing in the
pages of *Harper's Bazaar* at the same time as Betty Bacal.

Elizabeth was capable of a variety of poses, from exotic and sultry
to girl-next-door in sweater and shorts. Irving Hoffman, who worked
for columnist Walter Winchell, was impressed by her range. The Bronx-
born Hoffman was a Runyonesque character: an eccentric who wore
expensive clothes but never combed his hair, a columnist and radio interviewer, and a conduit to Winchell and the *Hollywood Reporter*. Hoffman, in fact, has been described as "the most direct link from Hollywood
or Broadway to Winchell" and the only one allowed to peruse Winchell's column before it went to press.[2]

Hoffman was supposedly the inspiration for the smarmy journalist
Sidney Falco in the film *The Sweet Smell of Success* (1957); and Winchell was the model for the reptilian J.J. Hunsecker. Actually, there is more
of Winchell in Hunsecker than there is of Hoffman in Falco. Sidney
Falco is a composite of both Hoffman and William "Billy" Cahn, whose
past was considerably more checkered than Hoffman's because he had
run afoul of Winchell when he took up with his daughter, Walda.[3] Hoffman, who lived with his parents when he was not working from his
West Forty-eighth Street office, was more interested in placing names
in columns than dabbling in the kinds of shady activities favored by
Cahn. And even if Hoffman had been interested in Walda, he knew how
to keep his distance.

Elizabeth Scott was another matter; to Hoffman, she was class. Eager to introduce her to those who could further her career, Hoffman arranged a twenty-first-birthday celebration for her at the Stork Club—Walter Winchell's favorite nightclub, where he had his own table. It was September 1943, and Wallis, who visited New York at least once a year to check out the current crop of plays, happened to be there that evening. Hoffman introduced Elizabeth to Wallis, who sensed enough potential to suggest a screen test. But the next day, she was asked to hop a train to Boston and take over the role of Sabina in the touring company of Thornton Wilder's *Skin of Our Teeth,* replacing Miriam Hopkins, who had become ill. Believing, as many stage actors did (and still do) that as an art form theater is superior to film, Elizabeth chose Boston. Perhaps if it had been a different play, she might not have felt so strongly about passing up a screen test. But Elizabeth had understudied Tallulah Bankhead in the role during the Broadway run, appearing in a walk-on ("The Girl") but at least getting her name, Elizabeth Scott, in the playbill. Hopkins recovered, however, and Elizabeth found herself back in New York.

But something significant had happened. En route to New York, she decided to drop the *E* from her name and become "Lizabeth Scott." "Elizabeth Scott" evoked a serious actress who could never rest until she played Shakespeare's Cleopatra and Ibsen's Hedda. "Lizabeth Scott" was the kind of name a studio executive might impose on an unknown if he wanted something that sounded chic and out of the ordinary, like Theda, Nita, or Lana. There were enough Elizabeths in Hollywood, with both an *s* and a *z.* But no Lizabeth. On the train that evening, Elizabeth Scott was not thinking Hollywood, only Broadway—and hoping she would remember her lines. But her desire to change her name to something unique suggests that she *was* thinking Hollywood without realizing it. Ironically, no further name change was needed when Lizabeth came to Los Angeles in 1944. Emma Matzo had already made the change.

Neither Wallis nor Lizabeth knew that a chance meeting at a celebrities' hangout would lead to a professional relationship that lasted almost fifteen years. Although Wallis considered Lizabeth Scott his personal discovery, she came to Hollywood through a circuitous route that owed less to him than to circumstances over which he had no control. In Hollywood, the agent is usually the liaison between artist and producer. Bacall's case was different; it was Nancy Hawks, a former model herself, who brought Betty Bacal to her husband's attention. Lizabeth's Hollywood entree was more typical; talent agent Charles Feldman spotted her picture in *Harper's Bazaar.* Feldman stood out in a business where talent agents were dubbed flesh peddlers. How many flesh peddlers read Henry James for relaxation and held a law degree from the University of Southern California? To pay his tuition, Feldman worked in the movies, eventually becoming one of John Ford's camera crew. As a lawyer, Feldman discovered he could negotiate the contract labyrinth for independent producers who could not distinguish between gross and net profits, having never studied the Hollywood version of Accounting 101. Soon stars such as Irene Dunne, Charles Boyer, Marlene Dietrich, and Claudette Colbert began flocking to his Famous Artists Corporation, which lived up to its name: by the mid-1940s Feldman could boast of having three hundred clients, including actors, writers, and directors.[4]

Feldman invited Lizabeth to the West Coast, going so far as to arrange for a screen test at his own expense. She did not have to be coaxed. Since Broadway was not beckoning, and modeling meant an income, not a career, she made the five-day trip to Hollywood, arriving in the summer of 1944. At first Lizabeth was delighted to be ensconced at the Beverly Hills Hotel—but sitting in a hotel room, however luxurious, was no substitute for working in pictures. Finally, Feldman arranged a screen test at Warners. After seeing the test, Jack Warner was characteristically blunt: "She's a second lead, and we have enough of those."[5] It might have been different if Lizabeth had come out to Hollywood in 1943 instead of trekking up to Boston for a few performances of *The Skin of Our Teeth.* In the meantime, Betty Bacal had become Lauren Bacall, making her film debut in *To Have and Have Not,* which was released in October 1944. Bacall's role, a lady with a past, would have been perfect for Lizabeth. While her acting style was different from Bacall's, the two were destined to be compared on the basis of their voices and screen personalities. Perhaps if Lizabeth had made her screen test in 1943, when Wallis was still at the studio, he could have prevailed upon Warner to give his new discovery a chance. At any rate, in the 1940s Warners would have been the ideal studio for Lizabeth Scott.

But by the time she arrived in Hollywood, Wallis was on the verge of setting up his production company at Paramount. Tired of waiting to hear from Feldman, Lizabeth was about to return to New York, when Minna Wallis, who occasionally worked for Feldman, arranged for a screen test, which she planned to show her brother. Lizabeth had not mastered the technique of movie acting. Given a monologue to prepare, she studied it as if it were a stage exercise. Minna cajoled the legendary director Fritz Lang to coach her. Despite his reputation as a martinet, Lang was understanding, once he realized that film was an alien medium to her. When Lizabeth went up on her lines, she asked to start from the beginning. Lang, however, told her to pick up where she had stopped, explaining that the flubbed line could be edited out.

Once Wallis saw the test, he was impressed. "If I could, I would put you under contract," he told her.[6] Believing that he was merely leading her on, Lizabeth was now determined to return to New York. At least she could model until a part in a play came along, which was more than she could do in Los Angeles. On the day she was scheduled to leave, Feldman rushed to the Beverly Hills Hotel to inform her that Wallis was officially at Paramount.

Her movie debut, *You Came Along,* began filming in January 1945. Lizabeth was naturally nervous, costarring with Robert Cummings, who had been in the business since the 1930s. Cummings was initially difficult but never rude. Gradually, he came to respect Lizabeth, who adapted surprisingly well to the camera. The director, John Farrow, was less gracious. Farrow had wanted Teresa Wright—a 1942 Oscar winner for best supporting actress in *Mrs. Miniver.* Unlike Cummings, who was teamed with Lizabeth again in *Paid in Full* (1950), Farrow remained distant throughout the shoot.

You Came Along was less expensive than either *The Affairs of Susan* or *Love Letters* for several reasons. First, it lacked "names" like George Brent, Joseph Cotten, Joan Fontaine, and Jennifer Jones, as well as supporting casts familiar to regular moviegoers (Dennis O'Keefe and Walter Abel in *Susan,* Anita Louise and Gladys Cooper in *Love Letters*). The star of *You Came Along* was Robert Cummings, billed above the title on the basis of his performances in *Kings Row* (1942), Hitchcock's *Saboteur* (1942), and Wallis's production of *Princess O'Rourke* (1943). Cummings was a competent actor, more adept at comedy than drama, but never a major star. For Lizabeth's debut, Wallis wanted an actor whom audiences would recognize but who would not substantially increase the budget. Robert Cummings fit the bill.

With three films in release in one year, Wallis had to establish priorities in terms of budget allocations. Of the three, *Love Letters* was the most expensive—and looked it. It was not that Wallis expected Liza-beth's star to shine through a modest production like *You Came Along*. It was that, as a commercial filmmaker with an eye for talent, Wallis found a vehicle for his new star that could be inexpensively produced while serving as her initiation into a new medium. To remind audiences that *You Came Along* heralded an actress's debut, he added a separate credit to the main title: "Introducing Lizabeth Scott."

You Came Along was the story of three fliers—one of whom is a war hero (Robert Cummings) on a bond tour, accompanied by a Trea-sury Department publicist (Lizabeth Scott). Her name, Ivy Hotchkiss, is the object of a running gag: everyone, including the fliers, assumes that "I.V. Hotchkiss" is a male. When the men discover the truth, their chauvinism surfaces, and it takes Ivy's tolerance (and Lizabeth's charm) to wean them into adulthood. Ivy is so successful that she marries the Cummings character, but they do not live happily ever after.

At Warners, Wallis produced several films in which the main char-acters were fliers: *The Dawn Patrol* (1930 and the 1938 remake), *Wings of the Navy* (1939), *Dive Bomber* (1941), and *Captains of the Clouds* (1942). He also made three films about terminal illness: *One Way Pas-sage* (1932), the remake entitled *'Til We Meet Again* (1940), and the acclaimed *Dark Victory* (1939). In each case, it was a woman who was terminally ill, fated to die from heart disease *(Passage)* and brain cancer *(Dark Victory)*. *You Came Along* interwove motifs from each genre: male bonding from the former and acceptance of death from the latter. It also switched the cancer victim's gender.

Until *You Came Along,* terminal illness was the prerogative of the woman's film. Men were hanged or shot or died in battle; otherwise, they dropped dead. While Hollywood still considers cancer a woman's affliction (*My Life* [1993] is a notable exception), Wallis was coura-geous enough in 1945 to suggest that the disease does not discriminate. In *Dark Victory,* Judith Traherne (Bette Davis) discovers that her brain tumor is malignant by stumbling upon her medical records. The situa-tion is complicated by her engagement to the surgeon (George Brent) who performed the unsuccessful operation and tried to conceal the truth from her. After wallowing in booze and self-pity, with a detour into anger and bitterness, Judith experiences the peace of resignation. She and the surgeon eventually marry, each accepting the inevitable, so that Judith can expire (one hesitates to say "die").

You Came Along is the flip side of *Dark Victory*. The cancer victim is a male, an Army Air Force major (Cummings), who learns he is terminal at the outset of the film. Since there is nothing for the major to discover, Ivy is the one who learns of his condition when a loose-lipped surgeon divulges more than he should. When Ivy and the major marry, she plays the role of army wife to the hilt, never even hinting that she knows the truth, even when her husband tells her he is being transferred to England, though he is really being flown to Walter Reed Hospital in Washington, D.C., to die. In *Dark Victory,* husband and wife both know the prognosis. In *You Came Along,* the husband tries to live up to his heroic image, which precludes admitting to his wife that he is dying of anything so unheroic as blood cancer.

The performances under John Farrow's direction were exemplary. As the doomed pilot, Robert Cummings faces his impending death with the forced nonchalance of someone who has put up a facade that he cannot allow to be penetrated. As his wife, Lizabeth acted with similar restraint, so that the film did not deteriorate into a "weepie." Although Lizabeth did not receive a rave from the (then) dean of newspaper critics, Bosley Crowther of the *New York Times*, the trades welcomed her as a promising star. A career seemed to be in the making, and Lizabeth's new contract reflected Wallis's belief in her. Lizabeth's original contract (June 1944) guaranteed her $150 a week for a minimum of twenty weeks; by January 1945 it was $200 for twenty weeks; by July 1945, $300 for not less than forty weeks. A year later, Lizabeth was making $750 a week.

After *You Came Along,* Wallis decided to feature Lizabeth in *The Strange Love of Martha Ivers* (1946), this time with a cast with real star power: Barbara Stanwyck in the title role; Academy Award winner Van Heflin (for best supporting actor in *Johnny Eager* [1942]) as Martha's childhood sweetheart, who reenters her life; and in the brief but memorable role of Martha's sadistic aunt, the eminent stage actress Judith Anderson, best known to moviegoers as the creepy Mrs. Danvers in Hitchcock's *Rebecca* (1940), for which she received an Oscar nomination. The name of Anderson's character—Mrs. Ivers—would not have been lost on 1946 audiences familiar with *Rebecca*.

Wallis also intended *Martha Ivers* as the debut film for his latest star-in-the-making, a stage actor by the name of Kirk Douglas, who would be playing Stanwyck's alcoholic (and ultimately suicidal) husband and accomplice in a childhood murder. Unlike Heflin's or Douglas's role, Lizabeth's—Toni Marachek, an ex-convict who becomes romantically involved with the Heflin character—is comparatively minor; it is not even part of the main plot, which is set in motion by young Martha's killing her aunt—an incident that haunts not only the action but also the lives of Martha and her husband. In fact, the prologue, in which the killing takes place on a staircase amid thunder and lightning, is the sequence that stays in the memory.

Stanwyck, who had been featured in leading roles since 1929, resented the billing in which her name, Heflin's, and Scott's—in that order—preceded the title. "I will not be co-starred with any other person other than a recognized male or female star," she wrote to Wallis.[7] Wallis's lawyer, Loyd Wright, replied that Lizabeth Scott was a "recognized star" and that her costar billing was not a breach of contract. Stanwyck quickly realized that a meaty role and an attractive salary ($10,000 a week) were too good to pass up because of pride; three days later, Wallis received a reply from the star's lawyer: "Miss Stanwyck . . . has no desire to injure Miss Scott's professional position."[8]

Lizabeth's part may have been peripheral, but the English did not think so. When she arrived in London for the British premiere of *Martha Ivers*, the moviegoers were so taken with her performance and her physical presence that they started to mob her. Graciously, she thanked them and was then escorted through the back door of the theater. Similar reactions occurred in Liverpool and Manchester.

That Wallis insisted on her being billed with the two leads was a clear sign that he was determined to turn his first contract player into a star. Lizabeth Scott became an obsession with Wallis. He had the power to authorize the kinds of products she would endorse in magazines and the interviews she would grant. Ads for Lux soap, Chesterfield cigarettes, designer clothes, and soft drinks were acceptable, but not endorsements for pressure cookers and dime store cosmetics. If she were to appear on radio, the show had to be "top grade" and her voice had to be recorded so he could hear it first. Wallis scrutinized all of her photos, demanding that some be retouched. When he learned that the October 1945 *Photoplay* would feature pictures of Lizabeth modeling clothes with captions indicating their cost, he vetoed the piece. Although the editor objected strenuously, Wallis would not approve anything implying that Lizabeth Scott's wardrobe was inexpensive. Stars do not scrimp.

An editor from Condé Nast, struck by Lizabeth's publicity shots, advised Wallis that she was "something special . . . a new type of movie girl . . . potentially a fine, fine actress . . . what every man in uniform wants his girl friend to look like."[9] Wallis knew even earlier that Lizabeth should not be subjected to the kind of portraiture that would make her look exotic but unreal: "I think the best way to shoot this girl is without makeup, except possibly for lipstick. . . . She seems to be the type that should go for this natural quality." Wallis's reasoning had more to do with expense than with her natural quality: the idea was "to save time, effort, and money, in the long run."[10]

That was before Lauren Bacall's film debut. Then the instructions changed dramatically. Instead of fretting about the products Lizabeth would endorse, Wallis should have devoted more time to finding her different material, particularly after the press began calling her "Wallis's Lauren Bacall." It would have been more accurate to call her "Wallis's Jennifer Jones," since he had become as single-minded about Lizabeth's career as Selznick was about Jones's.

Nuance, however, means little in Hollywood. Lizabeth Scott was no more a Lauren Bacall clone than she was a Tallulah Bankhead soundalike. Yet a Bacall clone is precisely what Wallis now wanted. He instructed his publicist, Walter Seltzer, to make sure that Scott's stills were "on the sexy, sultry side . . . on the order of the stuff that was done on Bacall."[11] The natural quality only emerged when Lizabeth had a chance to play someone other than a femme fatale or a seen-it-all chanteuse; otherwise it was the smoldering Bacall look, courtesy of Wallis, who treated Lizabeth the way some parents treat their firstborn: the child on whom much is lavished, and in return much is expected. Until she learned to drive, Lizabeth stayed at the Beverly Wilshire (now the Beverly Regent) and was taxied to the studio. She was even given $150 a week toward her hotel bill and living expenses.

In 1950 Wallis was delighted when Governor James Duff of Pennsylvania wanted Lizabeth for a seven-day tour of the state during Pennsylvania Week.[12] The tour was to have begun on 16 October in Harrisburg, ending a week later in Gettysburg. The logistics should have been simple, since Lizabeth's appearance as "Queen of Pennsylvania Week" would have coincided with the release of her latest film, *Dark City*. What Lizabeth did not know was that Wallis had arranged to loan her to Columbia for *Two of a Kind* (1951), which would commence shooting at the same time. Wallis, who was not informed about the date when Lizabeth was expected to show up at Columbia, was livid when he learned about the conflict, which apparently was caused by negligence on Hazen's part. Believing the truth should be told, Wallis informed the Pennsylvania press that Lizabeth had a commitment at Columbia. Some reporters, knowing that she had already made a film for Columbia, *Dead Reckoning* (1947), assumed that Wallis was counting on their ignorance of her career. The press did not know that Lizabeth was scheduled for *another* Columbia film. When Lizabeth learned of the snafu, she wired apologies to Governor Duff.

The press was less forgiving; Scranton, which for some reason was not included in her itinerary (probably because the tour bypassed the northeastern part of the state), threatened to boycott *Dark City;* and neighboring Wilkes-Barre agreed to do the same. It was an idle threat, made more out of frustration than vindictiveness. Ironically, the filming of *Two of a Kind* was delayed until 11 November.

Wallis thought he had a star in Lizabeth Scott; what he had was an talented actress whose range was never fully exploited, partly because Hollywood's postwar obsession with film noir darkened many of her films, which, ordinarily, would just have been considered crime movies or melodramas. Thus, while Lauren Bacall never became a noir icon (having never become a real *femme noire*), Lizabeth Scott did, joining the pantheon that included Marie Windsor, Ann Savage, Jane Greer, and Beverly Garland. In fact, according to *Film Noir: An Encyclopedia Reference to the American Style*, seven of her twenty-two movies qualify as film noir: *Martha Ivers, Dead Reckoning* (1947), *I Walk Alone* (1948), *Pitfall* (1948), *Too Late for Tears* (1949), *Dark City* (1950), and *The Racket* (1951).[13] Ironically, the best—*Reckoning, Pitfall,* and *Tears*— were loan-outs. In fact, almost half of Lizabeth's films were loan-outs, suggesting that the starmaker was not entirely certain about his astral touch.

Her first loan-out was Columbia's *Dead Reckoning,* in which she costarred with Humphrey Bogart. Wallis assumed Lizabeth would be the ideal partner for Bogart, who, the year before, had been paired with Lauren Bacall in *The Big Sleep.* Wallis loaned her out to Columbia at a salary of $5,000 a week for ten weeks, which was more than she was then making at Paramount ($750 for not less than forty weeks). Since Lizabeth would be working at another studio, Wallis had Paul Nathan run *You Came Along* for John Cromwell, the director of *Dead Reckoning,* so that he might know how Lizabeth should look. Since she would be playing a nightclub singer, Wallis insisted that her voice not be dubbed, but he was overruled. However, he managed to get approval of Lizabeth's portrait shots and the right to purchase them from Columbia.

The chemistry between Bogart and Bacall in *The Big Sleep* was never repeated between Bogart and Lizabeth in *Dead Reckoning.* It was not that Lizabeth was no match for Bogart; it was the script, which required her to play a *femme noire,* Coral Chandler, whose dark and murderous side made romance impossible. What chemistry can exist between a World War II vet (Humphrey Bogart) who is investigating his buddy's mysterious death and the buddy's former lover (Lizabeth Scott), especially when the vet feels more strongly about the buddy than the lover?

Lizabeth Scott and Lauren Bacall differed in other respects. Although Lizabeth played her share of lethal ladies, Bacall always remained on the right side of the law. In Bacall's four films with Bogart, there was no possibility of a tragic ending. It is hard to imagine Bacall's even doing a role like Coral, who must die to balance the scales of justice, as Bogart informs her on her death bed, reminding her that she must now join the others who have preceded her—not exactly the most comforting words for the dying.

As an exercise in noirism, *Dead Reckoning* had the requisite dark, smoky look, courtesy of Leo Tover's cinematography, which lent an air of rot to the Florida Gulf Coast setting, illuminated with the right amount of icy moonlight and neon glare. However, the subtext of *Dead Reckoning,* like that of *Double Indemnity* (1944) and *Gilda* (1946), was male bonding. The Bogart character, Rip, was more devoted to Johnny, his dead buddy, than he was to Coral, whom he perceived as a threat to the memory of their brotherhood. Although attracted to Coral, Rip was also wary of her, neutralizing her femininity by calling her "Mike." Given Rip's ambivalence, any scenes of intimacy between himself and Coral had to be so guarded—as indeed they were—as to be antiseptic. Lizabeth and Bogart understood the tension that existed between the characters and reacted to each other accordingly, sustaining a low level of eroticism while suggesting that the heat could rise at any time. However, Rip's obsession with justice, which he calls "John Law," and Coral's dark past even preclude sex by suggestion.

After *Dead Reckoning,* loan-outs became more common, especially after Wallis realized he could make more money on Lizabeth elsewhere. When Wallis loaned her to producer Samuel Bischoff for *Pitfall,* her salary was $7,500 for ten weeks' work; and for RKO's *Easy Living* (1949), she was guaranteed a minimum of $75,000. While neither was a major film, each succeeded on the B-movie level because of the professionalism of its director (*Pitfall's* André de Toth, *Easy Living's* Jacques Tourneur) and costars (Dick Powell and Jane Wyatt in *Pitfall,* Lucille Ball and Victor Mature in *Easy Living*). Although *Pitfall* now ranks as classic noir (French filmmaker Bertrand Tavernier considers it one of the genre's masterpieces), Wallis could not have known that in 1948; he simply believed that Lizabeth's appearing opposite Dick Powell, who showed his macho side in *Murder, My Sweet* (1944) and *Cornered* (1945), was right for a movie about a woman who ensnares a respectable married man in a web of deception and murder, from which he emerges repentant but not exactly on the best of terms with his wife. With Jane Wyatt as the sexless wife, one could understand why she would stand by her man and at the same time why her husband would be drawn to a considerably more sensuous woman.

Pitfall is a good example of the way Wallis handled loan-outs. He behaved like a combination agent–business manager, specifying salary and billing (always above the title), demanding script approval, and issuing specific orders about the way Lizabeth should be photographed (erase the shadows under the eyes, enlarge the upper lip). Despite her excellent performance, *Pitfall* did not enhance her appeal to audiences, particularly women. She was a home-wrecker in *Pitfall,* a murderer in *Dead Reckoning,* and the self-absorbed wife of a football player with a heart condition in *Easy Living.* Typecast as the dark lady, Lizabeth Scott never had the chance to display her gift for comedy, which was evident in *The Skin of Our Teeth.* But that was theater, not film. And theater was the medium for which she was yearning, as one movie role dissolved into another and all the characters merged into one.

Wallis never told Lizabeth that Jane Broder, a New York talent agent with whom he was in regular contact, wanted her for the role of Regina in Lillian Hellman's *Another Part of the Forest* (1946), the prequel to Hellman's earlier play, *The Little Foxes* (1939). The young Regina, some years before she became one of the foxes, seemed tailor made for Lizabeth, who could make the transition from vulnerable to predatory without having to suggest that the character went through an intermediate stage. Regina was Janus-faced; Lizabeth would have understood such women and, in fact, built a career out of playing them. Wallis, however, was so bent on turning Lizabeth into a star that he would not release her from her contract; thereby he deprived her of the chance to appear on Broadway in a play by America's preeminent female dramatist. Although *Forest* did not have a lengthy run, it launched the career of the then unknown Patricia Neal, who played Regina and went on to Hollywood, where she enjoyed greater longevity than Lizabeth did.

By 1949 Wallis thought differently about Lizabeth's return to the theater, particularly when he realized he could never make her into the star that Bacall had become at Warners. The comparisons that the press made between the two actresses were superficial: each had a throaty voice, although Scott's was more theatrical and Bacall's more studied. In her earlier films, Bacall sounded as if she had memorized her lines, with the inflections clearly marked to suggest a sense of cadence. Bacall also costarred with major talent, with Gary Cooper, Bogart, and Wallis's own discovery, Kirk Douglas, whose best roles—the opportunistic reporter in *The Big Carnival* (1951), the manipulative producer in *The Bad and the Beautiful* (1952), and Van Gogh in *Lust for Life* (1956)— were not even Wallis's productions. By contrast, Lizabeth was paired with actors nearing the end of their film careers: Dick Powell, Victor Mature, Alan Ladd; actors who never made Hollywood's A list (Robert Ryan, Dan Duryea, Dennis O'Keefe); and icons in the making (Burt Lancaster, Charlton Heston) in need of a female costar who would not give them competition.

In 1959, when Bacall realized that good movie roles were becoming scarce, she tried Broadway. George Axelrod's *Goodbye Charlie* (1960)—in which Bacall played a philandering playboy who dies and returns to life as a woman—capitalized on her androgyny, with the masculine side predominating until the end, when the woman emerges from the masculine chrysalis in which she was enclosed. Although *Goodbye Charlie* had a brief run, Bacall returned to Broadway with a trio of hits: *Cactus Flower* (1966), with which she remained for two years, never missing a performance; *Applause* (1970), the musical version of *All about Eve;* and *Woman of the Year* (1981), the musical version of the 1942 Spencer Tracy and Katharine Hepburn film. Despite Bacall's inexperience in musical theater, she won a Tony award for her performance in each show.

Movie audiences heard Bacall sing in *The Big Sleep,* but nobody in 1946 could have imagined Bacall in a Broadway musical. Fortunately, her singing, limited to the same kind of musical enunciation that non-singers use to their advantage, has been documented on original cast recordings. Lizabeth Scott's singing voice can also be heard on an LP that she cut in 1958, simply entitled *Lizabeth* (now a collector's item), which includes such pop standards as "He's Funny That Way," "Willow, Weep for Me," "When a Woman Loves a Man," and "It's So Nice to Have a Man around the House," which she sings as if she were winking at the same time. Hers is a far more natural singing voice than Bacall's; it is also considerably more melodic. Most of the numbers are romantic ballads and torch songs, which she personalizes as if they were experiences on which she is reflecting. When Bacall was ready to leave *Applause,* Lizabeth was rumored as a replacement. However, the producers decided to go with Anne Baxter, the Eve in the 1950 movie—an interesting bit of casting, in which Baxter would be playing the stage diva that, in the movie, she schemed to replace.

Lizabeth Scott might have enjoyed a career comparable to Bacall's, had Wallis not controlled her professional life as if he was an old-style mogul and she was a contract player—which she was, to a certain extent, although she did more films for other producers than she did for Wallis. By 1949 Lizabeth also sensed that, for all the fan magazine hype, she may have gone as far as she could in Hollywood.

Wallis must have thought so, too, since he allowed her to return to the stage to appear in a stock production of Philip Yordan's *Anna Lucasta.* Although Yordan had originally written *Anna Lucasta* about a black family, he revised it, making the family Polish so that the play could be performed by white actors. Anna, however, remained an ex-prostitute. At the same time that Lizabeth was receiving outstanding notices for her portrayal of Anna, Columbia Pictures released a sanitized movie version with Paulette Goddard in the title role, looking and acting trampy enough to suggest that she belonged to the world's oldest profession. Had Lizabeth been cast in the film, even with the Production Code in full force, she would have given the role the toughness that the wounded use as a defense mechanism, as the critics claimed she did when she played Anna in Hartford and Princeton.

Other stock companies wanted her, also, but Wallis was dissatisfied with the roles she was being offered. He turned down a request that she appear as Catherine Sloper in *The Heiress,* Ruth and Augustus Goetz's dramatization of Henry James's *Washington Square.* This was the same role for which Olivia de Havilland won an Oscar in the 1949 film version. Wallis must have thought that Lizabeth's playing an unattractive spinster, courted by the fortune-hunter Morris Townsend, would have been the ultimate in casting against type. He did not know that three years later, Lizabeth would be playing both a plain woman and the glamorous creation of a plastic surgeon in the British release *Stolen Face* (1952) and using two different accents—Cockney and standard American English—for the twin roles. Anyone familiar with Lizabeth's work could easily imagine her as Catherine, particularly in the final scene where she slowly ascends the staircase, kerosene lamp in hand, as Morris bangs desperately on the door that she has bolted—Catherine's revenge for the elopement that he had promised, until he realized that it would mean she would be disinherited.

In *Desert Fury* (1947) and *Dark City* (1950), Lizabeth was merely a decoration, the equivalent of a locker-room pinup; in the former, she adorned Burt Lancaster's locker; in the latter, Charlton Heston's in his film debut.

Lizabeth knew that what outsiders considered ruthlessness, Wallis would call expediency. "That's show business," professionals say with a shrug when faced with disappointment. When a career was not progressing as Wallis thought it should, and as Lizabeth's clearly was not, he looked elsewhere.

CHAPTER SEVEN

Interstellar Spaces

K RISTINE MILLER'S BACKGROUND was exotic enough to intrigue Wallis. Before she was Kristine Miller, she was Jacqueline Olivia Eskesen—born in Buenos Aires, the daughter of a Danish father and an American mother. The Eskesens emigrated to Denmark when Jacqueline was eight. In fall 1938, just before World War II broke out in Europe, the family set out for America, settling first in Long Island and later in California.

The young Jacqueline was anything but a budding actress. She had no interest in performing until she was cast in a high school production of George S. Kaufman and Moss Hart's *American Way* (1939), playing the same role that Florence Eldridge had played on Broadway. From then on, there was no stopping her. When a Warner Brothers talent scout, who was scheduled to attend a performance, failed to appear, Jacqueline dashed off a letter to the studio, along with a photo. In typical Hollywood fashion, a screen test followed, and Jacqueline Olivia Eskesen became Kristine Miller.

When nothing materialized at Warners, Kristine found herself at Paramount playing a bit part in *You Came Along*. Although she only had one line, that was enough to impress Jack Saper. Wallis then asked to see her, inquiring why she never told him she was in the film. Kristine replied spunkily, "You never asked."[1] Since she made her screen debut in the same film as Lizabeth Scott, their careers intersected at various points—first in *Desert Fury,* in which Kristine had a walk-on, even though she had billing; then in *Paid in Full,* in which Kristine was supposed to play Lizabeth's sister—a role that went instead to Diana Lynn. Even when *Sorry, Wrong Number* (1948) was being cast, Kristine expected to play the wife of the detective investigating a narcotics ring, in which the Burt Lancaster character had become so involved that he arranged for his wife's murder to pay his debts. That part, however, went to Ann Richards; instead, Kristine ended up as the girlfriend of the wife's doctor (Wendell Corey). Although Kristine did well with very little, the film belonged to Barbara Stanwyck. She received an Oscar nomination for her portrayal of the neurotic wife, who overhears a telephone conversation about a carefully planned murder that turns out to be her own.

Kristine Miller was typical of the kind of talent that Wallis claimed to discover but could not promote. After a while, she understood the problem: "He [Wallis] didn't know what to do with me."[2] Miller was in good company. Wallis did not know what to do with many of his contract players, except to find them a film and let the box office determine their fate. Kristine had someone other than Wallis championing her: Mark Hellinger, the journalist–movie producer (*The Killers* [1946], *Brute Force* [1947], *The Naked City* [1948]), who was convinced she could be a star. But his death in 1947 left Kristine no other choice but to freelance until the early fifties when marriage to media executive William Schuyler provided a second act to a life that otherwise would have been filled with doubt and regret.

Second acts were common for those for whom Wallis could not provide the careers he had envisioned. Lizabeth Scott's wise investments allowed her to follow Socrates' philosophy and pursue the life of the mind, taking courses at the University of Southern California and becoming a committed reader. Kristine Miller discovered her gift for choral song and public speaking, performing in masses and oratorios and lecturing on the movies of the 1940s and 1950s in Carmel, California, where she and her husband live.

Douglas Dick really made a career change, one that had nothing to do with acting—at least not in the traditional sense. When Douglas arrived in Hollywood in 1945, pursuing a Ph.D. in psychology was furthest from his mind. He was about to make his screen debut in *The Searching Wind* (1946), based on Lillian Hellman's 1944 play. Hellman had hoped Wallis would produce the film version when he was at Warners, since it would have been the logical follow-up to *Watch on the Rhine*. That was also Wallis's plan. But after Wallis's relationship with Jack Warner deteriorated, there was no hope of a Warners release.

Once he had settled at Paramount, Wallis made *The Searching Wind* a top priority, even though he knew that the play, which had a respect-able run of 318 performances on Broadway, never registered as power-fully with theatergoers as did *Watch on the Rhine*. Wallis's solution was simple: Hellman would write her own screenplay, and the cast would consist of familiar—but not big—names, to allow for an elaborate pro-duction. The action, framed by a prologue and epilogue, would occur in the form of flashbacks: Rome 1922, when Mussolini marches on the city; Berlin 1928, when the threat of Nazism is unmistakable; Madrid 1936, during the Spanish Civil War, the dress rehearsal for a world war that will erupt three years later; and Paris 1938, as Hitler is about to take over the Sudetenland.

Except for one role, Wallis had no difficulty casting *The Searching Wind*. Robert Young would play Alex Hazen, a career diplomat; Ann Richards, Emily, his socialite wife; and Sylvia Sidney, Cassie, his former lover, who tries in vain to instill in Alex a political conscience, only to witness his failure to alert Americans to the threat of a second world war. The role of the couple's son, memorably played on stage by Mont-gomery Clift, posed a problem. Wallis had wanted Clift to reprise the part of Sam Hazen, who must lose a leg from injuries sustained in the war—a fact Sam conceals from his parents until the denouement. But before Wallis had a chance to enfold Clift into his circle, the actor heed-ed Hollywood's siren call and headed west by himself; in 1948 movie-goers saw Clift first in *The Search* and then in *Red River*. Clift chose his first screen roles wisely; both were leads, even Matt Garth in *Red River*, in which he shared the spotlight with John Wayne. Sam, however, ap-pears only in the prologue and the epilogue—the latter providing him with a climactic speech that could be a career-maker. But then, it would all depend upon how accepting audiences would be of a son who chas-tises his parents for their indifference to fascism.

When Wallis was looking for a new face, preferably one from the theater, he usually called on Jane Broder, a New York theatrical agent, whose office on East Forty-ninth Street was one of his first stops when-ever he was in Manhattan. Broder recommended a strikingly handsome but inexperienced actor, Douglas Dick, for the part of Sam Hazen.[3] It was the right choice. Douglas rose to the occasion; his delivery resonat-ed with audiences, who might have found the film's love triangle te-dious but heard a point of view that was unusual for a 1940s movie: that knowledgeable Americans minimized the threat of fascism, insisting it would disappear with an economic recovery in Germany; that war would be averted and there would be "peace in our time" if Hitler were given the Sudetenland.

Douglas had no way of knowing that he would make his screen debut in a film directed by William Dieterle, whom Wallis had enticed to join him at Paramount. Since Dieterle was known for singling out one cast member—usually a newcomer—for derision, whether it was merited or not, Sylvia Sidney warned Douglas about Dieterle's habits. She advised Douglas to accede to the director's suggestions and then do what he wanted in front of the camera, particularly since Dieterle tended to forget his instructions, which were generally inspired by megalomania. Ironically, Dieterle refused to direct the concluding speech, perhaps because, politically, it was too far to the left, although it was basically what theatergoers heard in 1944. Sam voices his disillusionment with his father for advocating isolationism, and with his mother for consorting with Nazi sympathizers—implying that such irresponsible behavior and indifference led to a war that will cost him a limb. Sam's speech was pure leftwing rhetoric: appeasement and naïveté brought America into a war that it sought to avoid for all the wrong reasons, the dream of isolationism being the chief one. The speech was so powerful that many moviegoers may have missed the point: namely, that if Alec had listened to Cassie, he would have left Emily, spoken out against what he had witnessed in Europe, and at least have had the satisfaction of knowing he had taken a stand. When Dieterle backed out of shooting the last scene, Byron Haskins took over, granting Douglas Dick the wish of every newcomer—the final close-up.

Wallis was delighted with audiences' reaction to Douglas, whose first contract (10 January 1946) guaranteed him $650 a week. Once he signed with Hollywood's premier talent agency, MCA, his price went up. For his next—and last—film for Wallis, *The Accused* (1948), Douglas received $1,000 a week. *The Accused* reunited Douglas and Dieterle, this time in a film about a psychology professor (Loretta Young) stalked by a disturbed student (Douglas Dick), whom she kills in self-defense when he tries to rape her.

Both of them delivered powerful performances—Loretta Young cast against type and Douglas exuding a sexuality both enticing and menacing. When the student drives the professor to a desolate cliff overlooking the Pacific, the viewer does not know what to expect. Sex is obviously on the student's mind, especially after he decides to change to a tight-fitting bathing suit that offers a brief look at his abs and pecs in the moonlight. Loretta Young fans knew she would not undergo the ultimate indignity, but few expected her to grab a tire iron and clobber her would-be rapist over the head.

At the time Loretta Young was near the end of a long film career, which came to a close in 1953; she went on to a second life on television with *The Loretta Young Show* (1953–61). Although Douglas Dick was at the beginning of his career, Wallis had discovered two other male actors, one of whom projected a street-smart sexiness (Burt Lancaster); and the other, a patrician air that made him seem superior to his environment, regardless of what it was (Charlton Heston). Since Dick combined suave and sexy and lacked a towering presence, he could not fit into any of Lancaster's or Heston's roles.

After *The Accused,* there were other movie roles, but not in Wallis productions. And there was television, especially *Perry Mason.* Finally, in 1972, Douglas Dick decided that instead of ending his career as a character actor, he would begin a new one as a therapist. At fifty-two, when many men are contemplating early retirement, he changed professions, received his doctorate in psychology, and by the time he was sixty had succeeded in establishing a successful practice.

Douglas Dick was too handsome for character roles when he started out, but Wendell Corey was not.[4] Thus his career lasted longer. Corey had a deadpan look that could be either creepy or comic, depending on the role. His eyes rarely sparkled, and when he smiled, it seemed more like a grimace. He could appear with such stars as Lizabeth Scott, Barbara Stanwyck, Joan Crawford, and Katharine Hepburn without diverting attention to himself. Corey was simply a competent actor, whom Wallis discovered when he was costarring on Broadway with Betty Field in Elmer Rice's *Dream Girl* (1945). Wallis wanted him immediately but had to wait until his contract expired in June 1946.

What Wallis saw in Wendell Corey was not what he had seen in Douglas Dick, who had the potential to become a romantic lead of the heartthrob variety—or so his fan mail, which in 1947 exceeded Burt Lancaster's, implied. Corey was an journeyman actor, destined for neither greatness nor obscurity.

Corey's first love, however, was the stage; when he had the opportunity to play the only male role in the 1947 London premiere of John van Druten's *Voice of the Turtle,* Wallis not only encouraged him but also arranged passage for him and his wife on the Cunard line. Corey never experienced in film what he had in the theater. What one remembers about Corey's films are not his scenes but those with other actors. In his debut, *Desert Fury* (1947), he was upstaged by Burt Lancaster, who was upstaged by Mary Astor in a small but memorable role. It is hard to recall anything about *Sorry, Wrong Number* except Barbara Stanwyck's desperate phone calls as she tries to interpret an overheard conversation about a prearranged murder that she learns too late is her own. Movie buffs might remember Corey in *The Furies* (1950), but there he was eclipsed by the formidable trio of Stanwyck, Walter Huston, and Judith Anderson. If there is a scene in *The Furies* that lingers in the memory, it is the one in which Stanwyck hurls a pair of scissors at Anderson, striking her in the face and leaving her disfigured.

By 1950 Corey realized that his movie career was not advancing at the same pace at which he was making pictures. In three years he had made seven films for Wallis, none of which gave him the satisfaction or the reviews that he had received in the theater. In 1945 the 15 December *New York Times* called *Dream Girl* "an engaging and cheerful comedy," in which Corey was both "excellent" and "very well cast." Of his film debut in *Desert Fury,* the same paper (25 September 1947) noted that Corey and Mary Astor alone managed to "achieve any semblance of characterization" in "an incredibly bad" and "strangely incompetent motion picture." Hollywood was obviously not Broadway.

Since the recognition Corey anticipated in the movies never materialized, he became more difficult. Wallis suspended him in 1950 when he refused to do "Quantrill's Raiders," which underwent a name change and became *Red Mountain* (1951). Corey then found himself subject to the Wallis policy of suspension-extension: If an actor refused to do a film, his or her contract was extended for a minimum of six months; in the interim, the actor could be loaned out to another studio so that Wallis would not lose money. Thus, Corey was sent over to Columbia to costar with Joan Crawford in *Harriet Craig* (1950), a remake of *Craig's Wife* (1936) and based on the same source—George Kelly's Pulitzer Prize–winning play. Although Corey was playing the male lead—Walter Craig, who is so enamored of his wife that he stands by as she alienates his friends and transforms their middle-class home into a shrine—he was no match for Crawford, who discovered similarities between Harriet's deprived childhood and her own, tearing into the role as if she were the avenger of every woman who suffered at the hands of men. When Walter finally walks out on her, Harriet has the house to herself, just as Crawford has the last scene to herself. Crawford made the most of the fade-out as she slowly but majestically ascends the staircase to a bedroom where, it is implied, she has always slept alone—and apparently will continue to do so.

Harriet Craig was Crawford's film, and Corey knew it. Chastened, he returned to Wallis, who curtly reminded him that he was to report at 9:00 A.M. on 10 April for *Dark City* (1950). Corey did—reluctantly. But the lack of challenging roles continued to gall him. Realizing that unless he was lucky, he would always be a member of the supporting cast, he refused to do the Charlton Heston vehicle *Secret of the Incas* (1954), a Paramount release—but not a Wallis production. Corey made two final films for Wallis, *The Rainmaker,* in which he was overshadowed by Burt Lancaster in a bravura performance and Katharine Hepburn in a mannered but theatrical one, and *Loving You* (1957), in which he receded into the background whenever Elvis Presley, Dolores Hart, and Lizabeth Scott were on the screen. There were other roles at other studios, but there was also Corey's alcoholism, which led to his death in 1968.

Whereas Douglas Dick made a dramatic career change, Dolores Hart embraced a completely new life, that of a nun. Before she became Mother Dolores, Mother Abbess of Regina Laudis Abbey in Bethlehem, Connecticut, she was Dolores Hart, actress.[5] And before she was Dolores the actress, she was Dolores Marie Hicks, the daughter of Edmond and Harriet Hicks of Chicago. Although her parents were Protestant, Dolores was sent to St. Gregory's, a Catholic grade school, which had such a profound effect on her that she decided to convert to Catholicism at the age of eleven. That Dolores embraced Catholicism at such an early age—and by her own volition, as she has always admitted—suggests that even as a child she was seeking the kind of fulfillment that does not come from a career—particularly one in a business that disappoints more often than it rewards.

At the same time that Dolores converted, the Hickses, who had separated when their daughter was four, finally divorced, with Harriet receiving sole custody of Dolores. Mother and daughter relocated in Los Angeles, where Harriet remarried and Dolores continued her education. Meanwhile, Edmond Hicks, who had also moved to Los Angeles, became Bert Hicks, a movie actor, whose career was limited to bit parts. Whether her father's interest in acting had any effect on Dolores is unknown, although she enjoyed visiting movie sets. In retrospect, it seems that acting was a stage on her spiritual journey that began with her conversion and culminated with her decision to accept a role for which no profession could have prepared her: that of a cloistered Benedictine nun.

Even before she entered the convent, Dolores would have agreed that God works through others. One of the others was Donald Barbeau, whom she met at a dance in 1955 when she was a senior at Corvallis High School and he was a student at Loyola University, an all-male Jesuit institution in Los Angeles.[6] Barbeau, who planned to become a Trappist monk (but never did), sensed a spirituality in Dolores that he felt should be shared by others. Loyola's drama society was planning a production of Maxwell Anderson's *Joan of Lorraine,* in which Ingrid Bergman had astounded Broadway audiences in 1945 with her performance as Joan of Arc. Since the play required a female lead, Barbeau encouraged Dolores to read for the role, which became hers. However, Barbeau was not content with Dolores's just getting the part. He sensed a movie star in the making. But unlike an agent who measures talent in terms of his 10 percent, Barbeau was motivated by his desire for Dolores to share her gift with a mass audience. It is hard to know why Barbeau chose to contact Paramount about Dolores. Perhaps it was because it had not grown stodgy like MGM or Warner Brothers, perhaps because he knew that Wallis was cultivating new talent. Learning that Paul Nathan was Wallis's assistant, rather than write to Wallis personally, Barbeau invited Nathan to a performance of *Joan of Lorraine.* Actually, he did more than invite Nathan; he implored him: "Praying you will and enjoy the show, I remain, Donald J. Barbeau." Barbeau also included a photo of Dolores. Whether serendipity or providence intervened (Barbeau would have said the latter), Nathan was struck by a face that bore no trace of makeup and was a refreshing change from the glossies that crossed his desk.

Although Nathan did not attend the performance, he arranged a screen test for Dolores, envisioning her as the daughter in Wallis's production of *Hot Spell* (1958), not knowing that Shirley MacLaine was already slated for the part. Dolores was fortunate that *Hot Spell* had already been cast; otherwise, she would have been pitted against such pros as Shirley Booth and Anthony Quinn. Shirley MacLaine at least had a few films to her credit and could fend for herself, although, in truth, nobody could have saved *Hot Spell*, which was just an exercise in sweat and sex—the former rendered as perspiration, the latter off screen.

Once Wallis saw Dolores's picture, he agreed with Nathan: Dolores had potential—but then so did so many of his other would-be stars. When Dolores was awarded a contract, Barbeau expressed his gratitude to Wallis and Nathan in language that is rare in a business where gratitude is rendered materially or physically, but certainly not spiritually: "Within her is the inner radiance which causes all who meet her to love her. She is a natural actress because God has made her so. God love you."

Hazen, Wallis, and Nathan agreed: Dolores Hart was a natural actress. In her first film, *Loving You* (1957), Dolores played opposite Elvis Presley, who had only appeared in one other film, *Love Me Tender* (1956). Although Lizabeth Scott was in the supporting cast, Wallis saw to it that Lizabeth received costarring credit, thinking perhaps that it might be her last film for him, which indeed it was. Since Elvis was years away from the grotesque that he later became, his innocence combined with Dolores's gave the film an unusual freshness. Lizabeth went out of her way to be kind to Dolores, knowing what it was like to make one's screen debut in a leading role.

While Dolores was establishing herself as a film actress, she really longed for the stage, specifically Broadway. When Samuel Taylor's *Pleasure of His Company* (1959) was being cast, Dolores auditioned for the ingenue role: Jessica Poole, the daughter of an estranged globe-trotting father—a male Auntie Mame, who reenters her life as she is about to get married. Dolores was one of five hundred actresses who read for the part. After eight auditions in New York and two in Los Angeles, Dolores was hired to appear in the play with Cyril Ritchard, Cornelia Otis Skinner, Walter Abel, Charlie Ruggles, and newcomer George Peppard, who would soon be heading for Hollywood—as Dolores would after the run of the play, on the last leg of her movie career.

In her professional stage debut, Dolores held her own with what, by anyone's definition, was Broadway royalty, receiving a Tony nomination for best supporting actress. Although the deal Wallis had struck with producer Frederick Brisson allowed Dolores to appear in the play for at least six months, she stayed on for the entire run, once Brisson realized that audiences were more interested in seeing a movie star than

Broadway notables in the twilight of their careers. Brisson, the husband of Rosalind Russell and both a theater and film producer, also expected to capitalize on Dolores's popularity with a three-picture contract, which never materialized. Providence and Dolores had other plans.

Returning to Hollywood was a sobering experience. While she was on Broadway, she and Paul Nathan corresponded regularly. When Dolores wondered what lay ahead for her in the movies, Nathan refused to let her succumb to self-doubt. Jokingly, he replied that she could always work at a Poverty Row studio like Monogram, except that Monogram had gone out of business. Whatever premonitions she had were correct. The movie roles she had anticipated on the basis of her Broadway success were not forthcoming. Even before Dolores left for New York, she sensed that Wallis considered her loan-out material, since she only did three films for him: *Loving You, Wild Is the Wind* (1957), and *King Creole* (1958).

There was probably no connection between Fox's *Francis of Assisi* (1961), in which she played Clare—the thirteenth-century saint who founded the religious order known as the Poor Clares—and her decision two years later to devote the rest of her life to the service of God. More likely, it was another shoot that at least gave Dolores a taste of Italy.

Francis of Assisi required the cast to film on location. For Dolores, it was an exhilarating experience. Again, she and Nathan wrote back and forth to each other. Nathan had become her soul mate; he was frank about his drinking and analysis, and she would regale him with stories about director Michael Curtiz, particularly his abortive attempt to film a scene with pigeons flying from a church tower at the stroke of noon. When the shoot had to be rescheduled for 4:00 P.M., Curtiz thought that if the bell was rung twelve times, the pigeons would not know the difference. The pigeons knew.

On her return to Hollywood, Dolores realized she could never recapture the exhilaration of being on Broadway with stage veterans who were supportive of a talented newcomer. Nor was a location shoot a substitute for a challenging movie role. Dolores began losing part after part: *The Story of Ruth* (1960), *From the Terrace* (1960), *Return to Peyton Place* (1961). She could have appeared in Roger Corman's *Fall of the House of Usher* (1960), except that Nathan rightly thought such schlock was beneath her. Wallis debated about casting her in *A Girl Named Tamiko* (1962) but decided she was too young. The role went to

Martha Hyer, soon to become the second Mrs. Wallis. The last thrust of the knife occurred when the part of Jessica Poole that she had created in *The Pleasure of His Company* went to Debbie Reynolds in the movie version. Although Reynolds was hardly a star in 1962, her name meant more at the box office than Dolores Hart's. Despite these disappointments, Dolores was moving toward a decision that would bring her to a life that Hollywood could only glorify as ritual—the ceremonial taking of the veil in such films as *The Song of Bernadette* (1943), *Green Dolphin Street* (1947), and *The Nun's Story* (1959). On 26 June 1963 Dolores informed Wallis she was leaving the business; on 2 July her attorney was even more specific: "Her intention [is] no longer [to] render services in the entertainment industry."

In 1958, when Dolores learned she would be appearing in *The Pleasure of His Company,* she made a visit to Regina Laudis Abbey in Bethlehem, Connecticut, presumably for spiritual guidance. Whatever she experienced there carried her through the anxieties of a Broadway debut. Five years later, Dolores returned, this time to enter the order as Sister Judith. Hollywood was skeptical; June Haver also felt the calling but soon returned to the secular world. In the industry, for an actress to become a nun was the equivalent of taking a role in a costume drama—the difference being that there was no change of costume. When Sr. Judith took her final vows in 1970, she had made a lifelong decision, which led to her becoming Mother Superior of the convent. Now known as Mother Dolores, she was elected Mother Prioress of the abbey in February 2001.

Yet even in her new life, Mother Dolores has never severed her ties with Hollywood. The Hazens visited her regularly at Bethlehem, and Nathan, whom she addressed as "Brother Paul" in her letters, was a faithful correspondent. She has remained a member of the Academy of Motion Picture Arts & Sciences and receives tapes of the Oscar-nominated films, although she has chosen to refrain from voting.

Mother Dolores was profiled on ABC's *20/20* in March 2001, as was Don Robinson, a Californian to whom she was engaged at the time she left Hollywood. Devastated by her decision to enter the convent, he vowed never to marry; he visits Mother Dolores annually at Regina Laudis, believing that over the years "we have grown together like we would in marriage."[7]

Except for *Loving You* and perhaps *Wild Is the Wind,* Wallis was never able to capitalize on Dolores Hart's special brand of innocence, which stopped short of ingenuousness, implying a budding sophistication that the New York critics noted when she appeared in *The Pleasure of His Company*. Yet she will always be grateful to Wallis for making a dream become a reality until a higher reality presented itself: "He was one of the shrewdest producers there ever was. He didn't look down his nose at popular entertainment. He had a sense of what the people and the critics wanted."[8]

Wallis's inability to exploit the talents of Lizabeth Scott, Wendell Corey, Douglas Dick, Kristine Miller, and Dolores Hart does not lessen his reputation as a starmaker. After Wallis left Warners, he was desperate to recruit talent. At Warners, the talent was already there; what he had to do was to provide contract players like Humphrey Bogart, Bette Davis, Errol Flynn, and James Cagney with films with which they would be forever identified, like *Casablanca, Dark Victory, The Adventures of Robin Hood,* and *Yankee Doodle Dandy.* At Paramount, Wallis had to work from scratch, locating both the talent and the vehicle. Part of the problem was the pace at which Wallis recruited. A face, a voice, an aura, a presence, a build—and voilà, a contract. After that, it was sink or swim in a pool controlled by the public, whose taste did not always favor Olympic swimmers.

Wallis's first discovery, Lizabeth Scott, is an excellent example of what can go wrong with a career when a producer is more concerned with controlling his creation than nurturing it. While Wallis could provide Bette Davis with films such as *Jezebel, Dark Victory,* and *Now, Voyager* that enabled her to give memorable performances, he failed to come up with anything better than *You Came Along* for Lizabeth Scott's debut. If she excelled in roles like Sadie Thompson in *Rain* and Anna Lucasta and Sabina in *The Skin of Our Teeth,* either a sexy melodrama or a screwball comedy would have been the right choice—not a film about a terminally ill GI, around whom the action revolves. Wallis may have wanted the best for his debutante, but he failed to provide her with a vehicle that allowed for a starmaking performance.

Although *The Strange Love of Martha Ivers* is now considered classic film noir, Lizabeth's is a supporting role, despite the above-the-title billing. Wallis received a first-rate script from Robert Rossen that was well worth the $35,000 he was paid to adapt Jack Patrick's novel, *Love Lies Bleeding.* It was virtually impossible for Rossen to build up Lizabeth's role—Toni, an ex-con trying to go straight, since Toni's story was incidental to the main plot: the chance reunion of three childhood friends, whose lives were irrevocably changed by a murder committed twenty years earlier. The title character, a child murderer who grows up to be the predatory female of film noir, could have been tailored to fit Lizabeth, except that Wallis was more interested in showing off his latest discovery, Kirk Douglas (whose role is larger than Lizabeth's), and selling the film on the strength of the reputations of Barbara Stanwyck and Van Heflin.

Wallis was eager for Rossen to do the screenplay for *Paid in Full* (1950), basically a woman's film about two sisters—Jane (Lizabeth Scott) and Nancy (Diana Lynn). Jane is self-sacrificing, while Nancy is just selfish. All they have in common is their love for the same man, Bill (Robert Cummings). Jilted by a lover, Nancy marries Bill on the rebound, has a daughter, and grows so bored with her new life that she files for divorce. A freak accident, in which Jane backs out of a driveway and over her niece, leaves Jane so guilt-ridden that she proposes to Bill, hoping to provide him with a child to replace the one whose death she inadvertently caused. Once Jane becomes pregnant, she disappears, returning when it is time to deliver. Warned that she could die in childbirth like her mother, Jane accepts the inevitable. The delivery is successful, the child is a girl, and Bill and Nancy are reunited at Jane's deathbed.

Paid in Full was clearly not Rossen's kind of film; repelled by the subject matter, he sent a dismissive telegram to Wallis (15 November 1947), consisting of one sentence: "I disapprove of said basic material."[9] Rossen also expressed no interest in *Rope of Sand*, which also dismayed Wallis, who assumed Rossen might want to be reunited with the old Warners stalwarts: Paul Henreid, Claude Rains, and Peter Lorre.

Robert Blees and Charles Schnee took over the script for *Paid in Full*, making it into the prototypical woman's film—the ultimate in sibling rivalry, tragic wisdom, and self-sacrifice. Blees, who made the woman's film his specialty (*All I Desire* [1953], *Magnificent Obsession* [1954], *Autumn Leaves* [1956]), took an unusual approach to the genre. Rather than allow the characters to succumb to self-pity or go to the opposite extreme and declare themselves candidates for canonization, Blees and Schnee chose a frame narrative beginning with the preparations for Jane's delivery and ending with the birth of her daughter; enclosed within the frame was the main action, told in flashback. Jane's delivery by C-section is as graphic as the Production Code would allow and a 1950 audience could take. William Dieterle's direction complemented the script, keeping the tear ducts at capacity but always monitoring the level and maintaining the proper amount of sentiment. *Paid in Full* actually had more in common with a film like *Mildred Pierce,* which exploded the myth of mother love by pairing a loving mother with a daughter from hell, than with the more uplifting *Stella Dallas* (1936) and *Now, Voyager,* in which the female protagonists suffer but do not die, having already placed themselves on the altar of self-sacrifice. Jane's altar, in contrast, is the operating table.

Paired with Robert Cummings for the second time, Lizabeth was far more assured, working as hard as she could to ignite some fire in Cummings, who seemed oddly uncomfortable, perhaps because in this film, unlike *You Came Along,* his was not the dominant role. Cummings must have sensed that *Paid in Full* was not his vehicle; it belonged to Dieterle, Lizabeth Scott, Diana Lynn, and the team of Blees and Schnee, who came up with a ménage à trois unique in the woman's film: a husband, his second wife's sister (who had been his first wife before their divorce and whom he has now remarried), and the daughter of his (deceased) second wife, who, had her birth mother lived, would have been calling her new mother her aunt. Melodramatic? No more than the tangled skein of relationships in *Oedipus the King,* in which Oedipus's wife turns out to be his mother; his brother-in-law, his uncle; his daughters, his sisters; and his sons, his brothers. And no more than movies about unmarried mothers who give up their children for adoption (*The Old Maid* [1939], *To Each His Own* [1946]) and then experience the grand but brief reconciliation, which, from the child's point of view, is more like a recognition scene in Greek tragedy.

Wallis was sorry to lose Rossen, although he had no reason to be disappointed in *Paid in Full,* particularly since the theme was totally alien to Rossen. Even if Rossen had been tempted to try his hand at the script, he had his own agenda. Just as Wallis sought independence from Jack Warner, so did Rossen seek independence from whatever studio heads and production chiefs he could: Robert Rossen was seeking the freedom to write and direct projects of his own, working for others only when necessary. The days when Rossen was a contract writer at Warners were over. Wallis knew that Rossen had written the scripts for some of his best films, such as *The Roaring Twenties, Marked Woman,* and *The Sea Wolf;* Rossen knew that, too. But that was the Golden Age. Hollywood was now on the silver standard, even though both Rossen and Wallis were still prospecting and occasionally coming up with a nugget. After having written and directed *Johnny O'Clock* (1947) at Columbia, and then *Body and Soul* (1947) for United Artists, Rossen considered himself a writer-director. Although he had to endure the abuse of Harry Cohn, Columbia's president and head of production, he chose, wisely, to remain at the studio and both adapt and direct the movie version of Robert Penn Warren's *All the King's Men* (1949), which became a multiple Oscar winner, including best picture, best actor (Broderick Crawford), and best supporting actress (Mercedes McCambridge).

Paramount also had an Oscar winner in 1949—Olivia de Havilland for best actress in *The Heiress;* but that was a William Wyler, not a Hal Wallis, production. All Wallis could offer moviegoers in 1949 were *Rope of Sand* and *My Friend Irma.* Despite the failure of *Desert Fury,* for which Rossen wrote the screenplay, Wallis realized that he was a major loss. Yet whenever Wallis offered Rossen a film, he reneged, choosing to work elsewhere. Since Rossen was still under contract to Wallis-Hazen Productions, obligating him to write the script for one film and direct another, Wallis filed suit in 1948, and the suit was resolved in 1950. Rossen returned to Wallis-Hazen for a screenplay that was never produced. He continued to write and direct some extraordinary films, notably *The Hustler* (1961) and *Lilith* (1964), neither of which was for Wallis. The Wallis-Rossen relationship, which went back to the 1930s, ended abruptly, which was typical of most of Wallis's relationships. When it's over, it's over; no lady, fat or thin, has to sing.

While Rossen's career flourished in the 1950s and early 1960s, ending only with his early death in 1966, Lizabeth Scott's did not. She paid the price of being the equivalent of the firstborn. Oddly enough, she was not unpopular with audiences.

For his discoveries Wallis relied on Audience Research, Inc. (ARI), a unit of George H. Gallup's polling company, which boasted of being able, within three days, to provide studios with information about a film's popularity, its title, its domestic gross, and the appeal of its stars. The industry soon learned that there was no sure guide to a film's success, not even the first weekend's gross, which was only an indication of hype, not longevity. ARI developed a complicated formula based on audience anticipation and market penetration, which it would not divulge.[10] Wallis was still determined to learn about the popularity of his discoveries, particularly Lizabeth Scott. He was pleased to discover in 1948 that her popularity remained constant at twenty-seven, which ARI believed augured well for her career: "It is interesting to note that Miss Scott is one of the very few players we have measured over the past ten years, who has never, as yet, lost any ground between measurements. Her rating has climbed steadily except for two occasions when she showed no change."[11]

Like any polling company, ARI was not infallible. In the 1940s, moviegoers were less demanding than they were when the studio system was ending and when ticket prices were rising at a rate that alienated the same audiences ARI was courting. It is impossible to determine whether Wallis knew that ARI's ideal viewer was one who saw a movie at least every three weeks. Actually, in 1948, anyone who went to the movies every three weeks was not a moviegoer. True moviegoers went weekly—and many managed to get in two or three pictures per week. This was still a time when regular moviegoing was more common than it later became, and when children under twelve were more knowledgeable than ARI could have imagined. Moreover, the under-twelve population that ARI chose to ignore was still young enough to become future moviegoers, although many would transfer their allegiance to television and think not in terms of "movies" but "a movie"—"the" movie determined by the flavor of the month, which no one could predict.

Like any producer, Wallis was accustomed to sneak previews where questionnaires were filled out, which did not necessarily determine a movie's fate but could lead to a change of ending or a different marketing campaign. The only reason Wallis resorted to a service that used such simplistic categories as "Like," "Like Very Much," "Dull," and "Very Dull" to gauge audience response was his uncertainty about his discoveries, now that he no longer had access to the Warners talent pool. Although Wallis enjoyed an occasional reunion with some of the old gang, it was out of expediency, not loyalty. The industry was changing, and the enemy time was taking its toll on studio stalwarts who had now become character actors, good for a showy role if it came up or otherwise for billing near the end of the supporting cast.

Wallis needed the reassurance of a crystal ball that he suspected was cloudy but hoped would clear up. Advance reviews are never completely reliable, and ARI's were no exception. Rosalind Russell's efforts to depict the life of the Australian nurse who worked effortlessly to find a cure for polio resulted in the inspiring RKO release *Sister Kenny* (1946), which ARI lauded. However, the film failed at the box office. Since ARI tested titles, it might have suggested that RKO come up with something other than *Sister Kenny. Sister* in Britain and Australia means a nurse, not a nun; the other possibility would have been a different ad campaign explaining what *Sister* meant in the context of the film.

ARI was willing to do anything to make a movie a "want to see." But as the twentieth century approached midpoint, neither ARI nor Wallis could predict the future. Who knew what anyone would want to see? Wallis operated with a combination of instinct and inference, keeping himself attuned to the times and trusting to his starmaker's intuition. Usually, he was right; and even when he was not, he provided actors with careers—perhaps not long-lived, but at least not one-night stands.

Wallis had greater success making stars out of men than of women. The men who came out of the Wallis star machine were less malleable but also less vulnerable and insecure. Since they had confidence in their image, particularly in their brand of virility, they did not need Wallis's meticulous packaging. Burt Lancaster, Kirk Douglas, and Charlton Heston were Wallis discoveries who transcended stardom and in their own lifetime became screen icons—and in Heston's case, a public figure. While Wallis gave them their start, he could not claim credit for their popularity, which came from an almost perfect coinciding of person and persona. Each projected his own form of masculinity. Lancaster's was urban, forged of the streets; he also had a raw carnality that could explode in flamboyance whenever he had a chance to play a larger-than-life character, as he did in *The Flame and the Arrow* (1950), *The Rainmaker* (1956), and especially *Elmer Gantry* (1960). However, only *The Rainmaker* was a Wallis production, suggesting that perhaps the producer did not appreciate—or was put off by—Lancaster's devil-may-care side.

Douglas's persona began in his jaw and worked its way throughout his body. His grin and dimple belied the potential heel that lurked within, emerging in such classics as *The Big Carnival, The Bad and the Beautiful,* and *Two Weeks in Another Town* (1962)—none of which were Wallis's films. Whenever Douglas spoke through his teeth, one sensed it was because he was concealing something—perhaps an aspect of the character that the audience had to work to discover. Whether Heston was playing a cop, a gambler, a lawyer, or an explorer, he gave the character a lordly quality, as if everyone else was a social inferior. Wallis could claim to be responsible for the screen debuts of Douglas and Heston; Lancaster's was in *The Killers* [1946], the year before he became one of Wallis's actors. The only Wallis productions diehard Lancaster fans might recall would be *The Rose Tattoo* and *The Rainmaker*—certainly not *Desert Fury, I Walk Alone,* and *Rope of Sand,* which cannot compete with the actor's best performances, none of which were for Wallis: *The Killers, From Here to Eternity* (1953), *Elmer Gantry, Birdman of Alcatraz* (1962), and *Atlantic City* (1980). Douglas's two films for Wallis, *Martha Ivers* and *I Walk Alone,* pale alongside *The Bad and the Beautiful, Detective Story* (1951), *The Big Carnival, Lust for Life,* and *Spartacus* (1960). Heston, whose sole Wallis film was the forgettable *Dark City,* will never be anyone other than Moses and Ben-Hur even to those who have only seen *The Ten Commandments* and *Ben-Hur* on television. Yet although their best performances were not in Wallis films, two of the three actors—Douglas and Heston—admitted that Wallis made the path to stardom less rocky for them.

CHAPTER EIGHT

The Wallis Galaxy

O N THE SUGGESTION OF IRENE LEE, who had seen an unknown actor by the name of Burt Lancaster in Harry Brown's *A Sound of Hunting* when it was trying out in Philadelphia, Wallis arranged to see the play when it opened in New York on 20 November 1945. It closed five weeks later after twenty-three performances. The play, a World War II drama, was forgettable; Lancaster, however, was not. Wallis sensed that he was in the presence of a star. Accordingly, Lancaster was issued a star's contract, even though he had yet to make a picture: $1,250 a week for starters, then $1,500.[1] Lancaster's debut was to have been in the equally forgettable *Desert Fury,* but Wallis's assistant, Martin Jurow, suggested that the actor first be loaned to Universal-International for *The Killers* (1946), followed by *Brute Force* (1947) for the same studio. Jurow convinced Wallis that a film noir *(The Killers)* and a prison movie *(Brute Force)* would prepare audiences for the hunk they had under contract.[2] As it happened, both films were vastly superior to *Desert Fury,* which Lancaster truly despised, along with the critics and the public.

Lancaster had an uneasy relationship with Wallis, who had never before encountered anyone who knew his own mind after so short a time in the business. Initially, Lancaster's 9 April 1946 contract seemed acceptable to both the actor and his agent, Harold Hecht. For the next six years (9 April 1946 to 9 April 1952), Lancaster was expected to appear in twelve Wallis productions; however, during that period he was also free to make a total of ten outside pictures: one each in 1946 and 1947, two in 1948, one in 1949, two in 1950, one in 1951, and two in 1952.

In 1947 Hecht proposed that the number of Wallis films be reduced to six and the outside pictures increased to twelve. Hazen, who was handling the negotiations, offered a compromise: an additional outside picture for 1947; extension of the contract to 1953; reduction of the Wallis commitment to one picture each in 1950, 1952, and 1953; a 100 percent salary increase for the 1947–50 period; a 50 percent increase for 1951–52; and $75,000 for the 1953 film.

This was the deal that a newcomer's dreams are made of. However, since neither Lancaster nor Hecht was a dreamer, Hazen's counterproposal was rejected. Finally the parties agreed to a further compromise: Lancaster owed Wallis eight pictures during his option periods, with the possibility of postponements. There were indeed postponements, which were more like gaps. Yet Wallis eventually got his eight films, although rarely when he wanted them: *Desert Fury* (1947), *I Walk Alone* (1948), *Sorry, Wrong Number* (1948), *Rope of Sand* (1949), *Come Back, Little Sheba* (1952), *The Rose Tattoo* (1955), *The Rainmaker* (1956), and *Gunfight at the O.K. Corral* (1957). Of the eight, three were memorable, but not simply for Lancaster, who received stiff competition from his costars: Shirley Booth *(Sheba)*, Anna Magnani *(Tattoo)*, and Katharine Hepburn *(Rainmaker)*.

After *Desert Fury,* Lancaster wanted to break his contract with Wallis, but he stayed on with the understanding that he be allowed at least two outside pictures a year.[3] Certainly *The Flame and the Arrow* (1950), which he made for Warners, revealed a totally different Lancaster, an actor who had gone the Douglas Fairbanks–Errol Flynn route—reveling in derring-do, swinging from balconies, and crossing swords with villains.

Lancaster was never one of Wallis's favorites. Supposedly during a salary dispute, Lancaster shouted at Wallis: "I'm going to pick you up, you son of a bitch, and throw you out the window."[4] Wallis knew Lancaster probably could.

Around the same time that Wallis signed Lancaster, Lauren Bacall told him about another stage actor who, she believed, could become a major screen personality. The actor was Kirk Douglas; the play was Ralph Nelson's *Wind Is Ninety,* which enjoyed a modest run, opening on 21 June 1945 and closing on 25 September. It was a combination of *Our Town* and *The Human Comedy,* in which Douglas played the shade of the Unknown Soldier, accompanying the spirit of a dead pilot (Wendell Corey) on his return to earth, where the pilot learns how his family and friends remember him. When *The Wind Is Ninety* closed, Corey immediately went into *Dream Girl,* where he impressed Wallis far more than he did in *The Wind Is Ninety,* in which Douglas seems to have commanded the stage even in a secondary role.

Throughout the run, Douglas and Corey barely spoke. Corey was blatantly anti-Semitic, referring to Douglas as "that dirty Jew";[5] it probably did not help that Douglas received some highly favorable reviews. Douglas, however, was more interested in developing as a stage actor than in entrusting himself to a medium that, at the time, he considered inferior to the theater. On 24 July 1945, Douglas wired Wallis, declining his offer of a contract.[6] A week later Douglas had second thoughts; rather than burn his bridges, he explained to Wallis that his decision "was not to obtain better terms, but simply to fulfill a need to fully develop myself as an actor before going to Hollywood." However, Douglas could not have done more to endear himself to Wallis than to write at the close of his letter, "I would rather go to Hollywood under your auspices than any other. I feel certain we could work together and that I would trust my career in your hands. And so, if you want it then, you can have the first crack."[7] Wallis replied that he would be delighted to have "the first crack"—and he did.

Unable to land a part in a play, Douglas took off for Los Angeles, heading straight for Wallis's office at Paramount and into a $1,250-a-week contract, the same as Lancaster's. As attractive as the arrangement seemed, it allowed Wallis to exercise five options, each at a higher salary, so that if all five were exercised, Douglas would be making $5,000 a week. As a movie novice, Douglas knew nothing about loan-outs, nor did he realize that a long-term contract is an albatross for anyone who has made an auspicious debut, as he had in *Martha Ivers.* Henceforth it was a combination of Wallis productions and loan-outs; in 1948 it was both: Wallis's *I Walk Alone* and *My Dear Secretary* for United Artists.

I Walk Alone was the beginning of a lifelong friendship between Douglas and Lancaster, who were costarring in the film with Lizabeth Scott. Like Lancaster, Douglas soon learned the pitfalls of long-term contracts. Soon, Douglas's best films were loan-outs, for example, *Champion* (1949), which ranks high among such classic boxing films as *Body and Soul* (1947), *The Set-Up* (1949), and *Raging Bull* (1980); Joseph L. Mankiewicz's *Letter to Three Wives* (1949); and especially Billy Wilder's *Big Carnival* (1951). When Wallis realized Douglas's appeal, he tried to tie him to a seven-year contract, which Douglas considered "slavery."[8] Thereupon Wallis dropped his options, leaving Douglas free to appear in far better roles than the ones he could have offered him— roles, by the way, for which Douglas would be remembered: the manipulative movie producer in *The Bad and the Beautiful,* the unforgiving husband in *Detective Story,* the scoop-obsessed reporter in *The Big Carnival,* Van Gogh in *Lust for Life,* and the leader of the slave revolt in *Spartacus.* Since Wallis offered him good money for *Gunfight at the O.K. Corral,* Douglas agreed, provided Lancaster costar with him. Their teaming resulted in a well-made western, more accurate than John Ford's *My Darling Clementine* (1946), but, artistically, not in the same league.

In his autobiography, Douglas remembers Wallis as taciturn and remote. When Wallis heard that Douglas and Lancaster had become fast friends, staying up all night talking after a day's filming, he asked Douglas what they could possibly have been discussing. Douglas found the question revealing: "How sad that Hal Wallis, a great selector of talent, a man who knew people so well that he could pick stars, including Burt and me, had no friends with whom he could hold lengthy conversations after dinner. He didn't know that between friends the well of conversation never runs dry."[9]

Wallis, however, had no friends, if by "friend" one means a second self—or as Marlene Dietrich once defined it, someone you could call at 3:00 A.M. and would not hang up on you. Wallis preferred acquaintances; he had scores of them from all walks of life. He knew that loneliness was the starmaker's fate; all he could do was keep the Hollywood firmament ablaze with new additions to compensate for the black holes. There can never be a close relationship between star and starmaker; when the starmaker attempts to have one, it is usually injurious to the star.

Once an actor achieves stardom, particularly when it occurs overnight, obedience becomes a problem. Lizabeth Scott, Douglas Dick, and Kristine Miller accepted the roles they were given, whether in a Wallis production or a loan-out; if they felt underutilized, they remained silent. Lancaster and Douglas, however, were quite vocal.

When Wallis wanted Lancaster to costar with Lizabeth Scott in *Dark City,* he refused, having had his fill of unchallenging roles. The part he was to have played went to the unknown Charlton Heston, whom Wallis discovered after watching him play Heathcliff in a Studio One telecast of *Wuthering Heights*.

Heston also had a short-lived and turbulent relationship with Wallis, whom he nonetheless respected. Lancaster and Douglas may have been difficult, but Heston was impossible.[10] First, there was the matter of Heston's first name, which Wallis disliked but which the actor refused to change to "Charles" because Wallis thought "Charles" would be easier for audiences to remember. Then there was Heston's 11 January 1950 contract. From the outset Heston wanted one that would allow for outside pictures, particularly for Warners, which had been pursuing him at the same time that he signed with Wallis to make *Dark City* for $10,000. Wallis was willing to renegotiate, with the understanding that for every outside picture, Heston's contract would be extended for eight weeks beyond the time spent making the film. Heston's contract had become such a cause célèbre that it made Louella Parsons's column, in which the terms were so misrepresented that Wallis wired Parsons to explain that for the next seven years Heston would make two pictures a year for him and one a year for another studio—that studio being Warners for the next three years.

Early in 1953, both Heston and his agent, MCA's Herman Citron, who was known for driving hard bargains, knew that Wallis-Hazen productions was about to be dissolved.[11] Citron insisted his client not sign the "assignment of contract" papers permitting Wallis to sell Heston's services to another studio, arguing that even if Wallis-Hazen was dissolved, Hal Wallis Productions would exist; its address would be the same as Paramount's, 5451 Marathon Street; and Wallis and the studio could still draw on Heston's services. Meanwhile, Wallis had already determined Heston's next two films, both of which would be 1954 Paramount releases but not Hal Wallis productions: *The Naked Jungle* and *Secret of the Incas*. Citron's insistence that Heston's contract was for sale made the actor anxious, Paul Nathan furious, and Wallis combative. The contract, which had four more years to run, was still in effect, Wallis insisted. Heston can either appear in a Wallis production or be loaned out; if Paramount needs Heston, the studio must notify Wallis Productions, which has preemptive rights on any Heston film; and most important, the salary specifications remain the same without possibility of increase. Although Wallis knew that his association with Heston had ended, he was determined to make money on the actor, especially when

Paramount desired his services. Since Wallis was based at Paramount, it was more of a talent trade than a loan-out. But the talent was expensive, and when Paramount offered Heston $55,000 to appear in *Secret of the Incas,* Wallis had no objection—provided that he too was compensated.

The terms of Heston's contract were irrelevant, since the actor made nothing for Wallis after *Dark City*. Heston did, however, appear in several Paramount releases, two of which are among his most popular: *The Greatest Show on Earth* (1952) and his signature film, *The Ten Commandments*—both Cecil B. DeMille productions.

Although *Dark City* is hardly the film by which Heston would want to be remembered, Wallis took great pains to make it as memorable as he could. In fact, Heston's debut was more spectacular than Douglas's in *Martha Ivers*. "Introducing Charlton Heston" appears immediately after the title, *Dark City;* then comes "Starring Lizabeth Scott," which is more honorary than factual, since her character disappears for about a third of the film to make way for a subplot. Heston is the star—the only one. Heston is also part of the main title; as the credits appear, Heston is shown in close-up and medium shot, as the camera tracks him walking down a street. Rarely does a newcomer get to be part of the main title.

The rest of *Dark City* is Heston writ large. No neophyte could have asked for more close-ups. Heston was playing a variation on the tough-guy figure: a Cornell graduate sounding like an English major who dabbled in dramatics, played varsity basketball, chug-a-lugged with his fraternity brothers, joined the army, and after being discharged discovered easy money in cards and dice. Like most film noir, *Dark City* is overly complicated on the assumption that the audience will get so caught up in the action, which has no sense of place (the film ends in Las Vegas), that it will ignore the fact that the villain (Mike Mazurki) does not appear until the end. No matter. The center of attention was Heston, moving comfortably in the dark world of flashing neon, smoke-filled clubs, and cheap hotels.

Neither Lancaster nor Douglas received that kind of celluloid build-up. Since Lancaster had already made his debut in *The Killers, Desert Fury* was just another movie that did nothing for his career. When Wallis cast Lancaster and Douglas together in *I Walk Alone* (1948), Lancaster was a seasoned professional: in 1948 three Lancaster films were in release: *All My Sons* (for Universal-International), *Sorry, Wrong Number,* and *I Walk Alone.* By contrast, *I Walk Alone* was only Douglas's second film. The credits favored Lancaster, who got costar billing with Lizabeth Scott; Douglas and Wendell Corey were featured; and Kristine Miller's name topped the supporting cast in unusually large print, even though her character—the familiar classy dame on the make—was more decorative than functional. Conversely, Douglas should not have been given feature billing, since his role was equal to Lancaster's and bigger than Lizabeth Scott's.

Douglas played an unprincipled ex-bootlegger who lets his buddy (Lancaster) take the rap for violating the Volstead Act, which results in a fourteen-year prison term. When Lancaster is released, he wants satisfaction from Douglas, who has opened up a swank club, with Lizabeth as his star attraction. Since Douglas is unregenerate, he takes a different fall—a bullet-ridden one, while Lancaster and Lizabeth walk off together into the fog, presumably to a sunlit future. The three leads managed to hold their own, as did Kristine Miller as a sex-starved socialite who gave Lancaster a resounding slap in the face when he proved unreceptive to her charms. Nonetheless, *Dark City* was just a crime movie with noirish touches (neon signs, mirror-paneled bars, dingy rooms), not all that different from the melodramas that Warner Brothers produced in the thirties.

Wallis could only provide Lancaster, Douglas, and Heston with their entrée into movies, after which his services were no longer needed. That the iconic triumvirate outgrew Wallis's tutelage once they caught on with the public suggests that his role was like Miss Moffat's in *The Corn Is Green,* Emlyn Williams's play (made into a 1944 film) about a schoolteacher in a Welsh village who prepares her star pupil for Oxford, knowing that hers was a preliminary role in his development and that others would complete what she had begun.

Shirley MacLaine was another Wallis disappointment. Wallis always looked to the stage as a potential source of screen talent, aware that he might only be opening a door for one of his discoveries that would lead to a domain larger than his. Little did he know that the door he opened for Shirley MacLaine would be shut in his face. Although *42nd Street* (1933) was not a Wallis production, it still epitomized every understudy's dream: going on for the ailing star and scoring such a hit that there would be no more waiting in the wings. That was exactly what happened the night Wallis saw Shirley MacLaine in *The Pajama Game.*

When *The Pajama Game* opened on Broadway on 13 May 1954 for a run of 1,063 performances, the stars, billed above the title, were John Raitt, Janis Paige, and Eddie Foy Jr. However, it was the relatively unknown Carol Haney who stopped the show with her dancing in two numbers, "Steam Heat" and "Once a Year Day." Haney was a true gamine, a talented pixie with a quirky body that responded to Bob Fosse's unconventional choreography, which then was less erotic than it eventually became.

About a month after the premiere, Haney twisted her ankle, and her understudy, Shirley MacLaine, took over the role. Sexier and more attractive than Haney, MacLaine became the proverbial talk of the town. Wallis caught the show and was so impressed by MacLaine's performance that he went backstage to see her. In her autobiography, MacLaine recalls Wallis's backstage visit, noting that he had a "face like a suntanned pear."[12] MacLaine had nothing good to say about Wallis, accusing him, among other things, of chasing her around a desk, which Wallis denied in his autobiography—adding, however, that if he had, he could have caught her (*Starmaker,* 137). MacLaine also misrepresented their dinner at the Plaza when he broached the subject of a contract to her and her future husband, Steve Parker. Because Wallis only had Ry Krisp while they had steaks, MacLaine assumed he was a skinflint. Wallis explained that he had dined earlier and, assuming that she and Parker were not habitués of the Plaza, encouraged them to have whatever they would like. They did, ordering the most expensive entrées on the menu (*Starmaker,* 136–37).

What bothered Wallis was not MacLaine's allegations but her ingratitude. In June 1954 MacLaine signed a five-year contract, starting at $6,000 a picture and reaching $20,000 by the fifth year.[13] Because of frequent suspensions, the contract was extended to eight years. When MacLaine told *Look* magazine in 1963 that she had been "lured" into the movies with a "long term, mite-sized contract," Wallis rightly took exception. While it is true that MacLaine, like so many of Wallis's protégés, made her best films elsewhere (e.g., *Some Came Running* [1958], *The Apartment* [1960], *Sweet Charity* [1969]), she did extremely well for an understudy who was fortunate to go on the night a major film producer was in the audience. MacLaine, however, looks upon her years with Wallis as white slavery; if that was so, then victims of white slavery should have been so handsomely compensated for their services.

By 1963, having had her fill of being "owned" as if she were "a can of peas,"[14] MacLaine decided to buy her way out of her contract, paying Wallis and Hazen $150,000 in three installments over a three-year period (August 1964–March 1967). To her credit, MacLaine continued working at her craft; her efforts were recognized by her Oscar for *Terms of Endearment* (1983), which, along with *The Apartment,* represents her finest work.

The tension in their relationship resulted from each one's misconception of the other: MacLaine viewed Wallis as a mogul, and Wallis perceived her as an irritant. Like Creon and Antigone, each was right and each was wrong.

Shirley Booth was another matter. While she had been in the theater for over a decade, her breakthrough role occurred in William Inge's *Come Back, Little Sheba* (1950), from which she was nearly fired out of town. Anyone at the Broadway opening on 15 February 1950 would have wondered what the problem was. Along with Laurette Taylor's Amanda Wingfield in *The Glass Menagerie* (1944), Marlon Brando's Stanley Kowalski in *A Streetcar Named Desire* (1947), and Lee J. Cobb's Willy Loman in *Death of a Salesman* (1949), Booth's Lola Delaney ranks among the theater's legendary performances, although, as a play, *Sheba* was not on a par with *Menagerie, Streetcar,* or *Salesman.*

Wallis was determined to produce the film version of *Sheba* with Booth as Lola in her screen debut. He began negotiating with Booth's agent, the daunting Audrey Wood, early in January 1951.[15] Wood's terms were formidable: a seven-year contract beginning at $40,000 and gradually reaching $100,000. When Hazen heard Wood's demands, he could barely contain himself. Meanwhile, that April Booth was back on Broadway in *A Tree Grows in Brooklyn,* the vastly underappreciated Arthur Schwartz–Dorothy Fields musical derived from Betty Smith's novel, in which Booth played the free-wheeling (and free-loving) Aunt Cissy. *A Tree Grows in Brooklyn*'s fate was to open in the same season as Rodgers and Hammerstein's *King and I;* as often happens, there was not enough room for two major musicals. The victor was *The King and I,* which lasted for 1,246 performances.

Since Booth had a run-of-the-play contract, further discussion about the movie version of *Sheba* was delayed until *A Tree Grows in Brooklyn* closed on 8 December 1951 after a disappointing eight-month run. A year later, a compromise had been reached: Booth would receive $5,000 a week for eight consecutive weeks, which was another way of paying her $40,000. Wallis agreed to a six-year contract after *Sheba,* giving each of them picture approval in alternate years—Wallis in the second, fourth, and sixth; Booth in the third and fifth. The arrangement came quite close to what Audrey Wood had proposed, except for the money. Again, the contract became a moot point. Booth never became a screen star, although she later triumphed on television with the long-running sitcom *Hazel.* Her films for Wallis totaled four, including *Sheba.*

While Booth reprised her role as the slatternly Lola Delaney, calling plaintively each morning for Sheba, her lost dog, the part of her husband, "Doc" Delaney, posed a problem. The character is a former AA member who resumes drinking, partly because he cannot accept the frump his wife has become and, worse, because she has encouraged a romance between their boarder—a college coed, whom Doc regards as a surrogate daughter—and a sex-minded athlete. Although Sidney Blackmer created the role, his name would mean less to moviegoers than Booth's, which was not a household name, either, except to theatergoers and fans of the radio show *Duffy's Tavern,* on which she was a regular. Since *Rope of Sand,* Lancaster's last film for Wallis, the actor had been searching for parts that would reveal his talent for serious drama, not just swashbucklers and melodramas. And the movie version of a Broadway hit was precisely what Lancaster wanted.

Lancaster sought out Wallis, who offered him the role of Doc Delaney—not for old times' sake (Wallis was far from sentimental, especially when it came to Lancaster) but because the actor's name meant something at the box office. The film was so powerful, and Booth's performance resonated so deeply with audiences, that the miscasting of Lancaster did not throw it off balance. A drab business suit did not conceal the fact that a screen personality was wearing it, any more than the gray strands in Lancaster's hair suggested middle age. What mattered was that Booth gave an Academy Award–winning performance. On Oscar night, 19 March 1953, Booth was not at the Pantages in Hollywood; since she was appearing on Broadway in *The Time of the Cuckoo,* she watched the simulcast at the NBC Century Theatre in New York. When the award for best actress was announced, Booth was gracious in her acceptance speech. She would not have the opportunity to deliver another.

What could Shirley Booth do for an encore? Hers was a unique talent; in the theater she could shuttle between the bawdy and the poignant, playing characters as dissimilar as the much-unmarried Aunt Cissy in *A Tree Grows in Brooklyn* and the unfulfilled secretary hoping to find in Venice what she could not in the States (*The Time of the Cuckoo,* filmed as *Summertime* [1955] with Katharine Hepburn). Although Booth was not especially known for musical comedy, she did her share—for example, A *Tree Grows in Brooklyn, By the Beautiful Sea* (1954); and *Juno* (1959), Marc Blitzstein's musical version of Sean O'Casey's *Juno and the Paycock,* in which Booth played Juno Boyle. Booth gave a powerful performance, but *Juno* closed after a few weeks.

Wallis, however, saw Shirley Booth as a backstreet mistress or the neglected wife of a middle-aged stud. He knew immediately after *Sheba* that there would be problems finding suitable scripts for her. When Booth insisted upon doing a comedy as her next film, turning down *Ladies of the Corridor* because it was too morbid, Wallis tried to buy *The Solid Gold Cadillac*—a hit of the 1953–54 season—for her. Columbia's Harry Cohn beat him to it, and the comedy was altered to the comedic talents of Judy Holliday, who bore no physical resemblance to the character actress, Josephine Hull, who played the lead on Broadway. Booth, however, would have been more believable as a stockholder who, by asking a few pointed questions at a board meeting, ends up controlling the company. Glamour was a quality that Booth not only lacked but did not need. Booth would do a comedy, but not immediately—and not for Wallis. First, there was Wallis's production of *About Mrs. Leslie* (1954), a *Back Street* derivative, with Booth as the mistress of tycoon Robert Ryan. It was a well-made woman's film, with Booth as a more resilient Lola without an alcoholic husband. *Mrs. Leslie* was "adult" in the way 1950s movies tended to be: tastefully discreet without being prudish. *Mrs. Leslie* at least had style, but *Hot Spell* (1958), in which Booth was cast as the hand-wringing wife of womanizer Anthony Quinn, had only sweat. Her last Paramount film was not for Wallis, but it was a comedy: the movie version of Thornton Wilder's *Matchmaker* (1958), in which she revealed her old self—the Shirley Booth that Broadway took to its heart in *My Sister Eileen* (1940), *A Tree Grows in Brooklyn,* and *The Desk Set* (1955). Tossing off asides to the camera and occasionally winking at the audience, she invested the role of Dolly Gallagher Levi with a brash insouciance that would have been endearing on the stage—and was also on film, but only to audiences sophisticated enough to appreciate that they were experiencing a theater piece brought to the screen with its conventions intact. The audience for whom *The Matchmaker* was intended, however, failed to turn out en masse; and Booth's bravura performance went ignored.

There were more Broadway roles, but no triumphs. Realizing that the final curtain had been rung, Booth headed for television, where she created the title role in *Hazel,* costarring with Wallis alumnus Don De-Fore (*The Affairs of Susan, My Friend Irma, and Dark City*).

Since Shirley Booth had a wonderfully self-deflating sense of humor, she would have appreciated the irony of a Tony and Oscar winner known primarily as the title character in *Hazel,* the popular television series (1961–66), in which she played a wisecracking maid who brought order to an otherwise unmanageable household. Like other hit sitcoms, *Hazel* has enjoyed an afterlife on *TV Land* and *Nick at Nite.*

But in the 1950s, television was the furthest thing from Shirley Booth's mind. Having done radio, she was thinking film and theater. Audrey Wood sensed that there was a place for Booth in the new medium. Accordingly, Wood inquired whether her client could reprise *Sheba* for television, noting that "Shirley has resisted all television interests because she does not want to do television unless the vehicle is exactly right for her."[16] Shirley Booth's Lola Delaney is immortalized on film, not videotape or kinescope; and *Hazel* is only a footnote in a career that can never be as well documented as it should be, because Shirley Booth belonged to an age when memory, not technology, was the keeper of the flame.

The success of *Sheba*—and especially Booth's Oscar—attracted Wallis to another stage play, Tennessee Williams's *Rose Tattoo* (1951). Although Wallis never intended anyone other than Booth for *Sheba,* he knew he could not use Maureen Stapleton and Eli Wallach, the original stars of *The Rose Tattoo*. The roles of Serafina delle Rosa, a recent widow obsessed with memories of her rose-tattooed husband, with whom she enjoyed nightly sex; and Alvaro Mangiacavallo, a truck driver who woos her back to the world of the living (and presumably to the kind of lovemaking to which she had been accustomed), were played magnificently by two non-Italians: the Irish Maureen Stapleton and the Jewish Eli Wallach. To moviegoers, Stapleton and Wallach were merely names. Williams had written Serafina for Anna Magnani, the earth mother of Italian neorealism—a brilliant actress as well as a force of nature. But the earth mother's English was rudimentary, thus ruling out a Broadway engagement.

Magnani was Wallis's only choice for Serafina. By the time Magnani arrived in Hollywood, serious moviegoers knew her name. By the early 1950s, Italian neorealism had reached cities that ordinarily would have been impervious to European cinema, and Magnani's performance in *Open City* (1945) signaled a talent in the raw that did not require front lighting and sculpted makeup. Then, too, the *Miracle* case also brought her into prominence. Roberto Rossellini's *Miracle,* a forty-minute film in a trilogy entitled *Ways of Love* (1948), outraged Francis Cardinal Spellman, New York's archbishop, who denounced the film as obscene as well as an affront to Catholicism: Nannina (Magnani), an Italian peasant, is seduced by a bearded stranger (a nonspeaking role played by Federico Fellini), whom she associates with Saint Joseph, thereby becoming a quasi–Virgin Mary; when Nannina becomes pregnant, she assumes that, like Mary, she will experience a virgin birth. *The Miracle* was the distillation of Magnani's art: a deeply felt belief in the character, expressed in a face that knew suffering but not self-pity.

Cardinal Spellman mounted such a strong campaign against *The Miracle* that the New York Board of Regents declared the film "sacrilegious" and revoked the license that the New York State Motion Picture Division had issued to Joseph Burstyn, president of Burstyn-Mayer, Inc., which specialized in distributing foreign films.[17] When the Court of Appeals concurred with the Regents, Burstyn, believing his First Amendment rights had been violated, persisted in his quest for justice until the Supreme Court agreed to take up the case. In February 1952 the high court rendered a landmark decision, making film a form of protected speech within the context of the First and Fourteenth Amendments.

Even if Magnani had not starred in *The Miracle,* Wallis would have done everything in his power to persuade her to play Serafina. But the timing could not have been better; Anna Magnani not only was among Europe's greatest actresses, but she also appeared in one of the most controversial films ever made—at least by 1950s standards.

Serafina was different from any of Magnani's other roles. *The Rose Tattoo* is an earthy folk drama, which, if not played broadly—and it was *not* in the 1951 production—has a piquant charm that can camouflage some of the play's defects, one of which is the cartoonlike characterization of Alvaro Mangiacavallo. For Alvaro, Wallis wanted Burt Lancaster, again for reasons that had more to do with box office than with the actor's suitability for the role. Just as Wallis used Lancaster for Shirley Booth's debut in *Sheba,* he planned to do the same for Magnani's in *Tattoo.* Wallis's reasoning had not changed: Lancaster's name would attract those who knew Magnani by name or from *Open City;* and for the ones who had no idea who Anna Magnani was, there was the tantalizing prospect of seeing *grande amore* on the screen with Lancaster in his undershirt and his costar—the only real star—in a slip.

In fall 1954 Lancaster had just made the most important film thus far in his career, *From Here to Eternity* (1953); he had also reached a stage at which, like so many other actors, he decided that the real power lay behind the camera. When *Tattoo* was about to start filming, Lancaster was in Kentucky both starring in and directing *The Kentuckian* (1955).[18] Lancaster was so determined to succeed in his directorial debut that he chose to finish his own picture (which proved unmemorable) before starting Wallis's. In October 1954 Lancaster informed Wallis that he would not be available to start *Tattoo* until December. Wallis wired back that production could not be delayed for two months. He was adamant about Lancaster's arriving in Key West for location shooting by the end of October. Five days of rain prevented Lancaster from finishing *The Kentuckian* until October 29, after which Lancaster—who then had an aversion to flying (or so he said)—insisted on traveling by train to Key West, stopping off at Kansas City, supposedly to have his portrait painted (or so the press claimed). He finally arrived in Key West in early November, after having taken a train from Kansas City to Miami and driving the rest of the way.

Subtlety was not the hallmark of the movie version, which opened up the play with a vengeance. Everything was in-your-face ethnicity, conforming to what non-Italians thought about Italians and what Italians thought about some of their own. The folk element would have succumbed to primitivism, had it not been for Magnani's performance, which allowed some of Williams's humanity to shine through the faux Italian trappings. Magnani's Serafina was not nuanced but detailed, with the gestures of dismay, the wounded silences, the nervous "O.K.s" that meant just the opposite, and the sudden transitions from warmth to rage that made the viewer understand if not totally comprehend a woman so obsessed with the memory of a rose-scented and rose-tattooed husband that she has withdrawn into a world ruled by symbolism—the combined effect of Williams's language and Magnani's personal myth-making.

Lancaster's Alvaro was another matter. While Alvaro is a clown and at times a buffoon, he is as complex a character as Serafina. He has to be endearingly awkward in his courtship of Serafina, yet at the same time suggest that his interest is also carnal. Serafina is a slave to the eroticism of memory—something Alvaro cannot understand. He only knows that he can offer her love, primarily physical, unencumbered by the weight of the past. Lancaster, however, clowned, sweated, and swaggered his way through the picture as if everything depended on his personal magnetism. It was the difference between being lifelike (Magnani) and larger-than-life (Lancaster). Lancaster's exhibitionism worked better as the con artist in *The Rainmaker,* a role for which he begged Wallis after William Holden turned it down.

In *The Rose Tattoo,* Lancaster's flamboyance only highlighted Magnani's ability to do more with less, through a furtive glance, a hand at the breast or through the hair, a self-deprecating laugh that disclosed the pain it was intended to conceal, a walk that under stress turned into a stagger. Her art was rewarded at Academy Award time with a best actress Oscar, which she was not present to accept, having returned to Rome.

Wallis's professional relationship with Magnani was one of the most satisfying he had ever had with a star. Wallis was a complete pragmatist when it came to his discoveries: If a star could not generate enough brilliance to remain in the firmament, it was either the black hole or demotion to a lesser place in the heavens. The lucky ones (Lancaster, Douglas, Heston) managed to generate their own star power. With Magnani, it was neither a matter of discovery nor independence. Since Magnani was closely identified with Italian cinema, the idea of Hollywoodizing her was not only ludicrous but also impractical. She was in Hollywood for one reason: to make her American film debut in a part that was originally written for her. What happened later would depend on her acceptance by the moviegoing public. Like Shirley Booth's, Magnani's was a specialized talent as far as the Hollywood product was concerned. And finding the right material for Magnani would be just as difficult as it was for Booth.

Magnani seemed to adore Wallis; in her letters, he was "Hal dearest" or "my wonderful boss." When *Tattoo* was finished, Wallis had two

dozen red roses delivered to her stateroom when she sailed back to Italy. After her Oscar, Wallis sent her the jeep and trailer he had promised
her if the film turned out to be a success.

Magnani thanked "Hal dearest" for "the Hollywood experience," as
indeed she should. No Italian director would ever have come up with
such perks as a jeep and a trailer, which she needed so she could take
her crippled son with her when she went on location. But the "Hollywood experience" left her wanting more. As her next film, Magnani
tried to persuade Wallis to produce an English-language remake of the
Italian *Furia* (1947), based on Giovanni Verga's *La Lupa,* a lurid melodrama about a horse breeder, his adulterous second wife, and his daughter. The wife takes up with the groom; the father, thinking it is his daughter
who is sleeping with the groom, forces the two of them to marry, leaving the wife free to move on to other men. The husband eventually dies;
the wife is murdered by a spurned lover; and at the fade-out, the daughter and the groom realize that they love each other. This is the kind of
plot that gives naturalism a bad name.

Although Wallis knew an American remake of *Furia* would be a
mistake, he did not want to discourage Magnani from making another
American film. Wallis then tried to persuade her to star on Broadway in
Tennessee Williams's *Orpheus Descending,* playing an unhappily married woman who takes up with a drifter, resulting in both of their deaths—
his more violent than hers. It may not have been *Furia,* but there were
similarities. Magnani was interested, as was Wallis—but only in the
film version. The project escalated into a clash of egos. Magnani, who
did not think her English was up to eight performances a week, insisted
that someone else do the Wednesday and Saturday matinees, although
this may have been her way of saving face. Williams doubted he could
find a comparable actress for the matinees. Then Williams decided not
to write the screenplay. "I have never had so difficult or impossible a
deal put to me," Wallis complained to Magnani.[19]

To placate Magnani, whose services he did not wish to lose, Wallis
hired several writers, including Philip Yordan, to see if there was any
way in which *Furia* could be Americanized; but the best anyone could
come up with was transplanting the action to nineteenth-century Texas.
Finally, Arnold Schulman took over the project, but he soon realized it
was hopeless; he persuaded Wallis to consider a totally new script, which
he would write. Wallis agreed, and the script became *Wild Is the Wind*

(1957). However, when Schulman attended a sneak preview and saw the credits acknowledge an Italian writer's story as the basis of his original screenplay, he protested to the Screen Writers Guild, which agreed that Schulman should have screenplay and story credit. But since Magnani's contract specified that one of the adaptors of *Furia,* Vittorio Nino Novarese, receive a credit, Novarese's contribution was restricted to motion picture story. The irony is that whatever Novarese "adapted" was never used.

Although George Cukor was delighted at the prospect of directing *Wild Is the Wind,* which was a radical departure from the Spencer Tracy–Katharine Hepburn romantic comedies that had become his specialty, he was defeated by Schulman's script, which had all the earmarks of tragedy but not the tragic ending. Upon the death of his wife, the husband (Anthony Quinn) marries her sister (Anna Magnani) to perpetuate the wife's memory; however, the Magnani character becomes attracted to her younger son-in-law (Anthony Franciosa). In the language of high concept, it was *"Desire under the Elms* meets *Pagliacci."* However, in Leoncavallo's opera, the jealous Canio kills his wife and her lover; in Eugene O'Neill's *Desire under the Elms,* stepmother and stepson embark upon an affair that leaves the stepmother pregnant—the result being infanticide and shared guilt. *Wild Is the Wind* goes another route. Quinn finally stops thinking of Magnani as his first wife's stand-in; and Magnani realizes Franciosa is meant for a nonincestuous relationship with a younger woman (Dolores Hart). The result is more like *"Desire under the Elms* meets *They Knew What They Wanted"*; in the latter, the husband forgives his wife for her indiscretion, and marriage wins out over infidelity—real *(Wanted)* or potential *(Wild).*

The *Wild Is the Wind* denouement was obviously a sop to the Production Code Association, which would never have sanctioned a script in which the action progressed inexorably toward tragedy, unless the adulterous pair died at the end *(Pagliacci)* or went off to jail *(Elms).* Deciding to skirt retribution, Schulman opted for reconciliation. Even the Pygmalion myth was less complicated: Pygmalion fashioned his creation from his image of a perfect woman, not a real one; in *Wild Is the Wind,* the Quinn character seeks to preserve the memory of his former wife by staying within the bloodline. That Magnani and Quinn were able to convince audiences, at least for the duration of the film, that their marriage could possibly succeed was a tribute to their art but a blow to verisimilitude.

In 1957, the same year that *Wild Is the Wind* opened to less-than-ecstatic notices, *Orpheus Descending* arrived on Broadway and was greeted pretty much the same. Maureen Stapleton was again playing the "Magnani" role—the much abused Lady in need of a fling, which she has with a drifter in a snakeskin jacket with the symbolically portentous name of Val Xavier. *Orpheus Descending* is the kind of play beloved by academics who can mine it for its myths and symbols, both Greek and Christian; but what the play really cries out for is a production that ignores the Hellenic and pseudo-Christian trappings and concentrates on the characters, whose emotional needs go beyond anything even remotely scholarly. It was not until the late 1980s that *Orpheus Descending* was given the right staging—ironically, by a British director, Peter Hall, and a British actress, Vanessa Redgrave. Redgrave adopted an Italian accent that made Lady an outsider in the Deep South, a victim of discrimination like her lover, the poet-outcast Val Xavier. Hall's direction raised Williams's bid for intellectual respectability to the level of tragedy.

The same could not be said of the 1959 movie version of *Orpheus Descending, The Fugitive Kind,* which was melodrama masquerading as tragedy. Wallis had nothing to do with the film, a United Artists release directed by Sidney Lumet, who specialized in adaptations of stage plays. Magnani had another chance to do the movie version of a play that had been written for her; she also had a costar more iconic than Burt Lancaster: Marlon Brando as the inarticulate Val Xavier. Although it seemed that their acting styles would complement each other, the opposite turned out to be true. Magnani approached acting as if it were life lived on a more intense level, Brando as life viewed introspectively—an exercise in self-awareness. The combination was an uneasy blend of Italian neorealism and the Method. The presumed chemistry between Magnani and Brando, as the unloved wife and her scapegoat lover, was passion aestheticized in the service of myth—Orpheus as a Christ figure, restoring his Eurydice to the life of the body, only to lose her to the forces of intolerance and hatred that neither can withstand.

The Fugitive Kind was the underside of *The Rose Tattoo,* with carnality reduced to symbolism (snakeskin jacket, a guitar as the lyre, a burgeoning fig tree, evocations of Christ's Passion with the Orpheus figure experiencing his "crucifixion" on Easter Sunday instead of Good Friday).

Despite *The Fugitive Kind*'s lukewarm reception, Magnani wanted to work again with Wallis. In 1961 she wrote him about the title story in a collection called *Sagapo* by Renzo Biaison, believing it would make a good film. When Wallis demurred, Magnani was disappointed but would not allow her personal feelings to jeopardize their friendship: "Nothing has changed. I embrace you and hope to see you soon in Rome where you will be welcomed with the same joy and affection as ever. Kisses."[20]

Magnani's American career was more of a reflection on Hollywood than on Wallis's inability to come up with anything for her comparable to *The Rose Tattoo*. Although Magnani was older than either Lancaster or Brando, it was only by a few years. But she looked as if she had transcended chronology, so that what was age to others was experience to her. Magnani may have been forty-five when she made *The Rose Tattoo,* but the amount of living etched into her face could not be measured in years. Thus, she could only be earth mothers to men in need of a maternal lover, which was not exactly the most recyclable scenario. Even in Italian cinema, Magnani's features were unique; hers was the beauty of broken pillars and cracked frescos. It was a face with its own archaeology, best suited to a country like Italy where ruins are considered art.

CHAPTER NINE

Two Jokers and a King

W HEN THE INDUSTRY LEARNED that a team consisting of a crooner and a zany was Wallis's latest discovery, there was speculation that either the starmaker had lost his magic touch or it had been tarnished by his association with Paramount. Paramount had a reputation for farce and slapstick comedy; the Paramount brand, however, tended to include music, so that the result was not musical comedy so much as comedy interspersed with music. Thus, the Paramount comics— Gil Lamb, Cass Daley, Betty Hutton, and Eddie Bracken—often appeared in this anomalous kind of movie, in which there was singing, clowning, and the wisp of a plot (e.g., *Star-Spangled Rhythm* [1942], *Rainbow Island* [1944], *Out of This World* [1945], and *Duffy's Tavern* [1945]).

Wallis understood the Paramount tradition, which was never more apparent than it was in the *Road* movies, in which Bing Crosby, Bob Hope, and Dorothy Lamour went globe-trotting, sending up verisimilitude by making less-than-covert references to themselves, the studio, and the series. By the end of World War II, the series, which originated in 1940, was sputtering out, although there would be two more attempts to reunite the trio: *Road to Rio* (1947) and *Road to Bali* (1952); three, if one counts *Road to Hong Kong* (1962), in which Joan Collins was cast in the part that Lamour had hoped to play. Instead, Lamour was given the equivalent of a walk-on.

In 1948 Lamour's career was in a downspin; although Hope's and Crosby's would continue for two more decades, each would move in other directions—with Crosby achieving some degree of recognition for his attempts at serious drama, winning an Oscar nomination for his performance as an alcoholic actor in *The Country Girl* (1954).

In 1948 there was a vacuum at Paramount when it came to comedy. Preston Sturges had left the studio, Mitchell Leisen was biding his time, and Billy Wilder was upholding the Lubitsch tradition, in which there was no place for slapstick. Cass Daley's roles were getting smaller, as were Gil Lamb's; Eddie Bracken had reached his peak with two Preston Sturges films, *Hail the Conquering Hero* and *The Miracle of Morgan's Creek* (both 1944). That left Betty Hutton, who discarded her "blonde bombshell" image when she replaced Judy Garland in the film version of Irving Berlin's *Annie Get Your Gun* (1950) at MGM. After that she made only two more films for Paramount: *Somebody Loves Me* and *The Greatest Show on Earth* (both 1952), the latter arguably her best; Hutton's movie career ended with *Spring Reunion* (1957), a United Artists release.

Wallis never intended to fill the comedy vacuum at Paramount in quite the way that he did. His years at Warners taught him studio tradition. Once a studio has committed itself to a type of film, as Warners had to the crime film, the genre must be perpetuated. The comedy musical, as opposed to the musical comedy, had been a Paramount staple since the 1930s. Paramount embarked upon this new kind of movie with the coming of sound. It was neither a musical as such nor a conventional comedy, but a movie with musical numbers that were more often diversions than integrated with the plot: in short, not musical comedy, but comedy musical.

It was natural for this kind of film to originate at Paramount. Adolph Zukor, without whom there would have been no Paramount, began in exhibition—with an arcade on New York's Union Square, which had the usual coin-operated peep shows but also boasted of an area where those who preferred sound to image could listen to records. And so the visual and the aural were housed under the same roof. That practice continued even after the formation of Paramount Pictures. In 1929 Zukor acquired a half interest in CBS, which he had to give up a few years later when Paramount nearly went bankrupt.[1] However, at the time Zukor was thinking of an alliance between radio and film. Small wonder, then, that Paramount courted radio performers, such as George Burns and Gracie Allen, Bing Crosby, and Bob Hope, who had their own shows; and singers such as Martha Raye, Lanny Ross, and Shirley Ross, who appeared regularly on the air.

When Barney Balaban, later to become president of Paramount, went into exhibition in Chicago with Sam Katz to create the theater chain of Balaban & Katz, vaudeville became part of the bill at select theaters—specifically, the movie palaces with exotic names like the Marborough and the Granada. That tradition continued for many years at Paramount's flagship theater in New York, appropriately called the Paramount, at 1501 Broadway, whose stage door was thronged during the 1940s by screaming bobby-soxers waiting to get Frank Sinatra's autograph or a piece of his clothing.

Rather than make movie musicals, Paramount chose the flip side, the musical movie, which originated in 1929 with *Innocents of Paris* and the better-known *Cocoanuts;* the latter was the Marx Brothers' first film, based on George S. Kaufman's Broadway hit with songs by Irving Berlin. *The Cocoanuts* could no more be called a musical than *A Night at the Opera* (1935) could, despite excerpts from *Il Trovatore* and the presence of Kitty Carlisle and Allan Jones. To paraphrase the title of Victor Borge's popular one-person show, *The Cocoanuts* was a comedy with, not in, music. Except for such Lubitsch delights as *The Love Parade* (1929) and *Monte Carlo* (1930), the high mode was in short supply at Paramount during the 1930s and virtually disappeared after that. Lubitsch viewed life as if it were an operetta—a frothy affair, where people burst into song because, in certain circumstances, speech would be too banal. In *Monte Carlo,* Jeanette MacDonald, sitting in a train compartment in just her slip, looks out the window and suddenly breaks into "Beyond the Blue Horizon." The song was not exactly motivated, yet the sequence is undeniably charming. Paramount's lesser movies-cum-music of the 1930s followed the same "throw-in-a-song" format, except that they never brought viewers to such supremely giddy heights.

Many of the Paramount musicals of the 1930s starred Bing Crosby, whose first film for the studio, *The Big Broadcast* (1932), capitalized on the singer's public and private selves; Crosby was cast as a character with the name of "Bing Crosby"—an irresponsible boozer, a ladies' man, and such a loser in the game of love that he attempts suicide. Gradually, Paramount softened Crosby's image to fit the contours of a romantic lead, who looked so laid-back that he never seemed to have done a day's work in his life. In *Here Is My Heart* (1934), Crosby is able to retire in his thirties and do a Huck Finn—not on a raft but on a luxury liner, growing so enamored of Kitty Carlisle that he pretends to be a waiter. In *Waikiki Wedding* (1937), Crosby, who is supposed to be doing public relations for a pineapple company, behaves more like a beachcomber. Several of Crosby's musical movies were lesser versions of Lubitsch, lacking the touch that turned dross into silk; still, *Here Is My Heart* and *Waikiki Wedding* had the same operetta-like themes— rich man–poor girl *(Heart)*, and deceiving man–gullible girl *(Wedding)*— that Lubitsch could have made magical.

By the 1940s, slapstick had become part of the Paramount musical movie; actually, it had been introduced earlier in such truly lowbrow fare as *Many Happy Returns* (1934), *Mountain Music* (1937), and *Give Me a Sailor* (1938), which were really B movies with musical numbers and a good deal of horseplay.

Paramount legitimated slapstick with *Road to Singapore* (1940), inaugurating the *Road* series, which never sank into the bogs of the lowbrow because of the witty dialogue, inside jokes, and songs such as "Moonlight Becomes You" (*Road to Morocco* [1942]) and "Personality" (*Road to Utopia* [1945]) that went on to become standards. Originally conceived as *The Road to Mandalay*, perhaps with George Burns and Gracie Allen in mind, *Road to Singapore* was recast as a "two guys and a girl" movie, with Crosby and Hope as the guys and Lamour as the girl. In the early 1940s, the only major director at Paramount who did not think slapstick was infra dig was Preston Sturges; by adding slapstick to a blend of social consciousness, sentiment, and romance, Sturges created an idiosyncratic and highly personal kind of film.

With the coming of World War II, Paramount decided audiences wanted belly laughs, too, which would be delivered on a regular basis with the *Road* movies as well as lesser fare; the latter (e.g., *Nothing but the Truth* [1941], *The Fleet's In* [1942], *Sweater Girl* [1942], and *The National Barn Dance* [1944]) embellished with a few musical numbers to compensate for the threadbare plots.

The formula for the *Road* movies never varied: an exotic locale, a logic-defying plot, and a fade-out in which "the crooner [Crosby] gets the girl."[2] When Wallis arrived at Paramount in the summer of 1944, he was well aware of the series' popularity; when the *Road* series ended in 1962, Wallis would not have been surprised to learn that it had made Paramount $50 million richer; he already knew that the *Road* movies were the most popular series in film history. Had he lived to see the creation of the Library of Congress's Film Registry in 1989, he would have understood why *Road to Morocco* eventually made the list of films selected annually for their historical or cultural significance, thus becoming candidates for preservation. Audiences flocked to *Road to Mo-rocco*; before academics discovered intertextuality and intersubjectivi-ty, Crosby and Hope were tossing in allusions to their costar ("I'll lay you eight to five that we meet Dorothy Lamour," whom they had al-ready met in *Road to Singapore* and *Road to Zanzibar* [1941]); Crosby and Hope even took on Paramount in *Road to Utopia*, in which they poked fun at the studio's logo, the star-spangled mountain. Having seen his share of vaudeville, Wallis knew Crosby and Hope were the descen-dants of the straight man and the comic—a familiar combination but far more polished than the teams that played the circuits. Paramount's team consisted of America's favorite crooner and a deadpan comedian who was a consummate ad-libber with a way with a joke. Wallis, however, needed a younger—and considerably more hip—Crosby and Hope; "the girl" would not have to be the same actress, since he was not thinking of a trio but of a comedy act that could transfer to the screen.

Wallis knew that he had come to a studio where a successful formu-la existed and was waiting to be implemented. He intended to imple-ment it—not with Paramount's contract talent, but with his own.

When Wallis caught "the boys," as he called Dean Martin and Jerry Lewis, at New York's Copa in 1948, he immediately saw a way of con-tinuing the comedy musical at the studio that virtually invented it. Later that year, after he saw them again in Los Angeles at Slapsie Maxie's Café on Wilshire Boulevard (owned by ex-fighter Maxie Rosenbloom), he made an offer that apparently exceeded anything Martin and Lewis received from other studios: the usual seven-year contract that, if the options were picked up, would begin with $50,000 a picture and in-crease incrementally, reaching $125,000 in the sixth and seventh years.[3]

Martin and Lewis made their film debut in *My Friend Irma* (1949), based on the popular CBS radio show about the New York adventures of two young women—the practical-minded Jane and the scatterbrained Irma. Marie Wilson, radio's Irma, was also the film's; Wilson made a career out of playing "dumb blondes," despite the fact that she was a highly intelligent woman. Like Judy Holliday and Marilyn Monroe, she was destined to be stereotyped.

Although Wilson was playing the title character, she was upstaged by Lewis, who romped through the movie as if it were his private pre-serve. Everyone, including Martin, receded into the background while Lewis did his simian shtick, sprinting around with his hand in a clawlike position from squeezing too many oranges. While Martin was crooning and Wilson was doing her dizzy-dame routine, Lewis walked off with the picture, as even the venerable *New York Times* critic Bosley Crowther had to admit.

Because Lewis knew he could never be taken seriously either as a dramatic actor or a romantic lead, he compensated by feeding his ego so voraciously that he alienated Martin and finally Wallis. Lewis was also aware that his talent, undervalued by those who found farce inferior to drawing-room comedy, would be appreciated by others who never thought burlesque was beneath them. And for the ones who did, there was always the latest Billy Wilder or George Cukor movie.

Although Wallis has said that Martin was easier to deal with than Lewis, the truth is that both were victims of the sudden-success syndrome. The boys were not actors, or at least not when they started in pictures. They were still performers without the discipline or even the respect for the craft that make most overnight movie sensations proceed with caution, always careful to live up to the studio's expectations. Wallis had not expected loose cannons. Naturally, he was furious when the team appeared on NBC television on 3 April 1949, when *My Friend Irma* was a week away from completion, and performed a brief excerpt from the film without his permission. When Martin and Lewis were featured on the *Colgate Palmolive Comedy Hour* on 20 September 1950, they aroused the anger of the Council of Motion Picture Organizations because they poked fun at exhibitors; Wallis had no other choice but to issue an apology.

On rare occasions, Lewis could be humble. When Wallis tried to persuade him to tone down his antics in the *My Friend Irma* sequel, *My Friend Irma Goes West* (1950), Lewis realized he had exceeded even the flexible bounds of slapstick when he saw the rushes. Chastened, he sent off a note to Wallis: "I shall respect your decisions from here on in. Thanks, Boss."[4] Most of the time, however, Wallis was either appeasing the press or brushing up against Lewis's ego. When Maurice Zolotow wrote that Martin's role in *3 Ring Circus* (1954) was so small that Lewis insisted it be enlarged, Wallis fired off a reply, claiming it was not true.[5] Actually, it was true, and the reason Martin's role had become irrelevant was that Lewis kept insisting on adding comic business that was not in the script. Martin even wondered why he was in the movie, which revolved almost exclusively around Lewis.

Although in 1954 Martin and Lewis were two years away from breaking up, Wallis knew it was only a matter of time before they would go
their separate ways. After they decided how to play a particular scene,
Lewis did what he wanted anyway, making everything work to his advantage and thus upsetting Martin, who felt like the second banana in
burlesque. Lewis's behavior grew worse; the press dubbed him "the
problem child" after he walked off the set of *Don't Give Up the Ship*
(1959), interrupting filming for a half day. When he appeared at the
Sands in Las Vegas, he remained on stage for an hour and a half, making a second show impossible. While comedy has a long tradition of
being offensive, 1950s television audiences had not heard of Aristophanes
and commedia dell'arte. Television critic Jack O'Brien excoriated Lewis
for his tastelessness, particularly his tendency to ridicule people with
disabilities and physical shortcomings.[6]

Lewis knew he had become difficult but could not change. He was
determined to elevate his brand of slapstick, which he believed was in
the tradition of Chaplin and the other great silent clowns, to the level of
art. That French critics eventually agreed with him must have seemed
like vindication. But in the 1950s Lewis could not have known that he
would be lionized; he only wanted recognition, which meant taking
another route: directing, producing, and occasionally writing his own
films.[7]

In 1948, around the same time that Wallis had signed up Martin and
Lewis, their agent, Abbey Greshler, involved them in a seven-picture
deal with Screen Associates—the creation of the shady Ray Ryan, who
had deep pockets and a dark past. The following year, Greshler encouraged them to form their own independent company, York Productions,
which Greshler envisioned as a way of getting out of flesh-peddling and
into producing.[8] York, which was bankrolled primarily by Ryan, was
intended as a microcosmic Wallis-Hazen—a concentric entity within
the Paramount macrocosm. It was a hasty decision. Martin and Lewis
were not quick studies; Wallis had decided to go independent after years
of toiling under the yoke of Jack Warner, a fate Martin and Lewis were
spared. Unlike Harold Hill in *The Music Man* (1962), they didn't know
the territory.

It was a comic scenario worthy of Frank Capra: two Hollywood
neophytes getting suckered into independent production—their own
company and another's—while under contract to an Oscar-winning pro-

ducer at a major studio. Martin and Lewis must have been desperate to become independent—but of what or whom? Wallis, whom they hardly knew, or Paramount, where they had just arrived? It almost seemed as if Martin and Lewis regarded movies as the equivalent of gigs, where they would go from one engagement to another. There is an enormous difference between juggling club dates and honoring commitments to a production company at a major studio (Wallis-Hazen); at another (Screen Associates) that lacked a Hollywood pedigree, which Martin and Lewis were expected to provide; and at their own (York). If no one can serve two masters, serving three—Wallis-Hazen, Screen Associates, and York—would have required multiple personalities, of which Lewis was capable only on film. When Screen Associates realized that Martin and Lewis could not possibly deliver what they had foolishly agreed to, Ryan decided to cash in on the high grosses that *At War with the Army* (1950) was racking up and hit all the parties—Martin and Lewis, York, and Wallis—with a lawsuit.[9] Rather than become embroiled in litigation, Martin and Lewis gave up their majority interest in the film.

York continued for five more years, although none of the films Martin and Lewis made under the York banner did anything for either's reputation: *The Caddy* (1953), *Living It Up* (1954), *You're Never Too Young* (1955), and *Pardners* (1956), all of which were Paramount releases but not Wallis productions. However, Wallis, sensing that York might come up with some real moneymakers, met with Lewis on 2 February 1952 in Phoenix, Arizona. Wallis then wrote up an account of their discussion that he included at the end of his autobiography (*Starmaker*, 215–18), along with selectively chosen memos attesting to his extraordinary producing talent—to which archival material can attest.

It is a puzzling document, composed in the form of a memorandum without the name of the intended recipient, suggesting that Wallis wrote up the discussion for his own use and perhaps to share with Hazen in case of litigation. Wallis was aware of the Screen Associates suit that had occurred the previous year and took delight in reminding Lewis that, as a result, *Jumping Jacks* (1952), which was supposed to have been a York production, ended up as one of Wallis's.

At some point in 1951, Martin and Lewis wisely decided to switch agents, signing with MCA, then the most powerful talent agency in the entertainment industry. They were now represented by Lew Wasserman, MCA's president, and Taft Schreiber. No film neophytes could

have found a more formidable pair to do their negotiating. According to
Wallis's write-up after the Phoenix discussion, he sought a one-third
share in York and an arrangement whereby Martin and Lewis would
make one film a year for him and one for York. In a sense, the distinction did not matter, since all the films would be Paramount releases;
however, if there was money to be made, Wallis wanted his share. Martin and Lewis were, after all, his discoveries.

At first, Wasserman declined Wallis's offer to purchase stock in York;
Wasserman also wanted a drastic revision of the release schedule that
Wallis had prepared, which, if Wallis had consented, would mean a year
could go by without a Martin and Lewis film that was a Hal Wallis
production. That turned out not to be the case. The facts speak for them-
selves. From 1951 to their final appearance as a team in *Hollywood or
Bust* (1956), Martin and Lewis made two films for Wallis in 1951 (*That's
My Boy, Sailor Beware*); one in 1952 (*Jumping Jacks*); three in 1953
(*The Stooge, Scared Stiff,* and *Money from Home*); one each in 1954 (*3
Ring Circus*), 1955 (*Artists and Models*), and 1956 (*Hollywood or Bust*).
Interspersed with these were the York productions, which, after the *At
War with the Army* fiasco, were evenly spaced: *The Caddy* (1953), *Liv-
ing It Up* (1954), *You're Never too Young*) (1955), and *Pardners* (1956).

Apparently the York deal had no effect on the release pattern that
Wallis had worked out. It is impossible to know from his write-up whether
Wallis got his one-third of York Productions, although it is hard to believe that a shrewd deal-maker like Lew Wasserman would pass up such
an offer, especially since the stakes were far from high. Wasserman could
not possibly have believed that York would have the same longevity as
Hal Wallis Productions, much less Wallis-Hazen; and Wallis was too
clever to allow his latest discoveries to form their own production company while they were under contract to him, without getting his cut.

By the time York was dissolved, so was the team of Martin and
Lewis. After breaking with Martin, Lewis began moving further away
from Wallis and closer to the independence he craved. In 1957 he produced his first film, *The Delicate Delinquent;* the following year, he
produced two more: *Rock-a-bye Baby* and *The Geisha Boy*. As a new
producer, Lewis realized that he had often behaved badly in the past. He
wrote an eleven-page typescript, "Observations of a New Motion Picture Producer" (1958), a copy of which Wallis must have read since it
ended up in his Collection.[10] Had the text been circulated at the time, it

might have healed some wounds. But Lewis put down on paper what he would never say in person: "I would like to begin by making an apology to the producers whom I served as actor, for some of the headaches I gave them with my Katzenjammer antics while making their pictures." What followed was a catalog of generalities, culminating with "From Happy Operations Come Happy Pictures." If some of the individuals to whom Lewis had given such grief had read "Observations," they would have either laughed or emended the maxim to read: "From Unhappy Operations Come Happy Pictures at the Expense of the Unhappiness of Others."

In 1959, when Lewis was about to turn director with *The Bellboy* (1960), he decided to express his gratitude to Wallis in the form of a silver plaque: "There were tears in Lewis's eyes, none in Wallis'."[11]

Afterward, Lewis made only two more movies for Wallis, *Visit to a Small Planet* (1960) and *Boeing Boeing* (1965). Both originated as stage plays, with *Visit* starting as a teleplay by Gore Vidal, who later expanded it into a successful Broadway comedy with Cyril Ritchard in the lead. *Boeing Boeing* was a hit in London and Paris but flopped in New York. Lewis was not the lead in *Boeing Boeing;* that was Tony Curtis, playing a Don Juan who was able to juggle relationships with three different flight attendants until their schedules changed. As the sidekick, Lewis was curiously subdued; he obviously knew that he was playing a secondary role and behaved accordingly, which suggested that he either realized his place or sensed that Curtis was a bigger draw. *Boeing Boeing* did not suffer in its transfer to the screen; it was still a bedroom farce with the requisite number of doors. *Visit* lost virtually everything that made it an entertaining yet provocative comedy. Lewis could never step into a part created by Cyril Ritchard, a classical actor whose patrician voice turned everything he did into a Restoration comedy. Ritchard suggested that extraterrestrials had class; Lewis made it seem as if they all grew up watching the Three Stooges (or Lewis's earlier comedies with Martin).

Dean Martin made a few more films for Wallis after his breakup with Lewis—*Career* (1959), *All in a Night's Work* (1960), *The Sons of Katie Elder* (1965), and *Five Card Stud* (1968). While Lewis was struggling to create a place for himself in the comic pantheon, Martin was playing clubs, appearing on television, achieving notoriety as a member of the Rat Pack (which led to his making several films with "chairman of the board" Frank Sinatra), and starring in a string of movies that revealed a modest talent that could be exploited in serious drama, romantic comedy, caper films, and westerns. By the time Wallis was ready to make *Katie Elder,* Martin had become more popular than Lewis; he was also a tough negotiator. When Wallis approached Martin about the film, the actor asked for script approval because other studios were courting him. Eventually, Martin got his way, not only in terms of the script but also in delaying production for almost three months. No longer was Martin interested in long-term contracts; *Katie Elder* was a one-picture deal, followed by a two-picture contract that he fulfilled with two catastrophes, the unfunny *All in a Night's Work* and the western disaster *Five Card Stud.* Except for *Career* and *Katie Elder,* Martin's best films— Vincente Minnelli's *Some Came Running* (1958) and *Bells are Ringing* (1960) and Howard Hawks's *Rio Bravo* (1959)—were not Wallis productions.

By the late 1940s, Wallis had seen the future—and it was television, which was already encroaching on film. Variety shows such as *Broadway Jamboree, Arthur Godfrey and His Friends,* and *The Ed Sullivan Show* had reached the small screen; once such entertainment had been the preserve of the studios, which periodically mounted star-studded extravaganzas to show off their talent. Even radio was losing out to television; some shows succeeded in making the transition to the tube, such as *Burns and Allen, Arthur Godfrey and His Friends,* and *The Jack Benny Program;* others—including *Fibber McGee and Molly, The Fred Allen Show,* and *Lum and Abner*—were not meant for the cool medium.

By the mid-1950s, Wallis sensed he would be losing the team of Martin and Lewis; even if each stayed on with him, it would never be the same. Wallis needed a celebrity—a 1950s equivalent of a 1930s radio star. That meant television. Wallis realized that it was a gamble. Warners had gone that route earlier with "Mr. Television" himself, Milton Berle. But after *Always Leave Them Laughing* (1949), the studio realized it had made a mistake.

As for pop singers who appeared on TV variety shows, few of them found movies a congenial medium. Vic Damone did not last very long at MGM, although he sang beautifully in *Kismet* (1955); Peggy Lee won an Oscar nomination for *Pete Kelly's Blues* (1955), but then it was back to records, clubs, and television. Gogi Grant's contribution to Warners's *Helen Morgan Story* (1957) was providing the singing voice for Ann Blyth in the title role. Fox hired Johnny Ray for *There's No Business Like Show Business* (1955), but how could he compete with such pros as Dan Dailey, Ethel Merman, Mitzi Gaynor, Donald O'Connor, and the camera-savvy Marilyn Monroe?

Voice was not Wallis's chief requisite; magnetism was. There was no point in raiding sitcom talent, since television stars like Jackie Gleason and Lucille Ball would not bring in young audiences; the market Wallis was targeting was the same one that had earlier responded to Martin and Lewis. Either on Saturday evening, 28 January 1956, or on a Saturday in February, Wallis tuned into CBS-TV's *Stage Show* and found his answer. Since Wallis was never much for specific dates, it could have been 28 January, when a young singer by the name of Elvis Presley made his television debut. Many watched the show because the hosts were the venerable Dorsey brothers, Tommy and Jimmy, whom those of a certain age identified with the "big band" era. To others, the main attraction was the great jazz artist Sarah Vaughan. But the one who dominated the half hour was a rock 'n' roller from Memphis, who tore into "Heartbreak Hotel" like a wrecking ball—inspiring a new generation of swooning fans and going far beyond the Sinatra syndrome, genteel by comparison, to become a modern Dionysus. Whenever it was that Wallis saw Elvis on *Stage Show,* he knew he had found his answer to Martin and Lewis in one performer.

Sexual currents ran through Elvis's body, making his gyrations seem as though they came from a network below the waist that had been genetically programmed. Elvis's was a natural eroticism that, at times, was touchingly innocent. And it was that sexual innocence that endeared Elvis to those who were able to raise their gaze from his pelvis to his face, realizing that his body was only responding to the music.

Although Wallis has written that Elvis Presley was "a joy to work with, in every way" (*Starmaker,* 147), there is one biography of the entertainer that, while acknowledging Wallis's role in shaping Elvis's film career, also alleges that the producer "eventually ruined him."[12] Actually, Elvis ruined himself; what Wallis did was turn a rock 'n' roller into a movie star, whose iconic stature rests more on his recordings and documentaries about him than on his thirty-two films, only nine of which were for Wallis.

To Wallis, Elvis was a media celebrity who could easily fit into the movie-cum-music that had become a Paramount staple. Before meeting

Elvis in person, Wallis was determined to put him under contract. That
meant negotiating with his manager, Colonel Tom Parker, and convincing the Colonel that his protégé could become a film star. The Colonel
did not need much convincing. When Elvis and Wallis finally met, Wallis was amazed at the disparity between Elvis's public and private selves:
"[Elvis] was quiet, soft spoken, gentlemanly, and very modest."[13] On 23
March 1956 Wallis asked Frank Tashlin, who had just directed the Martin and Lewis movies *Artists and Models* (1955) and *Hollywood or Bust*
(1956), to test Elvis for a secondary role in *The Rainmaker*. Wallis thought
it best to proceed gradually—starting with a "gosh-darn" hayseed character, for which Elvis's natural drawl would be perfect. The problem,
however, was the leads: Burt Lancaster and Katharine Hepburn. Elvis
would be playing Hepburn's younger brother, which would make audiences wonder how two such dissimilar siblings, with totally different
speech patterns, could come from the same set of parents. As it was,
Hepburn was too old for the part, so that Lancaster found himself ro-
mancing an older woman again—this time a middle-aged virgin instead
of an Italian widow.

The screen test showed Elvis could act; that was the reaction of
both Wallis and Hazen—the latter believing that Elvis had more potential as an actor than a singer. If Wallis thought so, too, he could not
admit it. Wallis knew the public would never accept Elvis in straight
roles. They wanted the singer; if they could have the actor too, all the
better.

At first Elvis felt awkward around Wallis; when he kept declining
Wallis's luncheon and dinner invitations, Wallis sought an explanation,
not realizing that, despite his cool demeanor, Elvis was ill at ease among
film executives—especially someone with Wallis's credentials. It turned
out to be a case of mutual misunderstanding: Wallis thought Elvis was
snubbing him; Elvis, that Wallis was losing interest in him. When the
Colonel phoned Wallis to inform him of an Elvis concert, he was told
that Wallis was out of town, which was not the case.[14]

Wallis soon learned that Elvis preferred that he deal with the Colonel. Wallis had no problem with that, having experienced his share of
agents, managers, and hangers on—and the Colonel was all three. Wallis had great plans for Elvis; however, he was still using the gradual
build-up approach. When Elvis was given his first contract, Wallis assumed he would be making his film debut in *The Rainmaker;* hence the

meager terms in view of the role: $15,000 for one picture during the 1 June 1956–31 May 1957 period. When *The Rainmaker* was no longer a possibility, Wallis was at a loss to come up with a suitable vehicle, wanting to be certain that Elvis's first Hal Wallis movie revealed the "soft spoken" and "modest" young man along with his pelvic persona.

Meanwhile, Elvis's agents at William Morris were on the lookout for a film in which he would not be eclipsed by stars on the order of Lancaster and Hepburn. The Colonel concurred, wanting as little competition as possible for Elvis. When Fox offered Elvis $150,000 and third billing after Richard Egan and Debra Paget (neither of whom constituted a threat) for *Love Me Tender* (1957), Wallis reluctantly agreed to a loan-out, reminding the agency that he and Hazen had discovered Elvis's screen potential: "We were, in fact, the first motion picture producers to recognize his motion picture possibilities and also the first to enter into a contract with him."[15]

Love Me Tender was such a huge success that Wallis issued Elvis a new contract: $2,500 a week plus a bonus of $100,000. The contract was more than justified when Elvis's first film for Wallis, *Loving You* (1957), opened. *Loving You* had enough personal overtones (a press agent who discovers a guitar-playing youth and makes him into rock star) to convince audiences that the character of Deke Rivers (Presley) bore a vague resemblance to the actor himself. If so, Elvis, like his movie counterpart, was a paradox—a media-savvy country boy, a balladeer, and an exhibitionist; comfortable in jeans or gold lamé jackets, on dirt roads or city streets, on bandstands or in theaters. *Loving You* revealed all these facets, making them more complementary than contradictory. That Elvis often mumbled the lyrics did not trouble his fans, who considered them incidental to the real performance, which was Elvis himself: the uninhibited showman, with legs apart and pelvis thrust out; head slightly lowered to suggest covert eye contact with an audience he could not see but knew was looking back—if not above his waist, then below it. Yet when Elvis sings the title song in an outdoor setting, like a farm boy at a picnic, it is with such prayerlike simplicity and reverence that it seems like a wedding hymn.

Part of Elvis's art was his ability to give audiences double their money: he could be the sensualist, doing the equivalent of bumps and grinds; and the troubadour, strumming his guitar as if it were a lyre and he a poet.

Lizabeth Scott's performance as Glenda, the press agent capable of being both manipulative and compassionate, was as much a revelation as Elvis's. Although she had second billing, she was clearly the female lead and had a role as important as Elvis's. Looking trim and elegant, Lizabeth took a character that could easily have been unsympathetic and made her the kind of publicist any newcomer would welcome. But what was even more impressive about Lizabeth's performance was her rapport with Elvis, which revealed a deep respect for him and his talent. Deke's falling in love with Glenda might have seemed strained in the script, yet Lizabeth and Elvis interacted so well with each other that theirs became the natural attraction of a protégé toward a patron. The most powerful scene in the movie is the one in which Glenda and her discovery drive to a cemetery where she learns that the singer, who calls himself "Deke Rivers," took that name from a gravestone to assume a new identity after losing his parents. The naturalness with which Lizabeth and Elvis played the scene—he with the wrenching sincerity of an overdue confession, she with the humility of someone to whom another has bared his soul—suggests that, under different circumstances, each might have taken a different career route. Certainly Lizabeth had more roles in her, but there would be only one more movie, *Pulp* (1972), a cult favorite. And Elvis only had a few more opportunities to show that he really could act, even though his movie career lasted longer than Lizabeth's.

One such opportunity was his second film for Wallis, *King Creole* (1958), loosely adapted from Harold Robbins's *Stone for Danny Fisher,* which Wallis bought for a mere $25,000. To create a song-driven movie, the setting was changed from Chicago to New Orleans; hence, the more marketable title, *King Creole*. The plot, however, remained the same: street kid turned celebrity, this time from boxer to entertainer. Since Mike Curtiz had made a similar film at Warners, *Young Man with a Horn* (1950), with Kirk Douglas as a trumpet player who traversed a similar route—with detours into the wrong milieu and the wrong woman—Wallis knew his old friend was the ideal director for *King Creole*.

The problem was Elvis, whom the aristocratic Curtiz considered a phenomenon, not an actor. Still, Curtiz accepted the challenge, which resulted in mutual respect. Black and white may not have been the format Elvis's fans wanted, but it enabled Elvis to reveal a flair for melodrama that would have been undermined by color. Elvis found the key to Danny's character: anger, which Elvis possessed in abundance, often resulting in the destruction of whatever was at hand—from television sets to jukeboxes.[16] Whether Curtiz knew that the source of that anger was Elvis's growing awareness that he was becoming more of a commodity than a person—a transformation Elvis felt powerless to reverse—is problematic; Curtiz knew the anger was there and that he had to tap into it. In John Garfield, Curtiz had located a different kind of anger, which he exposed so powerfully in *The Breaking Point* (1950), another film about a decent man (Garfield) who is almost destroyed when his life spins out of control as a result of a single transgression.

The black-and-white photography gave a noirish look to the New Orleans streets, with the requisite flashing neon providing the contrast. Even Elvis's hair had a noir look, slicked up into a shiny blackness that matched the mean streets. He drew on the same combination of surliness and sensitivity that worked so well in *Loving You,* except that it had now acquired a volatility, so that one never knew if the surliness would turn into violence (it did) or the sensitivity into indifference (it did that also).

The songs ran the gamut from blues to ballads, revealing Elvis's best and worst qualities. The best were the guitar-accompanied renditions; the worst, the rock 'n' roll gyrations that took precedence over the lyrics, which he slurred into verbal mush. The sound was sexy, but the words were unintelligible. Elvis was surrounded by an especially strong supporting cast, notably Dean Jagger, Walter Matthau, Dolores Hart, and Carolyn Jones, who was especially convincing as Matthau's ill-starred mistress. Although Dolores Hart was again the love interest, her main function was to provide a contrast with the Carolyn Jones character, whose selfless devotion to Danny results in her death. In his scenes with both actresses, Elvis revealed that he could play hardboiled with Carolyn Jones and do the romantic bit with Dolores Hart. Contrary to reports that Elvis and Curtiz were constantly clashing on the set, the opposite seems to have been true. Mother Dolores Hart found that Curtiz was most supportive of Elvis, which corroborates what Elvis himself thought.[17]

The success of *Loving You* made Wallis and the Colonel fast friends. Hollywood friendships, however, are based on expediency. Colonel Parker was not above badgering Wallis about scripts and directors and specifying how bonuses were to be paid; if Elvis was to receive a $25,000 bonus, it would consist of \$5,000 for the first week and \$2,500 weekly thereafter for the next eight weeks.[18] By 1963 the Colonel wanted the same \$25,000 bonus that Elvis was given six years earlier.

Wallis had no difficulty indulging the Colonel, even when he asked to be technical adviser on one of Elvis's films, so that it would net him more money. The Colonel was even given an office on the Paramount lot. When Wallis forgot to arrange for a parking space and the Colonel was stopped at the gate, he soon heard about it.

Initially, the Colonel was pleased with the way Elvis's film career was progressing, as was Wallis. The two began exchanging gifts: the Colonel gave Wallis elephant figurines, while Wallis reciprocated with custom-made Sy Devore shirts and suits. Still, there was bound to be friction, especially since the Colonel was determined to get the best deal for his discovery as well as for himself.

Once Elvis became a movie star, the Colonel vetoed any tie-ins with television, including promos with Elvis singing numbers from his latest release. The Colonel wondered, "Why should anyone want to buy a ticket to see and hear a motion picture when they can hear the songs on television for free?"[19] That mentality, however, did not stop recording artists from singing or lip synching their latest single on both variety and talk shows; and if the song was from a film, all the better, since they could promote the soundtrack as well as the movie.

Although the Colonel did not have complete script approval, he was sent scripts as a courtesy. The Colonel was not a fast reader; he kept putting off reading the *Roustabout* script until Wallis had to press him for a response. Finally, the Colonel replied that after reading half of the script, he felt it was "too high class." The Colonel's concept of class was unusual, to say the least; there is nothing "high class" about a movie dealing with carnival people. Wallis decided to ignore the Colonel and put *Roustabout* (1964) into production; the result was the kind of film that neither enhances nor diminishes anyone's reputation.

To understand the impact Elvis had on American culture, one has only to look at the public's reaction to his being drafted into the army in 1958. Since 1973 the draft has been on hold, and generations of males have grown up without the slightest fear of interrupting their careers to serve two years in the military. In 1958 the draft inspired various emotions: fear in those who felt they could not endure regimentation; anger in the career-driven who cursed any obstacle in their way to the executive suite; and anticipation in those who believed the experience could work to their advantage. Elvis had become such a symbol of the American dream that any attempt to avoid serving his country would have been tantamount to treason, especially in cold war America. John Wayne could get away with not serving during World War II because his movies—especially *Flying Tigers* (1942), *The Fighting Seabees* (1944), *Back to Bataan* (1945), *They Were Expendable* (1945), and *Sands of Iwo Jima* (1949)—made it seem as if he had, albeit on the screen, which was the next best thing.

Elvis had enough self-confidence to endure a career hiatus, especially since his induction was a media event that meant continued coverage even in the army. The coverage started with his physical. In 1958 the average inductee was not photographed in his skivvies during a physical. Elvis was—and looked heavier than he did on the screen. No matter. Elvis was a son of Uncle Sam, more concerned about doing his duty than the state of his abs and pecs. Elvis was also America's poster boy. Paramount's foreign department handled the publicity for Elvis's arrival in Germany, where he would be stationed. Five thousand fans, along with newspaper, magazine, and television reporters, turned out in Bremerhaven to greet him.

Wallis was already making plans for Elvis's return by sketching out the terms of a new four-year contract: In addition to making four pictures for Wallis, Elvis would also be allowed to do two outside pictures the first year, one each in the second and third years, and two in the fourth. Financially, it was a good deal: $125,000 for each Wallis production, plus $50,000 per film for expenses. Each film would involve eight weeks of work; if longer, Elvis would receive two weeks' salary, with the expense allowance prorated. After that, it would be salary only, prorated for a five-day week, at $21,875 weekly.

Since Wallis intended to capitalize on Elvis's army experience in *G.I. Blues* (1960), he was disturbed to hear about the Colonel's negotiations with another studio. The Colonel had to be reminded that legally Wallis had the right to produce Elvis's first film after his discharge. An amicable resolution was reached when Wallis agreed to pay Elvis $200,000 plus an additional $50,000 for expenses.

Although *G.I. Blues* was minor Elvis, the star enjoyed working with the director, Norman Taurog, who made him feel confident about his acting. Thus Elvis wanted Taurog for his next film, *Blue Hawaii* (1961).

Wallis had no problem with Elvis's request; however, he did have a problem with his appearance, particularly since the Hawaiian setting required beachwear. After seeing Elvis in MGM's *Viva Las* Vegas (1963), Wallis was shocked at how "soft, fat, and jowly" he had become and how his hair had taken on a "wiglike inky blackness." Since *Roustabout* was ready to go into production with Elvis as a carnival worker, Wallis placed the responsibility on the Colonel to get Elvis back in shape: "When [Elvis] comes out here again I hope he will have trimmed down as this is a very serious concern for us and for him as it could have a detrimental effect on his entire career."[20] Wallis even went to far as to recommend the use of an ultraviolet lamp so Elvis could look tanned.

Getting a tan and shedding some pounds would not restore that sly sensuality that Elvis the innocent projected in *Loving You*. *Blue Hawaii* revealed a more worldly Elvis, who seemed at home in an environment where nature's lushness provides an incentive for easy living. The film was a popular success, some of which the Colonel attributed to Norman Taurog. The Colonel was eager to make Elvis and Taurog a team: "Taurog . . . works very easily with Elvis. Elvis has great respect for him. . . . You and I both know Mr. Taurog doesn't watch the clock and is a hard worker and knows what he is doing."[21] That may have been true, but for reasons unknown, Elvis got John Rich for *Roustabout,* his next film, whose chief attraction was the presence of Barbara Stanwyck; even in a supporting role, Stanwyck brought the star quality of the past into the present, which looked all the poorer by comparison.

As the 1960s progressed, the Colonel became increasingly prickly. While his relationship with Wallis had not deteriorated, it had begun to resemble the usual one between manager and producer. When the Colonel discovered that Honda executives managed to get hold of a print of *Roustabout,* in which Elvis was shown driving a Honda, he complained to Wallis, asking for an explanation.[22] None of Wallis's staff could come up with an answer. Since *Roustabout* was a Paramount release, someone at the studio, probably in distribution, had furnished Honda with a print.

Meanwhile Wallis went on paying bonuses, which the Colonel accepted. But that did not stop the Colonel from making further demands, proposing that in 1966 Elvis be paid $500,000 a picture, plus 20 percent of the profits. Wallis felt he could not authorize such an arrangement without consulting with Hazen, who was vacationing in Istanbul. Hazen naturally objected, although there is no way of knowing how the matter was resolved. Hazen knew Elvis's days as a movie star were numbered; an overweight rock 'n' roller might continue to perform in concert, but younger audiences, who had not experienced the Elvis phenomenon in the 1950s, would find nothing appealing about a chunky thirty-year-old. Approving a release date of Easter 1967 for *Easy Come, Easy Go* (1967), Hazen wrote: "I strongly believe that this will be Elvis's last good picture."[23] Actually, it was his last picture for Wallis, and it was not particularly good.

In 1965, when Elvis was about to make *Paradise, Hawaiian Style* (1966), he had no idea that two years later his association with Wallis would end. He had come to consider the Paramount lot as his and the Colonel's second home. Elvis had been using Jerry Lewis's former dressing room in a building whose ground floor could easily have been converted into a suite of offices for the Colonel's All Star Shows. The plan never materialized. After *Easy Come, Easy Go,* Elvis continued to make films, each as unmemorable as the last, until 1969. Eight years later, he died. In many ways, Elvis was the victim of an industry that was becoming so corporatized that talent was subservient to profits. In the mid-1960s, as Paramount was nearing the end of being an autonomous studio and about to become a subsidiary of Gulf + Western, Elvis was just a source of revenue. Realizing that Elvis's days as a movie star were drawing to a close, Paramount, which controlled the distribution rights, would reissue packages of his earlier films to coincide with the release of his latest feature. One such "Special Presley Package," *Girls! Girls! Girls!* (1962) and *Fun in Acapulco* (1963), was scheduled for February 1967, a month before the release of his latest movie, *Easy Come, Easy Go,* as if audiences could not get enough of Elvis. Hazen and Wallis had to explain to Paramount, which seemed to have no long-term memory, that during the two years (1958–60) that the star was in the army, there were no new Elvis pictures. Assuming that the summer of 1959 would be an ideal time for a rerelease package, Paramount reissued *Loving You* and *King Creole* with disappointing results; the revenues told the story: $74,000 for *Loving You,* $86,000 for *King Creole.*

To be brutally honest, after *Roustabout,* Elvis's appearance and the quality of his movies deteriorated noticeably. Innocence gave way to experience, and sensuousness to sleaze. The pace at which Elvis kept making movies—fifteen between 1965 and 1969—indicated that he had become a cash cow with limited milk. All that mattered to Paramount was getting exposure for the films, on television or in rerelease, before the distribution rights expired. That the country boy had become an overweight man made no difference, nor did the fact that he was doing less singing and more acting in his movies, as if preparing for the day when it would be just acting. Elvis, however, never had to worry about adopting a new image. With *Change of Habit* (1969) his Hollywood days were over.

Allowing Elvis to make thirty-one movies in twelve years (1957–69) was blatant exploitation, the culprit being not so much Wallis, for whom Elvis made only nine, as the Colonel, who complained that he never made as much from Elvis's movies as he did from his television appearances and recordings: "We do not mix our motion picture career in any way with a television career, especially if we are not in on the profits of a picture. This I learned from you [Hazen] a long time ago, and I am grateful for the teachings."[24] Even if Elvis had made all of his films for Wallis, the producer would never have given Elvis such over-exposure, because he knew it would result in surfeit. The correspondence between the Colonel and Wallis, and between the Colonel and Hazen, is filled with talk about bonuses, complaints about letters with no checks, accolades for Fox, where the Colonel received attention bordering on obeisance when Elvis was making *Love Me Tender* (gold cuff links from producer Buddy Adler, a chauffeur, an office and a secretarial staff). The Colonel had "gone Hollywood" in a way that Elvis had not. Wallis was right when he called Elvis "gentlemanly" and "modest." Such qualities, unfortunately, are liabilities in Hollywood. Wallis himself may have been gentlemanly, but he was never modest.

Despite the "happy days" (*Starmaker,* 152) that Wallis claims to have spent with Elvis, he could not have been other than saddened by the turn Elvis's career took in the early 1960s. Wallis was never one to wear his heart on his sleeve; rather than trash the films that Jerry Lewis directed and produced, he merely noted that "there is no reason to comment on their quality" (*Starmaker,* 146). And yet at the beginning, Wallis and Lewis were friends—at least to the extent that a producer and an actor can be, until the friendship ruptured because of a clash of egos. With his early discoveries, the scenario was simple: debut, loan-out, sink or swim. Although Wallis may have envied or even craved the kind of closeness that he observed between Burt Lancaster and Kirk Douglas, it could never be. If so many of his stars addressed him as "boss," it was because that's what he was. And no boss can be a friend to his employees. It is even difficult with a partner—especially someone like Joseph Hazen.

In 1944 the Wallis-Hazen partnership was the Hollywood version of Damon and Pythias. Initially, it was. Paramount even thought so, especially after the success of *My Friend Irma*, which was budgeted at $500,000 and made more than $5 million. In March 1950 Paramount renegotiated the Hazen-Wallis contract, giving the company 75 percent of the gross in North America and Hawaii, 70 percent in the United Kingdom, and 35 percent in all other territories. Payment would be withheld until Paramount recouped its investment and reimbursed itself for the production costs. Until then, Wallis-Hazen would receive $125,000 per film, with further profits divided 66⅔ percent (Paramount)–33⅓ percent (Wallis-Hazen).

Although in two years Wallis-Hazen Productions would be dissolved, it would emerge Phoenix-like under the Wallis banner, with Hazen very much a presence without a specific title. In 1952 Hazen informed the press, in effect, that he and Wallis had bitten off more than they could chew: "The history of the business proves that too many individual producers, using their own money as we do, have gotten into trouble and wound up broke because they didn't know when to quit."[25] This did not spell the end of the Wallis-Hazen partnership. There would still be joint ventures—but one picture at a time.

Hazen's explanation was consistent with what had been happening in the industry since the end of World War II. The growing popularity of television, the mass closings of theaters, the proliferation of drive-ins, the exodus to the suburbs, new priorities that placed education and home ownership above entertainment, and particularly the consent decrees that forced the studios to divest themselves of their theater chains were among the many factors that could be cited to show that Wallis-Hazen was irrelevant in a changing Hollywood, especially since it was just an umbrella for Hal Wallis Productions, which would remain intact when the umbrella collapsed.

Hazen, however, omitted some relevant information. Wallis-Hazen, Inc., was financed, according to Wallis (*Starmaker,* 114) by a revolving fund of $2.5 million arranged by Serge Semenenko, a curious figure in Hollywood history.

Born in Russia, Semenenko and his parents fled their native land when the Bolsheviks came to power in 1917. With many émigrés, the journey to America is a circuitous route. In the Semenenkos' case, there was a stopover in Constantinople en route to the States. The family seemed to have settled in New England. However, someone like Serge Semenenko always has gaps in his résumé. What is known is that Semenko graduated from Harvard Business School in 1926; his degree and a vice presidency at First National Bank of Boston ensured his entrance into the world of high finance. However, his tendency to lend money to companies in which he also held stock led to his being forced to resign in 1967. Until then, Semenko had been the financial wizard of Hollywood. After helping to finance Wallis-Hazen, Semenenko started buying up stock in Universal, which he then sold to Decca (at a profit, of course), facilitating Decca's takeover of Universal in 1952.[26]

The films that Wallis produced for Paramount, however, were another matter; they were financed by the studio through an arrangement that included profit-sharing. Thus Wallis was correct when he said that he did not bankroll his own films. Wallis-Hazen was a different entity. Paramount may have placed its facilities at Wallis's disposal, but production is only one aspect of the entire moviemaking process. In 1944 Wallis was thinking of a production company based at a studio where he could make his own films, including optioning properties and signing up writers. That required money; hence the need for Wallis-Hazen—at least initially. The studio itself was unimportant; that it turned out to be Paramount was merely the result of a confluence of circumstances that gave Wallis a permanent home for a quarter of a century. In 1944 he could not have known he would spending more than half of his career there. At the time Paramount was the distributor of his films and the home of his production company. Paramount had the easy part: it only had to finance Wallis's films, which would add a few more releases to its annual output. That Wallis encountered no interference and achieved the autonomy he desired was irrelevant. As far as Paramount was concerned, Wallis's films helped fill the pipeline.

There was a price to pay, which is often the case when one member of a team is more creative than the other. And there was no doubt that Wallis was that member. When Hazen realized his subordinate role, he retaliated with his own list of grievances. By 1952 Hazen had grown tired of languishing in obscurity while the lion's share of the publicity for what he considered "their films" went to Wallis. In his autobiography, Wallis would have one think that their friendship endured for the twenty-five years the two of them spent at Paramount.

In December 1952 Hazen fired off a letter to Wallis, accusing him, among other things, of taking the credit for discovering Martin and Lewis.[27] Judging from Wallis's four-page reply (10 December 1952), the letter was steeped in vitriol. Wallis was clearly hurt but rational. He admitted that Hazen may well have seen Martin and Lewis's nightclub act first; however, it was not until *My Friend Irma* was about to go into production that Wallis decided to hire the team, even though it meant adding two new characters to the script. Hazen was so desperate for recognition that he also criticized Wallis for not crediting him for drawing up their contract, as if Hazen should have been commended for doing what he was expected to do: "You are an attorney . . . and the negotiation and protection of our contracts and interests is definitely your function."[28]

Hazen regarded himself as far more valuable to Wallis than he really was. He chafed at being ignored by entertainment writers, most of whom had no idea who he was. Since Hazen chose to live in New York, he was removed from the epicenter of production, which is all that matters to journalists. Hazen was simply not good copy, and to a certain extent neither was Wallis. But Wallis's films were, and by extension so was he as their producer.

Wallis also implied that Lita Annenberg Hazen was in league with her husband: "You (and Lita) were cruel in hanging me without a trial."[29] But the bid for recognition was part of a larger scenario: the liquidation of Wallis-Hazen.

In 1951 Hazen requested a bigger stake in the company; at first Wallis was loath to offer it, but he finally agreed after the success of the first Martin and Lewis films. But Wallis drew the line at splitting the company 50-50, particularly since production required more money, time, and genius than drawing up contracts. As far as Wallis was concerned, it would remain 75 (Wallis)–25 (Hazen).

And so, when Hazen indicated that he wanted to dissolve the company, Wallis agreed. The demise of Wallis-Hazen, Inc., did not spell the end of Hal Wallis Productions nor the Paramount connection. In Hollywood, bridges are rarely burned, merely charred. Under the new arrangement, Hazen remained as the legal counsel of Hal Wallis productions and Wallis's occasional business partner. But they would

never experience the same camaraderie they knew when they were starting out. Hazen's sticking with Wallis, although in a much different capacity, was understandable; he would have been foolish to sever
connections with the business in which he had spent virtually his entire
career. Besides, Hal Wallis Productions needed someone to manage the
New York office.

By 1958 Wallis had second thoughts about New York. He had produced only two films that year, *Hot Spell* and *King Creole*—a far cry
from 1938, when he produced sixteen and thought nothing of it. The
glory days were over, and Wallis saw no need for Hazen to remain in
New York, since it was mainly the home of the advertising and sales
divisions. Nor was it necessary for Irene Lee to be a full-time story
editor, with so few films in production. Wallis practically begged Hazen
to move to Los Angeles, where he could be of more use, particularly
since, as he pointed out, the industry is really controlled by a dozen
actors who can command their own fees, making negotiating with agents
a complex and enervating task. Wallis wanted to be relieved of as many
legal responsibilities as possible.[30] Then Hazen was not amenable to
relocating, although later he and Lita bought a home on South Mapleton Drive near Wallis's. Even so Wallis continued to correspond with
Hazen, usually when he was in a quandary and needed a sounding board.
When he was desperate to cast the role of Alma, the sexually frustrated
spinster in Tennessee Williams's *Summer and Smoke,* he reeled off the
names of Audrey Hepburn, Eva Marie Saint, and Jean Simmons. He
was even reconsidering Shirley MacLaine, despite Tennessee Williams's
objections, and questioned the need to involve Williams in the casting.
Grudgingly, Wallis agreed to test Geraldine Page, who won the part that
brought her such acclaim when she performed it off Broadway in the
early 1950s. It was one of Page's finest performances. Wallis's reluc-
tance to think of Page first, particularly since she was the actress most
identified with the part, was characteristic of the new Wallis: the producer who thought in terms of "stars"—or rather the stars who, along
with their agents, controlled the business—leaving the rest to the new-
comers and those of a certain (or specific) age who came cheap, or
cheaper than they did in their salad days.

As Wallis and Hazen grew older, each became testier. During the
1960s their relationship kept deteriorating until, by 1971, the bridge
had become so badly burned that it was ready to be demolished. Wallis

expected Hazen to negotiate with television networks interested in leasing the rights to his films. Hazen, however, proved to be a disaster. Wallis was shocked to learn that Hazen settled for a mere $1 million from NBC for *Becket,* insisting that the arrangement should have been $1.75 million for two showings or not less than $2.25 million for three.[31]

Wallis needed a different partner—someone younger and craftier, who was capable of striking a hard bargain because he or she knew that cementing the deal was the first step to becoming a producer. However, Wallis had to rely on a man of retirement age who resented his partner's fame but did not mind profiting from it financially.

Since New York was Hazen's turf, he wanted an office of his own—not in the old Paramount building at 1501 Broadway, but at a different location, 1345 Avenue of the Americas. Wallis, whose unprivileged childhood was the reverse of Hazen's, questioned the move, especially since it suggested a dyarchy—with Hazen supervising advertising and publicity in New York and Wallis supervising production in Los Angeles. When Wallis chose to use an outside public relations firm to promote *Anne of the Thousand Days* and *True Grit* (both 1969), Hazen bristled at being bypassed. As far as Wallis was concerned, that was none of his business. The business was Wallis's.

Hazen continued to go his own way—making copies of vouchers to lessen Wallis's profits; submitting bills for a three-room suite in London for himself, Lita, and a maid, as well for car rentals. Ironically, the Hazens could have paid for the boondoggle themselves. By 1971, when Wallis was in his early seventies, he decided to unleash the resentment that had been building up for two decades: He accused Hazen of becoming independently wealthy through his efforts. That was not entirely true, given Lita's background, although even Hazen would have had to admit that he did better with Wallis than he could have on his own: "The pictures I have made have made you a wealthy man." "Wealthier" would have been more accurate, but there was no disputing Wallis's awareness of his place in film history: "My name has come to mean something in selling pictures. . . . I'm sure even your best friends would tell you your association with me was the deal of the century."[32] Wallis was then four years away from leaving the business and would die a decade later. Hazen would outlive him by six years.

That was the end of another dubious friendship.

Phoenix Rising

A s the 1950s came to an end, Wallis may have felt that his producing career was concluding also. After Shirley Booth and Anna
Magnani won their Oscars for *Come Back, Little Sheba* and *The
Rose Tattoo*, there was little else but Martin and Lewis; then there was
Martin minus Lewis, and vice versa; and Elvis. Few doubted that
Katharine Hepburn would be nominated for *The Rainmaker*, but only
diehard fans expected her to edge out Ingrid Bergman in her return to
the screen in *Anastasia* (1956). After Joanne Woodward's bravura performance in *The Three Faces of Eve* (1957), Anna Magnani did not
stand a chance with the poorly received *Wild Is the Wind;* her best actress nomination was the Academy's way of acknowledging her art in a
film that lacked it. Although Wallis prided himself on his ability to make
successful movies out of stage plays, a number of Broadway hits of the
1950s—for example, *Picnic, Cat on a Hot Tin Roof, Bus Stop, Witness
for the Prosecution, The Diary of Anne Frank,* and *Auntie Mame*—slipped
past him.

When Wallis finally decided to turn a play into a movie, he went off
Broadway. James Lee's *Career* may have had a decent run in Green-
wich Village; however, moviegoers, unfamiliar with the ways of the
theater, found little that they could identify with in the 1959 film version. The sacrifices an actor makes in his quest for fame had personal
meaning for Wallis, who knew from experience that sacrifice is a dou-
ble-edged sword, cutting the sufferer, who in turn learns to wield it against
others. The cycle of betrayal, disillusionment, regret, and a late but dubious triumph was one that Wallis knew too well. Wallis, however, was
in the minority; even the Academy ignored the powerful performances

of Anthony Franciosa as the actor on the rise, Shirley MacLaine as his alcoholic wife, Carolyn Jones as his agent, and Dean Martin as an unprincipled director. In 1959 there was one sure Oscar winner: *Ben-Hur,* which won in eleven categories, including best picture, best director, and best actor. The actor was Wallis's discovery, Charlton Heston.

The Wallis of *Casablanca; Now, Voyager;* and *Watch on the Rhine* seemed to have disappeared in the bogs of commercialism. By the end of the 1950s, Wallis was yearning for a return to the past, even though he knew that the forces that created the studio system could never recombine. Wallis's past was that of Warner Brothers, where he made most of his best films. What did he have to show for his Paramount period that was comparable to *Captain Blood, Dark Victory, The Roaring Twenties, The Letter, Sergeant York,* or *Yankee Doodle Dandy*—not to mention *Casablanca, The Maltese Falcon,* and *High Sierra*?

Naturally, there were enough Wallis productions at Paramount that, for want of a better word, are termed "interesting"—films with enough stylish touches, unusual plot twists, or creative camera work to distinguish them from typical genre fare. No film noir opened like *The Strange Love of Martha Ivers*—with a prologue culminating in a murder on a staircase, where the murderer is a child, the victim her hateful aunt, and the witness a boy, who takes part in a cover-up that sends an innocent man to his death. And there was never a woman's film like *Paid in Full,* in which a woman runs over her sister's child—and then atones by getting pregnant so she can make up for the tragedy, knowing she might die in childbirth. Although *Martha Ivers* may not rank with such classic noir as *Detour, Double Indemnity,* and *Scarlet Street,* it also cannot be dismissed as just another melodrama; nor can *Paid in Full* be written off as a weepie, even though it is no *Dark Victory.*

Wallis sought a comeback, and he found it on Broadway.

Despite his Anglophilia, Wallis made few films at Warners—and none at Paramount—that dealt with British history, particularly the monarchy; the closest was *The Private Lives of Elizabeth and Essex.* When Wallis saw Jean Anouilh's *Becket,* he knew he had to make the movie version. *Becket* opened in New York on 5 October 1960 for a run of 193 performances, featuring one of those dream casts—Laurence Olivier as Thomas Becket and Anthony Quinn as King Henry II—that producers rely on to sell a historical drama by a French intellectual. *Becket* did not duplicate the popularity of *The Lark* (1955), Anouilh's only play to enjoy a financially successful New York engagement. No doubt the subject matter of *The Lark*—the story of Joan of Arc—had more appeal than the complex relationship between Henry and Becket. But much of the credit was also due to Lillian Hellman, who adapted Anouilh's *L'alouette* (retitled *The Lark* by Christopher Fry, whose poetic translation was used for the London production). Unlike Fry, Hellman was a commercial playwright, not a verse dramatist. She made Anouilh palatable to Broadway audiences, minimizing the play's self-consciousness and emphasizing the character of Joan as a rebel who prefers death to compromising with mediocrity.

Becket needed someone like Hellman to turn debate into drama; instead, the production was given a stellar cast, an elaborate production, and a serviceable translation by Lucienne Hill, which was far closer to Anouilh's original than Hellman's "adaptation" of *L'alouette* was.

Oddly, *The Lark* never became a movie, perhaps because the last attempt to film Joan's life, *Joan of Arc* (1948) with Ingrid Bergman, fared so poorly at the box office. Wallis must have seen *The Lark* during the 1955–56 season but apparently found it unfilmable. *Becket* was another matter. For one thing, it was more of a traditional play than *The Lark,* which was conceived as a reenactment of Joan's life by actors aware of themselves as performers. *Becket* is relatively straightforward without the interplay of illusion and reality that characterizes so much of Anouilh; its only concession to theatrical convention is a framing device: the play begins and ends at Thomas Becket's tomb, where Henry is awaiting flagellation by Saxon monks in atonement for Becket's assassination, which he tacitly endorsed.

Wallis was so taken with the play that he saw it twice. He realized there were problems: the rhetoric needed a good purge; and the disquisitions on honor (the play is subtitled "The Honor of God") had to be simplified without obscuring Anouilh's thesis that the honor of God takes precedence over the duty to one's king. The Norman Conquest, a given in the play, needed to be clarified for moviegoers; an opening title would—and did—provide the background, along with the distinctions between Norman (Henry) and Saxon (Becket), both of whom had been reduced to conqueror and conquered, respectively. The historical Becket was a Norman, but that would not have served Anouilh's purpose.

There were several plays Wallis could have seen during the 1960–61 season that eventually reached the screen, but not under his aegis: *A*

Taste of Honey; Period of Adjustment; All the Way Home; Mary, Mary, Come Blow Your Horn; Critic's Choice; Send Me No Flowers; and *Under the Yum-Yum Tree.* Of all the plays he could have optioned, he chose *Becket.* Perhaps the play awakened his dormant Anglophilia, conjuring up images of on-location shooting. Perhaps, also, the relationship between Henry and Becket mirrored so many of Wallis's own failed friendships. Becket and Henry, former drinking and whoring companions, came from totally different backgrounds—not unlike Wallis and Jack Warner or, more so, Wallis and Joseph Hazen. Although Anouilh had taken on a historical subject, he was still a playwright, subordinating history to the cause of drama. Thus, it would have made no sense to make Henry and Becket Normans, even though they were. Becket was often misidentified as a Saxon and thus a victim of the Norman Conquest; however, he was a Norman from the merchant class—and a well-educated one at that. For the sake of contrast, Anouilh's Becket is a Saxon, whose father "collaborated" with the Normans in order to survive—a point that would not have been lost on French audiences familiar with their country's methods of dealing with its Nazi occupiers, who were shunned, resisted, or accommodated. Anouilh had created a similar subtext in his version of Sophocles' *Antigone* (1944), performed during the Nazi occupation, in which Antigone was meant to represent the French Resistance and Creon, collaborationist Vichy. The French may have gotten the point, but when Anouilh's *Antigone* reached Broadway in 1946, its appeal was not its political subtext, and much less its classical origins, but its stars: Katharine Cornell and Cedric Hardwicke.

Similarly, the collaboration motif was not muted in *Becket*'s New York production, although one wonders how many theatergoers made the connection with Vichy France. Lucienne Hill's translation has Becket and his father profiting from collaborating with the Normans: the father financially, the son professionally. Initially, Becket takes advantage of his relationship with Henry to enjoy the good life. However, after Henry appoints him chancellor of England and later archbishop of Canterbury, Becket cannot remain Henry's minion. The honor of God transcends all else. Like Joan, Becket achieves sainthood through martyrdom: Just as Joan refused to renounce her voices, Becket would not allow Henry to interfere in Church affairs. Each understood the risks of disobedience; each accepted the consequences.

When Wallis saw *Becket,* he must have felt waves of recognition washing over him, as he witnessed a relationship founded on servility that grew into friendship and deteriorated into antagonism. He had gone that route with Jack Warner, whom he tried to serve, until it became impossible to maintain his integrity and at the same time play prime minister to Hollywood's clown prince. But there was also a great deal of Henry in Wallis. Like the king, Wallis the producer expected obedience, particularly when it came to responding to his numerous memos, which were rarely commendatory. Usually they were critical; Wallis's pet peeves were directors who deviated from the script, did not adhere to shooting schedules, shot too many takes of the same scene, or failed to put in what he considered a day's work. Wallis knew the frustration of relying on others with skills that he lacked but sorely needed; he also experienced the loneliness that comes from imposing industry rules on artists who might have to break them to produce art, and with whom thereafter he can no longer be friends. A memo written after a director has shot a scene five different ways is merely a warning against future excesses—which, if the director is William Wyler, will not be heeded.

Wallis could appreciate Henry's frustration as Becket gradually moved out of his orbit and into that of the Church. Finally, as a producer who had to leave the studio that was home to him for two decades, Wallis, like Becket, understood the need to sever ties that bind too tightly.

Wallis was convinced that *Becket* would reinvigorate his career, which, for ten years, had lacked a truly prestigious film. He was determined that *Becket* would at least garner a best picture nomination (as it did), which would be his first since *The Rose Tattoo*.

Casting was paramount. Olivier and Quinn were far too old for their roles; Broadway audiences are willing to suspend disbelief more readily than moviegoers. For the film, Wallis wanted a Becket with matinee idol looks, a 1960s Errol Flynn. Only one actor qualified: Richard Burton, who, after playing Mark Antony in *Cleopatra* (1963), was still in a heroic frame of mind. For Henry II, Wallis pursued Peter O'Toole, who was the desert's equivalent of Melville's "handsome sailor" in *Lawrence of Arabia* (1962), leaping across the tops of trains with his robes billowing in the wind. It was assumed that Peter Glenville, who staged the New York production, would also direct the film version; Wallis and Glenville had worked together in *Summer and Smoke* (1961).

When Burton discovered that O'Toole, whom he admired, would

Silent star Louise Fazenda, Wallis's first wife. Private collection.

Martha Hyer in 1956, ten years before she became his second wife. Courtesy AMPAS.

Martha and Wallis on their wedding day, 31 December 1966.

The Wallises on their tenth anniversary.

(Above) President Reagan and the producer at the Wallises' Malibu home. (Below) The Wallises, President Reagan, and his wife Nancy at the Los Angeles County Museum's 1982 tribute to the producer.

(Above) Left to right: director George Cukor, Martha, director Anthony Harvey, and Katharine Hepburn (whom Harvey directed in *A Lion in Winter*) on the patio of the Malibu home. *(Below)* Martha, Wallis, and John Wayne with his black eye patch during the shooting of *True Grit* (1969), for which Wayne won his only Oscar.

(Above) The Wallises on location in Colorado for *True Grit. (Below) Left to right:* Bob Hope, the Wallises, Ronald Reagan, civil rights advocate Justin Dart, and Dolores Hope on New Year's Eve, 31 December 1962.

A treasured moment in 1972: Martha beaming as Queen Elizabeth II thanks Wallis for teaching Britons about their history.

The Wallis crypt at Forest Lawn in Glendale, California.

Lola Lane, for whom Wallis could do little to make her into a star. Courtesy AMPAS.

Corinne Calvet, a Wallis discovery whose physical attributes compensated for her limited talent. Courtesy AMPAS.

Lizabeth Scott, Wallis's first Paramount star. Private collection.

Kristine Miller as the glamorous Mrs. Richardson in *I Walk Alone* (1948). Courtesy Kristine Miller Schuyler.

Vanessa Redgrave as the ill-starred title character in *Mary, Queen of Scots* (1971). Private collection.

Douglas Dick, who played leading roles in Wallis's productions of *The Searching Wind* (1946) and *The Accused* (1948). Courtesy Dr. Douglas Dick.

Walter Seltzer, Wallis's director of publicity (1945–54), who enjoyed a second career as a successful producer. Courtesy AMPAS.

Michael Curtiz, Wallis's favorite director. Private Collection.

A *Casablanca* (1942) lobby card. Private collection.

Robin (Errol Flynn) and Maid Marian (Olivia de Havilland) in *The Adventures of Robin Hood* (1938). Private collection.

Burt Lancaster and Oscar winner Shirley Booth in *Come Back, Little Sheba* (1952). Private collection.

Lancaster and another Oscar winner, Anna Magnani, in *The Rose Tattoo* (1955). Private collection.

(Above) Drinking buddies turned adversaries: Henry II (Peter O'Toole, *left*) and Thomas Becket (Richard Burton) in *Becket*. Private collection. *(Below)* Two legends together on screen for the first and only time: Katharine Hepburn and John Wayne in *Rooster Cogburn* (1975), Wallis's last film. Private collection.

(Above) Dolores Hart and Elvis in *Loving You* (1957), the first of their two films together. Courtesy AMPAS. (Below) Reverend Mother Dolores Hart, Abbess, Abbey of Regina Laudis in Bethlehem, Connecticut. Courtesy Reverend Mother Dolores Hart.

be playing Henry, he committed himself wholeheartedly to the project.[1] In a piece written for *Life* magazine, Burton enumerated the challenges he faced as Becket, especially making the transition from collaborationist to church man, whose bed-hopping with Henry is only a detour on a spiritual journey that ends in martyrdom.[2] Once Becket becomes archbishop, he gradually distances himself from his king, friend, and patron, hoping that Henry will understand that he has been replaced by God in Becket's hierarchy. The film remains true to Anouilh's play, in which Becket and Henry are thrown into roles they have no other choice but to play: Becket, the former servant-turned-rebel, committing an act of disobedience in the name of the Church, and Henry, the betrayed monarch, who is unwilling to order Becket's death, preferring to entrust it to others. If anyone is a collaborationist, it is Henry; whether or not Henry knew of the assassination that the barons had planned for 29 December 1170, he used Becket's death to his advantage, winning over Saxon dissidents by performing penance and declaring Becket a saint.

In both play and film, Becket and Henry undergo a transformation that radically changes each of them. Burton believed that whoever played Henry had to understand the peculiar nature of the king's friendship with Becket; originally, it was one of inequality that might have remained that way had Henry not made Becket archbishop of Canterbury, thereby unwittingly forcing Becket into a role that required him to favor the interests of the Church over those of the Crown. The problem is that Henry had accepted his "role" as king earlier; Becket was then a member of Henry's supporting cast, not yet playing the lead. But when Becket took center stage, albeit in his own theater, he could no longer remain in the background.

Just as *Becket* had personal significance for Wallis, it became a mirror for Burton's own distrust of religion, which he inherited from his father and which haunted him throughout his life. Although he defined himself as an agnostic, Burton spoke eloquently of his empathy with Becket, "burned by the fury of his own awful and terrible belief"—a belief for which Burton also seemed to be striving.[3]

O'Toole had played his share of men who had seen their illusions shattered: *Hamlet* on the stage, T.E. Lawrence and Conrad's "Tuan (Lord) Jim" (*Lord Jim* [1965]) on the screen. Thus he had no problem understanding Henry with his penchant for revelry and sex, but it was his incredible bonding with Burton that produced the chemistry the film required. Both heavy drinkers, they swore off the bottle until they felt sufficiently acclimated to each other, at which point they hit the pubs. And if the banquet scene, in which Henry is completely besotted, seemed unusually realistic, it was because O'Toole had been drinking for twelve hours. Since union regulations would not allow filming after 6:00 P.M., and the banquet that degenerates into a free-for-all was scheduled for a 9:00 A.M. shoot, O'Toole spent the interim "preparing."[4]

What Burton and O'Toole brought to the roles, and what Olivier and Quinn did not, was the sense of a homoerotically charged friendship. In the scene where Becket washes and dries Henry's back and chest, it is evident that Henry enjoys the sensual experience of being bathed. The most moving scene in the film is not the murder in the cathedral, which is ritualized martyrdom, but the parting of Henry and Becket on the bleak Northumberland coast, each unable to clasp the other's hand, as they square off on horseback. Henry poignantly recalls the time when Becket used to bathe him. "I stink," Henry cries, admitting that he has not bathed since their estrangement. Theirs was a relationship that could never be consummated, since neither desired the other as a lover, but only as a friend, despite the Queen Mother's insistence that their bond was "unnatural." Actually, it was quite natural: Henry commanded, Becket obeyed. What the Queen Mother did not understand was that their greatest pleasure derived from each other's company. The wenching and boozing was perfunctory, the sort of thing expected of lusty males, whether they enjoyed it or not. In this sense the film is faithful to Anouilh's concept of theater as a *jeu*, a game, where the players enact the author's ideas—here, the idea that the pursuit of pleasure is only a diversion until something higher beckons. Thus both Becket and Henry played at being carousers, as scripted by the unknown scenarist who declared that males achieve manhood in the ale house and the brothel, and females achieve womanhood in the kitchen and their husband's bed.

The real tragedy in both play and film is not Becket's inevitable martyrdom but Henry's inability to step out of the role of king, in which he had been typecast by history. Becket's last words, "Poor Henry," are apt; Becket at least knows he has upheld the honor of God, but Henry must continue to court a clergy whom he despises, absolve himself from a crime that he encouraged by complaining to the barons about "the meddlesome priest," and finally realize that the days of his youth that could have continued indefinitely, if Becket were alive, were over—leaving in their wake a middle-aged king with an unloving mother, a shrewish wife, and a doltish son.

Since *Becket* was Wallis's bid for Oscar recognition, no expenses were spared. Knowing it was impossible to ascertain what Canterbury cathedral looked like in the mid-twelfth century, he instructed art director John Bryan to draw on whatever information he could find about church architecture of the period to construct a reasonable facsimile on stage H at Shepperton Studios, where most of the interiors were filmed.

From the first shot of Henry striding across the plaza and mounting the stairs of the cathedral, the camera moving with him until he reaches Becket's crypt, where he prepares to do penance, one is never in doubt about being in the presence of an epic film, perhaps not as grandiose as *Ben-Hur* but considerably more human. The opening was a harbinger of other epic touches, such as Becket's consecration as archbishop and his murder on 29 December 1170 as he was about to celebrate vespers. The vespers sequence evokes the same feeling of isolation and resignation that the evangelists describe in their accounts of Christ's passion when, on the eve of his crucifixion, he prayed on the Mount of Olives, asking his Father, if possible, to remove the cup from which he was to drink the next day; then, realizing the divine will was part of a divine plan, he conceded: "Not my will, but thine be done." A murder in a cathedral, whether Becket's in Canterbury or Archbishop Romero's in El Salvador, indirectly recalls Christ's passion. In *Becket,* when the barons interrupt the service, killing both Becket and the monk attending him, Becket cries out to God, "Oh, how difficult You make it all!" It is hard not to think of the agony in the garden when Christ, in effect, expressed the same sentiments but then acquiesced. Like Christ, Becket realized that the honor of God is a heavy cross to bear: "How heavy Your Honor is to bear!" the dying Becket whispers. Yet he bore it, as did Christ, Joan, and myriads in the world's martyrologies.

For a mass audience, many of whom would have found the film's theology both baffling and irrelevant, there were enough instances of ecclesiastical chicanery, including an opportunistic Pope Alexander III; bedroom bawdiness; family squabbles with Henry tongue-lashing his entire household; and debates on principles versus expediency that religion took a backseat to spectacle and human drama. There were apparently enough moviegoers who found themselves in Becket's or Henry's camp, or in both, to make the film a hit.

To make certain that *Becket* would be a Hal Wallis production, and not "A film by Peter Glenville," Wallis had no qualms about chiding the director for being behind schedule and cutting in camera, thereby giving the editor, Anne V. Coates (with whom Wallis collaborated closely) little to work with (*Starmaker,* 220–23). Eventually, Glenville understood what Wallis wanted and provided him with enough long shots for an epic ambience and enough close-ups and medium shots so that the human element would not be obscured by the pageantry.

Although *Becket* received twelve Oscar nominations, including best picture, best actor (both Burton and O'Toole), and best director, it only won for Edward Anhalt's screenplay. In a sense this was a triumph for Wallis, although few were aware of the extent to which he worked with Anhalt and Glenville. Wallis even thought of requesting coscreenplay credit but decided against it, preferring that Anhalt use as much of Lucienne Hill's translation as possible. At any rate, the reviews made it clear that the Wallis of yore had returned to the screen.

In 1960, while *Becket* was playing in New York, Robert Bolt's drama *A Man for All Seasons* was attracting audiences in London for its powerful writing as well as for Paul Scofield's towering performance as Sir Thomas More. When Scofield reprised the role in New York the following year, it became an immediate hit, winning Tonys for best play and best actor. As a play, *A Man for All Seasons* was far more popular than *Becket,* because Bolt's language never sounded lofty. The dialogue even became slangy at times; a character could say "goddamnit" without sounding anachronistic. When More bids farewell to his daughter Margaret, he reminds her of the inevitability of death, speaking as naturally as one would about an old friend. There was no rhetoric, or even poetry. Just eloquence, simple yet moving.

Very subtly, Bolt undermined verisimilitude through the use of a one-person chorus, more Shakespearean than Greek, called the Common Man, who addresses the audience directly at both the beginning and the end of the play. Initially, he is their guide to the sixteenth century, "the century of the Common Man"; but the common man must play many roles to survive. And Bolt's Common Man also functions as More's executioner. In the epilogue, the Common Man becomes the audience's mirror, inviting them to see themselves in what they have witnessed, asking where they would stand in a real-life conflict between conscience and expediency. He reminds them that More may not be breathing, but they are; and if they wish to continue breathing, "just don't make trouble." Because Bolt mixed tragedy, intrigue, and humor (however sardonic), the play enjoyed a much longer run than *Becket*—a phenomenal 637 performances.

It was not long before *A Man for All Seasons* arrived on screen. Since Bolt was also an Oscar-winning screenwriter (*Lawrence of Arabia* and *Doctor Zhivago* [1965]), he adapted his own play, which brought him a third Oscar. *A Man for All Seasons* proved as accessible to movie audiences as to theatergoers; the film had style without ceremonial bluster. Audiences warmed to Scofield's More, who in the film seemed even more of a family man than he did on the stage. At Oscar time, he was the logical choice for best actor, as was the film for best picture. Director Fred Zinnemann's ability to synthesize spectacle and drama merited him an Oscar also.

A Man for All Seasons could easily have been a Hal Wallis production. Yet Wallis seems not to have been interested in optioning the play, perhaps because the theme—disobedience to a king that results in death—seemed too close to *Becket*. The similarity was tenuous. *A Man for All Seasons* was less concerned with rendering to Caesar what is Caesar's and to God what is God's, than with choosing between the Church of Rome and the Church of England, the new creation of Henry VIII, who was both its head and its so-called defender. Becket did not have to make a choice between England and Rome; his was between being Henry's mouthpiece or speaking for himself (and supposedly God). Until his break with Henry, More was the consummate politician; yet even the politician could not swear allegiance to an institution in which he did not believe, and to a monarch who would, if possible, destroy a sixteen-hundred-year institution simply to beget a male successor.

A Man for All Seasons would have been a natural follow-up to *Becket*; that Wallis either passed on Bolt's play or did not even consider it (there is no mention of it in *Starmaker*) suggests that he may have been more interested in Henry VIII's sex life than in More's moral dilemma. Thus, instead of following a film about Becket and Henry II with one about Sir Thomas More and Henry VIII, he settled on one about Henry VIII and his second wife, Anne Boleyn.

During the 1948–49 Broadway season, Wallis saw Maxwell Anderson's *Anne of the Thousand Days* with Rex Harrison as Henry VIII and Joyce Redmond as Anne Boleyn. He paid little attention to it at the time, despite its favorable reviews and Harrison's Tony-award-winning performance. *Anne* was another one of Anderson's semiverse plays, which, with the right actors, could come off on stage (and did with Harrison and Redmond, who toured with it after the New York run). However, the text needed a prose makeover to work as a film. The late 1940s or early 1950s would have been a good time to make the movie version; there was a paucity of historical films then, and the few there were (e.g., MGM's *Quo Vadis* [1951] and *Julius Caesar* [1953] and Fox's *Viva Zapata!* [1952]) had great appeal. But at the time, Wallis was preoccupied with showcasing his latest discoveries, Dean Martin and Jerry Lewis, and looking for that Broadway nugget that could restore his Midas touch, which seemed to be working erratically.

Except for *The Rose Tattoo* and *Come Back, Little Sheba*, which returned him to class-act producer status, Wallis seemed indifferent to theater during most of the 1950s and early 1960s. When he finally optioned a Broadway play, it turned out to be a travesty of the original (*Visit to a Small Planet* [1960]). *Summer and Smoke* (1961) was a vast improvement, marking Wallis's return to the kind of theater he respected; although this reverential adaptation of Williams's chamber play received a couple of Oscar nominations, only one was significant— Geraldine Page, for best actress. Nonetheless, *Summer and Smoke* represented the kind of film Wallis should have been producing during that strange interlude in the 1950s, when so many plays found their way to the screen shortly after their Broadway runs—*The Glass Menagerie* (1950), *A Streetcar Named Desire* (1951), *Death of a Salesman* (1952), *Detective Story* (1951), *The Member of the Wedding* (1952), *Stalag 17* (1953), *The Country Girl* (1954), *Sabrina Fair* (as *Sabrina* [1954]), *Picnic* (1955), *The Bad Seed* (1956), *Witness for the Prosecution* (1959), and *Auntie Mame* (1959)—any of which Wallis could have produced but didn't. Maxwell Anderson's *Anne of the Thousand Days* was a major attraction of the 1948–49 Broadway season, yet twenty years elapsed before Wallis brought it to the screen.

With Wallis, it was always money. He could never shed the mentality with which he grew up, wondering where the next dollar would come from and making sure that when he had it, it was well spent. Even though Hollywood was experiencing retrenchment in the 1950s, there were still enough studio heads willing to gamble on bringing Broadway to the masses, and often without being condescending about it. Wallis, unfortunately, was not a studio head, only an independent producer with a studio base. Throughout his career he had always mingled highbrow with lowbrow, with an occasional upgrade to middlebrow; however, lately, he seemed to be opting for the latter, hoping that his crowd-pleasers would bankroll an occasional quality film. Until then, Wallis would promote the careers of performers, such as Martin and Lewis and Elvis, who could increase their audience base by appearing on television.

Seeing *Becket* in 1960 and making the film version in a historically rich environment reordered Wallis's priorities—at least in theory. Wallis, like any commercial moviemaker, could not commit himself solely to prestige films, which may or may not draw lines at the box office. The next play Wallis optioned after *Becket* was Marc Camoletti's *Boeing Boeing,* a bedroom farce that was a rousing success in London, where he must have seen it; in New York, however, *Boeing Boeing* lasted a mere twenty-three performances; the 1965 movie version is significant for being Jerry Lewis's last film for Wallis. As the 1960s were coming to an end, and Richard Burton was free to play Henry VIII in *Anne of the Thousand Days,* Wallis assumed Paramount would have been so pleased with the success of *Becket* that it would welcome a companion piece. But *Becket* was released in 1964, and by 1967 there was a new regime at Paramount.

Wallis must have sensed in the early 1960s that Paramount was headed for either ruin or rescue—the latter only with a deus ex machina strong enough to keep Herbert J. Siegel and Ernest Martin (the head of a talent agency and a Broadway producer, respectively) from gaining control of the studio. Their attempted takeover was an ongoing saga in the trades, which reported their loutish behavior at board meetings, at which they showed no respect for age or precedent.[5] But their failed coup called attention to the vacuum at the top: Paramount's president, George Weltner, was in his sixties, some ten years younger than his predecessor, Barney Balaban; more telling was the average age of the board: seventy.

As an independent producer, Wallis—then in his late sixties—probably never thought of Paramount as a gerontocracy; he may not have thought of himself as a senior citizen, either. He also expected it would be business as usual after Charles Bluhdorn, president of Gulf + West-

ern, saved Paramount from the clutches of Siegel and Martin by buying
them out and buying Paramount for himself, making it a subsidiary of a
conglomerate with interests in everything from auto replacement parts
and beef to cigars and life insurance.

Bluhdorn was an entrepreneur who had become a millionaire at
nineteen by specializing in commodities. Movies meant sexy starlets
and premieres. What he knew of quality could be seen in his favorite
Paramount films: *Is Paris Burning?* (1966), *The Adventurers* (1970),
and *Paint Your Wagon* (1969). Bluhdorn may not even have seen *Becket,*
since he had been known to walk out of a screening room if a picture
bored him.

Bluhdorn's problem was not so much *Anne* as Burton, whose name
was anathema to him after the actor tried to pull out of a commitment to
provide a voiceover introduction to a Paramount film. Finally, Burton
agreed, on the condition that Bluhdorn buy his (then) wife, Elizabeth
Taylor, a pair of diamond and emerald earrings that Burton could not
afford (*Starmaker,* 166). Burton's demand so infuriated Bluhdorn that
he vowed the actor would never work for him again. Either Bluhdorn
had a short memory, or he relented in 1974 when Burton was back on
the Paramount lot to make one of the worst films in his career or the
studio's history: *The Klansman* (1974). The story about the earrings
may well be true, but Wallis had told *Variety* earlier that Paramount
refused to meet Burton's salary demand of $1 million because the stu-
dio was committed to low-budget films.[6]

To Wallis, Paramount had become unrecognizable; it was no longer
the studio that had been his home for twenty-five years. Although it was
difficult to pull up stakes, there was no other alternative. It was time to
leave Marathon Street and head for the San Fernando Valley, the home
of Universal Pictures, which welcomed Wallis, as it had earlier welcomed Alfred Hitchcock, whose despair of understanding Paramount's
byzantine accounting methods prompted his own departure in 1962.
Universal became the last stop for both of them—Wallis winding up his
career there with *Rooster Cogburn* (1975) and Hitchcock doing the same
the following year with *Family Plot* (1976).

Universal had no problem with Wallis's making *Anne of the Thousand Days.* Budget was not a concern; in fact, *Anne,* which was shot in
thirteen weeks, came in $200,000 under budget. However, *Anne* was
not the artistic success that *Becket* was. There were ten Oscar nomina-

tions and one Oscar—for Margaret Furse's authentic costumes. *Anne* could never compete with *Becket* for a variety of reasons, chief of which was the reductive screenplay: a lecherous monarch so obsessed with begetting a son that he has his second wife, who could only give him a daughter, condemned to death on trumped-up charges of incest and adultery. As if that were not enough, the monarch has set his sights on another potential breeder even before he decides to rid himself of a wife who, according to his limited definition of fertility, is barren. The ultimate irony is that the daughter that Henry will not accept as his successor becomes one of the world's greatest rulers, Elizabeth I.

Anne of the Thousand Days succeeded on the stage because Anderson's combination of dynamic prose and free verse had a distancing effect, elevating the action to the level of conflict and debate—abstract enough so that empathy became a matter of side-taking, or how much one projected onto the characters. Anderson's language gave Henry a dignity that, combined with Rex Harrison's presence, made the play his tragedy more than Anne's. Anne, while obviously attracted to Henry, withholds her favors, demanding marriage and refusing to be a mistress and a mother of bastards—although after Henry's separation from Rome, papists brand Anne a whore and a heretic, and her daughter a bastard.

The fickle Henry is so taken with Anne's spiritedness, which he equates with a capacity for male progeny, that he is willing to accept excommunication to make her his queen. It is only after Anne bears him a daughter and realizes she can never give Henry a son that she rises to tragic heights, as Henry sinks into despondency and deviousness. Knowing that her husband will send her to an undeserved death merely to be free to marry another, Anne denounces him for his weakness, declaring that their daughter Elizabeth will surpass any male child of his. Anne is prescient; immediately after Anne's beheading, Henry marries Jane Seymour, who, after bearing him a son, Edward VI, dies twelve days later. Edward VI (1547–1553) is a mere nine years old when he succeeds his father, making his brief reign a form of puppetry with others pulling the strings.

Anne of the Thousand Days reached Broadway at the right time. That the Tony award for best actor went to Rex Harrison, and not Lee J. Cobb for his legendary Willy Loman in *Death of a Salesman,* suggests that bravura carried the day. The same was true about the Tony for best actress, which went to another star of the English stage, Martita Hunt (who later played Henry II's mother in the movie version of *Becket*), for her flamboyant performance in the title role of Jean Giraudoux's *Madwoman of Chaillot*. The 1948–49 season was eclectic; the big hits were *South Pacific* and *Death of a Salesman,* yet *Anne* and *Madwoman* proved that there was an audience for a type of theater that relied heavily on language, sometimes quite lofty, to make audiences listeners rather than mere spectators. That both *Anne* and *Madwoman* ran as long as they did—286 and 368 performances, respectively—suggests that post–World War II theatergoers could accept plays about wise fools taking on the establishment *(Madwoman)* and a queen sacrificed to the dubious cause of male succession *(Anne)*.

The ideal time for Wallis to have made the movie version of *Anne* was around 1954, four years after the end of the Broadway run. Burton had just made his second American film, *The Robe* (1953), looking properly heroic as a Roman centurion; had he played Henry then, he would have cut a more dashing figure on the screen than Harrison did on the stage, since he was seventeen years younger than Harrison. But time and drink had taken their toll; in *Becket,* Burton had not yet acquired the dissipated look that remained his signature throughout the rest of his relatively brief career. In fact, in *Becket* he looked almost ascetic. But by the time he played George in the booze-fueled *Who's Afraid of Virginia Woolf?* (1966), his face had become a craggy mask, which suited the character but not the classically trained actor who could have been the heir to Gielgud and Olivier.

By June 1968, when *Anne* was ready to go into production, Burton's complexion, never smooth to begin with, looked as if it had been buffed with sandpaper. But the voice could still make music out of words. In *Anne* Burton's voice may have been musical, but he seemed to be affected by a combination of lethargy and indifference. To watch Burton dance a galliard is to see a gifted actor going through the motions without really caring about the context. The reason, to which Wallis does not allude in *Starmaker,* is that Burton had second thoughts about the film and wanted to get out of his contract. It took the threat of a lawsuit to make him honor his commitment.[7] The reasons for Burton's change of heart will never be fully known, although they are inferable. When Elizabeth Taylor, whom Burton married in 1964 after his divorce from Sybil Christopher, discovered her husband would be playing Henry VIII, she immediately asked Wallis if she could be his Anne, although, at thirty-six, she would hardly have been the nubile creature that captivated Henry. When Burton pointed that out to her, she took it in stride.

Still, Elizabeth was curious about husband's new costar, particularly if he decided to live the role, which Wallis implies that Burton did not. Elizabeth, however, was taking no chances and occasionally dropped in on the shoot. Burton's Anne—and Elizabeth's imagined (or perhaps real) competition—was newcomer Genevieve Bujold, whose performance surpassed Burton's; Anne evolves from child to woman, while Henry devolves from man to child, willing to resort to the worst sort of treachery to be free of a wife who cannot give him a son. From the way Burton played Henry, it is hard to know whether the king's chief problem was the lack of a male heir or an overactive libido, which he thought would give him a son, provided he found the right woman. Meanwhile, Henry would sow his seed.

After *Becket, Anne* was an anticlimax, even though it was moderately successful—more so in Britain, where by November 1970 it had grossed over $1 million in London alone. Much had happened to Burton between *Becket* and *Anne*. In 1964 Burton returned to Broadway as Hamlet in a production directed by John Gielgud, who had the cast wear rehearsal clothes, implying that every *Hamlet* is a run-through for the ideal staging, which can only exist in the theater of the imagination. Audiences could care less about the absence of costumes or sets; they were treated to the equivalent of a lieder recital, with Burton in magnificent voice intoning the text. On those evenings when Elizabeth arrived in her limo to transport her husband from the Lunt-Fontanne theater to their ten-room suite at Park Avenue's Regency Hotel, Forty-sixth Street between Broadway and Eighth Avenue was a pedestrian nightmare. Gawking spectators lined up on both sides of the street to catch a glimpse of Burton entering the limo. Liz and Burton were Broadway royalty, courtesy of Shakespeare, whose contribution was secondary to their aura.

Next, Burton and Taylor were paired in the screen version of Edward Albee's *Who's Afraid of Virginia Woolf?* in which Burton gave one of his best performances. Each received an Oscar nomination—Burton for the third time. The winner, however, was Elizabeth—for the second time. Burton would never be so honored, although he enjoyed his share of nominations; anticipating an award for *Equus* (1977), which he had also done on stage, he could not disguise his disappointment when the Oscar went to Richard Dreyfuss for *The Goodbye Girl.*

To go from Shakespeare and Albee to recycled Maxwell Anderson was an anticlimax. After being directed by Peter Glenville, John Gielgud, and Mike Nichols *(Virginia Woolf),* Burton may have had second thoughts about Wallis's choice for *Anne*'s director, Canadian-born Charles Jarrott. After Burton agreed to Jarrott, he had misgivings. Jarrott, who had never directed a feature film before, had worked exclusively in television. Whether Burton knew that another Canadian, Genevieve Bujold, would be costarring with him as Anne, is uncertain. But Jarrott favored his own, particularly when his own had the freshness and authority that Burton, for the most part, lacked; there was some authority left, but it was largely in his voice.

Any actor reading John Hale and Bridget Boland's adaptation of Anderson's play would have assumed that the film belonged to Anne. Henry comes off as a monarch in a state of perpetual heat; early in the film, he pants as he presses his mouth against a reluctant Anne's as if he were trying to suck from her some knowledge of her fecundity. The play was quite different. Harrison's masculinity was low-testosterone, suave and calculating; Burton's was the opposite, boastful and treacherous. Harrison was a presence, Burton a force. If Joyce Redmond, who costarred with Harrison on Broadway, did not seem quite the tragic queen that Bujold did, the reason is that Anderson never portrayed Anne as Henry's victim. His Anne would have been more than willing to send Thomas More and John Fisher to their deaths for refusing to acknowledge Henry as head of the Church of England—which would, in effect, have meant demoting the pope to a quasi-bishop—provided Henry would acknowledge their daughter Elizabeth as his legitimate heir. It is Anne's concern for Elizabeth, which is both maternal and political, that drives the wedge between them.

Anderson left no doubt that if Anne had managed to live, the Tower of London would not have lacked for occupants. If self-knowledge is essential to tragedy, then Henry is the play's tragic figure. He realizes that he was only a catalyst in bringing about what was historically inevitable. Anderson gave Henry the final speech; alone, with Anne's ghost hovering behind him, he realizes that he and Anne were only agents in bringing about a revolution that would have occurred eventually; yet no matter when it happened, England would never be the same. Henry refers to himself and Anne as "puppets . . . the people dangled to a tune they were playing." Speaking with neither regret nor bravado, Henry knows that "the limb that was cut from Rome won't graft to that trunk again."[8] The rest is Reformation—and even greater bloodshed.

Denied such insights in the film, Henry becomes an oversexed monarch who lives by his libido, which, like a compass, points to potential bearers of sons. Even when the needle points toward Anne, she is at first unwilling to yield. When she learns that Henry has forbidden her to marry her fiancé, Harry Percy, because Henry wants her for himself, she plays hard to get; this is historically true, as are some other details. For example, it is clear in the film that Henry is no stranger to Hever Castle, the Boleyn family home in Kent. It was there that he saw Anne's sister, Mary, whom he promptly impregnated and then abandoned. This is only one of several authenticating touches in the film. However, if authenticity made a film a work of art, the staggeringly detailed *Tora! Tora! Tora!* (1970), which painstakingly chronicled the events of the December 1941 weekend that climaxed in the attack on Pearl Harbor, would have been a masterpiece, rather than a historical recreation.

What restricts the movie version of *Anne* to the category of romantic tragedy is Anne Boleyn's basic innocence, which was not the case in the play; given no tragic flaw, she becomes one of a succession of Henry's victims, who, when they cease to be of use, are either dismissed or convicted of high treason. An Anne like Anderson's, who admits that she concurred with her husband's purges, would have been a lesser version of Lady Macbeth: guilty but pathetic. By ignoring Anne's dark side, the film does everything but endow her with a nimbus. There may be intelligence in the film, but precious little drama—until the climax. In the meantime, viewers are given a textbook summary of the events leading up to Anne's execution—learning, for example, that Cardinal Woolsey fell from favor and was forced to leave Hampton Court, after failing to persuade Pope Clement VII to annul Henry's marriage to Catherine of Aragon on the spurious grounds that Catherine was Henry's sister-in-law, which made their union incestuous; that, although Pope Julius II had given Henry a dispensation to marry his brother's widow, Clement VII could not afford to antagonize Catherine's nephew, Charles V of Spain, especially after Catherine insisted that her marriage to Henry's brother, Arthur, was never consummated—but her union with Henry was; and finally that the problem was not Catherine's inability to bear Henry a child but that Mary, their child, was the wrong gender.

The film also credits Thomas Cromwell, chief minister to Henry and later lord chamberlain, with being the power behind the throne, encouraging Henry to break with Rome by appealing to his ego and inspiring the Act of Succession, which required an oath of allegiance to Henry as "sole protector and supreme head of the church and the clergy of England." At first, Henry desires Rome's approval of his union with Anne (whom he has already impregnated and secretly married). But soon he is willing to risk excommunication if Anne can bear him a son. Goaded on by Cromwell, who has convinced him that any form of disobedience to the king is an act of treason, Henry installs Thomas Cranmer as archbishop of Canterbury, who dissolves Henry's marriage to Catherine and legitimates his union with Anne (even though it has already been consummated).

If *Anne* has a villain, it is not Henry but Cromwell, who originally supports Anne but then abandons her when she falls out of Henry's favor. Anne made the mistake of acting like a queen, becoming as reform-minded as her husband. But when Anne realizes that Henry's roving eye has alighted on Jane Seymour, she banishes her rival from the court, agreeing to her return only if Elizabeth is next in line for the throne. Still son-obsessed, Henry refuses, planning instead to rid himself of the woman he once kissed shamelessly in front of her ambitious parents, who, if they were embarrassed, were too politic to show it. To do so would have called attention to the king's uncurbed lust, which subjects are expected to ignore. Having discarded one Boleyn daughter, Henry moves on to the next, who meets a far sadder end.

Wallis, as usual, collaborated with the screenwriters, making certain that *Anne* was the companion film to *Becket*. Anderson's play was framed by a prologue and an epilogue—the prologue spoken by Anne, the epilogue by both Anne and Henry, but with Henry getting the last word. *Becket* had a similar framing device, as Henry II recalled the past at Becket's tomb. To forge a parallel with *Becket,* Wallis retained the flashback structure of the original, but with a different narrator—Henry, reliving the time from his first meeting with Anne to her execution. Just as *Becket* opened with Henry's arrival at Canterbury cathedral, *Anne* begins with Cromwell rushing in to inform Henry that Anne, her brother George, and Harry Percy have all been executed—the cue for a flashback, after which the action returns to the present with a reflective but unrepentant Henry.

Anne ends with a shot of the four-year-old Elizabeth alone in the Tudor gardens. As she toddles up the path, unaware that she is motherless and, for all practical purposes, fatherless, Anne's offscreen voice proclaims, "Elizabeth will be queen, and my blood is well spent." The image was open-ended: Would there be a follow-up film? And is the shot of the child Elizabeth the bridge between *Anne* and the sequel?

Elizabeth I was no stranger to Wallis; thirty years earlier, he produced *The Private Lives of Elizabeth and Essex* (1939), which was also inspired by a Maxwell Anderson drama, *Elizabeth the Queen* (1930). Wallis wondered, however, if audiences had not had enough of Elizabeth. Mary Stuart was another matter; she, too, had been the subject of an Anderson play, *Mary of Scotland* (1933), the basis of John Ford's 1936 film, in which Katharine Hepburn played Mary, sounding more like an elocutionist than a queen.

Ford's *Mary of Scotland*, despite its lavish production, was a failure. Yet Wallis felt there was great potential in the story of Mary, Queen of Scots—a complex figure and a fine title for a movie; a better one, in fact, than *Mary of Scotland*, which sounded like *Anne of Green Gables*. Ever since Friedrich Schiller brought Mary and Elizabeth together on stage in *Maria Stuart* (1800), a meeting between the rival queens became a tradition, although the two had never actually met. But that did not stop Donizetti from having them confront each other in his opera, *Maria Stuarda*, or Maxwell Anderson from following suit in *Mary of Scotland*. Wallis felt similarly; he respected historical accuracy but was by no means a purist.

In 1969 Wallis was not the only one interested in interweaving the lives of Mary and Elizabeth. Robert Bolt was putting the finishing touches on another historical drama, *Vivat! Vivat Regina!,* which premiered at the Chichester Festival in 1970 and then transferred to the West End. Wallis had been in London during the 1970–71 season when *Vivat!* was playing; however, he was more interested in Terence Rattigan's *Bequest to the Nation,* which dramatized the affair between Lord Nelson and Lady Hamilton, perhaps because he was still fascinated by adultery among the upper classes. Wallis immediately bought the rights to *Bequest,* which never reached New York; *Vivat!,* however, came to Broadway in 1972 with Claire Bloom as Mary and Eileen Atkins as Elizabeth.

The play had a respectable run of 116 performances but never achieved the popularity of *A Man for All Seasons.*

Whether *Vivat!* inspired *Mary, Queen of Scots* is problematic, since Wallis claimed he became interested in a movie about Mary when he was making *Anne*. Still, *Vivat!* would have piqued his interest; it is hard to imagine Wallis's being in London and passing up a play that bore such a close resemblance to his own project.[9] At any rate, Bolt's play and Wallis's film have much in common, as would any two works about the same historical figures, if for no other reason than their dependence on the same source material. The chief difference is Bolt's fidelity to history (as one would expect from a former history major); Elizabeth and Mary occupy the same stage, but at different times, thus precluding the possibility of a meeting. This would not be the case in the film; from the outset Wallis wanted the two queens to meet, as they did in Schiller's *Maria Stuart.*

Still, *Mary* combined the right amount of history and invention to be taken seriously. Charles Jarrott, who was again the director, had now matured into a real moviemaker, far more secure in his craft than he had been in *Anne*. The transitions from the scenes with Elizabeth to those with Mary are seamless, as if the women occupy alternate pages within the same biography. Jarrott was no longer dealing with a theme as monolinear as Henry's obsession with a son, even though that obsession had repercussions that *Anne* only touched on. In *Mary* the issues went deeper: if the Reformation was inevitable, as Anderson's Henry VIII implies, it also turned men into sycophants, opportunists, rebels, and martyrs; and it forced a queen to play the dual role of monarch above reproach and woman in search of love, always fearful that her lover might view their liaison as an opportunity to seize the throne. The Reformation did not merely leave a cleft in the rock of the Church; it produced enough fissures to keep historians perpetually occupied.

Movie audiences were familiar enough with Elizabeth I to know her "virgin queen" sobriquet was dubious. As male history professors enjoyed saying in single-sex colleges in the 1950s, "Gentlemen, she was no more a virgin than you and I." Broadway, Hollywood, and opera felt the same, although Elizabeth's loss of virginity has never been documented. Still, an affair between Elizabeth and Robert Dudley has become an article of faith to those who believe that the queen needed a lover but was too strong-willed (and, one might add, intelligent) to make him her husband, always wondering when he might try to supplant her. *Mary, Queen of Scots* (1971) makes the same point; Elizabeth (Glenda Jackson) is first seen in Dudley's (Daniel Massey's) embrace, which, at the time, was enough to suggest intimacy. Elizabeth even demands that Dudley (affectionately called "Robin") sleep in the apartment above hers, in case she should need his "advice." By juxtaposing the lives of Mary (Vanessa Redgrave) and Elizabeth, the film becomes a diptych of two extraordinary women, who could have lived without men had they been immune to what proper folk called "Cupid's darts." Although Elizabeth might have wanted to marry Dudley, she knew his male ego would never tolerate being the queen's consort but not king. Dudley's ambitious nature made Elizabeth wary of him; wariness, however, does not mitigate desire.

Elizabeth also had to contend with Mary's claim to the English throne by virtue of being the granddaughter of Margaret Tudor, Henry VIII's older sister—Elizabeth being both a bastard and a heretic in the eyes of the Church. Since the death of Francis II left Mary a widow, Elizabeth believed her cousin would pose less of a threat if she remarried. Thus Dudley was sent off to woo Mary; if he succeeded, Elizabeth would at least know where he was, in case she needed his "advice." But Elizabeth's real purpose was to convince Mary that marriage to Dudley would strengthen, although not necessarily guarantee, Mary's right to succeed her. Since John Hale's screenplay downplays Elizabeth's ulterior motive, the queen's machinations are reduced to matchmaking.

Dudley held no appeal for Mary, but Lord Henry Darnley did. He was singularly handsome (but dissolute); he was also a Catholic—in name only. If love enters through the eyes, as the Elizabethan poets wrote, Mary no sooner saw Darnley than she was love's captive. Dewy-eyed lover was only one of Mary's roles; her others included grieving widow, professional Catholic, deceived wife, and treasonous queen, who would not even let death upstage her. Since Mary was not executed in a public space like Anne, only a small number of spectators gathered at Fotheringhay Castle at dawn on 8 February 1587 to witness her death. Despite the meager turnout, Mary did not stint on theatrics. Dressed in black satin, she entered the great hall where a makeshift stage had been constructed, walking slowly as if in a procession—a prayer book in her hands, a rosary around her wrist, and a psalm on her lips. The stage, complete with an executioner's block, became her venue. After she de-

claimed her motto, "In my end is my beginning," her attendants helped
her out of the dress. If there was a gasp from the onlookers, it was intended: Mary stood before them defiantly in a red petticoat. Before she
placed her head on the block, she intoned the sixth of Christ's seven last
words, "Into thy hands, I commend my spirit."[10] Compared to Mary's
coup de théâtre, Thomas More's execution was just a beheading preceded by a quip: as More sought assistance mounting the scaffold, he
joked, "Friend, if you'll help me to get up, I'll see to the coming down."
Mary did not turn a phrase; she gave a performance.

Since Mary is the dominant figure (hence, Redgrave's Oscar nomination for best actress) in a film that is biased in her favor, the uninformed
moviegoer might conclude that she was also the superior ruler. But the
truth is that of the two queens, only one was a born ruler: Elizabeth.

Mary played her roles well, except that of Queen of Scots, in which
she was miscast. If Vanessa Redgrave's Mary overshadowed Glenda
Jackson's Elizabeth, it was Redgrave's imposing stature and regal bearing—not to mention her attire, which was always tasteful, compared to
Elizabeth's ostentatious wardrobe that evoked the image of a blowzy
madam. If anyone looked like a "virgin queen," it was Mary, even though
her virginity had long been lost. However, anyone able to fill in the
lacunae in Hale's deliberately porous script could easily infer that Mary
was too deficient in statecraft and guided by emotion to rule any nation,
let alone Scotland.

Mary behaves as if she were the only true Catholic in Scotland,
which seems to have embraced Protestantism en masse. Even her half
brother, James Stuart, has sided with the Protestant lords. While James
and Darnley think nothing of switching faiths, Mary remains steadfast
in hers, although being both female and Catholic has made her queen-
ship a sinecure. Historians might argue that there was more at work
than male chauvinism, yet the treatment that the historical Mary received at the hands of men—her husband Darnley, her half brother James
Stuart, and the earl of Bothwell, supposedly her one true love—suggests that Mary's gender posed as much of a problem to Scottish males
as her faith, a point also underscored in the film.

After his marriage to Mary, Darnley underwent a rapid change from
ardent wooer to abusive husband, shaming Mary publicly and flaunting
his promiscuity, which led to syphilis (called "pox" in the film). Since
the historical Darnley was reputedly effeminate, Hale took advantage

of the recently interred Production Code, which forbade even the slightest suggestion of homosexuality, to make him bisexual. Timothy Dalton's Darnley, who looked like Billy Budd with the morals of Edward II, even imposes himself on Mary's secretary, David Riccio (Ian Holm), whose devotion to the queen leaves him no other choice but to play masochist to Darnley's sadist.

At several points in the film, Elizabeth admits she feels a kinship with Mary, as the historical Elizabeth also did, judging from her letters. The women shared a common bond: they were females who were also monarchs, forced to distinguish between affairs of state and those of the heart, subordinating the latter to the former, and hoping at least for an occasional "gaudy night" of the sort that Shakespeare's Antony envisioned with Cleopatra. If Elizabeth was the superior monarch, one reason is that she understood men better than Mary; as Henry VIII's daughter, she had a crash course in king-consort relationships. All she had to do to remain on the throne was to imagine herself as Henry. Thus the trappings of love—passionate embraces, bowing lords, clandestine meetings—were all Elizabeth could expect. Elizabeth could never be a tragic figure, because she already possessed the knowledge that should come at the end of the tragic process: namely, that any husband she chose would seek to replace her as "king," not realizing that she is one herself, but with a different spelling.

Elizabeth knew who she was: Henry's daughter. Thus she must rule as "king," even if it means defeminization. Mary, in contrast, grows more feminine as Elizabeth sinks into sexlessness, looking like a parody of a woman by the end of the film. Mary is a romantic, a Juliet who morphs into Cleopatra, suffering from both young love and midlife passion. No sooner is she mourning the death of Francis II than she is swept off her feet by Darnley until he becomes the husband from hell, forcing Mary to witness the murder of Riccio, whom Darnley believes is his rival. After falling madly in love with Bothwell, Mary is more than willing to be rid of Darnley. In the film, Mary is not directly implicated in Darnley's death, although she has no intention of preventing it, after he has become a syphilitic wreck. Despite his condition, Darnley embraces Protestantism to appease the Scottish lords, never realizing that if they wanted anyone as monarch, it was neither Mary nor himself but James Stuart.

Mary may have imagined Bothwell as her dream lover, but when danger reared its head, Bothwell left Mary to fend for herself and set sail for Denmark, where he remarried and died, supposedly insane. On these points Hale is correct; however, he omits the circumstances surrounding Bothwell's short-lived marriage to Mary, who had grown so enamored of Bothwell that she even agreed to marry him in a Protestant ceremony after his divorce, which was obtained in record time. The film makes no mention of a Protestant service (which would have denigrated Mary's image as quintessential Catholic). Yet Hale was so hopeful that audiences would understand Mary's infatuation with a married man that he included a scene in which Mary encounters Bothwell's nondescript wife. Although Mary is surprised that her lover is married, she has no qualms about sleeping with him before they are free to wed.

The scenes between Elizabeth and Mary should have been the film's highlights, yet compared to the death of Francis II and the grizzly murders of Riccio and Darnley, they were anticlimactic. Drama returned with Mary's execution, staged as a tableau in which the Queen of Scots did a star turn that Elizabeth would have envied, had she been there. The historical Elizabeth—and the film's, too—had no desire to kill her cousin; to do so would mean killing an anointed queen. Still, Elizabeth cannot dismiss the plots against her life, to which Mary admits she was privy. The film, eager to make Mary a tragic heroine, mitigates her involvement: "I know of the plans for your death," Mary admits evasively. Actually, Mary knew of several, including Anthony Babbington's, which she endorsed. Regardless, Elizabeth is willing to give Mary her freedom if she issues a public apology. Mary's pride—or, to be more exact, hubris—cannot allow it. And so, Elizabeth has no other choice but to send Mary to a death that her cousin willingly embraces; having playacted through most of her life, she is ready for her close-up, like Norma Desmond in *Sunset Boulevard.*

Mary had no way of knowing that she would inspire dramatists, librettists, and filmmakers; nor, for that matter, did Elizabeth, although she must have assumed her life was too eventful to end up in some dust-gathering tome. However, there were also screenwriters, playwrights, and librettists who were drawn only to Elizabeth, feeling no need to include Mary. Elizabeth does not share billing with Mary in such films as *The Private Lives of Elizabeth and Essex, The Virgin Queen* (1955), and *Elizabeth* (1998) or in such operas as Donizetti's *Roberto Devereux;* Rossini's *Elisabetta, Regina d'Inghilterra;* and Britten's *Gloriana.* Even

Maxwell Anderson gave the queen a play to herself, *Elizabeth the Queen,* although a few years later he capitulated to tradition and made her a character in *Mary of Scotland.* But, for the most part, Elizabeth herself was the muse, a role she would have relished. It is easy to imagine Elizabeth without Mary, but not the opposite. To paraphrase Mary's signature saying, "In Elizabeth's end is Mary's beginning."

Wallis was rewarded for his Anglophilia. At a Royal Command performance of *Anne of the Thousand Days* in November 1972, Elizabeth II whispered to the producer as she shook his hand, "Thank you, Mr. Wallis. We're learning about English history from your films" (*Starmaker,* 171). Compared to the average Hollywood biopic, *Anne of the Thousand Days* and *Mary, Queen of Scots* were the equivalent of a graduate seminar in Tudor history. A year later, Wallis was honored with the title of Commander of the British Empire (C.B.E.), by order of Elizabeth II.

After completing *Mary* in 1970, Wallis remained in Britain for another year to make two films, both based on plays: *The Public Eye* and *The Nelson Affair* (both 1972). *The Public Eye* was a decade old when it reached the screen. Written by Peter Shaffer when he was in his midthirties and produced in London in 1962, followed by an American engagement the following year, *The Public Eye* was the second play in a double bill, the first of which was *The Private Ear.* If Wallis managed to catch *The Private Ear* and *the Public Eye* while he was in London filming *Becket,* they left no impression. He felt the same ten years later after completing *Mary.* Wallis was more interested in the tragic love affair between Lord Nelson and Emma Hamilton than in Shaffer's one-acts about a cerebral male unable to attract women who share his interest in classical music (*Ear*) and a jealous husband who hires a detective to check on his wife, never suspecting that the wife will find the detective more fascinating than himself.

Universal felt differently, but only about *The Private Ear.* Originally, Ross Hunter, Universal's premier producer, planned to film both plays with Elizabeth Taylor and Richard Burton. When the Burtons insisted on directorial approval, Hunter abandoned the project. Meanwhile, Shaffer's reputation continued to grow, although his best plays, *Equus* and *Amadeus,* lay in the future.

When Hunter left Universal in 1970, neither one-act had been filmed. It was clear why *The Private Ear* wasn't; the play was an uninvolving tale of disillusion, ending with a spurned lover repeatedly dragging the arm of his phonograph across a record (in the London production, a *Madame Butterfly* LP), causing the audience to wince as the needle lacerated the vinyl. Understandably, Universal passed on *The Private Ear,* but not on *The Public Eye.* Universal asked Wallis to stay on in London and make the movie version, which he agreed to do purely as a favor to the studio that had given him such a warm reception after he left Paramount. Besides, he reasoned, it would be an easy shoot after *Mary.* Since *The Public Eye* was more of a Universal release than a Hal Wallis production, and its director was Carol Reed (which, to auteurists, would make it a Carol Reed film), Wallis made no reference to it in *Starmaker.*

The Public Eye is minor Reed, Wallis, and Shaffer. The playwright did his own adaptation, opening up the piece to include, among other locations, Covent Garden. It is easy to see why the play held no appeal for Wallis: it was literate, sophisticated, but too narrowly intellectual to be anything other than an exercise in cleverness: a private detective (Topol), hired by a jealous husband to spy on his wife (Mia Farrow), spends so much time following her around London that a silent attraction develops between them. For Shaffer, *The Public Eye* was a divertissement; of the two, the playwright probably favored *The Private Ear,* even though he knew it was a bittersweet vignette that most theatergoers would consider a curtain raiser, which is pretty much what it was.

After wrapping up *The Public Eye,* Wallis moved on to *The Nelson Affair,* which could never be mistaken for anything but a Hal Wallis production. Again, the playwright—this time, Terence Rattigan—adapted his own work, but with a different title. The original was *A Bequest to the Nation,* which would only make sense in context. A title with *affair* is always provocative, and in this case it was the one between Lord Horatio Nelson and Emma Hamilton. Their story had been told before— and better—in *That Hamilton Woman* (1941) with Vivien Leigh in the title role and Laurence Olivier as Lord Nelson. Although Glenda Jackson may have been a more believable Lady Hamilton, the character's selfishness, reflected in her indifference to her lover's military obligations, obscured the central theme of duty versus desire. After deciding to return to the fleet, Nelson ends up dying at Trafalgar, leaving Lady Hamilton as "a bequest to the nation," with the understanding that she will be provided for until her death. The bequest is denied, and Lady Hamilton is reduced to penury and alcoholism.

The critics came down hard on *The Nelson Affair,* as if by going from the Angevins and the Tudors to the Georgians, Wallis had abandoned his mission, which was assumed to be the mythologizing of British history, with enough background to make the films intellectually respectable and enough dramatic license to make them popular. Henry VIII's amours lay far enough in the past to take on a mythic patina. Whatever his excesses, Henry was the father of Elizabeth, whom Hollywood considered a bankable character.

Adultery among royalty is one thing; among peers, another. An audience's reaction to adultery is often determined by the parties involved as well their era. Because the Nelson-Hamilton affair seemed less remote to 1970s moviegoers than Henry VIII's wiving, it had not acquired the same mythology. The marriages of Henry VIII have proved to be perennially fascinating; the liaison between a naval hero and his mistress, less so. Horatio Nelson and Emma Hamilton may have engaged in *grand amore,* but audiences had their own idea of what upper-class infidelity should be; and that was not what they got in *The Nelson Affair.* Not so with *That Hamilton Woman,* which was released during World War II, when subordinating passion to patriotism was perceived as an obligation, at least to the British. Small wonder that *That Hamilton Woman* ranked among Sir Winston Churchill's favorite films.

The Nelson Affair was dismissed as a remake of *That Hamilton Woman.* The unrealistic battle scenes, which one critic believed were taken from "some old swashbuckler like *Captain Horatio Hornblower,*" further detracted from the passionate love story that lay at the heart of the film.[11]

That Nelson and Emma are unsympathetic lovers is not the point; Antony and Cleopatra were too, yet they move us. Emma moves us only at the end, and solely because of her plight. Had Elizabeth II seen *The Nelson Affair,* one doubts that she would have recommended it as a history lesson for her subjects.

CHAPTER ELEVEN

Brief Encounters

L IKE SO MANY GOLDEN AGE PRODUCERS, such as Louis Mayer, Harry Cohn, and Darryl Zanuck, Wallis was not monogamous. However, he was not a womanizer like Harry Cohn, whose office at Columbia had shelves of expensive perfumes and nylon stockings—payment for services rendered. The services were often rendered *in* his office, which was a study in white: white chairs, a white piano, and a white couch that may well have been the original "casting couch." With Cohn, sex was both a release of tension and an instrument of power. Like Mayer and Zanuck, Cohn fancied himself a starmaker; but there is a difference between using stars to light up the Hollywood sky and exploiting them for reasons having nothing to do with their luminosity. Wallis was not promiscuous; extramarital sex was dalliance, a by-product of the transformation process: Pygmalion creates Galatea and becomes enthralled with his creation, feeling not so much love as passion, and expecting the creation to respond accordingly. If, by some chance, passion turns to love, it can only be for the short term; otherwise, there is a marriage, or, in Cohn's and Jack Warner's case, divorce followed by remarriage.

Unlike Cohn and his former boss, Jack Warner, Wallis was discreet. While a few actresses were known to have spent inordinate amounts of time in his office, Wallis never boasted of what went on behind the closed—and, one assumes, locked—door. Wallis would have never humiliated an actress, as Cohn did, by asking her in the presence of a group of male executives if it was true that—to put it euphemistically, which Cohn did not—she was Hollywood's foremost practitioner of oral sex.[1]

There was another reason that Wallis needed an occasional lover, which had nothing to do with his transformative powers: it was the desire for a different kind of love—and a different kind of lovemaking—than he had in marriage. Although there is no doubt that Wallis loved Louise, it was a restrictive love—a love that bound them to their Valley farm, which was a haven for Louise and a combination editing room–study–theater for Wallis. Having no interest in the Broadway scene, Louise did not accompany him on his frequent visits to New York and rarely on location. And with the coming of sound, her roles became smaller and fewer, leading to retirement from the screen in 1939 and an indifference to the medium that brought her fame. There is no proof that Wallis ever considered divorce, nor would it ever have crossed Louise's mind. Eventually, the perfect producer's wife materialized in Martha Hyer, but only after Louise's death. Meanwhile, Wallis practiced discretion. If Louise found comfort in charitable work, it was her way of dealing with her husband's infidelity and, at the same time, playing the exemplary Christian. She may even have perceived herself as a Christian martyr, atoning for a wayward spouse. To Louise, everything was a corporal work of mercy, from visiting shut-ins whom she did not even know to inviting one of her husband's current liaisons for a visit, during which Louise interrogated her guest about the nature of the intimacies in which they had engaged thus far, as if she had a list of her husband's wooing techniques arranged in climactic order and was therefore able to prepare the newcomer for the next stage in their relationship.[2]

Wallis was raised in a household dominated by women. There was his mother, Eva, whose maternal warmth Wallis acknowledged in his autobiography; but it was a warmth that unfortunately dissipated in the wake of her ill health and her husband's desertion, which left Eva a single parent—tubercular and in need of medical attention and financial support. Wallis never portrayed himself as fortune's victim, one whose life was thrown into turmoil by an improvident father; however, it was, along with the lives of his mother and his two sisters, Minna and Juel.

The years of relocation, odd jobs, and the pursuit of whatever skills could guarantee a decent paying job left a void in Wallis's life that is traditionally filled by parents, siblings, and friends. When one parent has disappeared, the other is ailing, and the children are all working to pay the rent and the medical expenses, the void does not disappear but continues to exist like negative space that calls attention to itself. Since

Wallis and his sisters had to interrupt their lives—and in Wallis's case, his studies—to provide for Eva, they became quite close during those years in Chicago. It was a closeness that continued throughout their lives. As difficult as Minna was, Wallis endured her nagging—which was often public and more matriarchal than sororal—for one reason: Minna was family and remained such even after Wallis's film career ended in 1975. When her brother retired to Palm Springs, so did Minna, refusing to be deterred by anything as inconsequential as retirement. If Minna receives more space than Juel in *Starmaker*, it is because her life intersected with Wallis's more frequently than her sister's. Just as Wallis venerated his mother, Minna idolized her brother. If Minna had had children, she would have behaved like Mrs. Phelps in Sidney Howard's 1929 play *The Silver Cord* (filmed in 1933 with great fidelity to the original), dispensing "smother love" and making her children her devotees, as if she were the Mother Goddess and they were her minions. And if Minna's children showed the slightest sign of talent, she would have turned into the ultimate stage mother, *Gypsy*'s Mama Rose.

Once Minna became an agent, she found her forte—representing the talent that she firmly believed she discovered. And she never stopped telling her brother that it was she who introduced him to Jack Warner; actually, she introduced him to Sam Warner. Wallis did the rest by himself. Whatever Wallis may have felt for Minna, her obsession with his career, from which she felt excluded (and indeed was), exasperated him. Their relationship was emotionally claustrophobic for Wallis and remained so until his death, which occurred just two months after Minna's in 1986. She would have enjoyed having the first obituary, even though it was considerably shorter than her brother's.

Although Wallis does not play favorites in print, he clearly felt greater affection for Juel, who was "joyous" and "outgoing" (*Starmaker*, 9) and whose early death he laments. What Wallis fails to include about Juel is her humanitarianism and generosity of spirit that endeared her to all who knew her. If Minna had any interest in philanthropy, it remained dormant. Juel, in contrast, worked for the Damon Runyon Cancer Fund and the Jimmy McHugh Polio Foundation. During World War II she was instrumental in getting actors to appear at the Hollywood Canteen.

One of the photos in *Starmaker* is a group picture of the three women who had such an impact on the young Wallis. Since Eva, Minna, and Juel are fashionably dressed in the style of the 1920s, it must have been taken in Los Angeles after Wallis and his sisters were, so to speak, "in the money." Basic black and a choker could not conceal Eva's plainness; her daughters, however, seemed born to elegance, although Minna later began to resemble her mother. At the time, Minna had a vampish look; her cleavage was hidden by a V-shaped insert, but the concession to modesty only succeeded in being more provocative than discreet. Juel, the most striking of the three, is seated, looking pensive. But then, none of the women are smiling—the sober expression being typical of group portrait shots of the period. Except for his eyes, Wallis bore little resemblance to his mother and sisters, yet they were the ones who shaped his image of woman and who possessed qualities that, in the right proportion (and in moderation), would be ideal for the wife of a successful producer. Wallis would find the dream wife—but not at first.

Louise Fazenda embodied Eva's maternalism and Juel's love of life. Although Louise and Minna seemed to have little in common, they were both extremely pragmatic, a quality that Louise prized. Louise must have had some respect or perhaps even affection for Minna; although she left most of her estate to her husband and son, she left a piece of property on Foothill Road in Beverly Hills to Minna. Investing in real estate was Louise's avocation, which she passed on to Wallis. And if Louise could not play matriarch, as Minna did, she could at least get what she wanted. The interior of their Woodman Avenue home may have mirrored Wallis's tastes, but the idea of a moneymaking farm was mutual—and given Louise's background, more hers than her husband's. After the Fazendas relocated in Los Angeles from Indiana, Louise's father, John Altamar Fazenda, opened a grocery story, where, as a child, she often helped out.[3] The experience made Louise aware of Angelenos' dependence on local farmers. To Louise, everything had to be income-producing—from property to fruit. It is hard to imagine Wallis deciding to market dried apricots and walnuts by himself or buying an orange grove and arranging with Sunkist to pick and sell the fruit and share the profits with the grove's owners, namely, himself and Louise (*Starmaker*, 39). Playacting at being a gentleman farmer was a distraction from his producer's chores, providing a respite from moviemaking. Wallis and Louise did not really need another source of revenue. But each had a rainy-day mentality—Wallis, from experiencing privation firsthand; Louise, from working in a business that seemed modeled after fortune's wheel. Louise got what she wanted out of the Valley farm:

a refuge from the business in which she had toiled since she was a teenager.

The problem was the business. Wallis was constantly in the presence of stars, who had achieved the status of deities and in whose apotheosis he had played a part. If Hollywood is a "dream factory," those who create the dreams are dreamers themselves. Wallis dreamed of another life—not a different one but one that ran parallel to his own and was more representative of a Hollywood producer's. Like Robert Frost's traveler in the yellow wood, Wallis wanted to take both paths. Louise was attractive but neither beautiful nor sensuous. Had she been born a decade later, she would never have been a star; she would have been a character actress. Yet she always played the dutiful wife, even though Wallis never got home until well after 6:00 P.M.; and then he read scripts and edited films. It was obvious where his priorities lay. Still, she accompanied him at premieres and dinner parties; at the latter, Louise sometimes did silent comedy shtick—such as pretending to make off with the silverware. She may have gotten a laugh, but it was a couple of decades old.[4] Louise was astute enough to know that, when it came to adultery, the business had not changed. All that had changed was taste; and her husband's was a bit on the wild side.

At Warners, Wallis's fling with Lola Lane did not elude the studio publicists, who were naturally circumspect.[5] So were Wallis's lovers, except for Corinne Calvet, who decided to write a "tell all" memoir, *Has Corinne Been a Good Girl?* (1983), in which she may not have told all, but she certainly told a good deal. Physically, Lola and Corinne were similar; each had a voluptuousness that made them easy to cast. Their eyes promised the proverbial good time, the night of nights. Since Lola and Corinne gave the impression of "having been around," they often played ladies with a past. That their offscreen lives were even more colorful did not hurt their screen image.

It would be easy to accuse Wallis of lacking taste in his amours. Louise, for all of her strange ways, was above reproach. She may not have been the ideal producer's wife, but she could accompany her husband to a premiere without giving the impression that he had just picked her up. Any producer arriving with Lola or Corinne would make onlookers wonder what they did before they got there.

Lola Lane was the archetypal flapper, kin to Zelda Fitzgerald. One could easily imagine her at one of Jay Gatsby's legendary parties, drinking into the night and leaving with someone whose name she would not remember the next day. Lola was the oldest of five sisters, three of whom (Priscilla, Rosemary, and herself) achieved varying degrees of fame—and, in Lola's case, infamy—in Hollywood. Priscilla remained aloof from her sister's notoriety, which always made the papers, and concentrated exclusively on her career; as a result, Priscilla costarred in such films as Alfred Hitchcock's *Saboteur* (1942) and Frank Capra's *Arsenic and Old Lace* (1944).

Lola wanted desperately to be an actress. Physically, she evoked a buxom barmaid, who could look inviting or indifferent at will. Such natural ambivalence stood her in good stead when she played a "hostess" in a "clip joint" (read "whore" in "whorehouse") in Warners's *Marked Woman* (1937), a Wallis production. Wallis must have been aware of Lola's past, particularly the letters she had written to her agent, Arthur Lyons, when Lyons lodged a suit against her in 1930 for nonpayment of fees for the contracts he had negotiated.[6]

The press made much of the suit after Lyons produced letters showing that Lane's relationship with him went beyond the usual one between agent and client. "Love Notes in Suit on Lola Lane Bared," one 1930s headline read, hooking the reader on the story that followed, in which excerpts from the billets doux were quoted.[7] Lola was clearly writing to a lover: "Dearest, awake [*sic*] this morning and you were gone. Seems terrible without you." She also confessed to a checkered past: "Arthur, until now I have been a coquet [*sic*] and although I would perhaps be sincere at moments, at others I would not—perhaps it is due to my young ways and years." Whether Lola and Lyons loved each other ("You have given me peace of mind and a knowledge of your love") or whether her plaintive outpourings were a form of verbal seduction is impossible to know. At any rate, Lyons won his case and was awarded the $1,751 due him.

The letters revealed a vulnerable and insecure actress, a combination that would make her even more desirable to Wallis than if she had been one or the other. Hers was not a major role in *Marked Woman*, which was a Bette Davis vehicle that heralded Davis's return to Warners from a self-imposed exile in England because she refused to appear in the inferior films that she had been offered. *Marked Woman* resonated with female audiences who had previously found Davis too self-dramatizing; they now saw a different side of the actress in the role of a

woman willing to risk disfigurement (hence the title) to testify about
organized crime's infiltration of "clip joints." Still, Lola held her own
with the other "hostesses," looking more like one of them than Davis.
Lola persuaded Warners to put her sisters, Rosemary and Priscilla, under contract. Wallis was then saddled with the responsibility of finding
a suitable vehicle for them. Sister acts were common in vaudeville, the
theater, and film, but generally the sisters were a pair, not a trio: Rosa
and Carmela Ponselle, Lillian and Dorothy Gish, Joan and Constance
Bennett, Norma and Constance Talmadge. As a former publicist, Wallis
knew the importance of novelty; he also knew how to promote it.

Although Priscilla and Rosemary had appeared in Warners's *Variety Show* (1937), and Lola and Rosemary in *Hollywood Hotel* (1938),
the three had never worked together in a film until Wallis gave them the
opportunity in *Four Daughters* (1938). Since each had appeared on the
screen earlier, their debut as a trio was not quite the event Wallis had
anticipated, particularly since Lola had been in the movies since 1929.
Although *Four Daughters* received an Academy Award nomination for
best picture, as did Michael Curtiz for best director, the film was more
instrumental in launching the career of John Garfield than in furthering
that of the Lane Sisters. Garfield became an immediate box office favorite; even the Academy of Motion Picture Arts and Sciences acknowledged the arrival of a talented newcomer by nominating him for best
supporting actor. Although *Four Daughters* lost out to *You Can't Take It
with You,* Curtiz to Frank Capra, and Garfield to Walter Brennan, Wallis
realized he had a future star and insisted that Garfield appear in the
sequel, *Daughters Courageous* (1939). It was also directed by Curtiz,
who understood that the Warner Brothers male, typified by Garfield,
was unique. He was a city boy who grew up to be an urban male, never
forgetting the lessons he learned on the streets. Even Errol Flynn's derring-do was more a form of self-defense than a display of swordsmanship; Flynn was not the patrician duelist that either Douglas Fairbanks
Sr. or Jr. was. Garfield brought his own persona to the studio; unlike
Flynn, he was anti-Byronic; he was also sexier than James Cagney; more
proletarian than George Raft, less mannered than Paul Muni, scrappier
than Humphrey Bogart, and smart enough to sense that any attempt to
smooth out his rough edges would undermine his appeal. Curtiz sensed
this also, as did other directors such as Howard Hawks, Delmer Daves,
and Elia Kazan. By the time the fourth and final Lane sisters vehicle,

Four Mothers (1941), was ready to roll, Garfield had graduated to better roles, although, except for Priscilla, the Lane sisters had not.

Of the three, Priscilla could at least claim she worked with Hitchcock and Capra. When Rosemary figured out that she had no future in Hollywood, she headed for Broadway, where she won the lead in the musical *Best Foot Forward* (1941). However, when MGM bought the screen rights, her part went to Lucille Ball.

Lola was better known for her marriages than her films. She seemed to marry every few years. In 1931 it was actor Lew Ayres, from whom she separated the following year and whom she divorced in 1933 on the grounds that he kept late hours and virtually ignored her. In 1934 she eloped with director Alexander Hall; that marriage lasted until 1936. From 1936 to 1941 Lola was between marriages. It may have been during this period that her romance with Wallis began, after she appeared in his productions of *Marked Woman* and *Hollywood Hotel*. She was not only available but also eager to make her mark in a business where failure is more common than success. Lola could not have found a better patron than Wallis, who saw in her not a potential star but a "tough dame" on the order of Joan Blondell and Glenda Farrell; she would always be a clone, never the genuine article. Wallis's was the same combination of desire, compassion, and paternalism that drew director-producer Jospeh L. Mankiewicz to Judy Garland, who needed the security that Mankiewicz offered, until he could no longer satisfy her emotional needs—as if any one man could.

The Wallis-Lane romance ended in 1941 with the last of the Lane sisters movies. That year, Lola wed aircraft executive Henry Clay Durham, whom she divorced four years later. Lola did not have to divorce her fourth husband, director Roland West, who died in 1952. Nor did she have to wait long for a fifth husband. In 1955 she married lawyer Robert Hanlon. That was her longest marriage, lasting until her death in 1981. The reason was her conversion to Catholicism in 1961; for the next twenty years, Lola was so active in church affairs that she was awarded the Pope Pius X medal in 1967.

The only Lane sister Wallis mentions in his autobiography is Priscilla, "the buxom example of normal, middle-class, healthy womanhood" (*Starmaker,* 102). The "buxom example" appeared in more Wallis productions than Lola or Rosemary, and most of the time in major roles: *Love, Honor, and Behave* (1938), *The Cowboy from Brooklyn* (1938),

Four Daughters (1938), *Brother Rat* (1938), *Yes, My Darling Daughter* (1939), *Daughters Courageous* (1939), *Four Wives* (1939), *Brother Rat and Baby* (1940), *Four Mothers* (1941), and *Million Dollar Baby* (1941). Priscilla also made more films at Warners not produced by Wallis than either of her sisters, suggesting that her "healthy womanhood" lent itself to more scenarios than Lola's shady lady. "Normal, middle-class, healthy womanhood" held no appeal for Wallis, who was attracted to a different species. Under Wallis's patronage, Lola was a contract player at a major studio; without it, she was reduced to making movies such as *Miss V from Moscow* (1942) at PRC on Poverty Row—a feeble attempt to pay tribute to America's new, but short-lived, ally, the former Soviet Union; the film turned out to be "one of the worst movies ever made by any standards."[8] Lola's last credit was *Deadline at Dawn* (1946), in which she played a blackmailer who is so unprincipled that her murder by a taxi driver (Paul Lukas) seems almost justified.

Perhaps the best explanation for the Wallis-Lane affair appears in Tom Stoppard's play *The Real Thing,* in which a wife, an actress working in British repertory, explains to her cerebral husband that when two actors are thrown together, rehearsing daily and performing nightly, loneliness and desire can win out over fidelity. Trying to promote the Lane sisters as Warners's latest attraction put Wallis in contact with all of them. As Wallis's former publicist, Walter Seltzer, phrased it, "He shepherded them around." Lola, however, needed more than shepherding; she needed patronage, which Wallis provided—for a time.

Corinne Calvet was another matter. When Wallis decided to play Pygmalion to Corinne Calvet's Galatea, he found himself in the thrall of a minx, who, unlike Lola Lane, could be brazen, coy, mischievous, and cunning. Lola was none of these; she was ambitious but emotionally needy. Corinne was cut from gaudier cloth; she was the closest there was to a Hollywood coquette. Not surprisingly, Corinne entitled her autobiography *Has Corinne Been a Good Girl?* (1983), a question that studio publicists and executives must have asked constantly.

As Mae West put it in *She Done Him Wrong* (1933), "Goodness had nothing to do with it"—"it" being the goal and however it is achieved. Corinne's goal was stardom, once she realized that the law degree she had been pursuing at the Sorbonne was no substitute for the fame she was seeking. As it happened, she experienced more notoriety than fame. A few roles in a couple of obscure French films brought her to Hollywood—first to MGM, where she languished until her agent managed to persuade Wallis to look at her screen test. Wallis was drawn to actresses with a air of mystery about them; in Lola Lane's case it was her habit of changing husbands, with a brief hiatus between marriages, and her provocative looks that belied the insecurity that lay beneath them. With Corinne, it was the sense of abandon that she exhibited like a road sign: no danger ahead—a couple of detours but a great ride.

As a former law student, Corinne knew she was in the driver's seat; what she needed was a vehicle—the latest and most expensive model preferred. Eventually, Wallis provided her with the car that she insisted she must have.[9] But in 1949 the vehicle was a film: *Rope of Sand,* a misguided attempt to conjure up the spirit of Wallis's most famous movie, *Casablanca,* by reuniting some members of the original cast (Peter Lorre, Claude Rains, Paul Heinreid), with diamonds standing in for the letters of transit. Corinne, however, was having immigration problems, which could be solved by marrying an American citizen. Wallis had recently signed John Bromfield, a darkly handsome actor who became part of the pretty-boy brigade: actors whose looks signified more than their talent. Those with more than looks (e.g., Tony Curtis, Rock Hudson, Montgomery Clift) moved on to stardom; those with just looks (Troy Donahue, Tab Hunter) moved on to oblivion. Bromfield was one of that latter group.

Bromfield was slated for a minor role in *Rope of Sand,* with Corinne in the female lead. Corinne must have worked her magic, because her immigration problems were solved by her 1948 marriage to Bromfield. That marriage lasted longer than Lola's to Lew Ayres or Alexander Hall; Corinne divorced her husband in 1954, and Bromfield left the business two years later.

Meanwhile, Corinne had become Europe's latest export. While Wallis capitalized on her continental charm, to which she added more than a soupçon of wiliness, Corinne discovered Wallis's Achilles heel: his unwillingness to expose his human side for fear of endangering his reputation as a producer. Wallis was generous with her bonuses and loans, one of which was for $9,000 without interest. Although Corinne was grateful, she used the occasion to let Wallis know that she understood him thoroughly. Addressing him, as she always did, as "Dear Boss," she wrote: "I guess sometimes you have to look awfully tough to be a respected producer. But . . . inside, deep, inside you are very sweet and nice. A few times I saw that side of you—and it's like that I want to think of you when I do. Love, Corinne."[10] As the bonuses kept coming in, Corinne was effusive, but always with a request. Learning that another bonus was forthcoming, she asked if she could have it immediately: "I just saw a car I am mad about." This letter was signed "Love and Kisses, Your Slave Corinne."

Corinne was determined to make herself known throughout America. That meant television appearances. Wallis allowed Corinne and Bromfield to appear on the *Kate Smith Evening Hour* in November 1951, with the understanding that the $3,500 they would receive would be used to pay their expenses. The following year it was *The Dennis Day Show* for $2,250, which also posed no problem to Wallis. However, in 1953, when Corinne decided to appear on *The Colgate Comedy Hour* with the Ritz Brothers, whom Wallis considered in the same category as the Three Stooges, he was furious. But when Corinne started doing charades on local television, Wallis issued an ultimatum: no further television appearances without his permission.

Corinne knew she had become a star when she and Bromfield visited London in the fall of 1951. After attending a performance of *Antony and Cleopatra* with Laurence Olivier, Corinne was about to go backstage when she was mobbed by fans who clamored for her autograph. Even though she and Bromfield stayed in London for only two days, Corinne had achieved celebrity status.

Corinne's star power began to concern Wallis. Although she had caught on with audiences, he had little to offer her. She had become so convinced of her popularity that she would deliberately do a bad screen test for a film in which she did not wish to appear. Although MGM wanted her for a supporting role in *Quo Vadis,* she refused, despite the pleas from her agent.

Wallis had already loaned her to Fox in 1950. The roles were good: *When Willie Comes Marching Home* (1950) with Dan Dailey and *On the Riviera* (1951) with Danny Kaye. So was the pay: $25,000 for *Willie* and $30,000 for *Riviera*. Not bad for eight weeks per picture, with Corinne not even playing the female lead.

Even though Wallis knew Corinne could never be his Garbo or Bergman, she continued to appeal to him on a level that had nothing to do with her questionable talent. According to her autobiography, Wallis expected sex from her after *Rope of Sand*. When he propositioned her,

Corinne refused, calling herself a married woman. Wallis, however, knowing the circumstances of her marriage, allegedly called it one of convenience, which he himself had suggested.[11] Since Wallis was a pragmatist, one could easily believe that he recommended a union that would give him two attractive performers who could be marketed as a couple—but just in the press. Wallis was only interested in one of them—and not for long.

When Wallis dropped Corinne's option in 1953, Corinne wanted revenge, which she achieved in a perverse way after encountering Wallis at a club in New York. Corinne was afflicted with a sore throat and fever. Concealing her condition from Wallis, she accepted his invitation to join him in his room at the Plaza, where they proceeded to have sex. The next morning, Wallis awakened with a strep throat; shortly, four dozen roses arrived with a note: "Next time I'll give you something worse. Best wishes for your recovery."[12]

Whether the incident occurred as Corinne described it, or whether it was an attempt to embarrass a man who was three years away from death when her autobiography was published, is impossible to know. At least Wallis could claim that, as an actress, Corinne was not an embarrassment. She worked with some important directors (William Dieterle and John Ford) and major stars (Claude Rains, Paul Henreid, Danny Kaye, James Cagney, Deborah Kerr, Charles Boyer, Alan Ladd, and Joan Fontaine). Corinne was not Wallis's Anna Sten, the Ukrainian actress on whom Sam Goldwyn lavished a disproportionate amount of publicity and money to make into a star, only to see her career dissipate after a few films. Corinne's English may have been accented, but she never pronounced "earth" as "earse," as Anna did in *The Wedding Night* (1935), much to the amusement of her costar, Gary Cooper, who nicknamed her "Anna Stench."

CHAPTER TWELVE

His Last Girl

O N 6 AUGUST 1959, THE WORLD PREMIERE of Buena Vista's production of *The Big Fisherman,* a three-hour biblical epic based on Lloyd C. Douglas's novel about Saint Peter, took place at New York's Rivoli Theatre on Forty-ninth Street and Broadway. The ads promised a gala affair, "with guest stars of stage and screen." Two months before the premiere, Buena Vista dispatched one of the stars, Martha Hyer (who played Herodias to Herbert Lom's Herod), to New York to publicize the film—Frank Borzage's last and hardly the one by which the Oscar-winning director would want to be remembered.

Ordinarily, it would have been just another PR junket, or so Martha thought in June 1959 when she boarded American Airlines flight 2 from Los Angeles to New York. In the check-in line, she noticed a man, presumably a fellow passenger, who had already reached the counter, leaning against it in such a way that he faced her. He saw an extremely attractive woman; she, a man with armor-piercing blue eyes. For a moment their gazes interlocked. Each knew who the other was. To Wallis, Martha Hyer was the well-known actress and Oscar nominee for *Some Came Running* (1958). She had once auditioned for him when he was casting the female lead in *Gunfight at the O.K. Corral* (1957), which she failed to get because she was then under contract to Universal. Martha saw Wallis for the first time a decade earlier; the occasion was a brunch in Santa Monica to which her agent brought her just as she was about to begin her career as an RKO contract player. Wallis was there, along with other celebrities, including the Mexican-born Linda Christian, later to become Tyrone Power's second wife. As a 1940s columnist might have said, Linda was a "knockout." She also exuded a regal air that distinguished her from the typical Hollywood wannabes. Linda chose the pool to display her physical attributes.[1] For the myriads not at the brunch, Linda's aquatic talents were soon revealed in *Tarzan and the Mermaids* (1948). Wallis, who had a way of making eye contact with beautiful women, offered Linda a ride home. If Linda had been serious about a movie career, she would have inquired about her driver. Had she heard *"Casablanca,"* she would not have declined the lift. Barely into her twenties, Martha understood physical attraction; once she became the second Mrs. Hal Wallis, she enjoyed teasing her husband about the incident.

A Santa Monica beach house is one thing; Los Angeles International Airport, another. As an Oscar-nominated movie star, Martha was accustomed to craning necks, "Aren't you . . . ?" questions, autograph hounds, and wolf whistles. When Martha and Wallis caught sight of each other, she probably thought it was just another case of recognition. And it was—on both their parts, the difference being that Martha could recall the first time she ever laid eyes on Wallis, while he recognized her only from her films and the audition. If Wallis remembered anything about the brunch, it was Linda Christian.

Martha had no idea that a coast-to-coast flight would change her life; nor did the passenger seated behind her, who happened to be Hal Wallis. Both Martha and Wallis have written their memoirs; both allude to the flight; and both are off on the date—Wallis more so than Martha. Yet there is no doubt that within six hours their attraction had advanced from check-in to landing, from dinner to "courtship" (a term that each puts in quotes), and finally to marriage. If their story had been turned into a movie, it could have been called "Romance in Midair."

But in what year would it be set? According to Martha, it was "one sixties summer day" (*Finding My Way,* 83). Martha now admits that it was June 1959; as discreet in her way as Wallis was in his, she preferred a little white lie to the blatant admission that Wallis was still married to Louise when they met.[2] Readers familiar with the way writers create a subtext—concealing the truth beneath a deceptively glossy veneer that has been varnished to a sheen—would figure out that Martha was not being deceptive. In her filmography, she correctly cites the release date of *The Big Fisherman* as 1959, even identifying the studio as Disney's Buena Vista. In Wallis's filmography, however, *Saratoga Trunk* (1945), his last Warners production, is listed among his 1945 Paramount films, perhaps because it had premiered after he set up his production company at the studio. In view of the legal wranglings that ensued when Warner tried to deny Wallis credit for *Saratoga Trunk,* one wonders whether it was a memory lapse on Wallis's part or a deliberate attempt to divide his producing career into pre– and post–Warner Brothers.

A knowledgeable reader—which, for a work like *Finding My Way,* is someone cognizant of release dates—would rub off the veneer to get at the unvarnished truth—a process that Martha simplifies when she writes of accompanying Wallis on "location trips" (*Finding My Way,* 89), one of which was to Kauai for *Blue Hawaii* (1961), filmed in 1960, two years before Louise died. Although Wallis passed away four years before the publication of *Finding My Way* (and Louise had died twenty-eight years earlier), Martha chose prudence, a virtue highly prized in the Renaissance, over candor—the former requiring a slight shift in chronology without vitiating the truth: "Hal had another life," she explained (*Finding My Way,* 84). In 1959 he did—with Louise. But so did Martha, who said the same about herself—and in the same sentence: "I had another life."

Wallis is both specific and evasive about the date of their meeting. Louise does not receive her own chapter in *Starmaker.* While Louise is mentioned periodically, she is juxtaposed with Martha in a chapter appropriately entitled, "Louise and Martha." Wallis segues from Louise's death in 1962 to a "spring morning fourteen years ago" (*Starmaker,* 173) when, just before boarding his American Airlines flight to New York, he caught sight of an elegantly dressed woman, whom he recognized as the actress Martha Hyer.

"Fourteen years ago"—from *when*? From 1962? That would have been 1948, when Martha was just starting out at RKO at $150 a week and Wallis had no idea who she was. The only possible explanation is that the incident occurred fourteen years before Wallis decided to write his autobiography, which seems to have been around 1973. Wallis was not being cavalier about chronology; he simply believed that discretion was, in its own way, as much of an art as film. Until the Production Code was scrapped in the late 1960s, the real lovemaking took place offscreen; what moviegoers saw was metaphorical sex (the camera tracking back from recumbent or semirecumbent lovers; a fire going to embers; a rain-lashed window; the drawing of a shade that leaves only a silhouette; a fade-out followed by crumpled bedding). The classic example of sexual decorum was the long shot in *Gone with the Wind* (1939), with Rhett Butler carrying a reluctant Scarlett up the staircase to their bedroom, followed by a close-up of Scarlett awakening the next morning, looking thoroughly fulfilled. To Wallis, who guarded his privacy, watching people make love was voyeurism at its most infantile. In 1970, when the National Association of Theatre Owners honored him as Producer of the Year, Wallis used the occasion to inveigh against the "licentiousness and pornography" that had overtaken the screen. Movie sex in 1970 was mild compared to what it later became. But by then, Wallis was hors de combat.

Hal Wallis had his faults, but a penchant for sensationalism was not one of them. Just as generations of moviegoers never had to be shown what happened between the closing and opening of bedroom doors, the ideal readers of *Starmaker*—those astute enough to provide the right time line by connecting text and subtext—were expected to fill in the ellipses. Wallis provided the plot points, hoping they would be connected into as complete a narrative as possible. Martha did likewise in *Finding My Way,* perhaps following her husband's lead, but more likely her own instincts.

Wallis's account of meeting Martha was even more elliptical in an earlier version of *Starmaker,* in which he wrote: "Louise died in 1962. About five years later on a trip to New York, my seatmate on an American Airlines flight was an actress whom I had met briefly in Hollywood, Martha Hyer."[3] It was true that he met Martha when she read for *Gunfight at the O.K. Corral.* But that was in 1956, when Louise was very much alive. Either Wallis realized that he had made a chronological blunder, to which he was often prone; or, in an attempt to portray himself as an exemplary widower, he devised his own sequence of events. Once he figured out that there were readers, especially film buffs, to whom chronology is so sacred that a wrong release date can throw them into a tizzy, he decided to play by the rules.

In the final version of *Starmaker* (173–74), Wallis not only identified the woman on flight 2 by name, admitting that he recognized her—but not vice versa (little knowing that Martha possessed the better memory); he also pushed the flight back to spring 1959, when Martha "had just been nominated" for an Oscar. Wallis even acknowledged having read the 4 May 1959 *Life* profile on her.

June is not spring, which came late for Wallis in 1959. He was either off by a month or thinking symbolically of spring as the time of renewal. The facts are correct, but not the sequence. Martha was indeed an Oscar nominee for *Some Came Running*. However, by the time the *Life* piece appeared, the Oscars were a month old; they had been awarded on 6 April 1959, when Martha lost to Wendy Hiller for *Separate Tables*. That Wallis and Martha provided the bare facts—being specific in some cases, vague in others—implies that their meeting is what mattered, not when. Late fifties, early sixties; spring, summer—whenever. Their accounts are generally complementary. Being an actress (and a better writer), Martha is more vivid, as if she were fashioning a "meet cute" scene for a romantic film.

A treatment might begin like this: We FADE IN on Martha settling into her aisle seat on American Airlines flight 2. She takes a compact from her purse, catching a reflection of the passenger seated behind her. No surprise. The "Fasten Seat Belts" sign appears. After takeoff, Wallis taps Martha on the shoulder. Small talk. "I know your work," Wallis coos. "And I, yours," Martha replies. MONTAGE of more small talk, some without dialogue, followed by silences and CLOSE-UPS of each trying to become engrossed in a book—but not succeeding. Wallis finally takes the initiative: "What about dinner after we land?" "Sorry," Martha answers. "The next day?" Wallis inquires. "Prior commitment." Beat . . . beat . . . beat. Martha takes the initiative: "What about the night after that?"[4] To paraphrase the final line of *Casablanca*, that was the beginning—not of a beautiful friendship but of a classic romance.

What makes *Finding My Way* a more engrossing memoir than *Starmaker* is its structure: a framing device enclosing a flashback. *Finding My Way* begins in 1981 and ends five years later; in between is the author's life from her birth to Wallis's death. The chance meeting is also one of the great staples of the movie romance: on a boat (*Now, Voyager; An Affair to Remember* [1957]), a train (*The Major and the Minor* [1942]), a bus (*It Happened One Night* [1935]), a plane (*The High and the Mighty* [1954]), and even a stagecoach (*Stagecoach* [1939]). When life and art intersect, it is not matter of art imitating life, but of art dictating the plot points. On that memorable coast-to-coast flight, both parties played their roles to the hilt. Wallis certainly knew how to flirt, and Martha knew how to play the scene. She also knew how to direct it, pausing just long enough before giving him his cues.

Starmaker, however, is discursive—moving in and out of chronology, sometimes leaving huge gaps in the narrative. Both memoirs have one note in common: discretion. That each memoirist chose to describe his or her relationship prior to marriage as a "courtship" (quotation marks theirs) suggests that love took precedence over anything as reductive as chronology. When it came to affairs of the heart, Wallis and Martha practiced selective reticence. Until they married on New Year's Eve 1966, their relationship would remain a "courtship."

Martha entered Wallis's life at precisely the right time. Anyone following the Hollywood scene would have assumed that the 1950s were a glorious decade for Wallis: Oscars for Shirley Booth and Anna Magnani, the Martin and Lewis and Elvis phenomena. But then there was the news Wallis and Louise received about their treasured Valley farm: it had to make way for a junior high school. Worse, their house had to be demolished.

With his usual indifference to chronology, Wallis implies in *Starmaker* (112–13) that two major events in his life occurred in the 1940s: the loss of the farm and his departure from Warners. They occurred in reverse—the departure from Warners in late 1943, the demolition of the Woodland Avenue home much later—in the late 1950s.

The news about the home devastated Louise. To her, the farm was more than a home; it was a haven; to Wallis, losing it meant a change of address. Unlike Louise, who could luxuriate in retirement, Wallis spent his days dealing with the nitty-gritty of moviemaking. In *Starmaker* (112), Wallis described the effect of the property on Louise: "The shock . . . almost destroyed Louise [whose] health deteriorated rapidly."

In an early draft, Wallis was more explicit: "Her health was never the same."[5] Nor was their marriage. When Wallis was a Hollywood newcomer, marrying a star like Louise Fazenda was the equivalent of an announcement in the trades heralding his arrival. It helped that Wallis truly loved her, but it was a love that could never take the place of what, in Wallis's universe, was the equivalent of Dante's love that moves the sun and other stars: movies. Martha understood that love better than Louise, to whom moviemaking was a job that brought her fame, money, and eventually retirement. But it was also a love that Martha could share with Wallis, having known it to a far greater extent than Louise.

Realizing they would be soon dispossessed, Louise and Wallis made a move that neither would have considered in 1935: Beverly Hills—to a twelve-room mansion at 515 South Mapleton Drive, once the home of another producer and his actress wife, Walter Wanger and Joan Bennett. Since Brent was in his twenties, and Louise had long before retired, location was no longer a priority. Wallis was ready for a new life. His new address was also the equivalent of a calling card that read, "Hal Wallis Is Back Where He Belongs." And at a time when the industry was going through enormous change, the place was Beverly Hills, not in a cocoon. Louise did what she could by way of remodeling the house, but it took Martha to transform it into a producer's home. But that would only be after she became Martha Hyer Wallis. Until 31 December 1966, she was Martha Hyer, working actress.

Compared to Wallis's uncosseted childhood, Martha's was gilded. It was also idyllic in the way that storybook childhoods are supposed to be. Martha was born in Fort Worth, Texas, the daughter of Julien C. Hyer, a district court judge, and the former Agnes Barnhart, a Northwestern University alumna. She benefited from having parents who were education-conscious but also determined to give her and her sisters a traditional upbringing. It was Saturday afternoons at the movies or ball games with her father, Sunday services at the Methodist church, grace before meals, slumber parties, high school plays—in short, pure Americana. Her parents' respect for education brought her first to a junior college in Virginia, then to her mother's alma mater, Northwestern, from which she graduated with a degree in speech and drama.

Her next stop was the Pasadena Playhouse. Knowing that agents frequented the Playhouse in search of potential stars, Martha sent a letter to Milton Lewis, a Paramount talent scout, inviting him to a play in which she was to appear. Taken with her ability, Lewis arranged for an audition at Paramount, which did not lead to a screen test but nevertheless attracted the attention of several agents. Uncertain about the agent-actor relationship, Martha wrote to her father, then judge advocate of the Fifteenth Army stationed in Bad Nauheim, a well-known health resort in West Germany. It also happened that singer Ella Logan was entertaining the troops at Bad Nauheim and noticed Martha's picture on her father's desk. Learning that Martha was not the typical starstruck aspirant, Logan sent her a letter of introduction to her husband, a producer at Fox, who promptly told Martha to go back to Texas—the same advice that another fellow Texan, Mary Martin, was once given. Fortunately, neither Martha nor Mary heeded it.

In 1946 Ella Logan opened on Broadway in the classic musical

Finian's Rainbow; Martha's first movie, RKO's *The Locket,* appeared the same year. For the next few years, Martha experienced the slow, and at times arduous, ascent up the ladder of fame—looking up enviously at those above, sometimes watching them descend, and down at those below, stuck on the same rungs. While she never became a movie icon, she succeeded in a business where longevity is rarer than loyalty, gaining the respect of such costars as Tony Curtis, Rosalind Russell, Frank Sinatra, Dean Martin, and Cary Grant; and directors such as Mark Robson, Vincente Minnelli, Henry Hathaway, and Jean Negulesco. She remained in the industry for a quarter of a century, making sixty-eight films between 1946 and 1970—averaging two and sometimes three a year. Martha could have continued working after 1970 had she not decided to be the wife her husband expected her to be: one who would accompany him to premieres, exhibits, and opening nights, all of which she did gladly.

Given her upbringing, Martha had no problem playing the dutiful wife. Her first husband was aspiring filmmaker Ray Stahl, the son of director John Stahl. The son never achieved his father's fame, which rests on a handful of well-regarded films such as *Back Street* (1933), *Imitation of Life* (1934), *Magnificent Obsession* (1935), and *Leave Her to Heaven* (1945). When Ray decided the public was ready for a movie set in Japan during the American occupation, his wife agreed to play the lead. Japan proved an exhilarating experience for Martha, even though *Geisha Girl* (1952) was not. It was during the filming of *Geisha Girl* that Martha had the feeling that hers would not be an "until death do us part" marriage. Still, she continued to be supportive of her husband's abortive attempts at moviemaking.

When Hollywood seemed to be going native after *King Solomon's Mines* (1950) and *The African Queen* (1951), Ray headed for Kenya to shoot *The Scarlet Spear* (1953). Like the virtuous woman in the book of Proverbs (31:10–31), Martha girded her loins and joined him, even though it meant playing another thankless role as well as being upstaged by a python that draped itself around her shoulders like a stole. Although Martha found spiritual comfort in the African landscape, which seemed to be permeated with a divine presence, she realized that divorce was inevitable. There was another woman in Stahl's life with whom she could not compete: his mother. It was also a marriage that was destined to be childless because of Stahl's lack of interest in a family. The marriage lasted for two years, 1951–53. Six years after their divorce, Ray Stahl succumbed to cancer on 9 April 1959. He was thirty-eight.

By the time Ray Stahl died, Martha Hyer was a star. After only twelve years in the business, she was the subject of a full-page piece by the powerful gossip columnist Hedda Hopper, in which Martha was unusually candid about her devotion to art, readily admitting that she spent half of her salary on paintings: "Each time I get an assignment I feel I get two pictures—the film and the canvas I can buy from the money I can make on it."[6] Hopper easily concluded that Martha's love of art was consistent with a lifestyle dictated by the need to be surrounded by beauty in all its manifestations, from paintings and objets d'art to a hilltop house with a spectacular view. As Hopper concluded, "She's not a cold-water-flat type actress [and] likes to live luxuriously."

Just how luxuriously was revealed the following year when Martha was profiled in *Life*—a giant step from the syndicated Hopper, whose days of making and breaking stars were coming to an end. Pictures have their own form of eloquence, and those that accompanied the seven-page spread in *Life* revealed one of Hollywood's few genuine aesthetes: an actress who embraced beauty with all the temptations and snares awaiting those who worship at its shrine.[7] And although Martha prided herself on being a good Christian, even to the point of searching for and eventually finding a congenial congregation, she discovered a deity as powerful as the One she worshiped on Sundays: beauty.

"She loves, openly and single mindedly, only the nicest, most lusciously expensive things," *Life* proclaimed. The reader was treated to a tour of her home at 8868 Hollywood Boulevard with its panoramic view of Los Angeles, along with shots of Martha standing proudly at her Sheffield tea service, sipping champagne during a beauty treatment, and setting out for a stroll in a full-length mink. She conformed to the popular image of the movie star, who breakfasts on china, uses a Steuben glass in the bathroom, and, like the ethereal creature in Byron's poem, walks in beauty.

Like most celebrity pieces, *Life*'s was a combination of hype and fact. Drinking champagne while getting one's hair done is the public's idea of the good life, Hollywood style; and if such extravagant behavior can sell tickets, so be it. Although the profile exaggerated Martha's love of luxury, making her seem like a budding hedonist, it was accurate in its depiction of the actress as an art lover whose pursuit of beauty was subsidized by her work in film. Martha had not so much a love, as a passion, for art. At Northwestern, she vacillated between majoring in art or theater. She chose the latter, while continuing to paint for relaxation. When her film career started to take off, Martha began collecting, eventually acquiring originals by Rouault, Gauguin, Utrillo, Pissarro, Toulouse-Lautrec, and Renoir, which adorned the beige walls of her hilltop home above Sunset Strip. The *Life* piece also expressed her philosophy, which rang true: "The elegant life is living with a keen sense of beauty, exhibiting refined taste, which naturally includes comfort and suggests luxury." There were many stars who shared those sentiments about comfort and luxury but were clueless when it came to beauty and taste. Unlike most of her peers, Martha could invoke John Keats's equation of beauty and truth, even though she knew that the pursuit of beauty might require some tinkering with truth. How much tinkering she had yet to discover.

Although the *Life* profile did not give Martha's street address, it made her home easy for thieves to locate. On Halloween evening 1959, Martha attended a party at Merle Oberon's; when she returned home, she discovered that $80,000 worth of valuables were missing, including an Utrillo and a Renoir worth $25,000 and $15,000, respectively. Two years later, the paintings were recovered, but nothing else. The robbery did not sour her on collecting or neutralize her aesthetic sense. Martha simply became more cautious. But caution is often thrown to the wind, leading to a trail of deception ending in retribution. In Martha's case, it was retribution in the twofold sense of atonement and payment. But that would not be until 1981. In 1959 the dark side of aestheticism was far from her mind. Martha was an Oscar nominee who had held her own against Dean Martin, Frank Sinatra, and Shirley MacLaine in a film that validated her credentials as a serious actress. Fox wanted her for *The Best of Everything* (1958), a glossy exposé of the publishing world based on Rona Jaffe's best seller. Next came *The Big Fisherman* (1959), which indirectly (or providentially) led to a real "until death do us part" marriage.

If Wallis ever needed someone for the long term, it was in 1959. Louise was in failing health and would die of a cerebral hemorrhage three years later on 17 April 1962 while Wallis was on location in Hawaii filming one of Elvis's by-the-numbers vehicles, *Girls! Girls! Girls!* (1962). Brent did not turn out to be the son that Wallis had anticipated. Brent was a different breed. Had he shown an interest in Wallis's profession, as Richard Zanuck did in his father's, it might have compensated for the inevitable absenteeism that moviemaking imposes upon the families of producers. When Richard Zanuck was in the sixth grade, Darryl sounded him out on scripts and even brought him into the cutting room to view the rushes and offer suggestions.[8] When Brent saw his father editing films, he was so unnerved by the lack of continuity that he found the whole process repugnant, even frightening. Darryl and Richard Zanuck had a common bond that Wallis and Brent lacked. If such a bond had existed between Wallis and Brent, or even between Wallis and Louise, the schedule that Wallis maintained would not have mattered; father and son, husband and wife, could always talk shop in the evening. But since neither father and son nor husband and wife had much in common, Wallis's hours precluded the possibility of closeness.

Wallis arrived at the studio at 9:00 A.M. and left at 6:00 P.M., sometimes later. His daily indulgence was a visit to Jack Warner's exclusive barber shop on the studio lot, where he had water-soaked cotton balls placed on his eyes while he was getting a shave. By 6:30 P.M. Wallis was at home; after a quick dinner, he spent the rest of the evening reading scripts or viewing the dailies. Although he tried to introduce Brent to horseback riding, he preferred Michael Curtiz as a riding companion and even kept his horses at Curtiz's nearby ranch. Brent was not especially interested in deep sea fishing, either, Wallis's other passion.

Politically, they were at opposite ends of the spectrum, with Wallis growing increasingly conservative as Brent embraced diversity in its various aspects. There is no doubt that Brent respected his father out of the usual combination of fear and love that the children of the mighty feel for patriarchs. Wallis, however, was not the kind of father Brent needed. The bottom line was financial security, which Wallis provided and from which Brent profited. Had Wallis lived to see Brent's transformation of the foundation that he had set up in 1957, he would have been surprised. Except for some health-related contributions, the Wallis Foundation was relatively dormant during Hal Wallis's lifetime. Perhaps it was living and working in San Francisco during the 1970s and 1980s that made Brent sensitive to sexual and ethnic diversity as well as the need to espouse environmental causes. Among later recipients of Foundation money were the Los Angeles Gay and Lesbian Center; the San Francisco Zoo; UCLA outreach programs for prospective law school students from economically disadvantaged backgrounds; the Presidential Scholars Program at California State University at Hayward; the UCLA–Wallis Foundation Website for Learning Disabilities; less prominent museums such as the Santa Barbara Museum; the Center for Patient Partnerships at the University of Wisconsin, whose goal was to make doctors, health care providers, politicians, and educators more sensitive to patients' needs; and the Kennebec Coalition, which brought the fish back to Maine's Kennebec River once a dam had been removed and the river restored.

It is hard to imagine Wallis caring about gays, fisheries, the underprivileged, and mixed media art. Brent cared, as did the Foundation, which was now under his management. Although Wallis had made some movies about the downtrodden, his son went to the next level and attempted to improve their lot. Wallis made Brent's finest hour possible, although he would never have understood the route his son took to get there.

If Brent was the isolate that Wallis described in *Starmaker,* it could hardly have been otherwise with a father who was unavailable most evenings and a mother who spent her time visiting shut-ins and entertaining friends from her silent movie past. The chief difference was that Louise doted on Brent, the child of her prayers and pilgrimages and her personal refuge from a Hollywood that had become alien to her, but not to Wallis. Realizing she had no place in her husband's world, Louise found one of her own, embracing humanitarianism as if she had taken a lover, which, metaphorically, she had. A framed quote on her night table read: "May I never leave a lame dog by a stile, / but lift it to the other side / and make its life worthwhile." She applied the same principle to people, becoming a volunteer at the UCLA Medical Center, where her work so impressed the staff that a Louise Fazenda Memorial Fund was established shortly after her death.[9]

By extending her apostolate to Los Angeles's neediest cases, Louise made the acquaintance of Edward Bunker around 1950, just after he had been released from Los Angeles County Jail for stabbing a fellow inmate in the shower.[10] Bunker later achieved celebrity as a crime novelist after his first work of fact-inspired fiction, *No Beast So Fierce* (1972), was published while he was serving time in Folsom Prison for armed robbery; and as a film actor, who brought authenticity to his roles in *Straight Time* (1978), the film version of *No Beast So Fierce,* and Quentin Tarantino's *Reservoir Dogs* (1992).

To the courts, Bunker was a juvenile criminal, the product of foster homes, petty crimes, and parole violations; to Louise, he was a soul to be saved. In 1950 Bunker was seventeen, and Louise was fifty-four. At first, Bunker suspected Louise of being another lonely wife in need of a young lover; but he soon discovered that all that mattered to Louise was his spiritual regeneration, which "Mom," as Bunker called her, facilitated by introducing him to her library, many of whose books he had already read, and to her narrow circle of acquaintances, which included Charlie Chaplin and William Randolph Hearst. Louise often took him with her to the Hearst estate at San Simeon. In fact, he and Louise were at San Simeon the day Hearst died in 1951.

Louise's altruism did not have the desired effect. That same year, 1951, found Bunker back in jail, this time at San Quentin, where he spent the next five years. Imprisonment did not deter Louise, who corresponded with him, always encouraging him to pursue his goal of becoming a writer. When Bunker saw Louise again in 1956, he was shocked at her condition. The loss of the farm and, as she believed, her husband's love increased her dependence on alcohol. Bunker had hoped his friendship with Louise would lead him to Wallis and a screenwriting career. But Wallis literally barred Bunker from their home, and Louise's erratic behavior and subsequent nervous collapse precluded any possibility of further contact with her.

Had Louise not died in 1962, Wallis would not have left her, despite her deteriorating mental and physical health and his involvement with Martha. Unlike his father, Wallis had a sense of obligation. It may not have included fidelity to a spouse, but it did not allow for abandoning her, either. The concept of family meant much to Louise, who extended her own to embrace types ordinarily encountered by social workers, missionaries, and proselytizers. Louise had become all three, dispensing her brand of Christianity to the less fortunate. To Wallis, families were people in movies; he produced so many films about ideal families (e.g., *Four Daughters, Four Wives, Daughters Courageous, Yankee Doodle Dandy*) that the discrepancy between those and his own was a case of life mocking, rather than imitating, art. Wallis was always forthright in discussing his failures, by which he meant movies such as *About Mrs. Leslie* and *Wild Is the Wind* that did not live up to his expectations; whether he would have considered his attempt at being a husband and father a failure is problematic. Louise was the kind of wife Wallis needed when he was starting out in the business. Fortunately, his films were successful enough to make up for his indifference to socializing. That changed significantly with his marriage to Martha; then a world class producer burst out of the pod that had insulated him from a milieu for which he secretly yearned but could not embrace because of Louise. That marriage was, as Nina Leeds said of her life in Eugene O' Neill's *Strange Interlude* (1928), "an interlude of trial and preparation."[11] With Martha, the interlude had ended, along with the trial and preparation; it was a time for renewal.

The chance meeting on flight 2 returned Wallis to the producer he once was before he called a moratorium on art in favor of pop culture. Wallis had always wanted to make the movie version of Tennessee Williams's *Summer and Smoke,* which failed on Broadway in 1948 but enjoyed considerable success off Broadway in the early 1950s when a then unknown actress, Geraldine Page, under José Quintero's direction, recreated the role of Alma, another of Williams's mothlike prefigurations of *Streetcar*'s Blanche du Bois.[12] Like so many stage actors of the 1950s, including Paul Newman, Joanne Woodward, and James Dean, who heeded Hollywood's siren call, Page also headed west, winning an Oscar nomination for her film debut opposite John Wayne in *Hondo* (1953). For some reason, Wallis was skeptical of her drawing power, even though Page and Newman—she cast against type as a nymphomaniacal movie star who has seen better days, he as an opportunistic stud—were playing to sellout houses on Broadway in Tennessee Williams's *Sweet Bird of Youth* (1958). Because he had envisioned other actresses in the role, such as Deborah Kerr and Katharine Hepburn (who were considerably more bankable), Wallis held off on Geraldine Page. When none of his choices were available, Wallis yielded, earning the gratitude of those who had never seen Page play Alma off Broadway and now had the chance to see her recreate the role on film. Although Wallis knew that *Summer and Smoke* would not have moviegoers lining up at the box office, he was confident that the film would restore his credibility as a serious producer; it did, as Oscar nominations came in for Page, Una Merkel as her dotty mother, Hal Pereira and others for set decoration, and Elmer Bernstein for musical scoring. Although *Summer and Smoke* failed to win a single Oscar, it was the first time in six years that a Wallis production had received so many nominations; the last time was *The Rose Tattoo,* which had eight and won for three: best actress, best cinematography, and best art direction. *Becket* would do even better. But for the time being, it was important that Wallis's peers acknowledged his return from the ashes.

Wallis had become Broadway-bound. Seeing *Becket* in the fall of 1960 convinced him to make the movie version, which he did; *Becket* received nominations for best picture, actors (both Richard Burton and Peter O'Toole), director, adapted screenplay, cinematography, art direction, sound, musical score, editing, and costumes. This was the first time a Wallis production had been nominated in so many categories, even surpassing *Casablanca*'s nine. *Becket* may only have won for best adapted screenplay, but that was enough to restore Wallis to the producers' circle.

Martha was also riding high. Although she freelanced, making movies for various studios (*Ice Palace* [1960] for Warners, *The Man from the Diner's Club* [1963] for Columbia), Wallis decided it was time to make up for *Gunfight at the O.K. Corral,* in which the role she had hoped to play went to Rhonda Fleming, by casting her in *A Girl Named Tamiko* (1962) and *Wives and Lovers* (1963). At this point they were still unmarried, preferring to let a significant amount of time elapse between Louise's death and the beginning of their new life. That Martha accompanied him to Britain in 1963 when he was filming *Becket* was, in movie parlance, a "preview of coming attractions." It was after they fulfilled their film commitments, of which Martha had more than Wallis, that they chose a date that bespoke renewal: Wallis and Martha were married in a civil ceremony in Palm Springs on New Year's Eve, 1966. Brent and his wife at the time, Helen, attended. From that time on, the family shrank until it consisted of Martha and Wallis, with Minna as an unwelcome but grudgingly tolerated appendage.

Wallis was now thoroughly monogamous. To quote a Cole Porter lyric from *Out of This World* (1950), he had "thoroughly pitched the woo / from the heights of Valhalla to Kalamazoo." In Wallis's case the geography was different, but the sentiments were the same. The heyday in the blood had passed into myth and memory. "You're my last girl," he told Martha, meaning every word.[13]

Hal Wallis had finally come home. It may have been home to the same Holmby Hills mansion that he shared with Louise, but that dwelling would soon receive Martha's personal touch. After their marriage, Martha sold her Hollywood home, bringing her art collection with her to South Mapleton Drive. The combined collections of Martha and Wallis gave their home a uniqueness that was bound to attract the attention of *Architectural Digest*.[14]

Except for the picture-book gardens and Olympic-size swimming pool, the place was never exactly the same. It was rather like a museum with changing exhibits. The changes—some subtle, others dramatic—were inspired by whatever Martha experienced, saw, or purchased while she and Wallis were on location. If, in the early 1970s, their home had taken on a decidedly English air, it was the result of having been on location for *Anne of the Thousand Days* and *Mary, Queen of Scots*.

The house at 515 South Mapleton Drive—other than the living room—was a blend of styles, evoking a country house with seventeenth- and eighteenth-century furnishings, both British and American, that reflected their combined tastes. The living room was pure Martha, epitomizing her brand of elegance. Martha knew that one form of harmony came from the juxtaposition of opposites, spatially arranged so that they either complemented or played off each other. Anyone seated on the creamy white sofa would be framed between two blue-and-white, branch-filled porcelain jars. To the right of the sofa was a relic of ancient Rome, a female torso that was a gift of Anna Magnani. In one corner Monet's *Chrysanthemums* overlooked a Regency commode; in another, Renoir's *Young Girl with Flowered Hat* seemed to smile down on a Louis XV chess table. An attenuated Giacometti faced a Degas bronze nude. The combination of paintings, sculptures, and furnishings blended in such a way as to enfold a guest within the embrace of art. It was the kind of room that made a visitor feel all the better for having entered it.

"I was happier with Martha than I had been for many years," Wallis wrote (*Starmaker,* 175), recalling their "pre-honeymoon" days as they traveled together to such romantic places as Capri, Venice, and especially Hawaii. That happiness renewed Wallis's creativity, which the Hollywood community—even those who assumed he was passé—had to acknowledge when the 1969 Oscar nominations were announced. Wallis was back in the game, with two of his productions receiving twelve nominations: ten for *Anne of the Thousand Days* (best picture, actor [Richard Burton]; actress [Genevieve Bujold]; supporting actor [Anthony Quayle]; adapted screenplay [John Hale, Bridget Boland, and Richard Solkove]; cinematography [Arthur Ibbetson]; art direction [Maurice Carter, Lionel Couch, and Patrick McLaughlin]; sound [John Aldred]; original score [George Delerue]; and costumes [Margaret Furse]). Wallis's other nominated film was the John Wayne western *True Grit,* for which Wayne received a best actor nomination, as did the title song composed by the ubiquitous Elmer Bernstein. Few expected Wayne to get best actor, in view of his support for the unpopular Vietnam War and the movie he made (and codirected) that endorsed America's involvement in it, *The Green Berets* (1968). With Burton nominated for the third time—and on the same ballot with Jon Voight and Dustin Hoffman for *Midnight Cowboy*—it looked as if Hoffman and Voight would cancel each other out, and Burton would emerge as winner—Peter O'Toole being the dark horse for *Goodbye, Mr. Chips* and Wayne being an even darker one. And if Burton received the Oscar, as many believed he would, it would be a consolation prize for being passed over for *Becket* and *Who's Afraid of Virginia Woolf?*

Wallis read Charles Portis's novel *True Grit* in galleys that had been sent to a number of producers, including John Wayne, who had his own production company. A bidding war ensued, with Wallis offering $300,000. There may have been higher bids, but Portis wanted Wallis, perhaps because he was impressed by some of Wallis's westerns, such as *Gunfight at the O.K. Corral, Last Train from Gun Hill* (1959), and *The Sons of Katie Elder* (1965)—the last two being revenge westerns like *True Grit.*[15] Wallis knew there was only one actor capable of playing Marshal Reuben "Rooster" Cogburn, who was a truly Falstaffian creation: a one-eyed, hard-drinking, overweight ex-outlaw-turned-lawman hired by a teenager to avenge her father's murder. As in *The Sons of Katie Elder,* the grimmer aspects of the plot were leavened by rowdy humor—unlike, say, *Last Train,* which remained soberly focused on a marshal's search for the man who raped and murdered his wife.

Wayne had wanted to buy the property for himself but could only muster up $100,000. When Wallis phoned Wayne to tell him he had brought *True Grit,* the actor congratulated him. Then Wallis broke the news: he had purchased it as a vehicle for the only actor in Hollywood who could play "Rooster" Cogburn: "Duke" Wayne. Wayne and Rooster Cogburn were a perfect fit. Like Bette Davis in her later films, Wayne tended toward line readings devoid of shading and cadence, hitting syllables as if they were nails being driven in the plot pegs. That form of uninflected delivery, which had become his signature, was eminently suited to the character, whose breakfast often consisted of whiskey.

Rooster was also a mythic figure. Just as the Confederate overcoat, black neckerchief, saber, and rifle sheathed in fringed buckskin characterized Ethan Edwards of *The Searchers* (1956)—arguably Wayne's best role and greatest performance—as an anachronism in postbellum Texas, Rooster's eye patch in *True Grit* evoked the one-eyed Odin of Norse mythology, who traveled on horseback, albeit on an eight-legged steed. Rooster seems to have come from another world; he bears no resemblance to such cinematic marshals of the past as Henry Fonda, Gary Cooper, and Kirk Douglas; rather, he resembles an ex-warrior in the service of Bacchus, until he is roused out of his lethargy by a spunky girl, who turns out to be his youthful double: "She reminds me of me!" he finally exclaims.

Oscar night, 7 April 1970, did not bode well for Wayne. Signs proclaiming "JOHN WAYNE IS A RACIST" greeted the actor and his wife as they entered the Dorothy Chandler Pavilion at the Los Angeles Music Center. There was another reason why Wayne was not optimistic; his extraordinary performance in *The Searchers* and the film itself—now acknowledged as John Ford's masterpiece—had been ignored by the Academy fourteen years earlier. When Barbra Streisand, the previous year's Oscar winner for *Funny Girl,* opened the envelope to read the name of the best actor of 1969, cheers erupted from the audience when she announced, "John Wayne." Wallis may not have won for best picture (and it would have been hard to justify *Anne of the Thousand Days* over *Midnight Cowboy*), but it was the first time that an actor had won an Oscar for any of his productions since Gary Cooper did for *Sergeant York* (1941).

In 1974 Wallis, now at Universal, was interested in making a sequel to *True Grit,* with Wayne again as Rooster Cogburn. He wanted a plot that revolved around a trio, like the one in *True Grit,* which consisted of a grossly overweight marshal (and Wayne was now even heavier than he had been five years earlier); a girl who wants her father's killer brought to justice; and a Texas ranger, looking for the same man, who joins them on their quest. Since the formula had worked once, Wallis was convinced it could again—but with a much older woman and a Native American in lieu of the teenager and the Texan. Wallis envisioned a sequel with Katharine Hepburn as the woman seeking justice, so that two icons of Hollywood's Golden Age would be paired for the first— and, as it happened, only—time.

It was a tall order; not only were their work habits different (Hepburn being considerably more disciplined than Wayne), but so were their performing styles and the kinds of films with which they were associated. The closest Hepburn had come to making a western was *Sea of Grass* (1947), which was hardly her finest hour; *The Rainmaker* may have been set in the Southwest, but it is by no means a conventional western despite the presence of a sheriff and some cowpokes. Similarly, when John Wayne had been teamed with such screen personalities as Marlene Dietrich (*Seven Sinners* [1940], *Pittsburgh* [1942], *The Spoilers* [1942]) and Joan Crawford in the ludicrous *Reunion in France* (1943), his costars went their separate ways, taking with them their personas, which they either could not or would not discard.

Wallis knew that, to prevent the sequel from becoming a "John Wayne" or a "Katharine Hepburn" film, neither actor could dominate it; their characters had to mesh with the plot. That was not the case with the treatments that were submitted to him. Just as Wallis was about to abandon the project, Martha devoted a rainy weekend to fashioning a script that she believed would work. The formula would remain the same—a trio tracking down a killer; the Hepburn character would be a missionary's daughter, whose father had been gunned down by the leader of an outlaw gang. The daughter, then, is merely one of three, the most important of whom is Rooster; the credits, in which Wayne's name preceded Hepburn's, indicated as much.

Martha drew her inspiration from one of Hepburn's best films—the one for which her costar, Humphrey Bogart, received his only Oscar—*The African Queen* (1951), in which Hepburn played the spinster Rosie Sayer, a British missionary in East Africa during World War I, and Bogart played Charlie Allnutt, the alcoholic skipper of the *African Queen,* whose name belies its sorry state. After Rosie's brother is killed by the Germans, Charlie offers her refuge on his boat. Being a missionary, Rosie is not as bent on avenging her brother's death as she is on destroying a German gunboat, thereby turning the desire for personal satisfaction into an act of patriotism. Martha realized that the Bogart character was a prefiguration of Rooster and that Rosie could easily be Americanized, preaching and teaching in the postbellum West. The trio would be completed by Wolf, a Native American boy in her charge.

In principle, it might have worked. But Wayne and Hepburn had their own ideas on the way certain scenes should be played. When director Stuart Millar, who was basically a producer with scant directorial experience, realized he had lost control of the film, he gave up and allowed the stars free rein. *Rooster Cogburn* could have been a worthy sequel with a more seasoned director, such as Henry Hathaway, whose direction of *True Grit* was partly responsible for Wayne's Oscar. Hathaway knew there was poetry in the western landscape; when blanketed with snow, as it is at the end of *True Grit,* the landscape wears the mantle of mortality, suggesting a vast burial ground where Rooster will join the man whose death he has avenged. Visually, *Rooster Cogburn* is nondescript; the best that can be said is that it is pleasing to the eye. Although Wayne was only a few years away from death when he made *Rooster Cogburn* (and looked it), there were no intimations of mortality in Millar's landscape.

Hathaway had never directed Katharine Hepburn, yet he would certainly have had her respect, given his years in the business (which went back to the silent era) and his track record, which included *The Lives of a Bengal Lancer* (1935), *The Trail of the Lonesome Pine* (1936), *The House on 92nd Street* (1945), *Call Northside 777* (1948), and *Niagara* (1953). Furthermore, Wayne and Hathaway were not strangers, having worked together in *The Shepherd of the Hills* (1941), *North to Alaska* (1960), *Circus World* (1964), and *The Sons of Katie Elder* (1965). Similarly, Hathaway gave Wallis two of his most successful films of the 1960s, *Katie Elder* and *True Grit.* Although Hathaway went on to direct *Shootout* (1971) for Wallis, he showed no interest in continuing the saga of Rooster Cogburn, forcing Wallis to find someone else. Since Wallis preferred star power over director (a decision that may have been dictated by the budget), he went for the comparatively untried Millar. The results showed.

The *Rooster Cogburn* credits acknowledged "Martin Julien" as sole screenwriter. Both Judith Crist of *Saturday Review* (18 October 1975) and Pauline Kael of the *New Yorker* (3 November 1975) knew that was Martha's pseudonym. "Marty" was Martha's nickname, and Julien the name of her father, Col. Julien C. Hyer. For the most part, the script was Martha's, with contributions from Wallis and Hepburn, which she apparently incorporated. The script may have had promise, but what was lacking was a strong presence behind the camera. There were a few set pieces, such as Richard Jordan as the gang leader firing his revolver into the ground as Hepburn stands before him defiantly reciting the Twenty-third Psalm; but for the most part, it was just a retread. Although Wayne had the showier part, Hepburn in her own subtle way upstaged him, perhaps because she believed more in her character than he did in his. Although *Rooster Cogburn* turned out to be Wallis's last film, he never intended it as such. Nor did he think it would spawn such resentment from Paul Nathan, the only member of Wallis's staff to follow him from studio to studio—in Nathan's case from Warners to Paramount, and finally Universal.

Being in Wallis's presence for so long made Nathan yearn for his own production company. He also thought of himself as a writer. In 1949 Nathan attempted an adaptation of *Too Late for Tears* (1949) from Roy Huggins's novel, only to lose out to the author, who did his own screenplay. When *A Visit to a Small Planet* and *All in a Night's Work* needed rewriting, Wallis looked to Nathan. In July 1968 Wallis extended Nathan's contract for six months at $1,350 a week to serve either as associate producer or assistant to the producer of *Anne of the Thousand Days*. It must have been the latter, since *Anne*'s executive producer was Joseph Hazen. At any rate, Nathan's contribution is uncredited.

When Wallis was desperate to get a filmable script for *Rooster Cogburn,* Nathan, who was still his unofficial story editor, whipped up a treatment that, he maintained, entitled him to "original story" credit. Wallis did not agree, insisting that the final screenplay bore no resemblance to Nathan's treatment and that his sole contribution was acknowledged in the credits, where Nathan's name appeared as associate producer—a somewhat vague title that could mean anything from a troubleshooter and field officer to an alter ego and adviser. Associate producers were often assigned to on-location filming; thus Nathan probably handled whatever problems arose when the cast and crew were in Oregon. Since *Rooster Cogburn* was a Wallis production, Nathan would have relieved Wallis of the more mundane responsibilities such as lodging, transportation, and meals for the company.

Nathan had no quarrel with "associate producer"; it was story credit that he wanted. Nathan continued to badger Wallis about it until Wallis finally agreed to 5 percent of the profits, "even though I am not committed to do so."[16] Martha was unaware of Nathan's demand and Wallis's concession.[17] Rather, she suspects that Nathan may have encouraged his lover, Allan Weiss, to prepare a treatment after learning about Wallis's script problems. In the past Nathan had used his Wallis connection to find work for Weiss, whose credits were far from impressive: original story for *Blue Hawaii* and coscreenplay credit for *Roustabout, The Sons of Katie Elder,* and *Paradise, Hawaiian Style* (1966), all of which were Wallis productions.

The 5 percent was not enough. Feeling he had been treated shabbily, Nathan demanded 15 percent, arguing that he had paid the price for sticking with Wallis when he switched studios. Nathan boasted that Charles Bluhdorn, head of Gulf + Western, the conglomerate that took over Paramount in 1967, had had great plans for him: executive producer of *Love Story* (1970) and producer of *The Godfather* (1972)—opportunities he supposedly missed by remaining faithful to Wallis. Since Bluhdorn, "the mad Austrian," was known for being mercurial, he may have made such grandiose promises to Nathan, even though he already had an outstanding production team in Robert Evans and Peter Bart. More likely, Nathan was trying to convince Wallis of his own importance by invoking the name of Bluhdorn; at any rate, he seemed more anxious for Wallis's recognition than for his 15 percent. As it happened, Nathan received neither.

This was another end of a friendship founded on expediency. Nathan served Wallis well, although Wallis would have said that Nathan was only doing his job, for which he was well compensated. Still, Wallis did not want to lose Nathan, nor did Nathan want to leave Wallis. In January 1969 Nathan had a chance to produce *The Out-of-Towners* (1970) for Paramount. Since Nathan was with Wallis at Universal, he requested a leave, during which he would be off the payroll for twenty weeks. Wallis gladly consented, giving Nathan the opportunity to produce a film of his own, which also happened to be a crowd-pleaser.

When Wallis discovered workhorses like Jack Saper and Nathan, he tended to ride them hard. On some occasions, Wallis would assign Saper and Nathan tasks that were considerably beneath them; on others, he would seek their advice on professional matters, treating them like confidants. Since Wallis expected *Becket* to restore the luster that had been lost with the Martin and Lewis and Elvis films, he paid close attention to the script: "I spent months on the script myself," he confessed to Nathan.[18] It turned out to be a script of several hands, including those of the assigned writer, Edward Anhalt, who was working from Lucienne Hill's translation, and director Peter Glenville, who believed his contribution merited a cocredit. Wallis desperately needed advice: if Glenville was considering a shared credit, why not himself? Nathan was forthright: if Wallis and Glenville could prove that 60 percent of the completed script was theirs, they would have to share credit. However, if the script carried three names—theirs and Anhalt's—the case would have to go to arbitration. Since Wallis wanted the movie to adhere as closely as possible to Hill's translation, neither he nor Glenville asked for credit, thereby making it possible for Anhalt to win an Oscar for his adaptation—which was really an adaptation of a translation.

As it happened, *Rooster Cogburn* marked the end both of Nathan's association with Wallis and of Wallis's producing career. The film was neither an ignominious finale nor a glorious sunset. Few filmmakers depart in a blaze of glory. Sam Goldwyn may not have ended his producing days with a masterpiece like *The Little Foxes* (1941), but he at least had the satisfaction of bringing two great works of musical theater to the screen: *Carmen Jones* (1954) and *Porgy and Bess* (1959). David Selznick was less fortunate; his swan song was a remake of *A Farewell to Arms* (1957), with a miscast Jennifer Jones. Major directors such as D.W. Griffith, William Wyler, and Billy Wilder made less than grand exits with *The Struggle* (1931), *The Liberation of L.B. Jones* (1970), and *Buddy Buddy* (1981), respectively. Compared to any of these three, *Rooster Cogburn* is a masterpiece.

For Wallis, the film was also one of his happiest experiences in forty years of moviemaking. Much had to do with Katharine Hepburn, who became a true friend, one of the few who understood his ways. With Wallis, friendship came at a price. Everything augured well at the beginning; next came periods of tension, resentment, and ill will. Then it was THE END writ large. Wallis had gone that route many times: with Jack Warner, Jack Saper, Jerry Lewis, Paul Nathan, Joe Hazen. Hepburn was different. Even though she was on his payroll, their relationship was one of soul mates—but of a special sort. Neither needed the other for self-completion; rather, Wallis and Hepburn saw in each other their reflected selves, becoming more like kin than producer and star. That Wallis and Hepburn respected each other's artistic integrity is self-evident; they also respected each other's discretion in matters of the heart. Wallis and Hepburn had their lovers, but neither became tabloid fodder at a time when an extramarital liaison, such as Ingrid Bergman's with Roberto Rossellini, could lead to temporary exile from Hollywood. To them, the studio was the workplace where their careers were forged, not the temple of illusion that it was for Norma Desmond (Gloria Swanson) in Billy Wilder's *Sunset Boulevard* (1950). "Hollywood" was the mythic creation of the fan magazines and columnists who spun out fantasies for a public yearning for a world like Homer's Mount Olympus, where gods bled ichor and ate ambrosia; the equivalent was the magical restaurant that *Photoplay* readers associated with movie royalty: the Brown Derby, where the stars dined on Cobb salads and drank exotic cocktails like Pink Ladys, Orange Blossoms, and Brandy Alexanders. This was neither Hepburn's nor Wallis's Hollywood, nor did it bear any resemblance to the one they knew.

Each also avoided the limelight, Wallis less so than the reclusive Hepburn, who never attended the Oscars, even when she was nominated. She made one exception—on 2 April 1974, when she appeared in her signature attire, slacks and cap, to present the Thalberg Award to the distinguished MGM producer Lawrence Weingarten, who produced two of her films with Spencer Tracy, *Without Love* (1945) and *Pat and Mike* (1952). Forty years earlier, on Oscar night, 16 March 1934, Hepburn—then a mere novice—was a best actress nominee for *Morning Glory* (1934); the nomination meant so little to her that she made it a point to book passage to Europe that same evening. As it happened, she won; it was the first of four Oscars.

In Hollywood such indifference to ritual is either respected or condemned. Hepburn never had to worry about being told, "You'll never eat lunch in this town again," because she rarely did anyway. One suspects that Wallis secretly admired Hepburn's individualism that flew in the face of Hollywood protocol, because he too wished he could stay home on Oscar nights, pass up the obligatory banquets, and avoid the discomfort of interviews. But what really drew him to Hepburn was the sense of privacy that they shared. To them, privacy was the art of selecting what one wished to say, where one wanted to go, and with whom one wanted to be—permanently or temporarily. The rest is silence.

Starmaker contains an exquisite photo of Hepburn and Wallis, each of them smiling. While Wallis was looking straight at the camera, Hepburn, tilting her head to the side, glanced over at him—her face beaming with admiration. One suspects it was the same expression that she reserved for the great love of her life, Spencer Tracy—the difference being that Hepburn's feelings for Wallis never strayed from the platonic, and vice versa.

If Hepburn was Wallis's mirror self, Martha was his complement. The two were bipolar opposites. When it came to money, Martha did not share her husband's frugality or his financial secretiveness, which was such that he would not even let her see their joint income tax returns; he wanted her only to sign (*Finding My Way,* 4). Martha never denied her "extravagance," even quoting her father on the subject: "'Marty spends money like a drunken sailor'" (*Finding My Way,* 3).

The financial insecurity that plagued Wallis in his youth never disappeared. When Wallis decided to write his autobiography, he knew he needed a collaborator, who turned out to be Charles Higham. Once Macmillan agreed to be the publisher, the company issued a contract stipulating that nothing would be forthcoming for Wallis until Higham received $45,000. That being the case, Wallis believed Higham should pay for the typing, including the paper. However, if Macmillan decreed otherwise, Wallis would reimburse Higham for half of the cost if he were given enough to equal that amount. If not, Higham would be reimbursed in proportion to the lesser amount.[19]

Martha also had to contend with her husband's penny-pinching ways. Playing hostess and producer's wife cost money. By the late 1970s, the Wallises had three homes: the Mapleton Drive mansion, a Malibu beach house, and a ranch house on Halper Lake Drive in Palm Springs. Pieces from their art collection adorned each home. The ranch house, called Casablanca, looked like an adobe; it was distinctly Spanish with touches of Mexico and the American Southwest: red tile floors, wooden columns and arches, Plains Indian artifacts, and even some pre-Columbian art.

Wallis enjoyed their homes, leaving the upkeep to Martha but never suspecting the limits to which she would go to maintain their lifestyle. By 1980, Martha's getting and spending, about which she has always been open, had plunged her into such debt that she needed a deus ex machina, little thinking it would be her husband. Her profligacy had brought her into the netherworld of extortionists, loan sharks, and forgers—one that, until now, she had only experienced in movies:

I drove our Silver Cloud Rolls Royce into the seediest section of Los Angeles looking for loan sharks. . . . The people there were glad to lend me money. . . . When I got behind in my payments, I was used mercilessly. My signature was forged on documents I had never seen.

Loans I knew nothing about were made in my name with my collateral. (*Finding My Way,* 5–6)

The collateral was the art collection, some of which she used in August 1980 for loans from a Beverly Hills real estate investor, to whom she ended up owing $1.2 million.[20] Determined to keep Wallis from learning the extent of her indebtedness, Martha was successful until a far more threatening scenario developed. In January 1981 two con artists approached the Wildenstein Gallery in New York with paintings that Martha had given them in exchange for a $1 million loan: Monet's *Houses of Parliament* and Gauguin's *Siesta—A Brittany Landscape,* along with power of attorney authorizing them to sell the paintings for her.[21] The sale price turned out to be $650,000. The combination of the $1.2 million debt and the shady circumstances surrounding the Wildenstein sale convinced Martha that she had no other choice but to confess the truth to her husband, who could alone extricate her from the crazily spun web in which she was entrapped.

Wallis could never have imagined that Martha had gone to such extremes to give them the life a world-famous producer deserved; still, he must have realized that she had not acted selfishly. If Wallis was now hobnobbing with royalty, serving on the boards of museums, and socializing with a graciousness that he had never before displayed, the reason was Martha, who walked in beauty but had her feet planted firmly on the ground—at least most of the time. And when she ventured into the dark, it was to perpetuate the kind of life that she envisioned for both of them. Had Wallis managed to shed his pre-depression mentality (which is not much different from that of the familiar depression mentality), Martha might not have been reduced to doing what they should have been doing together: enjoying the life that hard work and good fortune had given them—and spending the money to ensure it. To paraphrase Wallace Stevens, beauty may be eternal and dust for a time. But unlike dust, beauty comes with a price tag.

Wallis had his own way of dealing with Martha's indiscretions; although he had no intention of seeing his wife implicated in a scandal that might result in a prison sentence, he wanted his paintings back. Furthermore, he did not intend to lose money on the transaction. Wallis was eighty-three at the time and a few years away from death; his faculties, however, were intact. But his diabetes was worsening.

In August 1981, when he began the retrieval process, Wallis had no idea how serious his condition was. Nor did Martha. What mattered to Wallis was recovering the paintings and saving his wife from a press that would have branded her a Hollywood Tosca, living for art and love and somehow confusing them, and himself as the octogenarian victim of her prodigality.

It took money and lawyers, but by April 1982 Wildenstein agreed to return the paintings in exchange for more than the original $650,000; Wallis wanted an additional $15,000 for "expenses" (presumably legal). Even though Martha's reputation was at stake, Wallis was determined not to lose money. Whatever money was lost—and it was a substantial amount—came from pursuing Martha's fleecers. If Martha recalled the song that her would-be sponsor, Ella Logan, introduced in *Finian's Rainbow,* "If This Isn't Love" ("the whole world is crazy"), she would have agreed with the sentiments. It was love—the love of a man for a woman who had erred and repented and was forgiven. One would like to think that Wallis believed Martha erred on the side of the angels. He probably did, even though he might not have admitted it. More important, Wallis provided restitution; Martha provided the support that Wallis needed when he had to confront something far more serious and potentially life-threatening: the loss of a limb.

CHAPTER THIRTEEN

Requiem for a Gentleman

T HE 1980S SPELLED THE BEGINNING of the end for Wallis. Martha knew there would be no more movies, even though Wallis acted otherwise. He may have bristled at the word *retirement,* but the truth was that he and Martha had if not "retired" to, then "moved" to, Casablanca, their Palm Springs home in Rancho Mirage. No sooner had the Wallises closed up their Holmby Hills and Malibu residences than Minna descended upon Palm Springs, aware that her Hollywood days were over—but also that her brother had taken up residence there. If Wallis felt the same about his Hollywood days, he would not have admitted it.

Minna never approved of her brother's marriage to Martha, whom at first she deliberately ignored, to the point of not speaking to her for a period of time. The only reason Minna never treated Louise that way was Louise's place in the Hollywood hierarchy. When her brother married Louise, Minna was just a secretary, and Louise was a star. Once Minna became an agent and a legendary party-giver, hierarchy no longer mattered.

Despite Minna's feelings toward Martha, she did not intend to be shut out of her brother's life. Fortunately, Minna found her own place in Palm Springs, which, happily, was not within walking distance of Halper Lake Drive. But that did not stop her from visiting Wallis and Martha. Being "family," Minna expected to be treated accordingly—which meant dinner, if not every night, then on a regular basis. Martha had to play chauffeur, driving Minna to Casablanca, where their Chinese chef would prepare a gourmet meal.[1] Since Minna enjoyed watching television while eating, the three of them would dine on trays set up in front of the TV. After Minna had had her share of food and entertainment, Martha would drive her back. Eventually, the all-enduring Martha reached her limit and began restricting Minna's visits. Restricting, not terminating. Only nature can terminate a force of nature—and that is what Minna was. Wallis, in contrast, was nature's victim.

In 1981 Wallis was driving through a familiar section of Palm Springs when he glanced down at the air conditioner and proceeded to plow into another vehicle. The accident left him hospitalized with head injuries. Even after he had recovered, he was plagued by misfortune. Wallis had earlier been diagnosed as a diabetic. In 1982 the disease returned with a vengeance. As in *Dark Victory* and *You Came Along,* there was no happy ending. Life imitated art, except that it was not the kind that he and Martha collected. It is hard to imagine any artist turning a leg amputation into an aesthetic experience.

Wallis had always assumed that his diabetes was under control. A discoloration of the toes on his left foot, however, proved otherwise. The toes had to be amputated. The extremities were not enough. The left foot was next. And finally the leg. Like many amputees, Wallis could not—or would not—use a prosthesis; in anger, he hurled it across the floor of the hospital room. Martha understood. Pride does not allow for an admission of mortality, much less disability, until the bell tolls.

And on 6 October 1986, the bell tolled for Hal Wallis.

During the ordeal, Martha never informed Minna of the gravity of her brother's condition, fearing a tirade against herself, the physicians, or maybe even life—depending on which scapegoat Minna in her dotage decided to target. At least Martha did not have to inform her of Wallis's death; the ninety-three-year-old Minna passed away on 3 August from natural causes.

Even if Minna had outlived her brother, she could have done nothing for him. Martha slept in a bed at his side, first at the San Francisco hospital, where his leg was amputated; then at the Eisenhower Medical Center in Palm Springs, where he recuperated; and finally at their home, where he was able to die in his sleep. His death was for the best. Martha could not bear to tell him that the right leg would be next.

Even before he died, Wallis anticipated the inevitable: he had purchased a crypt at Forest Lawn in Glendale for himself and his mother, sisters, and son in the Sanctuary of Truth in the Great Mausoleum. Since Eva and Juel had already passed away, he had their remains placed there.

What life denied, death provided; except for Jacob, the Wallises had become a family, however symbolically. The Sanctuary had a chapel-like serenity without suggesting any particular religion. The Wallis name loomed large over the gated crypt, where light passed through a window with a stained-glass border that looked faintly medieval. Enclosed within the border was an abstract design emblematic of a torso, perhaps a representation of the human form after death. Beneath the window was a stone bench, on which a visitor could place a flower. Martha would usually leave a single rose.

It was appropriate that Wallis was interred in the Sanctuary of Truth. To Wallis, truth had a specialized meaning: reality cloaked in illusion—its nakedness hidden under layers of finery, dressed to advantage, and transfigured as art. His favorite artists would have agreed; so would his favorite directors: Mike Curtiz, Irving Rapper, John Huston, Daniel Mann, William Dieterle, and Henry Hathaway.

Two days after Wallis's death, Martha arranged a private service at the Sanctuary, attended only by herself, Brent, Wallis's two secretaries, and the Chinese domestics who had served them faithfully in their Holmby Hills and Palm Springs homes. A violinist played "As Time Goes By," and Martha delivered a eulogy, after which the few mourners dispersed and Martha returned to Palm Springs.

Had Wallis agreed to a public memorial service, Martha would have accommodated him. But he wanted none, just a simple ceremony. He did not die the beatific death that artists deserve but rarely get. But he received a memorial that, by Hollywood standards, was the epitome of taste. No autograph hounds, stars hogging the spotlight, repentant enemies, or reporters asking for sound bytes to sum up a career that lasted almost half a century.

Although Martha was later besieged with calls from friends who had wanted to attend, she understood something about her husband that would have been lost on Hollywood's self-dramatizing chroniclers of their lives and loves: of all the great producers, Hal Wallis was the most private. The bottom line is the names of one's parents, which Wallis considered classified information. His standards of autobiography would have confounded the ancients, who, although renowned for their succinctness, would never have excluded parentage, even if they had to resort to conjecture—for which Wallis had no need. In his quest for selective anonymity—no one in the business can be totally "anon"—

Wallis disclosed little to anyone, including his lovers. Even Martha, whom he affectionately called "my last girl" after the heyday in the blood had subsided—and who nursed him during his last years—admits that he had sealed off the doors of his past.[2] In fact, it is amazing that Wallis decided to write an autobiography at all, even with a collaborator. But once he made the decision, he determined the form: a "tell some," not a "tell all," memoir.

The celebrity autobiography has always been a suspect genre, having been used to settle scores, catalog affairs, and immortalize images. Thus *Starmaker* is both refreshing and exasperating. The gaps are like chasms that beckon seductively but yield nothing substantive—just a few shards of information, the equivalent of outtakes or cutting floor remnants. In many ways, *Starmaker* recalls another decorous autobiography by a Hollywood celebrity, Rosalind Russell's *Life Is a Banquet* (1977), in which the actress tells the reader more about her upbringing than herself and her films, including her breakthrough movie, *Craig's Wife* (1936), which receives a mere mention. Although Russell knew she was terminally ill when writing *Life Is a Banquet* (which was published posthumously), she refrained from including anything—even downplaying the nervous breakdown she suffered in 1943—that would detract from the message implied in the title—a line from her signature film, *Auntie Mame* (1959).

Wallis was even vague—intentionally, it seems—about his art collection, which in 1985 consisted of about twenty-five paintings that had once been distributed among the Holmby Hills, Malibu, and Palm Springs homes. Unlike Martha, Wallis was not an aesthete; to him, art was an investment. If the paintings gave him pleasure, all the better. Beauty may be eternal, but it should still turn a profit.

Three years before his death, Wallis, ever conscious of taxes, transferred most of his paintings to the Wallis Foundation. Since the mid-1960s, Wallis had been a trustee of the Los Angeles County Museum of Art (LACMA), although his attendance at board meetings was erratic, depending, as it did, on his shooting schedule. It was not surprising, therefore, that Wallis specified that thirteen of his paintings were to be exhibited at LACMA "for a definite or indefinite period of time, appropriately evidenced as the Hal B. Wallis Collection."[3] It was an impressive collection that included Degas's *Sur la scène;* Cassatt's *Mother, Sara, and the Baby;* Bonnard's *Nu de profil, jambe droite levée;* Monet's *Asters* and *Le Parlement, coucher de soleil;* Fantin-Latour's *Vase de roses;* Pissarro's *Quai Saint-Sever à Rouen;* Vuillard's *Jeu des cartes;* and three Andrew Wyeths.

LACMA had been courting Wallis for two decades, even honoring him with a film retrospective in 1982. The Los Angeles tribute, however, was long overdue; London's British Film Institute hosted a retrospective in 1969, and New York's Museum of Modern Art did so the following year. Both programs were considerably more inclusive than LACMA's, whose purpose was to honor the prophet in his own land with the hope, if not the expectation, of being rewarded. Naturally, LACMA's director, Earl Powell, was delighted when the Foundation's president, none other than Brent Wallis, agreed to a "permanent loan"— with "permanent" defined as the period of time during which the paintings would be on display at LACMA, starting in January 1987 and ending on a date determined by the Foundation. To Powell, "permanent" meant long-lasting. In fact, the Los Angeles art community thought the same. The June 1987 issue of *Antiques & Fine Art* implied that the paintings were a gift. Powell had no idea that the permanent loan would be for only two years, from January 1987 to January 1989.

Although Wallis considered art the equivalent of blue chip stocks, he at least derived some joy and perhaps even aesthetic satisfaction from the collection; to Brent, art was a commodity of escalating value. In January 1989, when the Foundation discovered that the collection was worth five times what it had been two years earlier, the directors decided it was time for the curtain to descend on the Hal Wallis show at LACMA. Besides, as Brent and the Foundation's attorney reasoned, a loan is not a gift in perpetuity; the paintings belonged to the Foundation, which would determine their fate. And their fate was to go on the auction block at Christie's in New York.

Powell was furious, but the Foundation was adamant: the show had a two-year run, the equivalent of a Broadway smash. Now it was time to strike the set and sell it. Powell was then unaware that a document existed stating Wallis's expressed wish that the paintings be "exhibited at [LACMA] as a collection whether for a definite or indefinite period of time." The phrasing was crucial. However, on 10 May 1989, Powell learned of the document with the "definite or indefinite period of time" phrase through a series of events that went back to January 1981 when the con men, who fleeced Martha out of a Monet and a Gauguin, sold

them to the Wildenstein for $650,000. When the retrieval process final-
ly ended in April 1982, part of the settlement not only gave the Wildenstein first refusal rights on any sale but also the authority to act as
exclusive agent in any auction involving fifteen specified paintings from
the Wallis Collection. The consignment-rights provision was Wildenstein's way of making up for the profits the gallery lost—the return of
the paintings precluding the possibility of a sale.

The first violation of the consignment-rights clause occurred two
months after Wallis died—in December 1986, when Brent sold a Renoir
for $750,000, even though it was one of the paintings that the Wilden-
stein was empowered to auction. And when Wildenstein learned of
the 10 May auction at Christie's, the gallery decided it was litigation
time.

Rarely has the art world been embroiled in two such brouhahas
involving the same parties and the same paintings. There was Wildenstein versus Brent Wallis and the Wallis Foundation, which the District
Court of New York dismissed, invoking the common law rule against
unreasonable restraints on the alienation of property and arguing that
the settlement was a private restriction that did not adversely affect the
buying and selling of art. But the case that garnered the lion's share of
publicity was LACMA's $38.9 million suit against the Wallis Founda-
tion and Christie's.

On the morning of 10 May 1989, a lawyer for the Wildenstein Gallery, who had tried in vain to stop the auction the previous day, informed
LACMA about the existence of Wallis's "definite or indefinite period of
time" letter that would appear to support the museum's right to the
collection. Although LACMA's lawyers were encouraged by the news,
they felt that the Foundation could still have the upper hand. Accordingly, they decided against blocking the sale. Instead, knowing that
the Foundation directors were meeting at Christie's before the auction, LACMA faxed a letter, charging duplicity and fraud. LACMA
thought it had a case, especially since the Foundation had never revealed that it had such a letter in its possession, signed by Wallis, that
could be interpreted as granting the museum the equivalent of ownership. The fax did not stop the auction, which began promptly at 8:00
P.M. Within twenty minutes, it was over; the entire collection had gone
for $39.6 million.[4]

If this were a Frank Capra film, LACMA would be depicted as a citadel of culture, besieged by capitalists ready to despoil it for their own gain—as if the loss of some impressionist and postimpressionist paintings would jeopardize the fate of the museum (which had been doing well before the Wallis exhibit).

Capra was a mythmaker, not a realist. The Wallis Foundation was a nonprofit organization devoted to supporting worthwhile endeavors. Never a major philanthropic venture, it nevertheless contributed to enough causes, and sponsored enough programs, to have credibility. Although the Foundation was not as diversified in 1989 as it became during the next decade, it was still more than a footnote in the history of philanthropy, if for no other reason than its founder. Had Wallis been alive in January 1989 and learned that the Monet he had bought in 1971 for $215,000 was now worth $14 million, he might have decided that enough visitors had seen it at LACMA over the past two years and it was now time for an auction; and if the Monet's value had skyrocketed, what would the others net? The Foundation seemed to be acting in place of Wallis, whose instructions were not as ambiguous as they seemed. On the one hand, the paintings belonged to the Foundation; on the other, the Foundation had been given a mandate to display them either at LACMA or a comparable museum "for a definite or indefinite period of time." If Wallis had intended the collection as an outright bequest, he would have said so. He had bequeathed one painting to LACMA, Gauguin's *Field of Derout-Lollichon*.[5] If he had wanted the rest of the collection to go there, he would have insisted upon less ambiguous wording. Wallis knew that great art like his would not depreciate in value; he had too good a head for business to will the collection to a museum, where it would lie in state, like the Egyptian wing at the Metropolitan Museum of Art—never changing, always inspiring sighs but only generating income in the form of paid admissions. Wallis started collecting art for its commercial potential and perhaps for his own pleasure—more the former than the latter, although even he would have admitted that his paintings afforded a kind of satisfaction totally unrelated to either sex or moviemaking—both of which brought gratification of a different sort.

The pleasurable nature of art meant little to Brent and his associates at the Foundation, who believed the proceeds from the sale could be used for charitable purposes. Still, they were too conscious of popular opinion to ignore LACMA's suit, which, unless resolved, could reflect unfavorably on the Foundation. The case was eventually settled out of court with the establishment of a Wallis Foundation Fund that enabled LACMA to purchase some impressionist and postimpressionist art to compensate for its loss. One such painting was Cézanne's *Sous Bois,* which it bought for $13 million.[6]

The case had a curious side effect: it called attention to the fact that Hal Wallis had a son. Until then, few LACMA trustees knew Brent existed. In *Starmaker,* Wallis devoted exactly two pages to Brent, describing him as shy and reclusive and implying that his own greatest source of pride came not from a father-son relationship (which was nonexistent) but from Brent's Ph.D. in psychology. Apparently, Brent's 1961 marriage to Helen Sears Carpenter did not inspire the same pride, perhaps because the marriage ended in divorce before Wallis embarked on his autobiography. Anyone reading *Starmaker* would only know that Brent had married from a reference to his being present with "his wife Helen" at his father's marriage to Martha Hyer in 1966. When Wallis decided to tell his life story, however selectively, and chose Charles Higham as his collaborator, he had already determined how he wanted to tell it. The focus would be on himself: the devoted son forced to leave school and support his mother, the Hollywood novice en route to the executive suite, the producer who saw himself as the controlling force behind his films, the landowner who read farm magazines and grew produce for profit, the widower who proved that life's second acts make up for the mistakes in the first. Given Wallis's criteria for success, he would have considered the Christie's auction the Foundation's finest hour. How the Foundation allocated the money was subject to debate. Brent was fortunate; he did not have a debating partner.

At the end of Arthur Miller's *View from the Bridge* (1955), the lawyer Alfieri, a one-person Greek chorus, sums up the tragic Eddie Carbone as a man who "allowed himself to be wholly known." It was Eddie's inability to dissemble, to erect a facade, that made him transparent and therefore vulnerable. Unable to comprehend his incestuous love for his niece and his unformed but palpable attraction to her lover, Eddie traveled the familiar road to destruction, never knowing why he embarked on it in the first place. Wallis never allowed himself to be wholly known, even to those he loved; he closed off certain chambers of the past, as if he were sealing up rooms. His was not the fate of one who, knowingly or otherwise, ascends the tragic pyramid, falling headlong but gloriously, like Roy Earle (Humphrey Bogart) in his production of *High Sierra* (1941). In fact, Wallis's life was not tragic at all in the classic sense. He was not the victim of overweening pride or a fatal error, but of industrial change and deteriorating health; even if Wallis's diabetes had not worsened, he still could never have been the producer he was when "movies were movies." In 1975 *Rooster Cogburn* seemed more of an envoi to a bygone age than a western.

Wallis's was a fate that came out of life, not art, the sort that befalls millions with untreatable diseases or conditions that have spiraled out of control. How his diabetes began, no one—not even Martha—knows. Neither Juel nor Minna was diabetic; in fact, Minna's eating habits would have appalled the most progressive nutritionists. The only other possibility is Wallis's father. If diabetes ran in Jacob Walinsky's family, it visited his son with a vengeance.

Wallis never let himself be known because he never knew himself. He was not introspective, which might explain why he was so puzzled by Brent, who was—and who may have studied psychology in an attempt to understand his father. Wallis was too busy to be pensive or self-probing. There was something almost existential about Wallis; he believed in the *doing* and, until he found the profession that he wanted to embrace permanently, the gerund would not have a direct object. The "doing" could be selling stoves or writing copy; the goal was to do it well. Self-consciousness was not for Hal Wallis; his was the knowledge that came from accomplishment.

The only self-portrait Wallis has left behind is in his films—and not even in all of them. It is impossible to imagine Wallis's identifying with the Martin and Lewis movies that merely capitalized on the perennial need for mindless fun, which he was more than happy to provide. But films about facing terminal cancer without self-pity *(You Came Along)*; restoring an amnesiac's memory *(Love Letters)* or an introvert's self-esteem *(Now, Voyager)*; relinquishing a lover for a greater cause *(Casablanca)*; and assisting the helpless in their quest for justice *(The Life of Emile Zola, The Adventures of Robin Hood, True Grit, Rooster Cogburn)*—these reflected the kind of world Wallis would have wanted. Wise enough to know such a world could never exist in real life, he provided it on film. Yet Wallis also knew that life, both on and off screen, left a trail of shattered relationships *(Becket, Anne, Mary)* and loss *(Sheba)*, forcing one to settle for less, as Serafina does in *The Rose Tattoo*—

but even a clown for a lover is better than no lover at all. "Most of the time now we settle for half," Alfieri muses at the end of *A View from the Bridge*. Wallis would have understood.

If it had been possible, Wallis would have liked to maintain his association with Jack Warner, who—at the beginning, at least—was the kind of patriarchal figure that Wallis admired. Yet Jack Warner proved no less selfish than Wallis's own father, who walked out on his family when the going got rough. If the *Casablanca* incident had not soured Wallis on Warner, something else would have. Patriarchs maintain their authority by cultivating followers; by 1943 Wallis could no longer be a follower.

Fidelity meant much to Wallis; thus it pained him when long-standing relationships ended with recriminations, as did those with Joe Hazen and Paul Nathan, among others. Yet even if Wallis had acknowledged Warner's right to the *Casablanca* Oscar and remained at the studio, Jack Warner would never have thought of him as his equal—much less, as his superior, although Wallis was clearly the latter.

Loyalty meant little to Warner. When World War II made the former Soviet Union an ally, Warner rushed *Mission to Moscow* (1943) into production. Howard Koch was assigned to adapt the book of the same name by Joseph E. Davies, who had been the ambassador to the Soviet Union. The film abounds in inaccuracies, understandable in time of war, when the enemy is demonized and the ally, however suspect, is glorified. Among the many egregious reworkings of fact is Davies's (Walter Huston's) justification of the Soviet Union's "invasion" of Finland as a request from the Soviets to maintain a presence on Finnish soil in order to repel German aggression![7]

Never one to agonize over facts, Warner extolled *Mission to Moscow,* calling it "one of the most important films we ever made" and "a startling revelation."[8] It *was* a revelation, but only to those who knew about the show trials and the horrors of collectivization, including the famine in Ukraine. However, by "revelation" Warner meant his personal discovery that a nation that had embraced an economic system completely at odds with capitalism could join the Allied cause. What mattered was Russia's antifascism, not its totalitarianism, which, in the film, was nonexistent.

In 1947 when the House Un-American Activities Committee (HUAC) began investigating Communist subversion of the movie industry, singling out such films as *Mission to Moscow* as examples, Warner experienced a different epiphany; shamelessly cooperating with the committee, he admitted he would never have made *Mission to Moscow* in 1943, had he known what he knew in 1947. It scarcely mattered that few 1947 moviegoers would have cared about such an outdated piece of propaganda.

Since Howard Koch wrote the *Mission to Moscow* screenplay, Warner, who knew that HUAC was particularly interested in the way propaganda was injected into scripts, had a scapegoat. Totally ignorant of Howard Koch's politics, which were at most liberal, Warner told HUAC that Koch was among several writers at the studio with Communist sympathies, whom he proceeded to name, adding that Koch "always started out with big messages, and I used to take them out."[9]

If there was a message in *Mission to Moscow,* it was nothing that Koch had embedded in the script; the message, implicit in Davies's book, was that the Soviet Union had been misunderstood, that the purge trials were genuine, isolationism is folly, that the 1939 Nazi-Soviet nonaggression pact was necessary for Russia's survival, and that once Hitler violated the pact in 1941 by attacking Russia, the Western democracies had a new ally. All Howard Koch did was adapt a book that President Roosevelt wanted made into a film to honor the country that gave United States time to rearm by keeping the Nazis occupied: "Russia has given us time," Huston replies to a heckler who wonders what Russia has done for America. The "startling revelation" was not *Mission to Moscow* but Warner's betrayal of one of his best screenwriters, who, although never a Communist, ended up being gray-listed for almost a decade, thanks to loose-lipped Jack Warner.

Had Wallis produced *Mission to Moscow,* he would also have been on the receiving end of Warner's tirade against Soviet propagandists, even though Wallis was apolitical, having never felt the need to be a flag-waver like Warner. That Warner wrote an autobiography that barely mentioned Wallis, much less credited him for giving the studio the prestige it could not have achieved otherwise, was indicative of his megalomania. Warner betrayed Koch verbally and Wallis publicly. Wallis was fortunate; at least his career was not interrupted.

If Wallis felt so deeply about Lillian Hellman's *Watch on the Rhine* that he was determined to produce the movie version, it was not the play's antifascism that attracted him so much as the antifascists themselves: a family consisting of a freedom fighter; his wife, the daughter of a Supreme Court justice, who shares her husband's politics; and their three children, the oldest of whom knows that he must continue his father's work in the resistance if the inevitable occurs—and it is implied that it will. The family members are united by their belief in a cause that is worth any sacrifice that must be made. This was the kind of family that Wallis understood—one that rallied around a heroic father. It was quite different in Wallis's case; "sacrifice" was not in Jacob Walinsky's vocabulary.

Wallis's films abound with children who would have been any parent's dream: the title quartet in *Four Daughters,* Mattie in *True Grit,* and especially Sam Hazen in *The Searching Wind*. Although Sam criticizes his parents for their softness on fascism and their politics of appeasement, he genuinely loves them despite their failings; he even accepts the fact that he must lose a leg because of a war that might have been averted if men like his father had chosen honesty over diplomacy. Sam may have been naive, but naïveté is preferable to cynicism. Sam had "true grit," a quality Wallis admired; it was also one that is often concealed beneath the hide of disillusionment, as it was with Rick in *Casablanca*. But when it emerges, it gives off a lovely light.

Wallis's men are not the only torchbearers; the women light the way, too. Ilsa in *Casablanca* was ready to shoot Rick to get an exit visa for her husband; Sara in *Watch on the Rhine* gave up a comfortable life in America to become the wife of an itinerant resistance fighter; Julie in *Jezebel* accompanies her ex-lover, the victim of a yellow fever epidemic, to an island under quarantine where she can tend to his needs—something his wife cannot do. Wallis may have imagined himself as the idealized males of his films. But he did not have to conjure up a celluloid wife; Ilsa, Sara, and Julie all coalesced in Martha.

If Wallis possessed self-knowledge, it remained within him. He was not one to wear his heart on his sleeve for Hollywood daws to peck at. Wallis was never meant to play the family man or enjoy close friendships; he may even have assumed as much. But when it came to identifying himself as a producer, Wallis knew exactly what he was. Knowing that he was a producer—and one of the best—was the epitome of self-knowledge, everything else being just a heap of facts—or "a hill of beans," to quote Rick Blaine in *Casablanca:* "Many people still think the producer is the man who goes out and raises the money to make the picture. But that isn't the fact at all. A producer, to be worthy of the name, must be a creator."[10]

Charlton Heston would agree. Although Heston wrote that Wallis was "not a warm man," a fact others have corroborated, he understood Wallis because he appreciated the producer's role: "A real producer is a special combination, neither bird nor beast (or maybe both). He must have sound creative instincts about script, casting, design . . . about *film*. At the same time, he must have an iron-clad grasp of logistics, schedule, marketing, and costs . . . above all, costs. There really aren't a lot of guys who are good at all this. Hal was very good. Surely one of the two or three best of them all."[11] It is ironic that an actor, whom Wallis discovered and who only worked for him once, could provide such an accurate assessment.

In *The Genius of the System,* Thomas Schatz argued convincingly that during the studio years, film was a producer's medium, so much so that the greatest American films made between, roughly, the 1920s and the 1950s, would never have reached the screen—or at least not in their present form—had it not been for such producers as Irving Thalberg, Samuel Goldwyn, David Selznick, Darryl Zanuck, and, naturally, Hal Wallis: "These men . . . translated an annual budget handed down by the New York office into a program of specific pictures . . . coordinated the operations . . . conducted contract negotiations, developed stories and scripts, screened 'dailies' as pictures were being shot, and supervised editing until a picture was ready for shipment to New York for release."[12] They may have lacked the ability to impose their personal vision on a property they had optioned or a project they had green-lighted; that was the director's job. With all due respect to Wallis, the producer is rarely the creator; "procreator" or "prime mover" is more accurate. Producers cajole, sweet-talk, prod, nudge, arm-twist, or negotiate to get their film made. Auteurists who believe in possessory credit for directors (e.g., William Wyler's *Wuthering Heights* [1939]) should recall Samuel Goldwyn's distinction between producers and directors: "I made 'Withering [*sic*] Heights.' . . . Wyler only directed it."[13] With Goldwyn, it was hard to know whether he was playing the fool, being outrageous, or delivering a howler. Regardless, he was making a valid point. William Wyler's *Wuthering Heights* could not have been made without Goldwyn; someone else's *Wuthering Heights*, perhaps—but not the classic version that the American Film Institute ranked seventy-third among the one hundred best American films produced between 1896 and 1996.

Goldwyn, Thalberg, Selznick, Wallis. They were all different, except in one respect: their approach to moviemaking, which was the visual equivalent of beginning-middle-end narrative. The preamble to the Production Code made it unassailably clear that the primary function of motion pictures was entertainment. Wallis would concur, but with an amendment: "I look for projects I feel will make good entertainment. To me that is the primary purpose of a film, to entertain. Many of my films contains messages, but I try to see that the message is delivered entertainingly."[14] Wallis would also have subscribed to Wilkie Collins's advice to budding novelists: "Make 'em laugh, make 'em cry, make 'em wait."[15] However, Wallis would have added: "And make 'em better human beings."

While Golden Age producers understood that the best way to reach an audience was through linear narration and selective realism, they did not all achieve that goal in the same way. Those with a studio affiliation had an easier time; their films bore the studio's signature, so that, for example, *The Wizard of Oz* (1939) could not be mistaken for anything other than an MGM release; nor, with America's entry into World War II, could Paramount's *Wake Island* (1942) be confused with Fox's *Guadalcanal Diary* (1943). It was not a matter of "a war is a war is a war"; rather, it was a war waged in microcosm in southern California on two different back lots, with two different sets of actors, directors, and crews—not to mention screenwriters. Same war? Yes. Two more war movies? Only to the undiscerning.

All the studio films entertained in their own ways. And so did those of the indies. Since United Artists was a distribution company, even though it was considered one of the "little three" (along with Universal and Columbia), it lacked both a signature and a personality. A United Artists release could be anything from a classic (e.g., *Stagecoach* [1939]) to a forgettable bit of froth (*Getting Gertie's Garter* [1945]). The bottom line was entertainment, and producers, whether they worked inside or outside of mainstream Hollywood, adhered to the Code's mandate. The alternative was professional suicide.

Wallis was one of the industry's best entertainers, as his films attest. His years at Warners taught him how to work the marketplace without condescension and later turn problematic films such as *Becket* and

Anne of the Thousand Days into popular successes. Wallis could never have been an Irving Thalberg. First of all, unlike Thalberg, he was not based at MGM, Hollywood's premier studio, which boasted of having "more stars than there are in the heavens." The air at MGM would have been too rarefied for Wallis, who was meant for the studio of the tough guys, where actors looked as if they punched time clocks and moved through a haze of cigarette smoke on their way to makeup. One could hardly imagine Wallis working with Greta Garbo and Norma Shearer or, for that matter, Thalberg working with Edward G. Robinson and James Cagney. Wallis could no more have made *Camille* (1937) than Thalberg could have made *Little Caesar*—unless one can envision a *Camille* with Bette Davis or a *Little Caesar* with Clark Gable.

Thalberg refused screen credit for his MGM films, one-third of which came under his personal supervision, perhaps because he felt that the credit belonged to the those who helped him realize his intentions. Still, as one of his biographers has shown, Thalberg "was not merely the ringmaster of the collaboration required of filmmaking; he was a filmmaker himself . . . writing films, casting them, devising special effects, supervising the filming even to the point of directing sequences himself, and finally editing them."[16] Wallis was no different. Here is Wallis speaking on the following topics:

Budget: Based on my shooting script, I get a budget. I have always . . . come out pretty close to my budget figures.

Script: I work closely with the writer. If I buy an original story, I devote a lot of time to conferences for developing the screen treatment. . . . Then the director and I meet with [the writer] with our notes. We begin a series of conferences, rewrites, second and third drafts . . . until we come out with our final shooting script.

Editing: [Editing] teaches you construction and how a film goes together.

Dealing with Directors: When I work with a . . . talented director . . . I left him alone far more than I would a lesser man. . . . If there are scenes in the dailies I don't like . . . I have them done over. If I feel we need an added shot . . . I discuss it with [the director] and get what I want.[17]

The Golden Age producers would have agreed.

Thalberg, however, would have taken issue with a producer's receiving screen credit, although, had he lived to form his own production company, it would have been called the I.G. Thalberg Corporation.[18] That, for him, would have been acknowledgment enough.

But to most moviegoers of the 1930s, Thalberg was an unknown quantity; the buffs might have known who he was—not one of the industry's greatest producers, but the husband of superstar Norma Shearer. Thalberg was unusual in his willingness to hide his light under a bushel. The others subscribed to the "fame is the spur" philosophy. Recognition is what spurred Wallis on, as it did others, especially Jack Warner, who was hubristic enough to make his name part of the Warner Brothers logo. At least Carl Laemmle added his name to the main title, allowing the Universal globe to spin unimpeded by print.

When Wallis finally became an "independent producer," he was using the phrase in a specialized sense: someone whose production company was housed at a studio, where the producer could be truly independent, free to make only the pictures he wanted to make. Wallis always had a studio base: first Warners, then Paramount, and finally Universal. Thus he never lacked a distributor, nor did he have to go hunting for one.

Samuel Goldwyn never had the luxury of a studio berth. He was a real "indie." Samuel Goldwyn Studios on North Formosa Avenue was a "studio" only in the sense of being a production company. Unlike Wallis, Goldwyn always needed a distributor, generally United Artists or RKO, although his last two films, *Carmen Jones* (1954) and *Porgy and Bess* (1959) were released through Fox and Columbia, respectively.

Having had his share of the studio system, David Selznick went independent in 1936, first with Selznick International, then with Selznick Releasing. Selznick, too, needed distributors—the logical ones, again, being United Artists (for, e.g., *The Garden of Allah* [1936], *The Prisoner of Zenda* [1937], and *Rebecca* [1940]) and RKO (for, e.g., *Suspicion* [1941], *The Paradine Case* [1948], and *The Wild Heart* [1952]). Although *Gone with the Wind* (1939) is considered an MGM release, the reason is that Selznick—financially strapped and desperate to have Clark Gable, then under contract to MGM, for the role of Rhett Butler—cut a deal with his father-in-law, Louis Mayer, that gave him Gable and gave MGM the distribution rights and half of the profits in some territories, more in others.

Unlike Wallis, Walter Wanger was born under a wandering star. Wanger produced for various studios such as Paramount, Columbia, and MGM. However, his most famous productions—for example, Fritz Lang's *You Only Live Once* [1937], John Ford's *Stagecoach* (1939) and *The Long Voyage Home* (1940), and Hitchcock's *Foreign Correspondent* (1940)—were released through United Artists. Wanger was shrewd enough to hook up with Universal in the 1940s, providing the studio with B movies such as *Eagle Squadron* and *Arabian Nights* (both 1942), the latter being the studio's first Technicolor release, that were a notch above Universal's standard fare.[19] Around the same time that Wallis found his niche at Paramount, Wanger, his wife (actress Joan Bennett), and director Fritz Lang set up their own production company, Diana, releasing through Universal and providing the studio with the hugely successful *Scarlet Street* (1945).

The second, and last, Diana production, *Secret beyond the Door* (1948), was a disappointment and merits attention only because of its director, Fritz Lang. If Diana was short-lived, it was because Universal expected Wanger to cover 60 percent of the budget in cash and invest a minimum of $70,000 per film. *Scarlet Street* was worth the investment. But even Wanger's biographer admits that most of Wanger's Universal productions may have been "entertaining" but not "profitable."[20] Even so, Wanger was willing to take chances; Wallis's idea of taking a chance was settling in a safe house. By returning to his roots as a real independent producer, Wanger could at least leave the business with three impressive productions: *The Reckless Moment* (Columbia, 1949, remade as *The Deep End* [2001]), *Invasion of the Body Snatchers* (Allied Artists, 1956, remade in 1978), and *I Want to Live!* (United Artists, 1958), for which Susan Hayward won a best actress Oscar.

If Wallis had anything in common with a producer of his generation, it was with Zanuck. Before he left Warners, Zanuck not only had taught Wallis how editing could turn celluloid into narrative but had also determined the studio's specialty: urban realism, gritty and totally lacking in artifice. Wallis expanded the Zanuck model to include musicals, historical epics, domestic dramas, and exposés. Wallis had become Zanuck's alter ego—generating memos and fuming when his instructions were ignored, but perhaps sensing (never admitting it, though) that directors such as William Wyler and Anatole Litvak, who went their own way, did so for the good of the film, not for ego gratification. What

struck Wallis as an inordinate number of takes was Wyler's way of making sure he got the right one. Wyler's justification of his clashes with
Bette Davis is as revealing as his refusal to subscribe to Wallis's notion
of frugal filmmaking: "I have always felt that it is the director's responsibility to see the production as a whole and to know what is going to
serve to make a better overall film in the long run."[21]

Wallis, however, was not as adventuresome as Zanuck. In April 1933,
at the height of the Great Depression, Zanuck left Warners to become
part of a company that two years later became Twentieth Century–Fox.
It was not a rash decision on Zanuck's part, since he had several offers,
including one from MGM. Even if Wallis had been in Zanuck's shoes in
1933, he would have been too conscious of financial security to take
risks when the economy was in disarray. While Wallis's career spanned
three studios, and Zanuck's two, neither crossed over into the unpre-
dictable world of *real* independent production, Wallis's type being the
equivalent of social security or tenure. In Wallis's case, it was the desire
for a permanent address after a childhood marked by constant relocation. When Zanuck decided to make a short-lived (1957–62) excursion
into independent production with DFZ Productions, it was because he
was witnessing the slow death of the studio system and the erosion of
the production head's authority, as agents and stars rushed in to fill the
power vacuum. Although DFZ Productions would be headquartered in
Paris, the releasing company would still be Twentieth Century–Fox.
Zanuck may have left West Pico Boulevard in Beverly Hills, but he had
not severed ties with the studio that he reconfigured in his own image.
Of the seven DFZ productions, only two had merit: *Compulsion* (1959)
and *The Longest Day* (1962), Zanuck's recreation of the Normandy invasion, which remained definitive until Steven Spielberg's *Saving Private Ryan* (1998).

Since Zanuck had been a production head for most of his career,
one would have expected him to leave behind a distinguished body of
work, as indeed he did—chiefly, however, in the 1930s and 1940s. Wallis, though, ceased being a production head in 1944; he did not have the
advantage of heading a studio like Fox, with its own firmament of stars,
such as Betty Grable, Henry Fonda, Susan Hayward, Rex Harrison,
Gregory Peck, Gene Tierney, and Richard Widmark. Wallis had to draw
on Paramount's less impressive roster, discover new talent, and negotiate two or three picture deals with Golden Age icons such as Loretta

Young, Barbara Stanwyck, and Joan Fontaine, whose star power was diminishing but whose names still meant something at the box office.

Not every film Zanuck and Wallis made was of the same quality. Zanuck ran the gamut from *How Green Is My Valley* (1941) and *All about Eve* (1950) to *China Girl* (1942), for which he wrote the original story under the name of Melville Crossman (which he used again two years later for *The Purple Heart*) and *David and Bathsheba* (1951). It is not a question of *China Girl* or *David and Bathsheba*'s being inferior films; they are simply not outstanding examples of their respective genres, the war film and the biblical epic. Even at Warners, Wallis made his share of potboilers, as did every producer, studio-based or independent. Given the number of quality films that came out under the Hal Wallis banner at Paramount and Universal alone, it is amazing how many of them can stand up to the best of Zanuck's. And if the Warner Brothers pictures are included, Wallis and his former mentor would be equal.

Zanuck may have decided that the first CinemaScope film would be *The Robe* (1953), Fox's contribution to the wide-screen revolution, but Fox's historical epics (e.g., *The Robe, The Egyptian* [1954], and *Demetrius and the Gladiators* [1954]) are intellectually vapid compared to *Becket, Anne of the Thousand Days,* and *Mary, Queen of Scots.* If a producer, to use the show business idiom, "puts the package together," Wallis did more than that; frequently he gift-wrapped the package, so that it looked like an expensive present—which it often was.

Wallis's death resulted in a superabundance of obituaries, one of which bore a headline that best described him: "Hal Wallis: Gentleman" (*Finding My Way,* 125). "Gentleman" is an odd designation for Wallis. Certainly he does not fit Cardinal Newman's definition of a gentleman as "one who never inflicts pain." However, if that definition were applied unilaterally, there would be few gentlemen. Had Cardinal Newman written, "one who never *knowingly* inflicts pain," Wallis would qualify. He was never intentionally cruel; if some of his memos seemed harsh, it was because they were reprimands, intended for those who failed to do what was expected of them. Wallis assumed it was common knowledge that the movie business was not for the thin-skinned. Criticism, always; cruelty, never. Such was Wallis's credo. He would have agreed with Blanche duBois in *A Streetcar Named Desire:* "Deliberate cruelty is unforgivable."

His liaisons, of which there were few, were neither lovers' trysts nor lunch hour rendezvous. Since Louise knew that her husband tended to stray (although not as often, or as publicly, as Darryl Zanuck) and that his work took precedence over marriage and family, Wallis could hardly be said to be "cheating" on her. To be the kind of producer that Heston described and that Wallis considered himself to be required a set of commandments different from the Ten; "Thou shalt not commit adultery" was not in the producer's manual.

Moviemakers are born hagiographers, and those who believe that discretion is superior to revelation move to the next level: idealization. Reading *Starmaker,* one would assume that Wallis and Louise were moviemaking farmers. It was an idyllic picture: famous producer and his silent star wife as Hollywood homesteaders. That was the illusion. The reality was something else.

Despite his wide reading, Wallis was probably unaware of the courtesy books that were so popular during the Renaissance and dealt, for the most part, with the formation and education of a gentleman. But if he ever came upon Giovanni Della Casa's *Galateo* (1558), he would have agreed with the author's principles of gentlemanly conduct: a gentleman does not use objectionable language, nor is he verbose; he is never critical of religion, nor does he engage in scandal-mongering, lying, boasting, or displays of false modesty; he avoids rebuking and ridiculing others and disdains trivial and sordid conversation. According to these standards, *Starmaker* is a gentleman's autobiography, perhaps the most gentlemanly of any Hollywood self-chronicle.

"Hal Wallis, Gentleman" was a fitting headline; it would also have been a good epitaph. All that was missing was "Producer."

Notes

Chapter One. Child of the Tenements

1. Stephen Longstreet, *Chicago: 1860–1919* (New York: David McKay, 1973), 191.

2. "Hal Wallis Book," partial manuscript, 1, box 105, Hal Wallis Collection, Center for Motion Picture Study, hereafter abbreviated as HWC-CMPS.

3. Ibid.

4. Martha Hyer Wallis, telephone interview by author, 26 June 2002.

5. I am grateful to Russian scholar Dr. Irwin Radetzky for this information.

6. Wallis simply said they married "in the Old Country." "Hal Wallis Book," 27.

7. Donald L. Miller, *City of the Century: The Epic of Chicago and the Making of America* (New York: Touchstone, 1996), 457.

8. "We had very little money, but Mother managed to feed us very well." "Hal Wallis Book," 1.

9. Ibid., 2.

10. Box 105, tape transcript, side 2, p. 25, HWC-CMPS.

11. Box 99, "Miscellaneous Correspondence, 1944–50," HWC-CMPS.

12. Wallis provided dates of death for both parents when he had their names in-scribed in the memory book at Temple Israel in Hollywood. Wallis to Rabbi Merfeld, 20 October 1936, box 99, "Personal Correspondence 1936–37," HWC-CMPS.

13. Box 105, tape transcript, side 2, p. 20, HWC-CMPS.

14. Hal Wallis and Charles Higham, *Starmaker: The Autobiography of Hal Wallis* (New York: Macmillan, 1980), 3. Hereafter abbreviated as *Starmaker* with references placed in the text.

15. Charles Musser, *The Emergence of Cinema: The American Screen to 1907* (Berkeley: Univ. of California Press, 1994), 418.

16. Will Irwin, *The House That Shadows Built* (Garden City, NY: Doubleday, Doran, 1928), 274.

17. Ibid.

18. Box 105, tape transcript, side 2, p. 20, HWC-CMPS.

19. Ibid., p. 28.

20. Ibid., p. 20.

Chapter Two. Becoming Hal B. Wallis

1. This is the thesis of Neal Gabler, *An Empire of Their Own: How the Jews Invented Hollywood* (New York: Crown, 1988).

2. For background on the Warner family, see Charles Higham, *Warner Brothers: A History of the Studio, Its Pictures, Stars, and Personalities* (New York: Scribner's, 1975), 3–9; Michael Freedland, *The Warner Brothers* (London: Harrap, 1983), 3–17.

3. Jean Stein, "West of Eden," *New Yorker*, 23 Feb.; 3 Mar. 1998, quote on 153.

4. Higham, *Warner Brothers*, 6; Freedland, *Warner Brothers*, 12.

5. The literature on the MPPCo is extensive and often biased. Two of the most objective studies are Janet Staiger, "Combination and Litigation: Structures of US Film Distribution, 1891–1917," *Cinema Journal* 23 (winter 1984): 41–72; and Robert Anderson, "The Motion Picture Patents Company: A Reevaluation," in *The American Film Industry*, rev. ed., ed. Tino Balio (Madison: Univ. of Wisconsin Press, 1985), 133–52.

6. Wallis was more explicit on tape (box 105, tape transcript, side 2, pp. 23–24, HWC-CMPS), where he implied that it was Eva's brother who opened the luncheonette with his money. Wallis's decision to ignore his uncle's lack of business sense is consistent with his decision to reveal nothing in print that would reflect negatively on his family. Even his father's desertion is attributed to depression and gambling, rather than self-pity and irresponsibility.

7. Information on Louise Fazenda comes from her CMPS clippings file.

8. On the Vitaphone process and the making of *Don Juan*, see Cass Warner Sperling and Cork Millner, with Jack Warner Jr., *Hollywood Be Thy Name: The Warner Brothers Story* (Lexington: Univ. Press of Kentucky, 1998), 91–111.

9. Box 105, tape transcript, pt. 2, p. 23, HWC-CMPS. See also *Starmaker*, 16.

10. On Lubitsch at Warners, see Higham, *Warner Brothers*, 18–28.

11. Joan Fontaine, *No Bed of Roses* (New York: Morrow, 1978), 200.

12. "Biographical Note," Hal Wallis clippings file, CMPS. The same story is told in Maryls J. Harris, *The Zanucks of Hollywood: The Dark Legacy of an American Dynasty* (New York: Crown, 1989), 30–31.

13. Harris, *Zanucks*, 29.

14. Box 93, "Palm Springs Property—20 Acres," HWC-CMPS.

15. The house was profiled in *Architectural Digest*, 1 April 1991, 192.

16. Walter Seltzer, personal interview by author, 11 July 2001.

17. Lyn Tornabene, *Long Live the King: A Biography of Clark Gable* (New York: Putnam, 1976), 175.

18. Ibid., 176.

Chapter Three. At the Court of the Clown Prince

1. Edward G. Robinson, with Leonard Spiegelglass, *All My Yesterdays: An Autobiography* (New York: Hawthorn, 1973), 115.

2. Mervyn LeRoy, as told to Dick Kleiner, *Mervyn LeRoy: Take One* (New York: Hawthorn, 1974), 93–94. LeRoy also acknowledges Wallis as the film's producer.

3. Harris, *Zanucks*, 32.

4. Ibid.

5. See "Warners Finds Its Social Conscience," in *I Am a Fugitive from a Chain Gang*, ed. John E. O'Connor, Wisconsin/Warner Bros. Screenplay Series (Madison: Univ. of Wisconsin Press, 1981), 27–44; Mel Gussow, *Don't Say Yes Until I Finish Talking: A Biography of Darryl F. Zanuck* (New York: Pocket Books, 1972), 46–47.

6. "Warners Finds Its Social Conscience," 36.

7. Higham, *Warner Brothers,* 86.

8. Jan Herman, *A Talent for Trouble: The Life of Hollywood's Most Acclaimed Director, William Wyler* (New York: Putnam, 1995), 176.

9. Jack Warner to Wallis, memo, 8 June 1940, *The Letter* file, the Warner Brothers Collection, University of Southern California (hereafter abbreviated as WBC-USC).

10. Wallis to associate producer Henry Blanke, memos, 8 Jan. 1938, 4 Nov. 1937, 6 Jan. 1938, *Jezebel* file, WBC-USC.

11. Wallis to Warner, memo, 19 July 1940, *The Letter* file, WBC-USC.

12. Wallis to Blanke, memos, 23, 25, 29 Mar. 1939, *The Old Maid* file, WBC-USC.

13. Wallis to Blanke, memo, 4 Nov. 1935, *The Petrified Forest* file, WBC-USC.

14. Wallis to Blanke, memo, 14 Mar. 1939, *The Old Maid* file; Wallis to Wright, Westmore, and Blanke, memo, 7 Dec. 1938, *Juarez* file, WBC-USC.

15. Wallis to associate producer David Lewis, memo, 6 Apr. 1940, *All This and Heaven Too* file, WBC-USC.

16. Ibid., 15 Apr. 1940.

17. Wallis to Nugent, 3 Sept. 1941, *The Male Animal* file, WBC-USC.

18. Wallis to Arnow, memo, 13 Jan. 1937, *Marked Woman* file, WBC-USC.

19. Wallis to Curtis Bernhardt, memo, 27 Oct. 1941, *Juke Girl* file, WBC-USC.

20. Wallis to Wright, memo, 7 Nov. 1935, *Anthony Adverse* file, WBC-USC; for a case study of the production, see also Nick Roddick, *A New Deal in Entertainment: Warner Brothers in the 1930s* (London: British Film Institute, 1983), 29–63.

21. Wallis to William Koenig (general production manager), memo, 24 Oct. 1935, *Anthony Adverse* file.

22. Wallis to Wright, memo, 21 Dec. 1935, *Anthony Adverse* file.

23. Wallis to LeRoy, memo, 24 Jan. 1936, ibid.

24. Wallis to Blanke, memo, 17 Dec. 1935, ibid.

25. Wallis to Lewis, memo, 1 Apr. 1940, *All This and Heaven Too* file.

26. Wallis to Orry-Kelly (head of costumes), memo, 23 Jan. 1940, ibid.

27. Wallis to Bobby Agnew, memo, 22 Jan. 1936, *Anthony Adverse* file.

28. Wallis to Orry-Kelly, memo, 30 Apr. 1940, *No Time for Comedy* file, WBC-USC.

29. Wallis to Keighley, memo, 7 Mar. 1940; Wallis to Westmore, memo, 22 Mar. 1940, *Torrid Zone* file, WBC-USC.

30. Wallis to Michael Curtiz, memo, 23 Mar. 1943, *This Is the Army* file, WBC-USC.

31. Wallis to Orry-Kelly, memo, 7 Dec. 1936, *Marked Woman* file, WBC-USC.

32. Wallis to Blanke, memo, 8 Feb. 1939, *Daughters Courageous* file, WBC-USC.

33. Wallis to Blanke, memo, 27 Dec. 1940, *The Sea Wolf* file, WBC-USC.

34. Wallis to Warner, memo, 18 Sept. 1940, *High Sierra* file, WBC-USC.

35. On the making of *Dark Victory,* see "Introduction: The Fine Art of Dying," in Bernard F. Dick, ed., *Dark Victory,* Wisconsin/Warner Bros. Screenplay Series (Madison: Univ. of Wisconsin Press, 1981), 9–12.

36. Freedland, *Warner Brothers,* 113.

37. The telegrams and related materials are in box 50, Jack L. Warner Collection, University of Southern California, hereafter abbreviated as JLW Collection-USC.

38. Warner to Wallis, 4 Feb. 1935, JLW Collection-USC.

39. Wallis to Warner, radiogram, 21 Feb. 1935; Warner to Hazen, 19 July 1935, JLW Collection-USC.

40. Warner to Wilk, telegram, 17 Apr. 1943; Warner to Sears, memo, 16 Aug. 1939, JLW Collection-USC.

41. Wallis to Warner, memo, 28 Dec. 1935; Warner to Wallis, telegram, 21 Dec. 1935, JLW Collection-USC.

42. Warner to Berkeley, telegram, 25 Dec. 1935, JLW Collection-USC.

43. Einfeld to Warner, 29 June 1937, JLW Collection-USC.

44. Morris Ebinstein (lawyer) to Blanke, 28 Oct. 1938, *Juarez* file, Memos and Correspondence, WBC Collection-USC.

45. *Starmaker* typescript, 16, HWC-CMPS.

46. Bosley Crowther, review of *The Mad Empress*, *New York Times*, 15 Feb. 1940, 15.

47. Jack L. Warner, with Dean Jennings, *My First Hundred Years in Hollywood* (New York: Random House, 1964), 249.

48. On the making of *Confessions of a Nazi Spy*, see Bernard F. Dick, *The Star-Spangled Screen: The American World War II Film* (Lexington: Univ. Press of Kentucky, 1985), 51–61.

49. Warner to Wallis, 6 Mar. 1939, JLW Collection-USC.

50. Warner to Wallis, 25 Mar. 1939, JLW Collection-USC.

51. James C. Robertson, *The Casablanca Man: The Cinema of Michael Curtiz* (New York: Routledge, 1993), 34.

52. Wallis to Curtiz, memo, 30 Sept. 1935, in *Inside Warner Bros, 1935–1951: The Battles, the Brainstorms, and the Bickering—from the Files of Hollywood's Greatest Studio*, ed. Rudy Behlmer (New York: Fireside/Simon and Schuster, 1987), 24.

53. Wallis to associate producer Blanke, memo, 3 Nov. 1937, box 99, HWC-CMPS.

54. "From Legend to Film," in *The Adventures of Robin Hood*, ed. Rudy Behlmer, Wisconsin/Warner Bros. Screenplay Series (Madison: Univ. of Wisconsin Press, 1979), 32.

55. Bette Davis, *The Lonely Life: An Autobiography* (New York: Lancer/Putnam, 1962), 117.

56. Joan Leslie to author, 18 Sept. 2001.

57. Mother Dolores Hart, phone interview by author, 18 June 2002.

58. Aljean Harmetz, *Round Up the Usual Suspects: The Making of Casablanca—Bogart, Bergman, and World War II* (New York: Hyperion, 1992), 75.

59. Ibid., 64.

60. Vincent Sherman, *Studio Affairs: My Life as a Film Director* (Lexington: Univ. Press of Kentucky, 1996), 81.

Chapter Four. The End of a Dubious Friendship

1. Wallis to Jack Warner, memo, 12 Jan. 1942, box 102 (Warner Brothers), HWC-CMPS; Harmetz, *Round Up the Usual Suspects,* 18.

2. Roy J. Obringer (general counsel) to Col. J.L. Warner, memo, 29 Sept. 1942, in Behlmer, *Inside Warner Bros.,* 165.

3. On *Yankee Doodle Dandy*'s production history, see Patrick McGilligan, "Introduction: The Life Daddy Would Have Liked to Live," in *Yankee Doodle Dandy,* ed. Patrick McGilligan, Wisconsin/Warner Bros. Screenplay Series (Madison: Univ. of Wisconsin Press, 1981), 11–64.

4. William Cagney to Wallis, 13 Aug. 1941, *Yankee Doodle Dandy* file, WBC-USC.

5. Wallis to Irving Rapper, memo, 20 Apr. 1942, box 100, HWC-CMPS.

6. Patricia Bosworth, "Rebel with a Purse," *Vanity Fair,* Dec. 2000, 264.

7. Harmetz, *Round Up the Usual Suspects,* 18.

8. Harlan Lebo, *Casablanca: Behind the Scenes* (New York: Simon and Schuster, 1992), 13.

9. Rudy Behlmer, *America's Favorite Movies: Behind the Scenes* (New York: F. Ungar, 1982), 167.

10. Behlmer, *Inside Warner Bros.,* 206–7.

11. Ibid., 198; Harmetz, *Round Up the Usual Suspects,* 264.

12. Behlmer, *Inside Warner Bros.,* 196.

13. Behlmer, *America's Favorite Movies,* 167.

14. The best discussion of the *Casablanca* scripts is in Harmetz, *Round Up the Usual Suspects,* 35–60, 227–38.

15. Behlmer, *America's Favorite Movies,* 216.

16. Exactly when Wallis ordered his Oscar is unknown; according to the *Hollywood Reporter,* 23 May 1995, 6, the Academy files indicate only that it was after 1946. Quite possibly it was around 1951 when the Academy began awarding the best picture Oscar to the film's producer. Ironically, Wallis's Oscar was auctioned at Christie's on 14 June 1995 for about sixty thousand dollars.

17. Mason Wiley and Damien Bona, *Inside Oscar: The Unofficial History of the Academy Awards,* ed. Gail MacColl (New York: Ballantine, 1987), 73.

18. Warner to Wallis, memo, 5 Feb. 1943, box 103, HWC-CMPS.

19. *Cleveland Plain Dealer,* 2 Dec. 1942, 8.

20. On the making of *Watch on the Rhine,* see Bernard F. Dick, *Hellman in Hollywood* (Madison, N.J.: Fairleigh Dickinson Univ. Press, 1982), 86–93.

21. Various references in the *This Is the Army* file, WBA-USC, suggest that Berlin was opposed to Robinson's receiving screen credit. *Starmaker,* 82, implies as much. In an 8 Feb. 1943 memo to Jack Warner, *This Is the Army* file, WBC-USC, Wallis disparaged the Epsteins' contributions ("very unsatisfactory") and requested that they be removed from the picture. They received no screenplay credit.

22. Behlmer, *Inside Warner Bros.,* 233

23. Warner to Wallis, telegram, 21 Dec. 1942, JLW Collection-USC.

24. *Hollywood Reporter,* 5 Apr. 1944, 6.

25. Freedland, *Warner Brothers,* 161.

26. For the text, see *The 1941–42 International Motion Picture Almanac* (New York: Quigley, 1941), 775–88.

27. Hazen to Wallis, 25 Mar. 1944, box 83, HWC-CMPS.

Chapter Five. Starting Over

1. Wallis to Saper, memo, 8 Sept. 1944, box 96, HWC-CMPS.
2. Ibid., 27 Sept. 1955.
3. Nathan to Wallis, memo, 11 May 1951, box 92, HWC-CMPS.
4. Information on Walter Seltzer derives from the Walter Seltzer file, CMPS, and various interviews and conversations.
5. For the film's production history, see the *Love Letters* file, HWC-CMPS.
6. Rudy Behlmer, ed., *Memo from David O. Selznick* (New York: Avon, 1973), 406.
7. I owe this piece of information to one of the costars, Douglas Dick.
8. Dieterle to Wallis, 20 Feb. 1950, box 81, HWC-CMPS.
9. Joseph Hazen to Mike Levee, 13 Nov. 1953, box 81, HWC-CMPS.

Chapter Six. Morning Star

1. Information about Lizabeth Scott's life comes from personal interviews, her CMPS clippings file, and box 97, HWC-CMPS.
2. Neal Gabler, *Winchell: Gossip, Power, and the Culture of Celebrity* (New York: Knopf, 1995), 438.
3. Ibid., 360–67.
4. Cameron Shipp, "Portrait of a Hollywood Agent," *Esquire,* Mar. 1947, 81; see also Peter Biskind, "The Man Who Minted Style," *Vanity Fair,* April 2003, 210.
5. Lizabeth Scott, personal interview by author, 15 July 2001.
6. Ibid.
7. Stanwyck to Wallis, 4 Mar. 1946, box 97, HWC-CMPS.
8. M.B. Silberberg to Wallis, 7 Mar. 1946, box 97, HWC-CMPS.
9. Helen H. Wilkie to Wallis, 19 Apr. 1945, box 78B, HWC-CMPS.
10. Wallis to Steve Brooks, 6 Nov. 1944, ibid.
11. Wallis to Seltzer, 13 Mar. 1945, box 47, HWC-CMPS.
12. On the proposed tour, see *Daily Variety,* 4 Oct. 1950, 1.
13. Alain Silver and Elizabeth Ward, eds., *Film Noir: An Encyclopedia Reference to the American Style* (Woodstock, NY: Overlook Press, 1979), 80–82, 85–88, 142–53, 227–28, 236–37, 267–68, 292–93.

Chapter Seven. Interstellar Spaces

1. Information on Kristine Miller comes from a lengthy 13 Aug. 2001 phone interview by the author and from box 91, HWC-CMPS.
2. Phone interview, 13 Aug. 2001.
3. Information on Douglas Dick comes from personal interviews by the author and from box 81, HWC-CMPS.
4. Information on Wendell Corey comes from box 80, HWC-CMPS.
5. Information on Dolores Hart comes from box 83, HWC-CMPS, and from several phone interviews by the author.
6. In 1973 Loyola University and Marymount College merged to form Loyola Marymount University, a coeducational institution.

7. Highlights of the Mother Dolores segment can be viewed at abcnews.go.com/sections/2020/2020/2020_010323_motherdelores.html-58k, last accessed 24 Mar. 2001. *Dolores* is misspelled.

8. Mother Dolores, phone interview by the author, 30 May 2001.

9. Box 96, HWC-CMPS.

10. William Weaver, "Audience Research to Key Services to New Auction Sales Policy," *Motion Picture Herald,* 17 Aug. 1946, 28–29.

11. Jack C. Sayers, vice president, ARI, to Wallis, 1 Dec. 1948, box 96, HWC-CMPS.

Chapter Eight. The Wallis Galaxy

1. Unless indicated otherwise, information about Lancaster comes from box 86, HWC-CMPS.

2. Kate Buford, *Burt Lancaster: An American Life* (New York: Knopf, 2000), 61–64.

3. Ibid., 75.

4. Ibid.

5. Kirk Douglas, *The Ragman's Son: An Autobiography* (New York: Simon and Schuster, 1988), 128.

6. Douglas to Wallis, telegram, 24 July 1945, box 81, HWC-CMPS.

7. Douglas to Wallis, 2 August 1945, ibid.

8. Douglas, *Ragman's Son*, 142.

9. Ibid., 171.

10. Information on Heston's relationship with Wallis comes from box 84, HWC-CMPS.

11. The "dissolution," which was never as final as the term implies, is discussed in chapter 9.

12. Shirley MacLaine, *Don't Fall off the Mountain* (New York: Norton, 1970), 43.

13. Shirley MacLaine's contract file is in box 89, HWC-CMPS.

14. MacLaine, *Mountain*, 61.

15. Information about Shirley Booth comes from box 78, HWC-CMPS.

16. Wood to Wallis, 5 Aug. 1955, ibid.

17. On *The Miracle* decision, see Richard S. Randall, *Censorship of the Movies: The Social and Political Context of a Mass Medium* (Madison: Univ. of Wisconsin Press, 1968), 25–30.

18. Information on the making of *The Rose Tattoo* comes from material in box 96, HWC-CMPS.

19. Wallis to Magnani, 10 Sept. 1956, HWC-CMPS.

20. Magnani to Wallis, 7 July 1961, HWC-CMPS.

Chapter Nine. Two Jokers and a King

1. Bernard F. Dick, *Engulfed: The Death of Paramount Pictures and the Birth of Corporate Hollywood* (Lexington: Univ. Press of Kentucky, 2001), 18–19.

2. Ann McGuire, "Bing and Bob," *American Movie Classics,* December 1996, 6.

3. Unless otherwise indicated, information about Martin and Lewis comes from box 90, HWC-CMPS.

4. Lewis to Wallis, 8 Feb. 1950, ibid.

5. Maurice Zolotow, "The Great Martin-Lewis Feud," *American Weekly,* 20 June 1954.

6. *New York Journal American,* 21 Jan. 1957, 16; see also Jack Gould, *New York Times,* 8 Apr. 1959, 75.

7. For the definitive Jerry Lewis filmography, see Sean Levy's authoritative biography, *The Life and Art of Jerry Lewis* (New York: St. Martin's/Griffin Editions, 1996), 492–94.

8. Ibid., 115.

9. Ibid., 135.

10. A copy is in box 90, HWC-CMPS.

11. Army Archerd, *Daily Variety,* 29 June 1959, 2.

12. Alanna Nash, with Betty Smith, Marty Lacker, and Lamar Fike, *Elvis Aaron Presley: Revelations from the Memphis Mafia* (New York: HarperCollins, 1995), 75.

13. "Hal Wallis Predicts a New Elvis," as told to May Mann, box 94, HWC-CMPS. The piece was obviously intended for one of the trades.

14. Hazen to Wallis, memo, 26 Oct. 1956, box 94, HWC-CMPS.

15. Wallis and Hazen to William Morris Agency, memo, 10 Aug. 1956, ibid.

16. David P. Szatmary, *Rockin' in Time: A Social History of Rock-and-Roll,* 2nd ed. (Englewood Cliffs, NJ: Prentice-Hall, 1987), 56.

17. Mother Dolores Hart, phone interview by author, 20 June 2002.

18. Hazen to Wallis, memo, 17 Jan. 1957, box 94, HWC-CMPS.

19. The Colonel to Hazen, 7 Jan. 1963, box 93, HWC-CMPS.

20. Wallis to the Colonel, 10 Dec. 1963, box 94, HWC-CMPS; see also Alanna Nash, *The Colonel: The Extraordinary Story of Colonel Tom Parker and Elvis Presley* (New York: Simon and Schuster, 2003), 199.

21. The Colonel to Wallis, 7 Sept. 1963, box 93, HWC-CMPS.

22. Ibid., 20 Nov. 1964.

23. Hazen to Wallis, memo, dated only "September 1965," box 94, HWC-CMPS.

24. The Colonel to Hazen, 7 Jan. 1963, box 93, HWC-CMPS.

25. As quoted in Hazen's obituary, *New York Times,* 16 Nov. 1994, D25.

26. Bernard F. Dick, *City of Dreams: The Making and Remaking of Universal Pictures* (Lexington: Univ. Press of Kentucky, 1997), 158–59.

27. Information about Wallis's relationship with Hazen is based on material in boxes 83 and 84, HWC-CMPS.

28. Wallis to Hazen, 10 Dec. 1952, box 83, HWC-CMPS.

29. Ibid.

30. Ibid., 10 Oct. 1958.

31. Wallis to Hazen,, 22 Apr. 1968, box 84, HWC-CMPS.

32. Ibid., 11 Jan. 1971.

Chapter Ten. Phoenix Rising

1. Peter Glenville, "Reflections on Becket," *Films and Filmmaking* 10 (Apr. 1964):

7, claimed that the casting of Burton and O'Toole was his idea; but since the film was a Wallis production, with Wallis having optioned the play and selected a screenwriter, Wallis's account (*Starmaker,* 164) is more credible.

2. Richard Burton, "A Candid Look at 'Becket' and Myself," *Life,* 13 Mar. 1964, 85–86.

3. Richard Burton, interview, *Playboy,* Sept. 1963, 85.

4. Michael Freedland, *Peter O'Toole: A Biography* (London: W.H. Allen, 1983), 95.

5. On the Siegel-Martin attempted takeover of Paramount, see Dick, *Engulfed,* 92–103.

6. *Variety,* 3 Apr. 1970, 6.

7. Melvyn Bragg, *Richard Burton: A Life* (Boston: Little, Brown, 1988), 262.

8. Maxwell Anderson, *Anne of the Thousand Days,* in *Best American Plays, Third Series—1945–1951,* ed. John Gassner (New York: Crown, 1952), 591.

9. In the program notes for the 19 Sept. 1974 screening of *Mary, Queen of Scots* as part of the Los Angeles County Museum of Art's (LACMA's) Wallis tribute, Wallis is quoted as having told interviewer Rex Reed that "on stage it's OK if Mary never meets the queen . . . because you can see the two of them on opposite sides of the stage." That remark only makes sense if he had seen Bolt's play.

10. Most of the details in the film about Mary's execution are accurate; see Lady Antonia Fraser, *Mary Queen of Scots* (New York: Delacorte, 1969), 538–39.

11. Jay Cocks, review of *The Nelson Affair, Time,* 9 Apr. 1972, 85.

Chapter Eleven. Brief Encounters

1. I owe this piece of information to the late screenwriter Oscar Saul.

2. Much of what I have learned about Wallis's marriage to Louise derives from discussions with Walter Seltzer, who knew both of them well—or knew Wallis as well as anyone who worked for him could.

3. "Louise Marie Fazenda," *Dictionary of American Biography,* supplement 7, 238.

4. I am indebted to Walter Seltzer for this anecdote, which he related to me in a July 2002 conversation.

5. Walter Seltzer informed me about Wallis's relationship with Lola Lane in our July 2002 conversation.

6. Subsequent information about Lola Lane comes from the Lola Lane file, CMPS. Newspaper references are given in the text.

7. Excerpts from the Lane-Lyons correspondence in the Lola Lane file had been published in one of the trades, which seems to have been *Variety* (22 May 1930), although the name of the publication does not appear on the copy in the file.

8. Don Miller, *"B" Movies: An Informal Survey of the American Low-Budget Film, 1933–1945* (New York: Curtis Books, 1973), 305.

9. Unless otherwise indicated, information about Wallis and Corinne Calvet comes from box 79, HWC-CMPS.

10. The letter in box 79 is undated but was probably written around 1950–51.

11. Corinne Calvet, *Has Corinne Been a Good Girl?* (New York: St. Martin's, 1983), 161.

12. Ibid., 312–13.

Chapter Twelve. His Last Girl

1. Martha Hyer Wallis, *Finding My Way: A Hollywood Memoir* (San Francisco: HarperSanFrancisco, 1990), 30. Subsequent references are placed in the text. Other sources of biographical information used in this chapter are the Martha Hyer CMPS clippings file and the actress's article "What It Takes to Be a Starlet," *American Magazine,* Feb. 1948, 136–40.

2. Martha confirmed the June 1959 date in a 23 Feb. 2003 phone interview by the author.

3. *Starmaker*, box 105 (tape transcript 16), HWC-CMPS.

4. From the way Martha describes the incident, the flight was on a Saturday. In *Starmaker* (174–75) Wallis also speaks of a Saturday flight and dinner with Martha on Monday at the elegant Voisin, after she had declined his invitations for Saturday and Sunday evenings. According to Ralph Richardi, senior vice president of customer services at American Airlines, there was a flight 2 leaving Los Angeles at 8:45 A.M., arriving at what is now Kennedy (then Idlewild) Airport at 4:30 P.M. (10 Feb. 2003 e-mail to author).

5. *Starmaker,* box 104 (part 2 of 2), 209.

6. *Los Angeles Times,* 14 Dec. 1958,V3.

7. "Nothing but the Best," *Life,* 4 May 1959, 119–26.

8. Harris, *Zanucks,* 91.

9. President of UCLA Medical Center Auxiliary to Wallis, 19 Apr. 1962, Hedda Hopper Collection, CMPS, no. 715 ("Louise Fazenda").

10. Information about Louise's relationship with Bunker derives from material in Woody Haut, *Heartbreak and Vine: The Fate of Hardboiled Writers in Hollywood* (London: Serpent's Tail, 2002), 204–6; and Charles Waring, "Born under a Bad Sign— The Life of Edward Bunker," *Crime Time,* 23 Feb. 2003, http://www.crimetime.co.uk/features/edwardbunker.html, last accessed 23 Feb. 2003.

11. *Strange Interlude,* in *Three Plays of Eugene O'Neill: Desire under the Elms, Strange Interlude, Mourning Becomes Electra* (New York: Vintage, 1958), 221.

12. Although *Summer and Smoke* premiered a year after *Streetcar,* it was actually written first.

13. Martha Wallis to author, 1 May 2002: "He was a very private man—secretive even. He never spoke of the other ladies in his life—but did say to me, "You're my last girl.'"

14. "Architectural Digest Visits: Mr. and Mrs. Hal Wallis," *Architectural Digest,* Mar. 1978, 84–93.

15. *Dialogue on Film: Hal B. Wallis,* vol. 4, no. 6, Mar. 1975 (Beverly Hills, CA: American Film Institute/Center for Advanced Studies, 1975), 18; Wallis, *Starmaker,* 158–59.

16. Wallis to Nathan, memo, 16 June 1975, box 92, HWC-CMPS.

17. Martha Wallis, telephone interview by the author, 21 Apr. 2002.

18. Wallis to Nathan, memo, 29 July 1963, box 92, HWC-CMPS.

19. Attorney Jeffrey Glassman to Charles Higham, 23 Jan. 1979, box 105, HWC-CMPS.

20. See *Los Angeles Magazine,* June 1981, 66.

21. *Wildenstein & Co., Inc., Plaintiff,* v. *Brent Wallis, &C., Et Al., Defendants,* 9

June 1992, http://www.law.cornell.law.cornell.edu/ny/ctap/079_0641.html, last accessed 19 June 2002.

Chapter Thirteen. Requieum for a Gentleman

1. I am grateful to Martha Wallis for sharing with me the details of her husband's last years.

2. Martha Wallis phone interview by the author, 16 June 2002.

3. Mona Gable, "The Letter of the Law," *LA Business,* Oct. 1989, 6. This article is the best analysis of the dispute that occurred between LACMA and the Foundation when the latter decided to auction the paintings. See also *Los Angeles Times,* 19 May 1989, Calendar, 1; and *Los Angeles Herald-Examiner,* 18 May 1989, B1.

4. The Wyeths were sold separately on 25 May 1989 as part of an American paintings auction.

5. *Los Angeles Times,* 6 Feb. 1993, Calendar, F1.

6. Ibid., F1.

7. On the background of *Mission to Moscow,* see the exhaustive introduction and notes to the screenplay in *Mission to Moscow,* edited with an introduction by David Culbert, Wisconsin/Warner Bros. Screenplays Series (Madison: Univ. of Wisconsin Press, 1980), 11–41, 225–41.

8. Warner to Joseph Bernhard (president of the Warner Bros. Circuit Management Corp.), telegram, 22 Jan. 1943, JLW Collection-USC.

9. As quoted in Gordon Kahn, *Hollywood on Trial: The Story of the Ten Who Were Indicted* (New York: Arno Press/New York Times, 1948; reprint, 1972), 15.

10. *Dialogue on Film,* 7.

11. Charlton Heston, *In the Arena: An Autobiography* (New York: Simon and Schuster, 1995), 94.

12. Thomas Schatz, *The Genius of the System: Hollywood Filmmaking in the Studio Era* (New York: Pantheon, 1988), 9–10.

13. A. Scott Berg, *Goldwyn: A Biography* (New York: Ballantine, 1989), 333.

14. *Dialogue on Film,* 10.

15. As quoted in Walter Allen, *George Eliot* (New York: Collier, 1964), 84.

16. Roland Flamini, *Thalberg: The Last Tycoon and the World of M-G-M* (New York: Crown, 1994), 28; see also Schatz, *Genius,* 46.

17. *Dialogue on Film,* 4–6.

18. Flamini, *Thalberg,* 253.

19. On Wanger's financial arrangement with Universal, see Schatz, *Genius,* 350–52.

20. Matthew Bernstein, *Walter Wanger: Hollywood Independent* (Berkeley: Univ. of California Press, 1994), 236.

21. Gene D. Phillips, *Exiles in Hollywood: Major European Filmmakers in America* (Bethlehem, PA: Lehigh Univ. Press, 1998), 76.

Bibliographical Essay

A Wallis Bibliography

The standard histories of Warner Brothers—Charles Higham, *Warner Brothers: A History of the Studio, Its Pictures, Stars, and Personalities* (New York: Scribner's 1975); Michael Freedland, *The Warner Brothers* (London: Harrap, 1983); and Cass Warner Sperling and Cork Millner, with Jack Warner Jr., *Hollywood Be Thy Name: The Warner Brothers Story* (Lexington: Univ. Press of Kentucky, 1998)—include material on Wallis but, because of their focus, can only suggest the kind of production head he was. However, Rudy Behlmer, in his *Inside Warner Brothers, 1935–1951: The Battles, the Brainstorms, and the Bickering—from the Files of Hollywood's Greatest Studio* (New York: Fireside/Simon and Schuster, 1987), has assembled an invaluable collection of memos, letters, and telegrams, some of which are written by and to Wallis; Aljean Harmetz, *Round Up the Usual Suspects: The Making of Casablanca—Bogart, Bergman, and World War II* (New York: Hyperion, 1992), has written the (at present) definitive study of the classic film, documenting Wallis's significant contribution to its success; and Nick Roddick, *A New Deal in Entertainment: Warner Brothers in the 1930s* (London: British Film Institute, 1983), 29–62, has drawn on production files for a case study of *Anthony Adverse* (1936), revealing Wallis as a producer who left no doubt that he was boss; and as for those who thought otherwise, "they're not going to work here any more." However, when it came to an auteur like William Wyler, Wallis did not flex muscle; he simply aired his frustration in memos and hoped for the best. The best (*Jezebel* [1938] and *The Letter* [1940]) were worth overlooking Wyler's penchant for what struck Wallis as an inordinate number of takes; see Jan Herman, *A Talent for Trouble: The Life of*

Hollywood's Most Acclaimed Director, William Wyler (New York: Putnam, 1995), 177–78.

A Wallis Filmography

A. Scott Berg's *Goldwyn: A Biography* (New York: Random House, 1989) does not include a filmography, although the producer's films are highlighted in the "Notes and Sources" section at the end. Yet it would have been easier to compile a filmography for Goldwyn, who was a producer (but not a studio-based production head) than for Wallis, who began as a studio production head and then became a studio-based producer—first at Warners, then at Paramount, and finally at Universal. Wallis's elliptical autobiography, *Starmaker* (New York: Macmillan, 1980), contains a filmography consisting of 197 films spanning three studios—126 at Warner Brothers, 63 at Paramount, and 8 at Universal. There is one egregious error: *Saratoga Trunk* (1945) is numbered among the Paramount releases, but it was one of the very last films that he placed in production at Warners before leaving the studio in fall 1944. His filmography begins with *Little Caesar* (1930), in which his name does not appear in the credits, nor do the production files contain much information about his contribution to the film. (At the time he was just production manager.) Wallis also cites *I Am a Fugitive from a Chain Gang* (1932) as one of his productions, although enough evidence has been marshaled to award the credit to Darryl F. Zanuck. Thus, claiming that Wallis personally supervised these 126 Warner Brothers films from inception to completion is not entirely accurate. Although Wallis had something to say about each of them, his involvement varied: in some, he seemed mainly concerned about makeup and costumes; in others, editing and performance; and in those to which he was truly committed (that is, the best of the Warner Brothers releases of the period), no detail was too minor for his scrutiny.

I have discussed a number of Warner Brothers films in which Wallis was actively involved, such as *Captain Blood* (1935), *Anthony Adverse* (1936), *The Adventures of Robin Hood* (1938), and *Juarez* (1939)—not to mention *Casablanca* (1942). It almost seems ludicrous to call *Swing Your Lady* (1938) or *Yes, My Darling Daughter* (1939) Hal Wallis films. Wallis may have approved the script and determined the budget, but it is difficult to imagine his caring as much about them as he did about those in which he truly believed, such as *The Life of Emile Zola* (1937) and *Watch on the Rhine* (1943). It was not until 1942 that Wallis was able to move from production head at Warners to independent producer at the studio with the freedom to choose the movies he wanted to make—not the fifteen to twenty pictures a year that he was formerly expected to place in production. Even when Wallis left Warners for Paramount in 1944, he never went back to being a production head.

It would be better to distinguish between the films Wallis produced at Warner Brothers between 1930 and 1942 and the "Hal Wallis productions" (1942–75) that came after. The latter comprise the following:

Warner Brothers (1942–44): *Casablanca* (1942); *Now, Voyager* (1942); *Desperate Journey* (1942); *Air Force* (1943); *Watch on the Rhine* (1943); *This Is the Army* (1943); *Princess O'Rourke* (1943); *Passage to Marseilles* (1944); *Saratoga Trunk* (1945).

Paramount (1945–70): *The Affairs of Susan* (1945); *You Came Along* (1945); *Love Letters* (1945); *The Strange Love of Martha Ivers* (1946); *The Searching Wind* (1946); *The Perfect Marriage* (1946); *Desert Fury* (1947); *I Walk Alone* (1948); *So Evil My Love* (1948); *Sorry Wrong Number* (1948); *The Accused* (1948); *Rope of Sand* (1949); *My Friend Irma* (1949); *The File on Thelma Jordan* (1949); *Bitter Victory* (1949); *Paid in Full* (1950); *My Friend Irma Goes West* (1950); *The Furies* (1950); *Dark City* (1950); *September Affair* (1950); *That's My Boy* (1951); *Peking Express* (1951); *Red Mountain* (1951); *Sailor Beware* (1951); *Jumping Jacks* (1952); *Come Back, Little Sheba* (1952); *The Stooge* (1953); *Scared Stiff* (1953); *Cease Fire* (1953); *Money from Home* (1953); *About Mrs. Leslie* (1954); *3 Ring Circus* (1954); *The Rose Tattoo* (1955); *Artists and Models* (1955); *Hollywood or Bust* (1956); *The Rainmaker* (1956); *Gunfight at the O.K. Corral* (1957); *Loving You* (1957); *Wild Is the Wind* (1957); *The Sad Sack* (1957); *Hot Spell* (1958); *King Creole* (1958); *Last Train from Gun Hill* (1959); *Don't Give Up the Ship* (1959); *Career* (1959); *Visit to a Small Planet* (1960); *G.I. Blues* (1960); *All in a Night's Work* (1961); *Summer and Smoke* (1961); *Blue Hawaii* (1961); *Girls! Girls! Girls!* (1962); *A Girl Named Tamiko* (1962); *Wives and Lovers* (1963); *Fun in Acapulco* (1963); *Becket* (1964); *Roustabout* (1964); *The Sons of Katie Elder* (1965); *Boeing Boeing* (1965); *Paradise, Hawaiian Style* (1966); *Barefoot in the Park* (1967); *Easy Come, Easy Go* (1967); *Five Card Stud* (1968); *True Grit* (1969); and *Norwood* (1970).

Universal (1969–75): *Anne of the Thousand Days* (1969); *Red Sky at Morning* (1970); *Shootout* (1971); *Mary, Queen of Scots* (1971); *The Nelson Affair* (1972); *The Public Eye* (1972); *The Don Is Dead* (1974); and *Rooster Cogburn* (1975).

Archives and Special Collections

1. The University of Southern California's Warner Brothers Archives, acquired in 1977, is a repository of studio records from 1918 to 1968. Some files are more complete than others, and even if they cannot supply an answer to every question one might have about a particular film, it is still possible to reconstruct a fairly accurate production history from the screenplay drafts, memos, and contracts.

2. The Jack L. Warner Collection at the University of Southern California's University Park library (Cinema-TV division) contains enough material to show that Jack Warner was able to spend so much time away from the studio traveling because Wallis, who was intensely loyal to his "boss," kept him informed about virtually everything that was happening there.

3. The Hal Wallis Collection at the Center for Motion Picture Study in Los Angeles is easy to use because it has been cataloged alphabetically. Thus, if one is looking for information about a particular individual or organization, the meticulously prepared inventory provides the box number where the name can be found—Booth, Shirley, in box 78; Presley, Elvis in boxes 94 and 95, and so forth. Box 104, which contains early tape transcripts of *Starmaker*, was especially useful in learning the names of Wallis's parents, which, for some reason, he decided to omit from the book.

4. The Hedda Hopper Collection at the Center for Motion Picture Study should be consulted by anyone writing about Hollywood in the years before the studios were conglomerated. Primarily known as a gossip columnist, Hopper was a faithful correspondent. It is an erratic collection but never uninteresting. Sometimes a fact turns up that seemed impossible to track down—such as the date of a wedding or the full name of the bride. That information is possible because Hopper kept the wedding invitation.

Memoirs

Enough has been said about *Starmaker* to indicate its incompleteness. One wishes Wallis had been as candid as his second wife, Martha Hyer Wallis, whose autobiography, *Finding My Way: A Hollywood Memoir* (San Francisco: HarperSanFrancisco, 1990), is a true primary source.

Published Interviews

Wallis did not give great interviews, but he was also rarely asked probing questions. Two of the more informative are "Following No Formula," *Films & Filming*, December 1969, 4–7; and *Dialogue on Film: Hal B. Wallis,* American Film Institute, March 1975, vol. 4, no. 6, pp. 1–24.

Personal Interviews

It is a good sign when, after weeks of research, an interviewer finds a subject who knows more than he does. Conversations with Robert Blees, Douglas Dick, Reverend Mother Abbess Dolores Hart, Joan Leslie, Kristine Miller, Lizabeth Scott, and Walter Seltzer made it clear that time had not tarnished their memories—a fact that became strikingly evident after Lizabeth Scott, who had understudied Tallulah Bankhead as Sabina in Thornton Wilder's *Skin of Our Teeth* (1942), performing the role once in New York and several times in Boston, recited Sabina's opening lines flawlessly in July 2003 at a Santa Monica restaurant. And when Martha Hyer Wallis described her husband's final days with a vividness that only an eyewitness could muster, I knew I was in the presence of the keeper of the book.

Index

279

Wuthering Heights (1939), 253–54
Wyler, William, 34, 36, 236, 253

Yankee Doodle Dandy (1942), 64–66
Yordan, Philip, 109, 144
York Productions, 154–55
You Came Along (1945), ix, 89, 94,
    100–102, 122
Young, Loretta, 92, 114–15

Young Man with a Horn (1950), 162
Young, Robert, 113

Zanuck, Darryl, 19, 23–24, 33, 34,
    35, 41, 44, 83, 202, 224, 257–
    59, 260
Zanuck, Richard, 224
Zolotow, Maurice, 153
Zukor, Adolph, 14, 149